The Poetics of Empire

# The Poetics of Empire

## A Study of James Grainger's
## *The Sugar-Cane*

JOHN GILMORE

THE ATHLONE PRESS
LONDON & NEW BRUNSWICK, NJ

First published in 2000 by
THE ATHLONE PRESS
1 Park Drive, London NW11 7SG
and New Brunswick, New Jersey

© John Gilmore 2000

John Gilmore has asserted his right under the Copyright, Designs and
Patents Act, 1998, to be identified as the author of this work

British Library Cataloguing in Publication Data
*A catalogue record of this book is available
from the British Library*

ISBN 0 485 11539 5 HB
     0 485 12148 4 PB

Library of Congress Cataloging-in-Publication Data

Gilmore, John.
  The poetics of empire : a study of James Grainger's The sugar cane / John Gilmore.
    p. cm.
  Includes bibliographical references (p. ) and index.
  ISBN 0-485-11539-5 (alk.) -- ISBN 0-485-12148-4 (alk. paper)
    1. Grainger, James, 1721?-1766. Sugar cane. 2. Sugarcane industry--Caribbean Area--History--18th century--Poetry. 3. Plantation life--Caribbean Area--History--18th century--Poetry. 4. Sugarcane--Caribbean Area--History--18th century--Poetry. 5. Didactic poetry, English--History and criticism. 6. Imperialism--History--18th century--Poetry. 7. Caribbean Area--In literature. 8. Plantation life in literature. 9. Imperialism in literature. 10. Agriculture in literature. I. Grainger, James, 1721?-1766. Sugar cane. II. Title.

PR3499.G7 S95 2000
811--dc21                                                         99-054614

Distributed in the United States, Canada and South America by
Transaction Publishers
390 Campus Drive
Somerset, New Jersey 08873

All rights reserved. No part of this publication may be reproduced,
stored in a retrieval system, or transmitted in any form or by any means,
electronic, mechanical, photocopying or otherwise, without prior
permission in writing from the publisher.

Typeset by Columns Design Limited, Reading
Printed and bound in Great Britain by
Cambridge University Press

IN PIAM MEMORIAM
PATRIS OPTIMI

TERENTII JACOBI GILMORE

QUI IN ANGLIACA CIVITATE ESCAFELDAE
NATUS EST II° DIE MAII, A. D. MCMXVI

ET IN INSULA DE BARBADOS
UBI QUINQUE ET TRIGINTA ANNOS ARTEM MEDICAM
COLUIT
OBIIT XIII° DIE AUGUSTI A. D. MCMXCVIII

HANC EDITIONEM
OPERIS ALII CARIBBIENSIS MEDICI
FILIUS MOERENS DEDICAVIT

# Contents

| | |
|---|---|
| *Acknowledgements* | viii |
| *Abbreviations* | x |
| Introduction | 1 |
| Notes to Introduction | 67 |
| *The Sugar-Cane: A Poem* | 86 |
|    Grainger's Preface to the 1764 edition | 88 |
|    Book I | 91 |
|    Book II | 111 |
|    Book III | 127 |
|    Book IV | 145 |
|    Grainger's Notes to *The Sugar-Cane* | 165 |
| Appendix I: "Great Homer deignd to sing of little Mice" | 199 |
| Appendix II: Bryan and Pereene | 202 |
| Appendix III: Colonel Martin's directions for planting and sugar-making | 205 |
| Appendix IV: Ramsay's account of a plantation day | 208 |
| Additional Notes to *The Sugar-Cane* | 213 |
| *Bibliography* | 313 |
| *Index* | 333 |

# Acknowledgements

It has taken me almost as long as to produce this study of *The Sugar-Cane* as it took Grainger to write the poem and I am particularly grateful to The Athlone Press for their understanding and patience. Publication has been made possible by generous financial assistance from the Research and Development Fund of the University of Warwick and from the Centre for British and Comparative Cultural Studies and the Department of English at Warwick. The Centre's help with photocopying and expences of research trips is also gratefully acknowledged.

Special thanks go to Peter Jackson, who most kindly shared his transcripts of Grainger's correspondence with me and provided information or helpful suggestions on many points, and to Sean Carrington of the Department of Biological and Chemical Sciences of the Cave Hill Campus of the University of the West Indies, who helped with the identification of plants mentioned in the poem.

I have benefited from discussions, in person or in correspondence, with Tobias Döring (Freie Universität Berlin), Markman Ellis (Queen Mary and Westfield College, University of London), and with colleagues at the Centre for British and Comparative Cultural Studies at Warwick: Peter Davidson and Jane Stevenson have given me much help in my hunt for Grainger's unattributed quotations, and together with Susan Bassnett, David Dabydeen and Piotr Kuhiwzcak have provided constant encouragement.

Aspects of this material have also been presented at seminars or conferences organised by the Institute of Commonwealth Studies, the Luxury Project of the Warwick Eighteenth Century Centre, the Mahatma Ghandi Institute (Mauritius), and the Society for Caribbean Studies, and I am grateful to all those who took part in the resulting discussions.

The following kindly provided information or materials of various kinds: W. E. K. Anderson (Lincoln College, Oxford), Stephen Badsey (War Studies Department, Royal Military Academy, Sandhurst), Michael Ball (National Army Museum, Chelsea), Jo Currie (Special Collections, Edinburgh University Library), Geoffrey Davenport

(Royal College of Physicians), Henry Fraser (School of Clinical Medicine and Research, University of the West Indies, Cave Hill), Vincent Giroud (Beinecke Library, Yale), David J. Lewis (Lyman Entomological Museum and Research Laboratory, McGill University), John E. Mustain (Special Collections, Stanford University Libraries), Desmond V. Nicholson (Museum of Antigua and Barbuda), Victoria Borg O'Flaherty (National Archives of St. Christopher and Nevis), Felicity O'Mahony (Manuscripts Department, Trinity College Library, Dublin), Andrew O'Shaughnessy (University of Wisconsin, Oshkosh), Stephen Parks (Osborn Collection, Yale), David Pearson (Wellcome Institute for the History of Medicine), Ian Ritchie (National Portrait Gallery), Nicholas Rogers (Sidney Sussex College, Cambridge), Betty Shannon (Library of the Barbados Museum and Historical Society), R. A. H. Smith (British Library), Helen Watson (Scottish National Portrait Gallery).

I am also grateful to the staff of the following libraries and institutions without whose resources this project could not have been completed: the Bodleian Library and the Radcliffe Science Library, Oxford; the British Library; the Cambridge University Library, the Edinburgh University Library, the General Register Office for Scotland, the National Library of Scotland, the Public Record Office and the Warwick University Library. Over the years, my friends Andy and Myrna Taitt, of The Book Place, Bridgetown, Barbados, have helped to furnish my study with a significant part of the material used in this work.

My father-in-law, Grafton Browne, and my wife Marita have helped with a number of points of detail about Caribbean agriculture and rural life. Marita and our children Alex and Annabelle have lived with Dr Grainger for longer than they probably care to remember; I cannot give adequate expression to the gratitude I have for their tolerance and understanding. My mother and father made this book possible through their support of my education over so many years: it is dedicated to my father's memory.

John Gilmore

Centre for British and Comparative Cultural Studies
and
Centre for Caribbean Studies
University of Warwick

# Abbreviations

| | |
|---|---|
| 1764 | The first edition of *The Sugar-Cane* (London: Printed for R. and J. Dodsley ... 1764). |
| Bailey | N. Bailey, *Universal Etymological English Dictionary* ... (6th ed., 1733). |
| Bod. | Bodleian Library, Oxford |
| DNB | *Dictionary of National Biography* |
| E | Virgil, *Eclogues* |
| Errata | Errata list to *1764*. |
| G | Virgil, *Georgics* |
| Johnson | Samuel Johnson, *Dictionary of the English Language*, 4th ed. (1773) |
| n. | (and) note(s) [referring to Grainger's notes to the poem] |
| NLS Adv. MS | National Library of Scotland, Edinburgh, Advocates' Manuscript |
| TCD | Trinity College, Dublin, MS 880, a draft version (1762) of *The Sugar-Cane* in Grainger's hand. |

Full details of other works referred to by abbreviated titles are given in the Bibliography.

# Introduction

The name of James Grainger is known to most students of eighteenth-century literature in English. He rates a passing mention in most of the appropriate works of reference, and is represented in a number of anthologies. *The Sugar-Cane* enjoyed considerable success on its first publication (1764), and was reprinted with some frequency over the next seventy years. It is both a major work in the English georgic tradition, and a major work in the early history of Caribbean literature. There were many other eighteenth-century Caribbean poems, but *The Sugar-Cane* was the only one which for several decades found a place in the mainstream of 'English literature.' It is a skilled and successful poem of its kind, and as a document in cultural history it offers many points of interest: as an 'imitation' (in the eighteenth-century sense) of its Virgilian model, as an essay in the transculturation of a poetical form, as an important example of the literature of empire, and as a detailed and often illuminating exposition of plantation slavery and the attitudes which supported it.

For many years, however, *The Sugar-Cane* has been little read. Changes in taste (which are discussed below, and make an interesting study in themselves) have meant that the last complete edition was printed in 1836. It is also a poem which is better understood with some knowledge of the author's life, and of both its background in the literature of the period and the Caribbean context in which it was written: information which it has generally been difficult to find in combination. In the hope that current growing interest in a wider view of eighteenth-century literature and in the development of the literature of empire will win Grainger new readers, the present work offers a complete text of the poem for the first time in more than a hundred and fifty years, together with a detailed introduction and notes.

## 1. Biographical sketch of a 'Twofold disciple of Apollo'

> What is fame? an empty bubble;
> Gold? a transient, shining trouble.
> (Grainger, 'Solitude, an Ode,' ll. 96–7)

Less than 24 years after his death, Grainger's surviving daughter had a legal document registered in Edinburgh in an attempt to recover a small debt claimed to be still 'owing to umq[1]. [i.e. 'umquhill,' a Scots word meaning 'the late'] D$^r$ James Granger [sic] of the Island of S$^t$ Christophers at the time of his decease who died abroad upon the ... day of ... seventeen hundred and ... years'. As she had been only an infant at the time, Eleanora Grainger can be forgiven for being unable to supply the exact date or even the year of her father's death, but this is symptomatic of the problems facing anyone who seeks to write even the briefest account of Grainger's life.[1] Neither the date nor the place of his birth and death can be stated with certainty. A number of the details in published accounts of his life are mutually contradictory, and some are demonstrably erroneous.

Grainger's last surviving letter, to his friend Thomas Percy, was written on 4 December 1766 from Basseterre, capital of the Caribbean island of St Kitts (then as now officially referred to as St Christopher, but the shorter form was already in current use in Grainger's day).[2] This is the letter to which Percy refers when, writing to Grainger's biographer and editor Robert Anderson in 1805, he says 'Of the time of his death I was informed by the Captain of a Ship, who brought me a very kind Letter from him, and a present of a pig fed with Sugar Canes; But told me the writer had died just as he was leaving St Kitts.'[3] This suggests Grainger died in St. Kitts, as does the statement of a former acquaintance that he 'had been inform'd by those that knew' that Grainger died 'at his own House in the W[est] Indies'.[4] In the mid-nineteenth century the publisher and editor John Bowyer Nichols had a letter (apparently no longer extant) from Grainger's widow to Percy, 14 February 1770, which he quoted as saying 'he died on the 16th of December 1766, in the 39th year of his age.'[5] The nearest to a contemporary reference is in the *Gentleman's Magazine* (XXXVII, 95; February 1767) under 'List of Deaths for the Year 1766–7', which has '*Dec.* 24 Dr Grainger, physician at Antigua.'[6] His medical services were apparently in demand in other islands besides St Kitts[7], and there is nothing implausible in the suggestion that he died while on a visit to the neighbouring island: the distance by sea from Basseterre in St Kitts to St John's in Antigua would have been about 100 kilometres, or roughly 55 nautical miles. However, there appears to be no extant record of Grainger's burial in either St Kitts or Antigua, or any surviving tombstone or monumental inscription[8] – something he unwittingly prophesied in *The Sugar-Cane* (III, 654). Grainger's will[9], made in St Kitts 17 July 1763, was proved in that island 9 June 1767.

If his wife was correct in believing that Grainger was 39 when he died, this would mean he was born about 1727. Robert Anderson doubted this on the grounds that it was inconsistent with known facts about Grainger's life (though the examples he gives seem inconclusive) and he suggested that Grainger had been 'about 44' when he died[10], making him born about 1722. William Wright claimed that when he had seen Grainger in St Kitts in 1762, 'he appeared then, to be about 47 years of age'[11]; oddly specific for a judgement based on appearance, this would make him born about 1715, and mean that his wife's belief about his age was a dozen years out, which seems unlikely.

Robert Anderson never knew Grainger personally, but he does appear to have known the widow of Grainger's older half-brother William Grainger, or at least to have been provided with information by her. Some credence is therefore due to Anderson's suggestions that James Grainger was born at Dunse in Berwickshire, Scotland (now Duns in the Scottish Borders), and that 'He was the son of John Grainger, Esq. of Houghton-Hall, in the county of Cumberland; who, in consequence of some unsuccessful speculations in mining, was obliged to sell his estate; and having obtained an appointment in the Excise, settled at Dunse.'[12] The former English county of Cumberland (now part of Cumbria) was just the other side of the border between England and Scotland and on the other (western) side of the country. Grainger himself said 'I am the son of a gentleman of Cumberland' and that his father 'was ruined by his own extravagance, and that of his wives.'[13] Writing 35 years after Grainger's death, his friend Percy said he had 'understood his Father had a post in the Customs or Excise somewhere on the western English Border which he left thro' his attachment to the Stuart family in their unfortunate Year 1715' (or in other words, that in the Jacobite Rebellion of that year he had been among those who unsuccessfully supported the exiled claimant to the throne, 'James III', son of James II, rather than the new Hanoverian dynasty). A few years later, Percy specifically claimed to have had this information from Grainger himself. Percy also suggested that Grainger's father might at some point have settled in Annandale (just north of Cumberland, on the other side of the Anglo-Scottish border) but this seems to be no more than speculation based on a passage in *The Sugar-Cane*.[14] Anderson had the parish register of Dunse searched from 1719 to 1731, but 'no vestige of the name or family of Grainger' was found. In fact, there is now a computerised index to the records of the Church of Scotland (the Kirk, or the established church in Scotland, which was Presbyterian) which makes it a comparatively simple task to discover that there is no baptism of a James Grainger in the surviving records of the Kirk for the appropriate period anywhere in Scotland. Anderson suggested that Grainger might have been a member of the Scottish Episcopal Church, as his half-brother was, and Percy – himself a Church of England (Episcopalian) clergyman – agreed that this seemed to be the case: 'when he was my Guest which he was for several weeks in the Country, he always went to Church with me, nor did I ever discover that he differ'd from our established Episcopal Church in any point of Doctrine or Discipline.' This would explain his absence from the Kirk records, but the Episcopalian records for Duns only go back to 1853.[15] Whatever the exact circumstances of Grainger's birth, there can be no doubt that he thought of himself as a Scot, and that he was accepted by other Scots as such.[16] Grainger calls himself 'Scoto-Britannus' on the title-page of his *Dissertatio Medica Inauguralis* (1753), refers to Scots as 'my Countrymen' in a letter to Percy, and makes nostalgic references to Scotland in *The Sugar-Cane*. William Cuming, a Scottish physician living in England who met Grainger in 1754, believed that they were both 'born in Edinburgh' and said that he himself had been a pupil of Grainger's uncle, 'a genteel worthy Man, & an eminent Writing Master in that City'. William Wright, another Scottish physician who knew Grainger in the Caribbean, thought 'D$^r$ Grainger was the son of M$^r$ Grainger one of the ministers of Edinburgh,' while the Scottish General Melville, who never actually met Grainger, but who had corresponded with him while they were both in the Caribbean, believed him to be 'a native of Edinburgh'.[17]

## Introduction 5

According to Anderson, 'His father dying while he was young, the care of his education was kindly undertaken by his elder brother, by a former marriage, Mr William Grainger of Wariston, a writing-master in Edinburgh, and afterwards a clerk in the office of the Comptroller of Excise, who placed him at the school of North Berwick, under the tuition of Mr James Rae, formerly one of the masters of the High-School in Edinburgh, a teacher of eminent learning and abilities [...] After the ordinary course of education, he was put apprentice to Mr. George Lauder, surgeon in Edinburgh, and afterwards attended the medical classes in the University.' This last statement is apparently contradicted by Grainger himself, who said 'After being three years at the University, I was bound to an eminent surgeon-apothecary.' The earliest documented evidence about Grainger's career appears to be that in 1739 he matriculated at the University of Edinburgh in the class of John Kerr, Professor of Humanity. In the eighteenth century, students often started at a university at a much younger age than is normally the case now. Boswell went to the University of Edinburgh around the time of his thirteenth birthday, and many students matriculated there when they were about fourteen. Grainger is unlikely to have been much younger than this (which would suggest a date of birth around 1725). While Edinburgh has no medical matriculations extant before 1762, a James Granger was listed as attending the Anatomy classes of Alexander Monro, Primus, in 1741, 1742 and 1743 (the difference in spelling can be explained by the fact that Grainger himself signed the Arts matriculation, but the Anatomy lists were made by Monro or his clerk).[18] Grainger's own statement suggests that his attendance at the university's medical classes preceded, or possibly overlapped with, his apprenticeship to a surgeon.

The 1740s were a period of considerable upheaval in Scottish history. Britain as a whole was at war from 1739 to 1748; this was at first a conflict between Britain and Spain, popularly known as the 'War of Jenkins' Ear', but Britain was soon also fighting against France in the wider conflict of the War of the Austrian Succession, which involved most of the European powers. On 25 July 1745, Prince Charles Edward Stuart landed on the Scottish mainland, hoping to make good the claim of his father James Francis Edward Stuart (known to his supporters as 'James III' and to his opponents as the 'Old Pretender') that he, rather than George II (the representative of the Hanoverian dynasty), was the rightful king of Great Britain and Ireland. This was the beginning of what came to be known as the second Jacobite Rebellion, or 'the Forty-Five.' The prince had brought some arms and ammunition with him, and managed to raise enough men among Scottish supporters of his cause to create a viable military force. He reached Edinburgh on 17 September and defeated a Hanoverian army at Prestonpans on 21 September. At the end of October, the prince marched south into England, reaching as far as Derby (5 December) before retreating to Scotland, reaching Glasgow on 26 December.

By this time Edinburgh had been reoccupied by troops loyal to the Hanoverian government. While support for the Stuart family was certainly greater in Scotland than in England, it should not be exaggerated; a large proportion of Scots were either indifferent or active supporters of the Hanoverian side. Nevertheless, we should not assume that the defeat of the Rebellion was inevitable – it did not seem so at the time. On 17 January 1746, some 8,000 men under Prince Charles Edward routed a slightly larger Hanoverian force at Falkirk Muir, about halfway between Glasgow and Edinburgh. However, the prince was unable to make good his victory or keep his almost entirely irregular troops together (the British navy had ensured that most of the reinforcements of regulars he had hoped for from France had never reached Scotland), and he began to retreat northwards. While he had some further successes, particularly the capture of Inverness on 17 February, after Falkirk Muir a reorganised Hanoverian army under the command of the Duke of Cumberland (a younger son of George II) began to take the initiative. On 16 April 1746, Cumberland won a decisive victory over Prince Charles Edward's army at the Battle of Culloden, and put an effective end to the rebellion.[19]

According to Anderson, Grainger 'was surgeon in Pulteney's Regiment, at the battle of Falkirk.' This is certainly incorrect (apart from the fact that Anderson assigns the battle to the year 1745) though it is possible that Grainger was at the battle as a surgeon's mate with Pulteney's. Also known as the 13th Foot, this was a regiment of regular troops in the British army.[20] Grainger was a surgeon's mate with Pulteney's at Culloden, and wrote a letter to his brother William about the battle and its aftermath which shows that (whatever his father's sentiments about the Jacobite cause might have been) he himself was strongly pro-Hanoverian: 'You may be sure it gave me infinite joy to see those who threatened ruin to our glorious Constitution of Church and State dead on the field'.[21]

The anti-Jacobite campaign no doubt gave Grainger opportunity to demonstrate whatever medical skills he had acquired as a result of attending the university's classes and from his apprenticeship – though the 13th Foot had only 14 casualties at Falkirk Muir and none at Culloden. The regimental surgeon, John Hadzor (or Hadzer) may have been old enough to find active service a bit much for him, as he had been with the regiment since at least 1715. Presumably Grainger continued with the 13th Foot when it and other regiments were sent after Culloden to Perth, where they arrived about 14 May. From 28 June 1746, Grainger officially ranked as Surgeon in the 13th Foot, and would have been with the regiment when it and others were marched to Burntisland at the beginning of August to embark for Flanders. They took part in various campaigns in the Low Countries in 1746 and 1747, including the Battle of Val (or Lauffeld), 2 July 1747. Grainger's commission as Surgeon in the 13th Foot (replacing Hadzor) was dated 19 September 1746. This represented more than a simple promotion, for a regimental surgeon was a commissioned officer (which a surgeon's mate was not) and was therefore entitled to wear a sword and be considered as a gentleman – though Grainger may have felt he enjoyed this status anyway, as (at least in later life) he claimed the right to a coat of arms.[22]

In November 1747 the 13th Foot returned to England, where the regiment was employed on anti-smuggling duties on the south coast, although Grainger himself seems to have remained with the army in Flanders. The war ended the following year with the Treaty of Aix-la-Chapelle (18 October 1748). Anderson says Grainger left the army after the peace in 1748, and this statement is repeated by later writers, such as Gordon Goodwin in his *Dictionary of National Biography* article on Grainger. While it can be shown that Grainger remained in the army for several more years, it seems probable that he obtained an extended period of leave after the peace and that he devoted this to travel. He later said he had 'made the tour of Europe' and it is difficult to see when else during his life this could have been done. His minor poems include 'Three Elegies written from Italy,' there are references to Italy in *The Sugar-Cane* which suggest personal experience, and one of his book-reviews suggests that he either had or claimed to have a good knowledge of Italian, and that he had seen Goldoni's *Padre di Famiglia* acted at the Venetian carnival of 1750.[23] Later that year he probably rejoined the 13th Foot, as he made notes on the illness of a soldier's wife at Aberdeen in 1750, though 'Little is known of the movements of the Regiment about this period except that from 1751 to 1753 they were in Scotland.'[24] He subsequently published a paper on 'An obstinate Dysentery cured by Lime-Water'[25] describing the case of a soldier he had treated over a continuous period of 14 months in Scotland and northern England, from November 1751 to January 1753. On 14 March 1753 he presented his dissertation for the degree of Doctor of Medicine at the University of Edinburgh; published the same year with a dedication to John Craufurd, the Lieutenant-Colonel of the 13th Foot, this was in Latin (as was usual for the period) and discussed the use of mercury in the treatment of syphilis. By now at least in his late twenties, Grainger could at last consider himself fully qualified: the Edinburgh MD remained a first degree until after the Medical Act of 1858. Also in 1753, he published another Latin work giving his observations of the fevers he had observed among his army patients in the Low Countries from 1746 to 1748, but the former physician-general to the British forces in Flanders, John Pringle, had published his *Observations on the Diseases of the Army* the previous year, and Grainger's offering was unable to compete with this: a contemporary review noted 'indeed it is possible, this performance may appear to a somewhat greater disadvantage by succeeding one that has been so deservedly well received', but said that while Grainger had 'displayed a profusion of reading, very little is offered that can be esteemed new, or capable of contributing very greatly to the improvement of medicine'.[26] In October 1753 the 13th Foot left Scotland for the south of England, where they were at first engaged on more anti-smuggling duties along the Sussex coast, before proceeding to Salisbury. At some point in late 1753 or early 1754, Grainger, as he himself put it, 'sold out of the army', i.e., sold his commission (according to the frequent practice of the period), presumably to George St Clair, his successor as surgeon of the 13th Foot, whose commission was dated 19 February 1754.[27]

Grainger, who 'had but a few hundreds' of pounds to his name, settled in London about this time and practised medicine there, becoming a Licentiate of the College of Physicians on 20 March

1758. However, this was not his only resource. By 1754 (and probably during that year) he had become acquainted with a young man of about 16 called John Bourryau, who was admitted a fellow-commoner of Trinity College, Cambridge, on 21 August 1754 and matriculated at Michaelmas 1755, though it is not clear how long he remained at the university and he never took a degree. Bourryau's father, Zachariah Bourryau (who had died in 1752) was a London merchant who owned an estate in Lincolnshire and property in St Kitts, where he may have been born. John Bourryau was described as Grainger's 'pupill', and Grainger referred to him as 'my patron' and said that he 'had in a great measure, the superintendance of his Studies' – presumably some payment was involved. From May 1756 until May 1758, Grainger was also a regular contributor to the *Monthly Review*, one of the most successful and best regarded periodicals of the day. It also had a reputation for comparatively generous payment – at a slightly later date (1771) it paid contributors four guineas for each printed sheet, against the two guineas a sheet paid by its rival the *Critical Review*. Grainger reviewed a military treatise, medical works, books of travel, translations, contemporary poetry and miscellaneous works in a manner which suggested extensive reading not only of English literature from the seventeenth century onwards (especially poetry), but also of European medical and general literature from classical antiquity and the Renaissance, as well as a fairly good knowledge of contemporary French literature and at least some acquaintance with Italian and Spanish. He may also have found other ways to employ his pen: one example we know of is that in 1757 the publisher Andrew Millar (a fellow Scot) got him to write the second volume of a bulky folio work on *The History and Antiquities of Scotland* which had been left unfinished by the death of William Maitland, the original author.[28]

Whatever Millar paid him, there was little prestige to be had from this sort of anonymous hack-work and the contributions to the *Monthly Review* (like nearly all reviews of the period) were also anonymous. However, in 1755 the well-known London publisher Robert Dodsley brought out a fourth volume of his *Collection of Poems ... By several hands* (which first appeared in three volumes in 1748) and the new volume included (pp. 233–43) a poem called 'Solitude. An Ode.' Like many of the pieces in Dodsley's *Collection*, it was at first unattributed, but it came to be known that it was the work of Grainger, and it won him some degree of recognition – doubtless helped by the fact that Dodsley's *Collection* went on to become one of the most popular anthologies of the century and that his name was printed with the poem in later editions. More than twenty years after its original publication, Samuel Johnson could repeat the opening of 'Solitude' from memory to Boswell, and describe it as 'very noble.'[29] Some later critics have found it interesting as a 'pre-Romantic' poem, or dismissed it as 'simply one more pseudo-Miltonic poem of sensibility,' but as Phillip B. Anderson points out, there is rather more to it than that. The opening address to Solitude as 'romantic maid' may indeed seem like 'a poem solidly in the tradition of Collins or the Wartons', and the poet-speaker goes on to imagine 'a series of quiet landscapes which palpably breathe an air of pseudo-Miltonic melancholy' (the Milton of *Il Penseroso*, whose tetrameter couplets are imitated here, as they had earlier been imitated by Joseph Warton) and 'a gothic desert which is full of knells, gloom, and charnals and which is worthy of Young.' Then there is a change 'unique in the poetry of the mid-eighteenth century' for Solitude 'not only speaks, but speaks in heroic couplets.' By contrast, 'None of the personified figures of Collins or the Wartons speaks, for their poetry is not a poetry of statement.' And 'The message of Solitude is consistent with her medium' for she points out sternly that however pleasing the thought of retirement from the world may be, this is form of self-indulgence which is incompatible with the duties which divine command has given man to fulfil – only at the end of life, when duty has been done, may Solitude 'Allay the pangs of age.'[30] Grainger's emphasis in 'Solitude' on the importance of society and the reciprocal nature of human obligations ('God never made an independent man/ 'Twould jar the concord of his general plan') perhaps prefigures his emphasis on the rôle of commerce in *The Sugar-Cane*, just as the idea that 'The height of virtue is to serve mankind' not only reminds us of Grainger's medical background, but also to some extent looks forward to his discussions of the care and treatment of slaves, both in *The Sugar-Cane* and his prose *Essay on the more common West-India Diseases*.

During the summer of 1756, Grainger was introduced to the Rev. Thomas Percy, a young clergyman (born 1729) of literary tastes who in a distinguished old age did his best to preserve and foster Grainger's reputation: nearly all of Grainger's surviving letters are to Percy, and much of what we know about Grainger's life and works ultimately depends on Percy himself or on the encouragement he gave to Robert Anderson. By this time Grainger was well connected in literary London, and it was he who introduced Percy to Samuel Johnson (who had published his *Dictionary* in 1755) and later to Oliver Goldsmith (still a virtually unknown hack).[31] Grainger himself was ambitious of literary fame: one of his earliest letters to Percy has a seal showing a hand holding a quill and the Latin motto 'Penna perennis erit' ('The pen shall be eternal').[32] Eighteenth-century medical men often were, or at least aspired to be, gentlemen of wide general culture as well as practitioners of a specific scientific discipline: Sir Richard Blackmore (c. 1655–1729), Sir Samuel Garth (1661–1719), John Armstrong (c. 1709–79), Mark Akenside (1721–70) and Grainger's friend Goldsmith were only some of the medical practitioners who acquired a reputation as poets. The double rôle of Apollo as god of medicine and poetry was something of a cliché: an anonymous contemporary versifier, for example, hailed Akenside as 'Twofold Disciple of APOLLO!'[33] Grainger was preparing for the press a translation of the poems of Tibullus, a Roman poet of the first century BC, which he had begun while still in the army, and he discussed this in detail in his correspondence with Percy, who made many suggestions and supplied parts of the translation as it finally appeared. The two of them also began work on a collaborative translation of the *Epistolae Heroidum* ('Letters of Heroines') of Ovid, a classical poet more popular in the eighteenth century than Tibullus; this was never finished, possibly because of the appearance of another translation of the same work.[34]

Although dated 1759 on the title-pages, the Tibullus translation appeared towards the end of 1758 and soon involved Grainger in a heated controversy with the novelist and critic Tobias Smollett (1721–71, another Scottish medical man), who was the editor of the *Critical Review*. The controversy is extremely revealing about attitudes to translation in the period, and some of the arguments about Grainger's choice of words, particularly the assumption (taken for granted by both Grainger and Smollett) that the correct language for poetry is the language of a London literary public are of interest in view of Grainger's somewhat ambivalent championship of the use of both 'terms of art' and Caribbean vocabulary in *The Sugar-Cane*. Similarly, Tibullus is not simply a love-poet; he –

and Grainger as his translator – is very concerned about the significance and importance of money in his society and about its effect on human relations. This concern is developed in the theme of the importance of commerce in *The Sugar-Cane*. Tibullus's rôle as a poet of husbandry and of cultivated landscape is also one which is central to Grainger's concerns in *The Sugar-Cane*. Particularly noteworthy is the fact that the translation is dedicated to John Bourryau, who may have paid for its publication; while in the notes and translation Grainger emphasises the importance of slavery in ancient Rome (rather more than is apparent in the original), the general effect is to suggest that contemporary slavery in the Caribbean is much less harsh than ancient Roman slavery. In spite of Smollett, Grainger's translation enjoyed some success, and continued to be reprinted into the twentieth century.[35]

Tutor and pupil were associated in another literary venture, for Grainger contributed 'The Cyclops of Euripides' to a collaborative translation from the French of *The Greek Theatre of Father Brumoy* edited (and mainly written by) his friend the novelist Charlotte Lennox, while Bourryau contributed the 'Discourse on the Cyclops of Euripides, and Theatrical Representations of the Satyric Kind.'[36] By the time this appeared in 1759, Grainger had decided on a major change in his life. Bourryau had reached the age of 21 in August 1758, and thus had control of his fortune. He now proposed to Grainger that 'as a strict Intimacy had long subsisted between us', he should accompany Bourryau on his travels for a period of four years, promising to settle on him in return an income of £200 a year for life. Although Grainger claimed 'my Business was exceeded by that of no young Physician in Town,' his income from his medical practice and his literary efforts was clearly not enough to enable him to resist the prospect of this annuity and 'the patronage of Noblem[en] of Interest, whose Good-will I may haply acquire abroad.'[37] Presumably what was intended was the conventional 'Grand Tour' of Europe, for which Grainger would have been excellently qualified as a travelling companion, but it was decided that first they should spend some time visiting Bourryau's Caribbean property, and by early April 1759 Grainger was on his way to St Kitts.[38] He 'arrived there 6 weeks from England, after a tolerable good passage'[39], probably about the end of May or early June. While there were other persons of the name of Grainger or Granger in St Kitts in the eighteenth century, there is nothing to indicate that there was any family connection or that Grainger himself was even aware of this, far less that it in any way influenced his decision to accompany Bourryau.[40]

Percy heard nothing directly from him for over a year, but eventually received a letter Grainger had written from St Kitts, 1 June 1760, informing him that he was now 'a settled physician in St Christopher w[i]t[h] a family.' On the voyage out, he was asked to go to another ship in the fleet to attend a widow who was suffering from smallpox, and found himself attracted to one of her daughters. Shipboard romance led to an engagement, and they got married sometime after they arrived in St Kitts. Grainger's wife was Daniel Mathew Burt, whose masculine-sounding Christian names were those of prominent Caribbean families to whom she was related. She was almost certainly the 'Mathew dau. of [...] Pym and Louisa Burt' whose baptism was recorded at St Anne's, Sandy Point, St Kitts, sometime in August 1738, which would make her about ten years or more younger than her husband (though baptisms in the Caribbean at this period did not always take place soon after birth, and could occur up to several years later). Her father William Pym Burt (died 1750) had been Chief Justice of St Kitts, and her paternal grandfather William Burt (died 1707) had been President of Nevis. Her mother's father Sir William Mathew (died 1704) had briefly been Governor of the Leeward Islands, while her mother's brother, another William Mathew, had held the same office for more than 20 years at his death in 1752. Her brother, William Mathew Burt, had been a member of the St Kitts Council and later became a member of the British Parliament (for Great Marlow, 1761) and Governor of the Leewards (1776–81). Her older sister Penelope was married to James Verchild, President of St Kitts (1759–69) and later Governor of the Leewards (1766–8). Not surprisingly, as she 'was of the first family in these Islands', Grainger assumed that 'She must be provided for as a Gentlewoman; I was accordingly Easy on that Head.'[41] However, it is possible that Grainger at first hoped she was wealthier than she turned out to be: when her brother later suggested that Grainger was an unsuitable match, apparently implying that he had been a fortune-hunter, he retorted (perhaps protesting a little too much) that 'Her fortune could be no temptation. A Doctor of Physic who had 200*l*. a-year, independent of practice, could never be tempted by the paltry consideration of 1000*l*. currency, and three or four negroes.'[42]

Nevertheless, although Grainger had been, as he himself admitted to Percy, 'a medical Traveller w[i]t[h] a Mistress in every place,' he does seem to have become not just 'a settled Physician' but also a family man who was genuinely devoted to his wife, and later to his daughters.[43]

Grainger began to look for medical work in St Kitts, having dissolved his arrangement with Bourryau. The parting was apparently amicable, although Johnson and others were to suggest there was a quarrel – Grainger and his family certainly remained on good terms with Charles Spooner, who was John Bourryau's uncle as well as being married to Grainger's wife's sister Mary, and when Bourryau died in 1769 he left £1,000 to Grainger's daughter Louisa.[44] Soon after his arrival Grainger wrote to Bourryau's brother-in-law, who reported to Percy that 'I find the D$^r$. picks up the pistoles very fast'[45] and about a year later he claimed that he could make £1,000 a year 'by Business', i.e. from his professional services and the fact that, 'as I must keep Drugs for my own practice,' he could also expect to make a profit from the sale of medicines. He expressed the hope of many British adventurers who went out to the Caribbean in the period: 'I therefore may reasonably expect to be able to return in a few Years w[i]t[h] an easy fortune to London.'[46] He had married into the group his contemporaries referred to as the Creoles, and modern historians call the plantocracy, that is, the local elite of European descent whose wealth and position was dependent on the ownership of plantations and of the slaves of African origin or descent who cultivated the land in sugar-cane and processed the cane into sugar for export to Britain. With an area of 68 square miles, St Kitts was one of the smaller British colonies in the Caribbean. In 1756 it was reported to have 21,891 slaves and 2,713 white inhabitants. On the other hand, its cane-lands had a reputation for exceptional fertility; the later eighteenth-century Caribbean historian Bryan Edwards described the dark grey loam found in much of the island as a soil 'more especially suited to the production of sugar than any other in the West Indies' and claimed that average production there was 'nearly two hogsheads of sixteen cwt. *per* acre for the whole of the land in ripe canes [...] a prodigious return, not equalled I imagine by any other sugar country in any part of the globe.' The years of Grainger's residence in the island were not only years of comparatively high production, but also of good prices for sugar on the London market, which could be twice as much as they had been in the 1720s and 1730s (though not as high as they reached later in the century).[47] Grainger was not only connected by family ties to the slave-based economy of St Kitts, but directly dependent on it for his income. His wife's cousin, Daniel Mathew, and some of his other relatives by marriage employed him to look after the slaves on their estates. The Rev. James Ramsay, who lived in St Kitts from 1762 to 1781, noted that 'A surgeon is generally employed by the year to attend the sick slaves. His allowance per head varies from fourteen pence to three shillings; in a few instances it rises to three shillings and sixpence sterling, besides being paid for amputations.' Grainger could also have expected to earn fees from attendance on white patients. However, these too, and things like the payment of £189-16-6 Grainger received in 1765 'for his attendance on the sick and wounded prisoners in the gaol' were indirectly dependent on the slave economy.[48] Some Caribbean doctors of the period were wealthy: the will of Dr George Crump, who died in Antigua in 1761, disposed of two plantations and legacies of several thousand pounds in money (though he was well connected and some of this may have been inherited). By contrast, Dr Thomas Fraser, who died in Antigua the same year, appears to have enjoyed a rather more modest prosperity.[49] However, Grainger gave great care to the exercise of his profession. The *Essay on the more common West-India Diseases* which he published in 1764 was the first work from the English-speaking Caribbean specifically devoted to the diseases and treatment of slaves. Dr William Wright, who had known Grainger personally in the Caribbean and who was himself an eminent physician, praised the *Essay*, saying that not only owners and managers of slaves, but also 'the Physicians and Surgeons profited much by it; both in the knowlege [sic] of diseases, and the virtues of many native plants in the Westindies [sic].' Wright also claimed that Grainger 'was in great repute' as a physician in St Kitts, and that 'He was often called, to Patients in the neighbouring Islands, and consulted by letter, for other Patients in distant West India Islands.'[50] Grainger's hopes of making a fortune were therefore not unrealistic.

However, his ambitions were not only financial. Little over a year after his arrival in St Kitts, he was writing to Percy that 'This Island affords a great fund of new poetical Images, which I am storing up in my mind to produce on a proper Occasion'.[51] The reference in

*The Sugar-Cane* (II, 174–7) to General James Wolfe appears to have been written before news of his death at the capture of Quebec (13 September 1759) reached St Kitts[52], and suggests that Grainger must have begun work on the poem very soon after he settled in the island. In June 1762, Grainger wrote to Percy that he had 'completed it, at least for the present, though no less than a Georgic, and in four books too [...] I now send you the whole; only as I have seen no hurricane, and have not yet had time to arrange my remarks on a fire by night in a cane field, those parts in the second book are incomplete.' He talked of publishing it by subscription 'on the finest paper,' with engravings.[53] The next month he sent Percy 'some Additions', mentioning that he had 'made many verbal Corrections of the whole' which he was not sending until he had received Percy's opinion of the earlier version, and that 'The preface, Arguments to each Book, & Dedication are also finished'.[54] In September 1762 Grainger was ill, and wrote a note in a copy of the poem requesting that, if he died, his nephews should transcribe it and send the fair copy to Percy. Grainger lived, and presumably the transcript was never made, but the copy itself eventually ended up in the library of Trinity College, Dublin. The only surviving manuscript of the poem, this is, as a cataloguer describes it, a 'foul copy, much corrected' but it clearly represents an intermediate stage between the version Grainger sent Percy in June 1762 and that finally published. It includes a version of the hurricane passage in Book II, and one of the cane-fire, not in Book II, where Grainger had originally thought of placing it, but in Book III, as in the published version. Long sections are substantially the same as the version eventually published, though there are numerous minor variations, and some significant differences in structure. For example, the Montano episode was in Book II rather than Book I, and the Junio and Theana episode is at the end of the volume, though there is a note (f. 42$^v$) suggesting it should be placed in Book I (rather than at the end of Book II). There is a dedication to the Earl of Bute, a fellow-Scot who was then prime minister; by the time the poem was published Bute had been out of office for a year, and it appeared without a dedication. There is comparatively little in the way of the annotation which is so prominent a feature of the published poem.[55]

In April 1763 Grainger wrote to Percy that 'I have now completed the Cane Piece, such as I could wish it to appear; but I shall not transcribe either my corrections or additions for England without first hearing from you.' He complained that he had heard nothing from Percy for more than fourteen months and was particularly disappointed to have had no response to the poem. On the other hand, he must have had some favourable comments from his friend the poet and landscape gardener William Shenstone (1714–63), for the 'Advertisement' to Book II of *The Sugar-Cane* says that Book was 'originally addressed to' Shenstone, 'and by him approved of'. Shenstone had died 11 February 1763, a fact of which Grainger was still unaware in April. On the other hand, the Seven Years' War was now over, and the terms of the peace (concluded by the Treaty of Paris, 10 February 1763) were known in the Caribbean. Grainger mentioned that 'Mr. Bourryau has bought a vast estate in Grenada' and that 'many of my friends have purchased large plantations' there. He himself hoped to be able to buy land either in Grenada or in one of the other Caribbean islands, such as St Vincent, which had been ceded to Britain by the Peace, but was handicapped by a shortage of ready cash, having 'converted all my money into negroes.'[56] The purchase of slaves who were then hired out for the benefit of the owner was popular with small investors. It is possible that they were domestics or artisans, but Grainger's ambition to be a planter makes it likely that they were agricultural labourers whom he would have hoped to use on a plantation of his own eventually, and that he had bought or built up what was known as a 'jobbing gang' of slaves who would be hired out to plantations which needed additional labour on an occasional basis, particularly in crop-time. As it was in the interest of the hirer to get as much work out of hired slaves as possible, while reducing the burden on the slaves he owned himself, the members of jobbing gangs had a notoriously hard life.

Around September or October 1763, Grainger left St Kitts for the British Isles. At the end of November, he wrote to Percy from London to say that he had just arrived from Scotland, where he 'had been on family business for some weeks.' He mentioned he had brought 'a corrected copy' of *The Sugar-Cane* 'which received the approbation of Lord Kames', the well-known Scottish judge and philosophical author who had a special interest in agricultural matters and whose *Elements of Criticism* had been published in 1762. Grainger told Percy, 'My time is short, and yet I must see you.'[57] He went to Easton Mauduit in Northamptonshire, where

Percy was vicar, travelling in some style: Percy noted on 16 December 1763, 'D<sup>r</sup>. Grainger came this ev[enin]g in a Post Chaise, w[i]th his Mulatto servant'. The next day Percy recorded that 'The D<sup>r</sup>. & I began to read over & correct the D<sup>r</sup>.'s Poem the Sugar-Cane. Lib. 1' (i.e. the first Book). The following day was Sunday, and Percy was busy with his clerical duties, but they read Book II on the Monday. They spent Tuesday with friends, but on the Wednesday and Thursday they read the third and fourth Books of the poem. After that, the rest of the visit seems to have been given to relaxation and seeing friends. Percy went fox-hunting on 23 December, and the next day Grainger read to him William Somervile's *The Chace*, a popular poem on hunting first published in 1735. Grainger was 'not well' on Christmas Day, but seems to have recovered quickly, and he returned to London on 30 December.[58]

He wrote to Percy three weeks later from Sonning in Berkshire (not far from London), where he was staying with Charles Spooner. He said 'I am come to no absolute determination with regard to "The Sugar Cane." I will not, however, risque its publication at my own expense.' He suggested Percy might mention it to Jacob Tonson (d. 1767) a well-known publisher of the day, and also said 'Sam Johnson has got the second book, but whether he has yet perused it I know not; perhaps it may lie in his desk untouched till I call for it.' He was missing his family, and said that at Spooner's 'we talk of scarce any thing else but dear St Christopher.'[59] While his 'family business' in Scotland seems to have been a major reason for Grainger's visit to Europe, it is unclear what was now keeping him in England past his originally intended departure, unless it was that he was anxious to see *The Sugar-Cane* in print.[60] He visited Percy again in Northamptonshire on 21 February and stayed until 17 March. He inoculated Percy's two daughters against smallpox, and Percy later recalled that 'During this or his former Visit he wrote his Ballad of Bryan and Pereene' – apparently at Percy's request – to be inserted in what became the *Reliques of Ancient English Poetry*, the collection which made Percy famous as a student of traditional ballad literature.[61]

A week after his return to London, he wrote to Percy, indicating that *The Sugar-Cane* was then in the process of being printed. It was described on the title-page as 'Printed for R. and J. Dodsley' and Grainger must by now have come to an agreement with James

Dodsley, who had taken over the publishing business from his brother Robert in 1759. The details are unknown, though Grainger's letter to Percy suggests that he had agreed to pay for 300 copies for his own use.[62] It was presumably sometime in this period between about November and March that there occurred the well-known incident recorded by Boswell, when *The Sugar-Cane* was 'read in manuscript at Sir Joshua Reynolds's' (see Appendix I). While Grainger had a substantial library in St Kitts[63], he may also have used this time and the libraries of friends and acquaintances to work up some of the more obscure information included in the footnotes to the poem.

The printing was going 'slowly' when Grainger wrote to Percy again at the beginning of April, though 'Sam Johnson says he will review it in the Critical.' At the end of the month Grainger was busy getting ready to return to the Caribbean, but on 14 May he was still at Southampton, detained by unfavourable winds and miserable at still being away from his family. He told Percy 'The Sugar Cane is printed, but when it will be published, I know not.' In May 1764, the leading London printer, William Strahan (1715–85 – another Scot) charged James Dodsley £20 18s. for printing 750 copies of *The Sugar-Cane*, and another £2 14s for 'Extra Corrections in D[itt]o throughout', which suggests that one reason for the slowness of the printing had been that Grainger kept making last-minute alterations. The *Gentleman's Magazine* for June 1764 included it in the 'List of Books lately published' and in its next issue printed the whole of the Junio and Theana episode.[64]

By this point, Grainger would have been well on his way back to the Caribbean. He found his family well but 'the person to whom I had intrusted the management of my little Concerns had wholy [sic] neglected them so that instead of having Money to receive, I found myself greatly behind hand.' His wife became seriously ill, and soon after she began to recover, he heard that his brother had died in Scotland.[65] He wrote to Percy over the next several months, asking how *The Sugar-Cane* had been received in England, and full of enthusiasm for the idea of buying a plantation in St Vincent or one of the other 'neutral islands' (St Vincent, Dominica, St Lucia and Tobago) which had been ceded to Britain by the Treaty of Paris, and where land could now be bought from the British government on easy terms. He thought of selling the property his brother had left him in Scotland in order to buy land in St Vincent, convinced it would be a lucrative venture: 'I have got a good number of fine young negroes, and, as I am well acquainted with West India agriculture, I cannot help thinking it will be worth my while to sacrifice a few more years in this climate, to the leaving behind me of a little fortune of four or five hundred a-year to my family.'[66] By the end of the year or early in 1766, he had changed his mind and was now 'perswaded the *first* Adventurers there, will *all* be ruined.' He was worrying about money, and uncertain whether to stay in St Kitts or return to England: 'What my Brother left me is not sufficient to maintain my Family w[i]t[h]out Business; & I do not know, how far I should be able to get into any, should I again make London the place of my Aboad. It is certain I can not only live here but also save some small matter yearly by my profession. But then I am lost, murdered for want of Company, & w[i]t[h] all my Sweat, I never can expect to make an independent fortune by physic.'[67]

Almost a year after that, he wrote to Percy again, apparently much happier and more settled. He grumbled that the *Annual Register* had not mentioned *The Sugar-Cane*, but he was pleased to have heard from a friend in Edinburgh that it had 'been greatly applauded at Paris by the authors of the *Gazette Litteraire de l'Europe*.' He reported 'I have at last got into a house of my own, and I now write to you in a library thirty-six feet long and twenty wide. It is at the end of a very pretty garden, and commands a complete prospect of the bay and beautiful vale of Basseterre, which is, at this moment, more verdant than any English meadow in the month of May. From this you will easily conclude that I mean to remain some years longer in the torrid zone.'[68] Whatever Grainger might have hoped to accomplish in that library – the composition of a West Indian epic would have been a logical progression from *The Sugar-Cane* – was never to be, as he died before the month was out.

Grainger's widow mentioned a portrait of him in a letter to Percy in 1771, though it was not in her possession. Percy did not remember this in 1800 when Robert Anderson was trying to trace a portrait in order to have it engraved for his proposed edition of Grainger's works, and the portrait would appear to be now lost, or at least no longer identifiable. An anonymous attack on Mrs Grainger in 1773 described her late husband as 'a man of modesty and reserve', suggesting that he was shy in company until drink loosened his tongue: 'his friends were indebted to the inspiring juice of the grape to make him throw off the *mauvais* [sic] *honte* so prejudicial to his own merit; for, when warmed with the enlivening juice of the true Falernian, in spite of a broad provincial dialect, he was extremely pleasing in his conversation.' It went on to say, 'He was tall, and of a lathy make; plain featured, and deeply marked with the small pox; his eyes were quiet and keen; his temper generous and good-natured; and he was an able man in the knowledge of his profession.' From personal acquaintance, however, William Cuming insisted that this could not have been written by any one who actually knew Grainger, as 'D$^r$ Grainger was not deeply markt with the small pox, D$^r$ G. had none of that *mauvaise honte*, that required a degree of Intoxication to call forth his powers; he had no broad provincial Dialect when I knew him [...]'[69] Of his general character, 'Johnson said, that Dr. Grainger was an agreeable man; a man who would do any good that was in his power.'[70]

## 2. 'West-India georgic' – imitation and innovation in The Sugar-Cane.

> A perfect Judge will *read* each Work of Wit
> With the same Spirit that its Author *writ*,
> [...]
> In ev'ry Work regard the *Writer's End*,
> Since none can compass more than they *Intend*;
> And if the *Means* be just, the *Conduct* true,
> Applause, in spite of trivial Faults, is due.
> (Pope, *An Essay on Criticism*, ll. 233–4, 255–8)

Grainger began the Preface to the published version of his poem with the statement that 'Soon after my arrival in the West-Indies, I conceived the design of writing a poem on the cultivation of the Sugar-Cane.' This may have been prompted to a greater or lesser extent by his desire for literary fame, or hints from previous writers. On the title-page of his MD dissertation he had quoted from the *Syphilis* of Girolamo Fracastoro (?1478–1553), one of the most famous Latin poems of the Renaissance, which includes myths set in the Caribbean and an idealised account of Columbus's first voyage.[71] In *The Seasons* (final version published 1746), one of the most popular poems of the eighteenth century, James Thomson (another Scot) had described the natural riches of the tropics and hymned the praises of British commerce.[72] Grainger had reviewed John Dyer's *The Fleece* (1757), whose similar encomiums on trade include passing references to 'the Caribee isles, whose dulcet canes/Equal the honey-comb' and 'Those sea-wrapt gardens of the dulcet reed,/Bahama and Caribee'.[73] There was a significant quantity of earlier poetry written in the Anglophone Caribbean or by writers of Caribbean origin, but while Grainger seems unaware of this, there is in fact no earlier poem comparable to his own in scale or aspirations. The most substantial earlier effort is that of Nathaniel Weekes, a Barbadian by birth, but in the 1006 lines of his *Barbados: A Poem* (1754), Weekes devotes only a little over a hundred lines to the sugar industry.

Grainger told Percy that what was to become *The Sugar-Cane* 'was composed mostly in my rides to the different parts of the island to visit my patients'. Some aspects of the poem are simply the result of observing what was around him with a keen eye. In these we may include the descriptions of the St Kitts landscape and its flora and fauna. He mentions a wide range of plants, nearly all of them recognisable and identifiable in terms of modern scientific nomenclature, while a twentieth-century entomologist who made a special study of Grainger's references to insects and helminth parasites of man was led to describe him as 'a sane, careful observer.'[74] However, personal observation was certainly followed (or perhaps preceded) by library research. He refers in his Preface and notes to a number of well-known writers on the Caribbean and the wider Americas, and he almost certainly examined others he neglected to name. For example, he probably consulted not only Hans Sloane's *A Voyage to the Islands [...]* with its bulky and heavily illustrated account of the natural history of Jamaica in English, but also the same author's much shorter preliminary *Catalogus Plantarum* in Latin, which gives much more in the way of both Latin synonyms and common names, and more extensive references to other authors, although the actual descriptions of the plants are considerably briefer. He never mentions Griffith Hughes's *Natural History of Barbados*, but a few of the details in his notes may have been lifted from this source (see notes in this work, e.g. on I, 132–3, n.).

In his Preface, Grainger went on to say that his 'inducements' to the 'arduous undertaking' of composing such a poem 'were, not only the importance and novelty of the subject, but more especially this consideration; that, as the face of this country was wholly different from that of Europe, so whatever hand copied its appearances, however rude, could not fail to enrich poetry with many new and picturesque images.' Immediately afterwards, he emphasised that 'the precepts contained in this Poem' were 'the result of Experience, not the productions of Fancy.' Accordingly, 'though I may not be able to please, I shall stand some chance of instructing the Reader; which, as it is the nobler end of all poetry, so should it be the principal aim of every writer who wishes to be thought a good man.' He later refers to both 'pleasure and profit', though there seems to be more emphasis on the practical, such as the way he concludes the Preface by referring to his 'mention of many indigenous remedies'. Indeed, in a draft of the Preface he described the poem as 'principally intended for Instruction' (*TCD*, f. 103$^v$). However, we should also look at other indications of what Grainger thought he was doing.

His claims for his work begin on the title-page, with the Latin epigraph:

> Agredior primusque novis Helicona movere
> Cantibus, et viridi nutantes vertice sylvas;
> Hospita sacra ferens, nulli memorata priorum.

Chosen from the *Astronomica*, a lengthy poem on astrology and the appearance of the heavens composed early in the 1st century AD by the Roman poet Marcus Manilius, this may be translated: '... and I am the first to attempt to stir with new songs Helicon and its green-topped, nodding woods, bringing strange mysteries, proclaimed by none before me.' Taken at face value, this assertion of what he goes on to refer to in his Preface as the 'novelty of the subject' is bold enough, but it will repay closer attention. The word *sylva* normally means a wood or forest, and is unquestionably used here in this sense by Manilius, but it can also mean vegetation in general (compare for example Virgil, *G*, I, 152–3, where it is used with reference to burs and thistles). It is at least possible that Grainger, and some of his readers, saw in the *viridi nutantes vertice sylvas* not just the woods of Manilius, but a field of canes waving in the breeze, an interpretation reinforced by the picture of a cane-plant on the frontispiece opposite the title-page. Grainger is not only going to 'stir' Helicon (the mountain in Bœotia sacred to Apollo and the Muses in classical mythology) with his 'new songs,' his poem on a new subject, he is going to clothe it in cane-fields instead of pine-woods: the choice of quotation stresses Grainger's claim in the Preface for the 'importance' as well as the 'novelty' of his subject, and the belief on which the whole poem is based, that the cultivation of the sugar cane is a dignified and suitable subject for poetry.

In the Latin, the word *et* ('and') both connects and separates Helicon and its woods. Grainger's use of the quotation may have the further implication, which is also present in his Preface, that he hoped to appeal not only to a British literary public, but also to readers in the West Indies.

Both the novelty and the importance of his subject are given further emphasis by the final line, where Grainger applies to himself Manilius' claim that he is 'bringing strange mysteries, proclaimed by none before me.' The 'strange mysteries' are 'strange' in the sense of 'foreign, exotic' to a British literary public because they have never had a poem written about them before – indeed, as Grainger points out, little of any kind had been written on the subject. They might even be 'strange' in the sense of the term which Grainger applies in his Preface to the 'appearances' of 'this country' (by which he means the West Indies in general and St. Kitts in particular); the 'strange mysteries' are perhaps 'rude,' that is, 'rough, coarse, unpolished' (in Bailey's definition), perhaps even barbarous. But what are they? Grainger can only be applying the phrase to what his entire poem is describing, the different processes involved in the cultivation of the cane-plant and the production of sugar. These processes would indeed have been 'strange' in many senses of the word to most of the readership Grainger is addressing, but he calls them *sacra* – not mysteries in the sense of the secrets of a craft, though something of this is involved, but 'sacred things' – using a word which has the connotation of religious rites.

The choice of Manilius for the epigraph itself has programmatic implications. In the first place, it is an ostentatious indication of Grainger's view of himself as a learned poet. Although Manilius had been given a comparatively recent edition (1739) by the illustrious English classical scholar Richard Bentley, he was never as widely read as more famous Latin authors such as Virgil, Horace or Ovid. Nor, in fact, is there any need to suppose that even Grainger had read all of the *Astronomica* – the quotation comes from the very beginning of the poem.[75]

We may contrast the ending of Book I of Akenside's *The Pleasures of Imagination* (ed. Dix, pp. 108–9):

> Genius of ancient Greece! whose faithful steps
> Well-pleas'd I follow thro' the sacred paths
> Of nature and of science; nurse divine
> Of all heroic deeds and fair desires!

Akenside claims to be content to follow, but while Grainger has his *Vos sequor* ... in the Preface, and talks about following Virgil at a distance (II, 132–3), he also expresses the hope that he may transcend his classical models (I, 77–83). Akenside intends to 'tune to Attic themes the British lyre' but Grainger hopes that the 'new songs' he refers to in his quotation from Manilius will achieve rather more than that. Grainger does sometimes go in for conventional modesty – e.g. 'My imperfect strain' (II, 451); 'my weak song' (III, 591) – and he may wonder if he has achieved what he set out to do and seem anxious in his letters for the approbation of his friends, but there is no doubt that he is aiming high.[76]

The other important indicator of what Grainger thinks he is doing is his reference in the Preface to his poem as a 'West-India georgic.' In other words, he is attempting a work within a tradition of didactic poetry on agricultural and rural subjects which goes back to the classical period of European civilisation – he explicitly cites Hesiod and Virgil among his models – and which had achieved a renewed popularity in eighteenth-century Britain with works such as John Philips's *Cyder* (1708), William Somervile's *The Chace* (1735), Christopher Smart's *The Hop-Garden* (1752) John Dyer's *The Fleece* (1757) and, of course, James Thomson's *The Seasons* (1730), all of which Grainger refers to.[77] As with the other modern writers of this type of poetry, Grainger's main model is Virgil, and he says in a draft of his Preface (*TCD*, f. 104$^r$) that 'If the good natur'd Reader shall discover any thing praiseworthy in this poem, it must be ascribed to my having studied Virgil with some Attention.'

The literary culture of eighteenth-century Britain (and Europe in general) set a very high value on Virgil. Akenside, whose *The Pleasures of Imagination* (1744) was a didactic poem of a very different and non-agricultural sort, referred to Virgil in his Preface as 'the faultless model of didactic poetry'. What Akenside had in mind was not the pastoral poet of the *Eclogues*, or the epic poet of the *Aeneid*, but Virgil as poet of the *Georgics*, which is – on one level – as the etymology of the title shows, a poem about the agriculture of Italy in the first century BC. In a well-known and influential essay which Grainger quoted in his review of Dyer's *Fleece*, Joseph Addison (1672–1719) called the *Georgics* 'the most complete, elaborate, and finisht piece of all Antiquity.' One translator, Joseph Trapp (1679–1747), went a step further and called it 'the most *finish'd* and *perfect* Poem in the World.'[78]

This high estimate is difficult to understand if we believe (or think eighteenth-century critics believed) that the *Georgics* was, as a twentieth-century writer has suggested, 'written basically as a treatise on Italian agriculture.'[79] Virgil does describe aspects of the Italian countryside with the attentiveness of a careful observer, and he does dispense practical advice on farming (some of it highly unreliable). However, the *Georgics* is certainly not a versified textbook on how to be a farmer, even if it has sometimes been treated as such. Virgil is extremely selective about what he includes and what he leaves out, and what are usually referred to as his digressions are very much part of his overall plan. The theme of the poem is not the detail of agricultural practice, but the much grander one of the relationship between man and nature as a whole, set against a longing for stability and an end to the political upheavals of the period in which the work was composed. If there is any one passage which can be said to sum up the poem as a whole, it is perhaps the famous *labor omnia vicit/improbus et duris urgens in rebus egestas* (*G*, I, 145–6: 'unceasing toil overcame all things, and pressing need among hardships'). Modern classical scholarship has suggested Virgil intended a much more pessimistic reading of both this passage and the entire poem, pointing out, for example, that *improbus* can mean not only 'unceasing' but also 'harsh, grim' or even 'disgraceful, demeaning,' emphasising the grinding toil humanity is now forced to endure in order to survive, in contrast to the mythical golden age when a bountiful nature provided everything without the need for work. However, a traditional approach which was long accepted adopted a much more optimistic interpretation, exemplified in the version of this passage in the 1697 translation by John Dryden: 'What cannot endless labour, urged by need?'

Agriculture was indeed a struggle between man and nature, but aspects of Virgil's poem, such as the plague at Noricum in Book III, which suggested that (at least some of the time) man was utterly helpless in the face of the assaults of nature, were played down in order to suggest that the struggle was a heroic one in which (at least most of the time) man was triumphant.[80]

Both the optimistic and pessimistic versions depend on the fact that Virgil constantly reminds us that agriculture is the basis of human existence. He does this by treating agriculture – something which in pre-mechanised times could seldom be thought of without remembering that it was basically grubbing around in the dirt – in self-consciously lofty terms. For eighteenth-century writers and their public, there was a contradiction here. Addison defined a georgic as 'some part of the science of husbandry put into a pleasing dress, and set off with all the Beauties and Embellishments of Poetry.' Unfortunately, husbandry, by its very nature, put the poet in danger of 'letting his subject debase his stile, and betray him into a meanness of expression.' As Joseph Warton put it in the introduction to his 1753 translation of Virgil's *Georgics*, 'The coarse and common words I was necessitated to use in the following translation, viz. '*plough* and *sow, wheat, dung, ashes, horse* and *cow*' etc. will, I fear, unconquerably disgust many a delicate reader.' Addison claimed the answer to the problem was that 'nothing which is a Phrase or Saying in common talk, should be admitted into a serious Poem; because it takes off from the solemnity of the expression, and gives it too great a turn of familiarity: Much less ought the low phrases and terms of art, that are adapted to Husbandry, have any place in such a work as the *Georgic*, which is not to appear in the natural simplicity and nakedness of its subject, but in the pleasantest dress that Poetry can bestow on it.' Virgil had achieved this, said Addison, by the use of 'a pomp of verse' and 'a solemn air', so that 'He delivers the meanest of his precepts with a kind of grandeur, he breaks the clods and tosses the dung about with an air of gracefulness.'[81]

It was, as Virgil himself described it (*G*, III, 290) a matter of *angustis hunc addere rebus honorem*, of conferring dignity upon things mean in themselves. Eighteenth-century writers of georgic followed the precedent set by Philips's *Cyder* by attempting to do this 'in *Miltonian* Verse' – not so much the language of *Paradise Lost* as a special adaptation of it, full of grammatical inversions and elaborate paraphrases intended to avoid the necessity of calling a spade a spade by calling it instead a 'Metallic Blade, wedded to ligneous Rod/Wherewith the rustic Swain upturns the Sod.' This example, from Erasmus Darwin's *Botanic Garden* (1791), is perhaps an extreme one, and while eighteenth-century 'poetic diction' is not to the taste of most modern readers, this should not blind us to the fact that there were poets who could use it skilfully and to some purpose – or to the fact that some aspects of it which may strike us as especially peculiar were a normal part of scientific prose in the period. We also need to realise that there is sometimes an entirely conscious element of self-parody and mock-heroic in this kind of writing – it was not for nothing that the author of *Cyder* was also the author of *The Splendid Shilling* (1701), the first and most successful of many burlesque imitations of the Miltonic style. In many cases, the effect sought by the poet and the pleasure derived by the reader depend on an elaborate game in which something 'low' is deliberately introduced for the express purpose of being given 'the pleasantest dress that Poetry can bestow on it.' The rules of the game were well-established and could be taken for granted by both the poet and the reader in the eighteenth century; the modern reader needs to make an effort to learn them in order to make any serious attempt to '*read* each Work of Wit/With the same Spirit that its Author *writ*'.[82]

Where many eighteenth-century poets differed from the classical writers who were their ultimate inspiration was in their view of the relationship between the country and the city. Many classical writers (including Tibullus) compared the two in a manner which suggested that, at least as an ideal, rural simplicity was something far removed from urban sophistication and greatly to be preferred to it. By contrast, many of the eighteenth-century poets who claimed to follow in the steps of their classical predecessors, saw agriculture as a part, or even the foundation, of a commercial system which involved not only the nearest town, but the national capital and trade on a global scale. In Book III of *The Fleece*, for example, Dyer's contemplation of 'the labors of the loom' and 'How widely round the globe they are dispers'd' leads to a picture of London, 'where lofty trade,/Amid a thousand golden spires enthron'd,/Gives audience to the world' and the rapturous conclusion: 'What bales, what wealth, what industry, what fleets!/Lo, from the simple fleece how much proceeds.' This was an outlook congenial to Grainger, with his belief in the planter's 'honest purposes of gain' (III, 319). Not everyone was quite so enthusiastic: Grainger's friend Goldsmith, in his poem *The Traveller* (published in the same year as *The Sugar-Cane*) characterised international trade as 'The wealth of climes, where savage nations roam,/Pillag'd from slaves, to purchase slaves at home', while Johnson's vigorous denunciation of the city's corruption in his *London* (1738) – significantly, an imitation of the classical Roman poet Juvenal – associated 'vice and gain'. However, modern critics like Bonamy Dobrée and David Dabydeen have demonstrated that the celebration of British commerce was a frequent theme in eighteenth-century poetry, where it was often regarded as not only good in itself, but as a major contributor to the glory and importance of the British nation – a nation which was itself largely a construct of this period, as Linda Colley has shown. A large and valued part of British commerce, and one whose morality was generally unquestioned before the later part of the century, was the triangular trade between Britain, Africa and the Caribbean, in slaves and slave-grown sugar.[83]

By calling *The Sugar-Cane* a georgic, Grainger is explicitly aligning himself with this tradition. However, he does more than appropriate a label, for form and content are inextricably entwined in the poem. As many of his contemporary readers would have recognised (and as the notes to this study endeavour to show), many aspects of *The Sugar-Cane* are based on conscious imitation of Virgil's *Georgics*. These begin with the structure of the poem in four books, which begin with the soil itself and progress to the slaves and their treatment, in the same way that in the four books of his poem Virgil had, as Dryden put it, 'taken care to raise the subject of each Georgic', beginning with 'dead matter' and then moving on to vegetables, from vegetables to animals, and from animals to bees, 'the most sagacious of them'.[84] Grainger's hurricane is in many ways reminiscent of the storm in Virgil, just as his cane-field on fire echoes Virgil's fire in a grove of olive-trees. There are verbal resemblances (e.g. at II, 356) which suggest – unsurprisingly, in view of other evidence of Grainger's wide-ranging knowledge of classical literature – that while he was probably familiar with translations such as those of Dryden and Trapp, he certainly had Virgil's Latin text very much in mind when he was composing his own poem. Grainger makes conscious use of Shakespeare and Milton, and was also familiar with the work of contemporary poets in the georgic manner; among these it is Philips's *Cyder* which seems to have been drawn on most heavily. Sometimes a particular resemblance may be the result of the process by which writers can unconsciously absorb a phrase or two from somebody else, and later use this themselves, sincerely believing it to be their own: this may be the case with the lines Grainger recycled with only slight adaptation in his 'Solitude' from Joseph Warton's 'Ode to Fancy.'[85] On the other hand, when we find that Grainger's description of the slaves' dance is modelled on Philips's account of English rural festivities, the verbal echoes are so many that it is hard to believe that the process of adaptation was not a deliberate one (see IV, 582–605 and this writer's note). However, as with many other eighteenth-century writers, Grainger's use of imitation is not the result of laziness, plagiarism or lack of imagination, but a genuinely creative process which was consciously intended to achieve a particular effect.[86]

To imitate Virgil was to imitate the most illustrious model possible. Grainger's doing so was intended to establish the dignity and importance of his subject, and this would have been understood by his contemporary readers. The same is true of his choice of language: when we find Grainger calling the carnation 'More gorgeous than the train of Juno's bird' (I, 524) rather than 'prettier than a peacock's tail,' we know we are reading somebody who knows the rules of the game. Although he later dropped the lines, in one draft (*TCD*, f. 32$^r$) he adapted Addison's summary of Virgil's method by saying 'The Muse on Lowliness can Worth impart:/ And scatter Dung with conscious Majesty.' Grainger's choice of his form depends on more than his desire to make a name for himself by writing a poem of a kind which (however little it may appeal to modern tastes) enjoyed a considerable vogue in the eighteenth century. It enables him to move beyond the sort of conventional description of Caribbean scenery through the eyes of a temporary resident which is to be found in, for example, the anonymous poem 'The Pleasures of Jamaica' (1738).[87] Grainger's subject is, on the one hand, as he proclaims it in the opening lines of his poem (I, 1–4), the Caribbean landscape in its socio-economic context. On the other hand, he emphasises in his Preface not only the 'novelty' but also the 'importance' of his subject, the place of sugar in British commerce – as he puts it, 'Its vast importance to my native land' (I, 302). The form and style of his poem, the use of Miltonic blank verse and poetic periphrasis are not extraneous to his purpose, but an assertion that his subject in all its aspects – from the choice of soil for planting to the choice of slaves, from the treatment of chiggers and guinea-worms which ail the slaves to the extirpation of the rats which damage the crops – is a dignified and important one, because 'Supreme of plants, rich subject of my song' (I, 23), the 'imperial cane' (II, 100) is the source of much of the wealth and commerce of the British empire. From the beginning of the poem, where we see the 'huge casks, in order due,/Roll'd numerous on the Bay' (I, 27–8), to the end, with its vision of the mutual dependence of the metropolis and its colonies (IV, 654–83), we are repeatedly reminded that the cultivation of the sugar-cane is not a matter of growing some rather peculiar plant in a few small islands a long way from anywhere important, but the basis of a prosperous trading system which spans the Atlantic. Grainger's correspondence indicates he had a sense of humour, and it has been suggested that in parts of *The Sugar-Cane* he makes use of the mock-heroic mode in the same way as other eighteenth-century georgic poets, such as Smart in his *Hop-Garden*.[88] This is a possible interpretation, but Grainger never loses sight of the seriousness of his purpose. Even the rats, which in Boswell's well-known anecdote (see Appendix I) excited the ridicule of some of Grainger's contemporaries, are taken very seriously as destroyers of valuable canes. They, and the other pests of the cane, like the diseases of slaves which echo Virgil's plague at Noricum, contribute to the image of cane-growing as a heroic struggle between man and nature as much as the more obviously epic descriptions of the hurricane and the fire. He expresses it rather more subtly, but Grainger's message is the same as that of Nathaniel Weekes, who, when he says that Barbados is entitled to a decent price for its sugar, is demanding economic justice, not aid hand-outs:

> Much Labour and Fatigue is yet to come,
> Tho' now the *Sugar*'s made; To cure it well,
> No small Care is us'd. Grudge not then to give,
> Ye ever grumbling, discontented Men!
> A gen'rous Price for what supports us All.
> The Risk, the Danger, Trouble, and Expence,
> In this Commodity from first to last,
> Demand a Profit, and your Thanks beside.[89]

*The Sugar-Cane* is not only a georgic, it is also avowedly 'a West-India georgic'. Grainger uses 'terms of art' (i.e., technical terms) peculiar to the sugar industry, and defends this in his preface as necessary, even if they 'look awkward in poetry'. (We may recall that Johnson condemned even Milton for 'his unnecessary and ungraceful use of terms of art'.[90]) He may call the peacock 'Juno's bird', but he calls the humming-bird a humming-bird. Among the conventional poeticisms of naiads and dryads for streams and woods, we find Caribbean plants and animals which are – in defiance of Addison's injunction that 'nothing which is a Phrase or Saying in common talk, should be admitted into a serious Poem' – called by their common names. Grainger had been rebuked by Smollett for using neologisms in his translation of Tibullus, and even as successful a writer as Thomson could be criticised by Somervile for using vocabulary from beyond the boundaries of conventional poetic diction (with a dig at Thomson's Scottishness thrown in for good measure):

> To coin new words, or to restore the old,
> In southern bards is dangerous and bold;
> But rarely, very rarely will succeed,
> When minted on the other side of Tweed.[91]

Griffith Hughes was even criticised for using common names in a prose work on the natural history of a Caribbean island, names which were criticised for being not only English rather than Latin, but also 'the very worst English of West-India planters'.[92] In a review of *The Cadet: A Military Treatise*, Grainger himself apologised for using 'manœuvre', which he italicises: 'We adopt this word with reluctance, for want of one equally expressive in our own language.' He also condemned *The Idea of Beauty, according to the Doctrine of Plato*, not just for its errors in translating Greek but for language which 'abounds in low phrases, and North-British modes of expression, to a degree that is equally intolerable to a judge of the original, or of the English.'[93] When we find Grainger introducing yams, okras and bonavist into his georgic, there is more than 'novelty' to it, there is an artistic boldness which should not be underestimated. It is clear he had come to some understanding of the idea that a poem about the Caribbean could not be written in a manner that was entirely European. When *The Sugar-Cane* was still in draft, he was anxious to have his friends' views of it, so that he could use these criticisms as a means of improving the poem: 'I desire my work should be as perfect as possible; they therefore cannot be too critical in its perusal.' On the other hand, however much he might respect their judgement in literary matters, he knew his subject and they did not: 'as the subject is foreign to any thing British, it is possible they may think alterations necessary where it would take away from the truth of the poem.'[94]

At the beginning of the *Georgics*, Virgil invokes Octavian, the future Emperor Augustus who will bring the longed-for peace and stability to the Roman world. At the beginning of *The Fleece*, Dyer invokes King George II in appropriately Homeric terms as the 'people's shepherd.' Grainger mentions 'Imperial George' (King George III), but it is not royal patronage he asks for. Rather, he hopes his poem will 'win the Public ear;/And not displease Aurelius' who is identified as 'him to whom,/Imperial George, the monarch of the main,/Hath given to wield the scepter of those isles' (I, 18–21), or in other words, not the king, but his local representative, easily identified as the governor of the Leeward Islands, who happened to be George Thomas, a Creole. Although Grainger's Scottishness generally goes unmentioned by modern commentators[95], it was of real significance. It meant that he belonged to a nation which was – particularly in the aftermath of the 1745 Jacobite rebellion – to some extent a victim of an English cultural imperialism in the same way as the sugar colonies in the Caribbean. The Celtic regions of the British Isles were impoverished and peripheral, and Grainger himself seems to have accepted a hierarchical ordering of the nations subject to the British crown: after a visit to Ireland in 1758, he wrote of 'the common Irish' that 'they are as far out done by my Countrymen, as the English surpass us'.[96] Linda Colley's argument that the eighteenth-century development of a sense of Britishness which could include not only the English but the Scots as well was largely a negative one – being British was largely a matter of not being French and to a certain extent of not being Catholic – can be applied to Grainger. His hostility to 'False Gallia's sons' (III, 455) is made explicit in several passages of *The Sugar-Cane* and there are indications of a conventional anti-Catholicism in his contributions to the *Monthly Review*.[97] However, while Grainger is pro-Hanoverian and loyal to the crown, he constantly reminds his readers that Britain is more than England, and that the British empire is more than the British Isles. The invocation of 'Aurelius' is part of this, but his choice of other figures is also significant. He mentions prominent Englishmen, such as Jethro Tull (I, 290), Wolfe (II, 175) and Townshend (III, 595–8, n.), but also the Scottish General Melville (IV, 25). The British peer Lord Romney is introduced (III, 289), not at random, but because he is married to a Kittitian heiress. Like 'Aurelius', 'Amyntor' (I, 329–30), who is probably Ralph Payne, is veiled under a classical pseudonym in accordance with a common convention, while 'M * * *' (III, 31) may be either Samuel Martin or Daniel Mathew, but it is clear from the context that West Indians are intended. The Junio and Theana episode proclaims that Creoles are capable of the finer emotions, and the praise of Theana makes the point that beauty is not confined to Europe, for (at least to Junio) she rivals the Venus de Medici (II, 475–7), and Grainger boasts that the virgins of St Kitts are 'far more beautiful [...] and more chaste' than the Proserpine of classical mythology (I, 71–2). He adapts (III, 577 ff.) Virgil's famous *O fortunatos* passage to suggest that the Caribbean can rival or surpass whatever Europe has to offer. The symbolic (and perhaps entirely imaginary) figure of Montano (I, 579–646) has an important rôle to play as a representation of the ideal planter. 'Heaven bless'd his labour' – he is happy in the enjoyment of wealth legitimately acquired, and the fact that he is the 'lov'd master' of 'a numerous gang of sturdy slaves' is no bar to this, for 'good Montano; friend of man was he'. Grainger's portrait manages to combine classical images of rural felicity with suggestions of a biblical patriarch: Montano is the 'father' of 'all the Cane-lands'. The stress on Montano's humanity, on the smiling master who treats his slaves 'like men', is not a response to anti-slavery propaganda (which does not become a serious force until the 1780s) but to a rather different set of attitudes. At the time Grainger was writing *The Sugar-Cane* there were not that many people like his friend Johnson, who 'had always been very zealous against slavery in every form'.[98] However, it was possible to regard both the trade in slaves from Africa and the reliance of the British Caribbean colonies as lawful and necessary, and still think it a somewhat unsavoury business, rather like the Westminster MP who admitted in 1791 that the slave trade was 'an unamiable one' but claimed, 'So also were many others: the trade of a butcher was an unamiable trade, but it was a very necessary one, not withstanding.'[99] The fact that many people in Britain profited indirectly from slavery did not stop them from regarding those who were more directly involved with a fastidious, if somewhat hypocritical, distaste. The stereotypical view of 'the West Indian' was not of the plantation slave, but of the planter, as a colonial exotic, whose ability to command his slaves' obedience to his every whim gave him autocratic ideas and habits which were supposedly un-British, and whose excessive wealth was potentially a corrupting influence. The year *The Sugar-Cane* was published also saw the production at London's Haymarket Theatre of Samuel Foote's *The Patron*, with the author taking the rôle of Sir Peter Pepperpot, 'a West-Indian of an over-grown fortune,' an absentee planter who has bought his way into the Westminster parliament by bribing the electors of his pocket borough with gifts of West-India turtle. Richard Cumberland's play *The West Indian*, first staged in 1771 and popular for 50 years, both responded to and depended on the stereotype, by portraying the title-character, a planter newly arrived in London from Jamaica, as having 'rum and sugar enough belonging to him, to make all the water in the Thames into punch,' but also as a sort of noble savage, whose natural goodness is enough to overcome the fact that he is 'accustomed to a land of slaves', at least when he has spent long enough 'in England; at the fountain-head of pleasure, in the land of beauty, of arts, and elegancies.'[100] While Grainger puts the fact that 'Here, crouching slaves, attendant wait your nod' among the advantages of living in the Caribbean rather than in Britain (III, 582), he is also concerned to suggest that the region can rival Britain as a 'land of beauty, of arts, and elegancies.'

*The Sugar-Cane* can be seen as a far-reaching attempt to rewrite the prevailing cultural discourse which, just as it relegated Scotland and Scottish concerns to a secondary position, in effect dismissed Caribbean society as an unfit subject for literature. In his 'West-India georgic', Grainger is not only a doubly colonial writer – as a Scotsman by birth and a Kittitian by adoption – asserting the dignity and importance of the Caribbean, he is also appropriating a well-established form in contemporary English literature, and seeking to make it into something which is more than English. Just as it can be argued that a number of eighteenth-century Scottish writers reacted against the English cultural hegemony by creating a literature which sought to be British rather than English,[101] so Grainger seems to seek an Imperial literature in which the Caribbean will be as much entitled to a place as what he is careful to refer to as Britain rather than England.[102]

### 3. From 'tuneful Grainger' to 'stuffed owl': reception of The Sugar-Cane

> Short is the Date, alas, of *Modern Rhymes*;
> And 'tis but just to let 'em live *betimes*.
> No longer now that Golden Age appears,
> When *Patriarch-Wits* surviv'd a *thousand Years*;
> Now length of *Fame* (our *second* Life) is lost,
> And bare Threescore is all ev'n That can boast [...]
> (Pope, *An Essay on Criticism*, ll. 476–481)

'What does the W[orld say] of the Sugar Cane?' Grainger asked Percy in a letter from St. Kitts, almost a year after the publication of the poem.[103] When the *Gentleman's Magazine* for July 1764 printed the Junio and Theana episode, it presumably expected that this would be pleasing to its readers, but as was often the case with such extracts reprinted in its pages, there was no editorial comment. In the same month, however, three successive issues of the newspaper, the *London Chronicle*[104], gave the best part of a page to long extracts from the poem, interspersed with comments. The introduction said that 'America' (an expression which then normally included the islands of the Caribbean) 'is well known to be the habitation of uncivilized nations, remarkable only for their rudeness and simplicity. The plains and mountains of the Western hemisphere afford no monuments of ancient magnificence, nor any exhibitions of modern elegance: the life of their vagrant inhabitants, insecure and unfriended, can only shew how labour may supply the want of skill, and how necessity may inforce expedients.' This sweeping generalisation, which casts into oblivion the achievements of pre-Columbian societies and their 'Incas and emperors' who are acknowledged by Grainger (IV, 185), seems to include not only the Amerindian peoples, but the colonists of European descent and their African slaves in the category of 'uncivilized nations', unless we are to suppose that the colonists are responsible for their transformation into the 'enlightened regions' mentioned later. It is a good example of the sort of claim for the cultural superiority of Europe which *The Sugar-Cane* is in some ways attempting to combat. On the other hand, the difference of the exotic has its attractions: 'Nature has filled these boundless regions with innumerable forms, to which European eyes are wholly strangers.' Grainger, it seemed, deserved praise for introducing some of these to a European readership:

> The qualifications of an American traveller are knowledge of Nature, and copiousness of language, acuteness of observation, and facility of description. It is therefore with that pleasure which every rational mind finds in the hope of enlarging the empire of science, that we see these enlightened regions visited by a man who examines them as a philosopher, and describes them as a poet.
>
> The subject which he has chosen to illustrate, demands by its commercial value the attention of a mercantile, and by its physical curiosity, that of a philosophical nation. And it is reasonable to expect, that all to whom SUGAR contributes usefulness or pleasure, will be willing to know from what it is produced, and how it is prepared.

Since 'Every author is best recommended by himself,' the review went on to 'subjoin some examples of the descriptions and precepts, both physical and moral, with which this poem abounds.' It was said that 'They are not selected as superior in excellence to many other passages in the poem, but as more easily separated from the rest, and more intelligible when the connection is broken.' The reviewer chose part of the description of soils (I, 128–50); part of a description of St Kitts (I, 376–95), said to be 'a scene which will equally strike Europeans by its grandeur and its novelty'; a 'moral sentiment' of Grainger's which 'arises so naturally from a physical observation, that we cannot but wish it may be generally read' (I, 458–67); 'the Carnation-hedge and Humming-bird' (I, 520–31, quoted with Grainger's footnotes) which would be 'Equally new to the readers of this hemisphere'; most of the hurricane (II, 270–426); the cane-fire (III, 55–91); and the beginning of the fourth Book (IV, 1–17), described as a 'fine personification'. 'After this', we are told, 'the Poet gives a curious account of the genius and disposition of the different negro nations; and proceeds to recommend mild treatment to their masters. In which the generosity of the Author's temper, and the ingenuous liberality of his sentiments will be admired and approved by every humane reader.' The review then quotes IV, 211–43 before mentioning the 'enumeration of the several ails to which the negroes are peculiarly liable, with their cures' and noting 'The wild opinions and customs of this sable race are also described; particularly the grand negroe dance on festival occasions.' The conclusion of the poem (IV, 635–83) is quoted and described as 'an address to the mother country [...] with a premonition of the dangerous consequences likely to arise from that independency, to which the northern colonies are gradually advancing.'

The review appears to have been written by Johnson, at the prompting of, and in collaboration with Percy. Johnson did not share the fondness of so many of his contemporaries for didactic poetry, as can be seen from the dismissive comments in his 'Life of Dyer' or the exclamation about *The Sugar-Cane*, reported by Boswell: 'What could he make of a sugar-cane? One might as well write the "Parsley-bed, a Poem" or "The Cabbage-garden, a Poem" ' – though one may note that these remarks lead up to one of Johnson's typical anti-Scottish jokes at Boswell's expense and may have been made for that purpose.[105] Johnson told Boswell 'that Dr. Percy wrote the greatest part of this review' though Boswell thought 'he did not recollect it distinctly, for it appears to be mostly, if not altogether, his own.' Johnson also said 'I only helped Percy with it, and was in jest.' Percy later told Robert Anderson that 'as D$^r$ G's Sugar Cane was published while Johnson was at my house he joined with me in drawing up a favourable but just account of it for the public Papers.' This must refer to Johnson's visit to Percy at Easton Mauduit, 25 June to 18 August 1764, and to the review in the *London Chronicle*. In spite of Johnson's remarks to Boswell, the critical parts of the review do suggest Johnson's style and, less subjectively, they do (as Bertram H. Davis points out) 'survive in a manuscript in Johnson's hand.' Possibly, as Davis suggests, 'Percy selected the illustrative quotations and prepared a first draft for Johnson's revision.' The major part of the review consists of quotations, and the comments are generally favourable rather than wildly enthusiastic – its format may have been the result of haste, as it must have been sent to the *London Chronicle* during the first week of Johnson's visit to Easton Mauduit.[106]

Grainger's old home as a reviewer, the *Monthly Review*, devoted some thirteen pages of its issue for August 1764 to *The Sugar-Cane*.[107] The review was by John Langhorne (1735–79), mainly remembered as editor of the works of William Collins (1765) and translator, with his brother William, of 'Langhorne's Plutarch' (1770). He began with two long paragraphs on georgic poetry in general, contrasting the 'utility' of Hesiod with 'His more elegant and more artful Imitator, Virgil,' and suggesting that, whatever might have been the case in Hesiod's time, simplicity and utility in a poem were no longer enough for Virgil's readers, or indeed, the readers of the eighteenth century: 'the learned and ingenious Author of the Sugar Cane [...] knew, surely, that the Ascrean simplicity was by no means characteristic of these days, and that to write more like Hesiod than like Virgil, would be to write in vain.' After such an introduction, it was fairly damning to continue with 'whether Dr Grainger meant it as a compliment to the genius and disposition of his country, or whether something like ancient simplicity may not really exist in our Western Colonies, it is certain that he has made his Sugar Cane rather an useful than an entertaining poem.' For Langhorne, 'the novelty of his subject, a manufacture unknown in the European world,' far from being any advantage, 'loaded it with many difficulties.' He claimed that 'Terms of art to which the ear has never been accustomed, have a peculiar uncouthness in poetry'. He objected to Grainger's use of Caribbean names for Caribbean things, complaining that the 'Indian' (that is, West Indian) 'names of trees, and herbs, and fruits, are unpleasing even to the eye.' Instead, he suggested, the 'botanical names' (the Latin scientific names) 'would at least have appeared more classical, and are incomparably more harmonious'. The most he was prepared to concede was that 'probably, there might be some local reasons against this.' Mention of 'the terms of vegetables' led Langhorne to applaud Grainger for 'the liberal and diffusive pains he has taken, in his Notes on this poem, to enlarge the knowledge of the West-Indian botany', and to the rather double-edged compliment that 'These Notes may, indeed, be considered, both in their medical and botanical capacity, as a very valuable part of the work; and, possibly, there are few parts of it more entertaining.'

However, Langhorne went on to quote some long passages to which he was willing to attach some more favourable remarks. The description of St Kitts (I, 60–83) seems to have been quoted together with Grainger's footnote only in order to question the detail about 'the fabulous legend of the Devil's carrying St Christopher on his shoulders', and the 'panegyric on Columbus' (I, 97–126) was said only to follow 'naturally' from the mention of Jamaica. The next passage quoted was 'The description of a Caribbean Shower' (I, 348–75), which was allowed to be 'extremely poetical, if we except an image at the beginning, which, in our opinion, is rather too low' – presumably a reference to the 'housewives' with their 'spouts and pails'. With its suggestion of the collection of rainwater for drinking and also of leaky roofs, this is precisely the kind of naturalistic detail which might earn Grainger forgiveness for a few of his more artificial passages from anyone who has ever (like the present writer) lived in an old-fashioned Caribbean house where puddles formed on the living-room floor with every downpour. But we must remember that Langhorne would have been far from alone among eighteenth-century critics in thinking that naturalistic detail was not necessarily what poetry was about.

On the other hand, Langhorne quoted much of what Grainger had to say about hurricanes (II, 303–61) 'as an European, who has never been in the West-Indies, can form no idea of them' and called it a 'well-wrought description'. Similarly, the 'sketches of an earthquake' (II, 391–424) were quoted as no less 'dreadfully just'. Once more, the Junio and Theana episode was reprinted, as 'a very tender story of two Lovers, which, we suppose, may be more generally acceptable to our Readers than any precepts of cultivation contained in this poem'. Readers were then told 'The Cane-Harvest, and the process of Sugar-boiling, make the Argument of the third book' and informed that 'Every poetical circumstance that attends these, is artfully introduced, and much philosophical, chemical, and medical knowledge is displayed.' The 'digression in favour of Rum' (III, 489–506) was quoted approvingly, as was 'The West-Indian prospect, after the crop is finished' (III, 538–76), which was introduced as 'perfectly poetical and picturesque' and afterwards the reader was assured that 'Most of the above-quoted verses are delightfully melodious, and not a little recommended by the novelty of the scenery.'

Proceeding in order, Langhorne came to Book IV, the subject of which was bluntly summarised as 'the management of Negroes, in treating of which our amiable and ingenious Author gives no less agreeable proofs of his humanity than his poetry.' As proof, Langhorne quoted IV, 211–43, saying 'Hear how pathetically he pleads in favour of those poor wretches, and THE LIBERTIES OF MANKIND!' The 'description of a Negroe dance' (IV, 582–605) was then quoted, before the statement that 'In the midst of all these exotic amusements, the Author, like a genuine Poet, never loses sight of his native country' introduced the invocation to the

Thames (IV, 635–53). Langhorne's conclusion certainly seems more favourable than his beginning: 'The Reader had no need of these quotations to inform him of Dr Grainger's poetical abilities, which were already sufficiently known: we have quoted them for his entertainment, as well as to do the Author justice; and hope, that in neither of these respects we have laboured in vain.'

Grainger had given Johnson at least part of the poem to read in manuscript (though whether Johnson actually read it at that point is uncertain), and before its publication had secured a promise that Johnson would review it in the *Critical Review*. The *Critical Review* for October 1764 duly gave some seven pages to *The Sugar-Cane*.[108] The opening was off-putting: 'There are some works in which the exertion of a poet's genius may be very great, and yet his success but moderate [...] what is there in the title of the *Sugar-Cane* to allure the multitude, or what can a subject so seemingly barren promise to repay the purchaser?' However, the review then moved on to praise, and high praise at that:

> Yet, after all, the reader must not be deterred by the title-page, since the most languid will here find his passions excited, and the imagination indulged to the highest pitch of luxury. A new creation is offered, of which an European has scarce any conception; the hurricane, the burning winds, a ripe cane-piece on fire at midnight; an Indian prospect after a finished crop, and nature in all the extremes of tropic exuberance. It is, indeed, a little extraordinary how regions so poetically striking, and so well known to the merchant, have been so little visited by the muse: and that while the Spaniards boast their Garcilasso, and the Portuguese their Camoens, we have been destitute till now of an American poet, that could bear any degree of comparison.

Although the reviewer appears to confuse Garcilaso de la Vega (c. 1501–36) who was one of the most celebrated poets of the Spanish *Siglo de Oro*, but who neither visited nor wrote about the Americas, with the Inca Garcilaso de la Vega (c. 1535–1616), an equally celebrated historian – in prose – of Peru and Florida, and although the *Lusiads* of Luis Vaz de Camões (1524–80) is an epic of Portuguese triumphs in the East rather than of Brazil, the implication is clear: in Grainger the British have finally found a worthy poet of their own empire.

Both the difficulty and the success of Grainger's attempt to create 'a West-India georgic' were noted:

> [...] throughout the whole poem, he keeps Virgil in his eye: nor should this be objected to him as a fault; since it was not an easy task to reconcile the wild imagery of an Indian picture to the strict rules of critical exactness. This, notwithstanding the difficulty of the undertaking, our author has happily effected; and although he treads upon unclassic ground, yet maintains a classical regularity.

After quoting two passages from Book I – the shower (I, 348–75) and about half of the Montano passage, where 'The character of a good planter is beautifully described' and noted as reminiscent of Virgil – it is suggested that Grainger has been more successful than other modern writers of georgic:

> It has been remarked of Virgil that he rises in every book: on the contrary Dyer, Philips, and some others, who have pursued his plan, grow languid as they proceed, as if fatigued with their career. Our poet happily improves in his progress; and as the *tædium* of reading increases, he makes the interest increase proportionably.

The pests of the cane in Book II are mentioned with some detail about the monkeys' cunning, but no critical comment other than what is implied by the following, 'The poet then displays his stronger powers in the description of an hurricane,' which, says the reviewer, echoing Langhorne, 'as it greatly differs from our European tempests, we shall give at length.' This leads to the comment that 'In one particular, namely, that of extending the bounds of natural history, while he seems only to address the imagination, we may safely assert that doctor Grainger has the advantage of many poets'. After quoting III, 23–8, we are told that in the description of crop, Grainger 'gives, with all the graces of poetry, several rules which may amuse an European reader even in prose', and III, 391–7, is given as an example. The description of 'the savage pastimes of the Negroe slaves upon concluding the task of the day'[109] is mentioned before proceeding to a discussion of Grainger's 'celebration of Rum' (III, 489–506):

*Introduction* 43

[...] which, it is probable, no other poet has dignified in verse before him; and tho' this liquor, together with punch which is made from it, would, at first sight, seem more adapted to the comic muse, yet has he maintained his description without sinking, and the poet has elegantly described a liquor which yet he seems ashamed to name.

Elegantly describing that which one seems ashamed to name is perhaps as good a definition as any of what the poetic diction of the period is all about. The reviewer also found 'much local propriety' in the landscape of III, 540–51, which is quoted.

Calling the beginning of Book IV 'a striking invocation to the genius of Africa', the reviewer found fault with the 'proper instructions for the buying and choice of Negroes':

[...] here we think that tenderness and humanity, with which the former part of the poem seems replete, is, in some measure, forgotten. The poet talks of this ungenerous commerce without the least appearance of detestation; but proceeds to direct these purchasers of their fellow-creatures with the same indifference that a groom would give instructions for chusing a horse.

The lines at IV, 74–7, are quoted as evidence of this, and Grainger's suggestions that the slaves should content themselves with the thought that the miners are worse off is met with the observation that 'it is but a small alleviation to our misery to find conditions in life still more miserable than our own.' The comments on slavery, so very different from Langhorne's on the same material, suggest that the review is indeed by Johnson, as does the early reference to a 'new creation', which echoes the quotation from La Condamine at the beginning of the review in the *London Chronicle*, which talks about seeing 'new plants, new animals, and new men' in the Amazon.[110] The review ended, however, on a positive note: 'The poet had an untrodden country to clear; and though he may not have entirely subdued the native rudeness of the soil, yet he certainly has opened a delightful tract for future cultivation.'

At the end of the year, another review appeared in the *Gazette Littéraire de l'Europe*, published in Paris.[111] This was much shorter than the other reviews, mainly because there were no illustrative quotations, perhaps because of the language difference. It began by commenting on the ancient association of agriculture and poetry, with the inevitable mention of Hesiod and Virgil, and went on to note that changes in society, particularly the growth of distinctions in rank, had rendered such poetry much more difficult, especially in France:

> [...] où le Culivateur est si fort avili par sa profession, les détails de la vie champêtre emportent avec eux une idée de bassesse incompatible avec la nature même de la Poésie. Les noms propres de la plûpart des instrumens de labourage choqueroient l'oreille des gens de goût; le mot de *vache* ne pourroit entrer dans un Vers.
>
> [... where the farmer is so debased by his profession, the details of rural life are charged with an idea of lowness incompatible with the very nature of Poetry. The actual names of most instruments of tillage would shock the ears of people of taste; the word *cow* cannot be permitted in a line of verse.]

As a result, French georgics were almost impossible. Things were rather different in England where, said the reviewer, fashionable people lived more in the country, agriculture was more respected, and 'la Langue est plus populaire, moins délicate & moins gênée par les idées de noblesse & de bassesse' [the language is more popular, not so over-refined, and less restricted by the concepts of nobility and lowness]. English poets were thus able to write about rural subjects; some had done so with success, and the author of *The Sugar-Cane* was an example of this, though it was true that

> [...] il a trouvé dans ce sujet des avantages que ne lui auroient pas offert les détails de la culture ordinaire. La différence du climat, du sol, des mœurs, &c. lui fournissent une multitude d'objets nouveaux, frappans & très-favorables à la Poésie.
>
> [... he found advantages in this subject which the details of ordinary farming would not have afforded him. The difference of climate, soil, customs, and so forth, furnished him with a multitude of new and striking subjects, extremely suited to poetry.]

The reviewer gave a brief précis of the first three books (though nothing is said about the details of slave management or slave diseases in Book IV, or, for that matter, about Grainger's anti-French comments) and concluded by saying:

> Les préceptes & les descriptions didactiques sont relevés par un grand nombre de tableaux très-poétiques & de digressions intéressantes. Le Poëte Anglois a eu toujours Virgile devant les yeux & a souvent imité avec succès ce grand modele. Les tempêtes, les ouragans, les tremblemens de terre, & d'autres phénomenes communs dans les Isles de l'Amérique sont peints avec beaucoup de chaleur & de force. De riches paysages, les danses des Negres, & d'autres objets agréables contrastent avec les premiers tableaux. L'Auteur a joint au texte des notes instructives sur les différens objets de Géographie, d'Histoire Naturelle, de Physique, &c. Cet Ouvrage mérite d'être connu, & suppose beaucoup de connoissance, de travail & de talent.

> [The precepts and didactic descriptions are relieved by many most poetical scenes and interesting digressions. The English <sic> poet had Virgil constantly in mind, and has often imitated this great model successfully. Storms, hurricanes, earthquakes and other phenomena common in the islands of America are portrayed with much liveliness and vigour. Fertile landscapes, Negro-dances and other attractive subjects set off the first scenes. The author has added to his text informative notes on various points of geography, natural history and medicine. This work deserves to be known, and shows much learning, industry and talent.]

Grainger had good reason to write from St Kitts that 'I am perfectly satisfied with the reception the "Sugar Cane" has met with.' It did of course help to have friends with some influence in literary circles, and he told Percy he was 'greatly obliged to you and Mr. Johnson for the generous care you took of it in my absence.'[112]

Matters were somewhat different in the Caribbean. Grainger had told Percy in 1762 that 'Reading [...] is the least part of a Creole's consideration. It is even happy if they can read at all; spell few of them can; and when they take up a book, modern romance, magazines, or newspapers are the extent of their lucubrations.'[113] Both in *The Sugar-Cane* and in his correspondence it is clear that he missed the intellectual companionship of his London friends, and at one point he was driven to say he could not bear the thought of leaving his bones 'in this country of Vandals.'[114] Any examination of the amount of literature actually produced in the Anglophone Caribbean in this period suggests that Grainger was guilty of some exaggeration, but it does seem probable that it would have been more difficult to find suitable readers among the Creoles of Basseterre or St John's than among a London literary public for a highly allusive poem like *The Sugar-Cane*, or, as he put it, that 'few here can relish it.'[115] He summed up the local reaction for Percy by saying 'The planters say, it is impudent in a Scot to pretend to teach planting' and complained that he had 'only a bare Dozen' subscribers in St Kitts when he had the poem advertised 'for a charitable purpose'. Nevertheless, he claimed he had had 'a numerous and important subscription' at Antigua,[116] a difference perhaps to be explained by the fact that Antigua was both more populous than St Kitts and the seat of the Leeward Islands government. Nor was interest confined to the Leewards: a copy survives which was bought in Jamaica in August 1764; the purchaser read it with enough attention to make the corrections called for in the errata and a few other minor annotations, and thought it was worth having it bound.[117]

*The Sugar-Cane* also had some influence on other writers in the Caribbean. John Singleton, a member of an English troupe of actors touring the region, seems to have been inspired by it while composing his own *General Description of the West-Indian Islands*, described as 'Attempted in Blank Verse' and first published in Barbados in 1767:

> Come, pow'rful genius of these fertile isles,
> [...]
> Inspire me now, nor let my languid pen
> Disgrace those climes, which late thy fav'rite son,
> Thy tuneful Grainger, nurs'd in Fancy's arms,
> So elegantly sung: Him (happy bard!)
> Delighted thou hast led with list'ning ear;
> Through each enliven'd scene his sprightly muse
> Rejoic'd to traverse [...][118]

In Jamaica, Bryan Edwards (1743–1800), the later historian of the British West Indies, 'at a very early period of life, presumed to sketch out a West-Indian Georgick, in four books,' and actually wrote the first and most of a second before abandoning the project. The first book of 'Jamaica, A descriptive and didactic poem' was eventually published in Jamaica in 1792 as part of a volume called *Poems, written chiefly in the West-Indies*. Although he does not mention Grainger by name, the resemblance of his 'Advertisement' to the plan of *The Sugar-Cane* is striking:

> This little Poem is imperfect in every sense of the word. It is presumed, however, that the subject of it is as happily adapted for descriptive and didactic poetry, as any that can be imagined. The magnificent scale whereon natural objects in this part of the globe are in general formed, the beauty and novelty of the scene, could not fail to supply an able artist with many new, striking, and picturesque images. These, and various collateral topics (among others, the first voyage and discoveries of Columbus – the subsequent conquests and cruelties of the Spaniards – the productions of the soil, and method of cultivation – the slavery and superstitions of the African negroes – the diseases of the climate – the great irregularities of nature, and the devastations which are sometimes occasioned by floods, hurricanes, and earthquakes) afford rich materials for a Poem, that might prove at once original, instructive, pathetic, and sublime.[119]

In the preface to his *Barbadoes, and other poems* (London, 1833), the Barbadian writer Matthew Chapman said he was 'not aware of any poem expressly on the West Indies, excepting Mr Grainger's on the "Sugar-Cane." '[120] A number of passages in the poems of Edwards and Chapman which appear to have been influenced by *The Sugar-Cane* are detailed in the notes to this study.

The anonymous author of *Jamaica, A Poem, in three parts*, which is (sign of things to come) a strongly anti-slavery piece, written in Jamaica but published in London in 1777, says 'But how can I forget the sugar cane?' He refuses, however, to give it any extended discussion:

> Here could I sing what soils and seasons suit,
> Inform the tap'ring arrow how to shoot;
> Under what signs to plant the mother cane,
> What rums and sugars bring the planter gain;

> Teach stubborn oxen in the wain to toil,
> And all the culture of a sugar soil:
> Th'ingrateful task a British Muse disdains,
> Lo! tortures, racks, whips, famine, gibbets, chains,
> Rise on my mind, appall my tear-stain'd eye,
> Attract my rage, and draw a soul-felt sigh;
> I blush, I shudder at the bloody theme,
> And scorn on woe to build a baseless fame.

Although the author nowhere mentions Grainger by name, this looks like a reaction to *The Sugar-Cane*.[121]

After the first edition of 1764, there were new editions of *The Sugar-Cane* in Dublin and London in 1766 (though these may be different issues of the same edition, as they are apparently identical except for the title-page, and the London imprint may be spurious). It was reprinted in Jamaica in 1802, both separately and as one of a collection of 'scarce and valuable tracts' on West Indian agriculture. It also appeared as part of Grainger's works (and as the only others included were 'Solitude' and, in three out of four instances, 'Bryan and Pereene', it was by far the most prominent of his works) published in multi-volume collections of standard British authors in 1794 (London and Edinburgh), 1810 (London), and 1822 (two entirely separate editions, published in Chiswick and Philadelphia). It seemed that *The Sugar-Cane* had achieved canonical status. In the early nineteenth century, the Edinburgh critic and editor Robert Anderson aimed to produce a definitive edition of Grainger's works, and corresponded extensively on the subject with Thomas Percy, by then Bishop of Dromore in Ireland, who supplied him with points of information and manuscript materials by Grainger (though these did not include any part of *The Sugar-Cane*, which Anderson simply reprinted from the 1764 edition). Anderson's new edition (he had been responsible for the 1794 publication of Grainger in his collection of *The British Poets*) was announced as 'Speedily will be published [...]' as early as 1802, and Anderson referred to it as 'in the press' in 1804, saying 'The publishers are impatient.' However, Anderson kept delaying in the hope of getting additional information from Percy, the original publishers went out of business, and the edition did not finally appear until 1836, six years after Anderson's death.[122]

It was to be the last attempt at a collected edition of Grainger's

# Introduction 49

works, and the last complete edition of *The Sugar-Cane* before the present one. The poem was overtaken by a number of changes in literary taste. The age of Wordsworth and Coleridge was hostile to the poetic diction of the previous generation, and while the readers of Tennyson were prepared to enjoy long poems, and still read Thomson, didactic poetry was no longer in fashion and the frank celebration of wealth had come to seem vulgar. As early as 1810, the critic and editor Alexander Chalmers (1759–1834) said of *The Sugar-Cane* that

> [...] what lessens the respect of the reader for the poem in general, is the object so often repeated, so unpoetical and unphilosophical, *wealth*. Yet, this, too, is a necessary evil arising from the choice of subject, for although our author frequently says,
>
> ..... the planter, if he wealth desire ...
>
> it would be difficult to find many instances of planters who desired any thing else.

If wealth was 'unpoetical and unphilosophical', wealth based on slavery was even more so. Beginning in the 1780s, a campaign against the slave trade and later slavery itself transformed British public opinion from indifference or acquiescence to active hostility. An important contributing factor was the publication in 1784 of the Rev. James Ramsay's *Essay on the Treatment and Conversion of African Slaves in the British Sugar Colonies* which offered a much grimmer picture of slave life in the British Caribbean colonies in general, and St Kitts in particular, than that given in *The Sugar-Cane*. Britain abolished its slave trade in 1807 and freed its slaves in 1834. All of this told against Grainger. The change in taste was summed up by Richard Alfred Davenport (?1777–1852) in 'The Life of James Grainger' he wrote for an edition of his works published in 1822:

> In selecting as his theme the cultivation of the sugarcane, Grainger was neither fortunate in his choice of a subject, nor of a species of poetry. The didactic poem is, perhaps, that kind of poem which is least calculated to become popular. It is only when it ceases to be didactic that it begins to please. The Muses

are fastidious, and cannot easily be induced to be teachers of manual processes. [...] But if we can derive no pleasure from home scenes of manufacture, far less can we be charmed by the picture which brings before our eyes the kidnapped slave, wielding the hoe, under a burning sun and the lash of a taskmaster, or feeding the mill which, should his faculties chance to be overpowered by momentary slumber, may mutilate or destroy him. It is too, an unfortunate circumstance for the work of Grainger, that his subject, which was always a repulsive one, has been rendered by time still more hateful to the feelings of humanity than it was at the period when he adopted it. The horrors of the slave-trade, and of the slave system, have so often been depicted to us in vivid colours, that to read of the culture of the sugarcane inevitably calls up a succession of the most painful ideas.

By the time of Emancipation, what the British reading public wanted, if it wanted poetry on slavery at all, was not advice 'How [...]/Afric's sable progeny to treat' (I, 3–4) but self-congratulation of the sort exemplified by the verses of the popular writer Charles Mackay (1814–89) on 'The Abolition by Great Britain of Slavery in her Colonial possessions':

> No more for me shall helots till the soil —
> Stripes their reward, and pain and hopeless toil;
> No more shall slaves produce vile wealth for me —
> Joy! Afric, joy! thy swarthy sons are free!
> [...]
> The wealth is cursed that springs from human woe,
> And he who trades in men is Britain's foe [...]

Finally, there was the problem that – whether or not we accept Eric Williams's classic argument that the slave trade and slavery were abolished only because they had ceased to be profitable – after Emancipation most of the British Caribbean colonies slid into economic decline and a position of much less importance to the British Empire as a whole. New industries and new forms of trade rivalled sugar as creators of wealth, and new producers of sugar relegated the British Caribbean colonies to a position of comparative insignificance in the world market. In the 1760s Grainger could justifiably claim attention because of his subject's 'vast importance

# Introduction 51

to my native land' (I, 302); a century later this was no longer the case. The beginnings of the change are already visible in 1810, when Chalmers could say

> [...] it will not be easy to persuade the reader of English poetry to study the cultivation of the sugar-plant, merely that he may add some new imagery to the more ample stores which he can contemplate without study or trouble. In the West Indies this poem might have charms, if readers could be found; but what poetical fancy can dwell on the economy of canes and copper-boilers, or find interest in the transactions of planters and sugar-brokers?[123]

While in 1802 William Wright could refer to Grainger as 'the celebrated author of *The Sugar-Cane*, and other ingenious performances', by 1860 George Gilfillan (1813–78), a Scottish clergyman who was then an influential literary critic, could include him in his *Specimens with Memoirs of the Less-Known British Poets* (in distinguished company which included Gavin Douglas, Sir Philip Sidney, John Donne, Jonathan Swift and Christopher Smart).[124] While the 1875 edition of *Chambers' Eminent Scotsmen* could still describe Grainger as 'a physician and poet of some eminence' (though it regarded *The Sugar-Cane* as 'an ill-judged attempt to elevate things in themselves mean and wholly unadapted for poetry'), many later anthologies, reference works or critical studies of Scottish literature either ignore Grainger entirely or give only brief and inaccurate summaries of his career.[125]

Often he has not fared much better south of the border. Edmund Gosse (1849–1928), a popular if often sloppy English critic, in a *History of Eighteenth Century Literature* first published in 1889, claimed that 'There is no section of our national poetry so sterile, so unstimulating, as [...] the poetry of the third quarter of the eighteenth century.' He allowed Grainger to have written 'one fine lyric' – that is, 'Solitude' – 'before he began to sing of canes and swains in tedious couplets'.[126] If Gosse thought *The Sugar-Cane* was written in couplets rather than blank verse, he had not read it with much attention.

D. B. Wyndham Lewis and Charles Lee mocked Grainger in their *The Stuffed Owl: An Anthology of Bad Verse* (1930). They included 'Bryan and Pereene,' saying that 'with its affecting parting not only of the lovers but of the lover himself', it was 'pretty enough'. They also included several short extracts from *The Sugar-Cane* (I, 218–24; II, 201–15; III, 455–62; IV, 72–80, 103–7, 112–22) which, torn from their context, they found easy to hold up to ridicule. They seem to have found particularly amusing 'the poet's bland counsel to slave-owners desirous of profit [...] entirely at one with the sentiments of the pious citizens of Bristol, who made such fortunes in the trade', though the composts and dungheaps were also thought sufficiently ridiculous.[127]

A generation later, Ronald Knox made a more extended attack in an essay called 'A Neglected Poet.'[128] Where Grainger's contemporaries praised him for what they saw as his successful imitation of Virgil and Milton, Knox clearly thought there could be nothing worthwhile in this form of imitation at all: 'The selection and grouping of the matter is bad Virgil. The style is bad Milton.' Knox has no sympathy for eighteenth-century poetic diction, singling out Grainger's description of the mill (III, 240–8, 252–4) for the comment 'Oh admirable faith of the eighteenth century, which would fit the classical key to every lock!' He suggests (sometimes with justice) that Grainger does not always reach as high as he was aiming, finding, for example, that I, 322–6, 'falls, somehow, short of the heroic note.' He accuses him of repeated bathos: 'Even where his subject is such that it might have been securely treated by a less adventurous hand, a fatal rhetorical instinct betrays the poet to his fall; and he rises heroically from one ditch only to trip in another.' The phrases 'of this amazing plant' and 'and much the largest part remains' in the description of cane-cutting (III, 120–7) are offered as examples. Knox sums up what he sees as the matter with Grainger by saying

> [...] that the subject of his choice is a process incurably pedestrian, the result of which can only be sugar or (at the best) rum: that while the Mantuan [i.e., Virgil] reaps corn Grainger hoes yams, while the Mantuan treads grapes Grainger must peel bananas; that local colour demands the superseding of the ash and the pine by the coconut; that machinery, which Grainger is far too conscientious to leave undescribed, does the greater part of the manufacture; that the human labour involved is not that of jolly Apulian swains but that of negroes looted from the Gold Coast, whose presence has begun to need some explanation, even

to the easy conscience of the eighteenth century. The situation cries for bathos, and gets it.

It is perhaps being pedantic to point out that in his brief references to yams (I, 236–43, and n., 595, 596 n.; IV, 94, 449) Grainger – who knows rather more about Caribbean agriculture than Knox – does not make the improbable suggestion that yams are reaped with hoes,[129] and that his passing mentions of bananas (I, 604 n.; III, 533; IV, 569–71) say nothing about peeling them. Of more importance is the fact that Knox never tells us why grapes should be more poetical than bananas, or the ash and pine more poetical than the coconut; he simply assumes (much as Alexander Chalmers had assumed a century and half earlier) that European topics are suitable for poetry while Caribbean ones are not. Even his remarks about Grainger's treatment of slavery and the later suggestion that 'It is possible that we might have to recognise in him the father of propaganda' are not as unproblematic as they might at first appear: they conceal a similar Eurocentric bias which will be further explored below.

In more recent decades, Grainger has benefited from a growing tendency (at least in academic circles) towards a more favourable reassessment of eighteenth-century literature and a greater willingness to consider the poetry of the period on its own terms. 'Bryan and Pereene' and part of 'Solitude' are included, for example, in the Penguin Classics *Eighteenth-Century English Verse* edited by Dennis Davison (first published 1973), while Roger Lonsdale's *New Oxford Book of Eighteenth Century Verse* (1984) includes two extracts from *The Sugar-Cane*.[130] Phillip B. Anderson's interesting study (1985) of 'Solitude' has already been mentioned. John Chalker's 1969 survey of *The English Georgic* gives significant space (pp. 55–64) to a generally sympathetic analysis of Grainger's approach to his material, seen as 'the epic aspect of Man's struggle against Nature.' Astonishingly, Chalker manages to avoid any mention of slavery, and says little on Grainger's treatment of the relationship between Britain and her colonies. For other critics, from the Caribbean and elsewhere, these topics have been central to any discussion of *The Sugar-Cane*.

### 4. 'Canes and swains': slavery, poetry, and the modern reader

> Whipp'd, and enchain'd, I'll plough the stubborn Land!
> Grainger, *A poetical translation of the Elegies of Tibullus*,
> (Book II, Third Elegy, l. 58)

In a 1970 article on 'West Indian Consciousness in West Indian Verse: A Historical Perspective',[131] Arthur D. Drayton noted 'It is surprising how much writing (its quality is another matter) went on in the islands in the eighteenth century and indeed how much local publishing there was.' However, he sees this as derivative and evasive. Most of the writers in and from the Caribbean during this period, says Drayton, 'shared the orientation towards England and its selectivity: they may invoke Pope, Prior and Thomson, but on the whole they are taking the name of the English Muse in vain. In general, they avert their gaze from the Negro, from the great distinctive (and disturbing) fact of their way of life, and from all the consequent problems.' In a brief survey of *The Sugar-Cane*, Drayton says that Grainger's 'need to offer technical advice to the planter permits him to depict actual conditions, even to chide at times', but 'Concerned as he seems for the well-being of the slaves, his interest in them is only economic. He comes close to a sense of justice and inhumanity, and yet contrives to draw back from the brink of condemnation.' He sums up the poem by saying

> In its acceptance of slavery and its pictures of slave life it is part of that century's apology and rationalization. Thus we are shown slaves as happy workers 'panting' to get on with their job, 'the laughing, labouring, singing throng'. But it looks forward to the following century in another way, in the impulse to put the West Indies on the literary map.[132]

In the same year, in an important article on 'Creative Literature of the British West Indies during the period of slavery'[133] Kamau Brathwaite (whose opinions as a poet as well as a cultural historian command attention) gave qualified praise to *The Sugar-Cane*: 'In many respects, it is an impressive poem. It is unified by its very West Indian theme of sugar; the verse, despite the regularity of the cadences, is well managed over its considerable length.' He quotes Grainger's statement in his Preface that 'that, as the face of this country was wholly different from that of Europe, so whatever hand copied its appearances, however rude, could not fail to enrich poetry with many new and picturesque images' and calls this 'a wholly admirable intention', saying that 'The roots of a distinctive West Indian writing cling to the truth of this realization.' After quoting a number of passages (I, 1–6, 317–20; II, 156–66, 354–6, 358–9; III, 111–19, 526–9), Brathwaite says 'All this is certainly «wholly different from ... Europe», though spoken with a European, post-Miltonic voice. But the voice is crucial. It can transform the scene, even though its elements are local, into something quite «other».' With something like Grainger's description of the beginning of the year (I, 427–433), says Brathwaite, 'we find ourselves in English autumn, anticipating Keats'. He continues: 'This view of Nature, which dominates the poem (despite hurricanes, fires and insect swarms), comes also to dominate Grainger's view of the people who move within it – the tenders of the cane, the slaves. [...] In the end, we are left with a vision of nymphs and satyrs dancing.' Quoting Grainger's description of the slave dance (IV, 582–601), he notes:

> [...] we come face to face again with the tyranny of the model. There can be no doubt that Grainger actually saw slaves dance. The wheeling circle is there, the dancers in the centre; the custom of bestowing coins on a favourite is described. But «frisk» and «caper»? The dancers are moving to the wrong rhythm. This really is a Scottish reel or a Maypole dance. No wonder the performers seem «aukward».

After mentioning Grainger's passing reference to 'Fell acts of blood, and vengeance' (IV, 605), Brathwaite says that 'To have lifted his poem out of the ordinary [...] Grainger would have had to have been capable of counterpointing the picturesque and sylvan against the harsher realities of his society; and he would have had to produce verse capable of expressing these realities.' He concludes by quoting from the anonymous author of *Jamaica, A Poem, in three parts*, the lines about 'Th'ingrateful task a British Muse disdains,' apparently suggesting that Grainger remained too British to write a truly Caribbean poem.

This point is taken up by Keith A. Sandiford in a 1987 article, 'The Sugared Muse: or the case of James Grainger',[134] where he says that 'The verse itself appears sometimes to be straining to deny the landscape and its contents their indigenous character and shape, constraining West Indian nature to behave like English nature.' Sandiford criticises Grainger for invoking his Muse too often – this was a standard eighteenth-century practice, for which the example of Pope, among others, could be cited, but Grainger does rather overdo it, and critics as early as Chalmers and Davenport had complained of this.[135] Sandiford draws attention to III, 526–76, where he finds 'five examples of litotes concentrated in thirty-seven lines' and says of what he interprets as 'a compulsive resort to understatement' that 'The choice of such rhetoric bespeaks less than complete satisfaction with the natural and social order he so much wants to legitimize' – though one of the examples he uses is a clear misinterpretation of what Grainger actually says.[136] Although he acknowledges the poem's 'revisioning of St. Christopher into Grainger's ideal of a New World paradise', he finds the poem inconsistent, sometimes suggesting that 'the definition of colonial value, even in the undisputable domain of indigenous nature, must remain the prerogative of the metropole' and sometimes proposing 'a West Indian aesthetic which supplants the European aesthetic in the new order of Grainger's vision.' He accuses Grainger of having a 'fractured resolution', a 'perverse disposition to dissociate himself from the inherent logic of his work' and 'inchoate semiology'. The 'net result', concludes Sandiford, 'is a repudiation of georgic itself, a misappropriation of the form that finally asks of the work only that it serve the conventional moral ends of poetry, and of the reader only that he think the author a good man.'

In a book-length study of 'Poetry, Politics and Commerce in British America 1690–1750', David S. Shields gives a brief survey of *The Sugar-Cane*. He perhaps over-emphasises the didactic aspect, arguing that 'Grainger made instruction his highest purpose' and drawing attention to the bulk of Grainger's notes:

> The result is the most informative account of a staple that survives from the colonial era, also the most curious. Its oddity arises in part from its ordering of subjects. The design begins coherently, but soon shows signs of distraction [...] While the descriptions of sugar production in Books I-III employ the logic of chronology, the episodes and digressions interspersed through the descriptions and the final book reveal the tensions that dis-

turb the heroic simplicity of the georgic mode. The poem presented no progress toward civility or triumph over the wilderness. In the culminating book, where the vision of [an] accomplished estate should be, Grainger provided an extended discourse on the most problematic aspect of planting – slave management. Here conflicts between man of science and man of feeling became acute in the narrator's persona. The welter of cross-purposes dramatized the predicament of a progressive man, ambitious to serve as spokesman for the material improvement of mankind brought about by imperial expansion, yet compelled by economic circumstance to employ and justify slavery.

Shields's comment that 'It is instructive how little Grainger treats trade in his very long book' is rather strange in view of the repeated emphasis on the significance of sugar as an export crop. However, there is something in Shields's suggestion that for Grainger to have described in detail the logistics of the triangular trade would have 'too blatantly revealed the complicit immorality of his existence in St Christopher Island' [sic], and his comment on 'Grainger's obsessive concern with the character of the planter.' For Grainger, Shields argues, 'Only the government of virtue held at arm's length the horrors of the mines and the transformation of the planter into a tyrant', but in spite of the portrait of Montano, 'The problem was that in the eyes of most of the world, and indeed among themselves, West Indians exemplified all that was extravagant, arbitrary, and presumptuous in human nature. He was the tyrannical nabob; she was the capricious belle.'[137]

Gosse's jingling association of 'canes and swains' sums up much of what nineteenth- and twentieth-century critics have said or suggested about Grainger: that his treatment of the slavery somehow combines with his use of the georgic mode and the poetic diction of his period to ensure that his poem can be safely dismissed as inferior, or at least as failing to achieve what it sets out to do. This argument deserves further consideration.

One does not have to be much of an economic determinist to feel that Grainger, married into the plantocracy and dependent on the slave system for both his living in the present and his hopes of becoming rich in the future, was unlikely to be an abolitionist. In the 1760s not many white people in Britain or the Caribbean were. *The Sugar-Cane* includes a good deal of what was intended as practical advice on the choice and treatment of slaves. Grainger suggests that to treat his slaves well is in the planter's interest (e.g., IV, 421–7) and can discuss the slave trade with the detachment of one recommending slaves from different parts of Africa as best suited for different jobs (IV, 38–118) – as Johnson put it, directing 'purchasers of their fellow-creatures with the same indifference that a groom would give instructions for chusing a horse' or, in Davenport's similar condemnation, 'directions he gives with all the coolness, and with much of the phraseology, of a jockey or a grazier.'[138]

However, when he asks the planter, 'Must thou from Africk reinforce thy gang?' (IV, 72) he not only gives pragmatic instructions but also shows at least some awareness of what was involved in kidnapping victims for the slave trade (IV, 211–24). Nevertheless, he is anxious to show slavery and the plantation system in as good a light as possible, and their more unsavoury aspects are ignored or displaced. We are shown cattle being whipped, 'A better fate deserving' (I, 182–5), but not slaves. The suggestion that slaves *might* suffer the 'horrid whip' is laid at the charge, not of the planter or his white overseers, but of 'the driver, Æthiop authorized' – authorized by whom is a question readers must work out for themselves (III, 141–6), and this is, incidentally, an interesting example of poetic diction at work. Some slaves, 'alas!', end up receiving 'blows', but only because 'so stubborn is their kind' (IV, 209–10). Grainger talks about English sheep receiving the 'impress' of 'Their master's cypher' (III, 135–6) but nothing is said about the branding of Caribbean slaves.[139] Slaves sometimes get maimed in the mill, but only because they are 'incautious' – it is due to the victim's own 'imprudence or sleepiness', not to that fact that his master was overworking him at night (III, 168, n.). If anything really gruesome is mentioned, such as the idea that owners might turn loose worn-out slaves to starve, it is a case of 'Muse suppress the tale' (III, 179), just as Grainger is careful (III, 168 n.) to play down as much as possible Labat's reference to grinding slaves to death. The only suffering on the plantations which Grainger is prepared to discuss at any length is that caused by the diseases which he as a physician can cure, or at least alleviate. We get the affecting tale of Junio and Theana, and mention of the charms of white Kittitian virgins, but nothing is said of the sexual exploitation of black women by white men which was an institutionalised part of the plantation system.

*Introduction* 59

On the contrary, Grainger describes slaves laughing and singing at their work (III, 146) and enjoying themselves afterwards (IV, 582–601). Letting them have a drum instead of the 'wild banshaw' or permitting them 'vinous spirits' (presumably rum was all right) might lead to 'Fell acts of blood, and vengeance' (IV, 602–5) – but vengeance for what? Grainger does not tell us. His West Indian readers would not need to be told, and his British ones (or most of them) probably did not want to know. The only other real suggestion of slave resistance is the hint of the possibility of arson in the description of the cane-fire (III, 54). Grainger would have us believe the slaves are happy, and happy slaves do not revolt – even though the Leewards had seen a major slave conspiracy in Antigua in 1736 and there had been a large-scale slave rebellion in Jamaica in 1760–61, while Grainger had been writing *The Sugar-Cane*.[140]

A much starker picture of Caribbean slave life in the period can be had from other accounts, such as Ramsay's (see Appendix IV), and our suspicion of poetical descriptions of happy slaves is sharpened when we recall the rather later words of Mary Prince, one of the few Caribbean authors of the type of slave narrative better known from North America:

> I have been a slave myself – I know what slaves feel [...] The man that says slaves be quite happy in slavery – that they don't want to be free – that man is either ignorant or a lying person. I never heard a slave say so.[141]

Yet Grainger's description of the slave dance repays closer examination. Kamau Brathwaite's suggestion that 'The dancers are moving to the wrong rhythm' has already been noted. In fact when we look at one of Grainger's models, Philips's *Cyder*, we discover that some of Grainger's details are taken from Philips's account of the festivities of English agricultural labourers (see this writer's notes on IV, 582–605). There are two ways of looking at this. One is to feel that Grainger's literary model has got the better of him, and that the European form in which he has chosen to write is preventing him from seeing, or at least from describing, what was actually in front of his eyes in St Kitts. Another is to wonder if we are not seeing an essentially humane man who realises that he is compromised by his economic dependence on the fundamentally inhumane system of slavery, and who is trying to reinterpret this fact in a manner which is a little more palatable, much as he endeavours to convince his readers and himself (IV, 165–82) that Caribbean slaves are better off than Scottish miners – who were, it is worth remembering (even as we bear in mind Johnson's comment that 'it is but a small alleviation to our misery to find conditions in life still more miserable than our own'), tied to the mines in which they worked by a hereditary bondage for a generation after Grainger's death. The black Caribbean slave and the free white British agricultural labourer are placed on a common plane of humanity by Grainger's literary borrowing. As a writer, Grainger is a member of a self-conscious literary elite and he is writing for an elite audience. He feels superior to the slaves who form a large part of his medical practice in St Kitts, but this is at least partly in the same way he feels superior to English agricultural labourers – both groups are, as he calls the Caribbean slaves, 'uninstructed swains' (IV, 229). Class and race are much more closely intertwined in Grainger's St Kitts than they were in Britain, but his sense of superiority is arguably based as much on the one as on the other.

Grainger has been criticised for calling the slaves 'swains' (I, 165; I, 584; IV, 229) and the word has been used as evidence of the poem's 'unimaginative imitation of popular literary forms in Western Europe.'[142] But he also uses the word to refer to the Greek and Roman farmers of classical antiquity (I, 9; I, 314) and to English shepherds (III, 133). When we come across 'the masterswain' (I, 405) and 'Britain's honest swains' (III, 458), the reference is to the West Indian planters, who are also called 'swains' plain and simple (I, 286; III, 287 – note that this passage goes on to include a British peer among the 'swains' of St Kitts). There is even a passage where it is far from clear whether the word refers to the masters or the slaves (III, 48–54). The word thus appears as simply an aspect of the way in which Grainger uses his blank-verse form and consciously lofty poetic diction in a manner easily understood by his contemporaries to portray the cultivation of the cane as an epic struggle between man and nature. The ills which menace the cane, whether minute insect pests – 'Bugs of uncommon shape; thrice hideous show!' (II, 215) – or 'The all-wasting hurricane' (II, 271), are treated in the same elevated style. The labour of the swains is a battle in which planter and slave may not occupy the same rank – the sort of distinction of which Grainger, a former regimental surgeon, was very aware —but they are shown as being on the same side. Digging cane-holes is described in terms of military metaphor (I, 266–77) and the 'master-swain' supervising the planting (I, 400–15) is described in terms of Hephaestus forging the shield of Achilles, when 'The swarthy Cyclops shar'd the important task' – in endeavouring to confer heroic status on the planter, Grainger to some extent does the same for the slaves.

He tells his fellow slave-owner that 'thy slaves are men' (III, 178), a point he has to insist upon since 'insensate some may deem their slaves,/Nor 'bove the bestial rank' (IV, 421–2). He is prepared to admit the slave-trade can cause its victims 'heart-felt anguish' (IV, 68), and he can talk of 'tyrannic sway' and 'heart-debasing slavery' (IV, 235–6). Grainger was, said Johnson, 'a man who would do any good that was in his power', and he claims that he would if he could 'give to man,/Of every colour and of every clime,/Freedom, which stamps him image of his God' (IV, 236–8). But it is clear from the context that he knows he has no such power. Grainger is sincerely convinced of the slave's humanity, and considers that freedom for the slave is perhaps desirable in the abstract, but is something unlikely to happen for a very long time. In the meantime, it is enough to enjoin, 'planter, let humanity prevail' (IV, 211).

The fact that Grainger admits his slave to be a man does not mean he acknowledges him to be an equal. He is fascinated by what he can discover of Amerindian names for plants, and uses Amerindian names like Liamuiga and Karukera for some of the islands in his poem – a bold stroke – and introduces the Amerindian myth of the origin of cassava (IV, 449–53). Nevertheless, it is clear he felt culturally superior to the region's indigenous inhabitants. When Percy enquired if Grainger might be able to supply him with any indigenous songs to add to his collection of old ballads, his reply was that 'no Body can tell me any Thing of the Charibbean poetry; indeed from what I have seen of these Savages; I have no Curiosity to know ought of their Compositions.'[143] Similarly, while both in *The Sugar-Cane* and his *Essay on the more common West-India Diseases* he is fascinated by local plants 'and the Remedies which that Country itself produces', he is reluctant to acknowledge any medical expertise on the part of the slaves, though one might suspect not a few of the local remedies he advocates came to his knowledge or that of earlier European doctors in the region from the practice of the slaves. In his *Essay*, he says the slaves were 'sufficiently expert' at extracting teeth, and that they could treat the 'adhesion to the surrounding membrane' of 'the liver and spleen præternaturally swelled.' He also mentions 'A variety of external applications [...] recommended by the old Negroes' in cases of yaws, without saying whether he thought these were effective.[144] In *The Sugar-Cane*, he merely invites 'the laughing world' – that is, white readers of georgic poetry – to derive amusement from his description of obeah (IV, 365–405). As a man of science and a poet, Grainger is confident of his own superiority, and thus feels safe in suggesting that, in an ideal world, 'Servants, not slaves; of choice, and not compell'd;/The Blacks should cultivate the Cane-land isles' (IV, 242–3). As far as he is concerned, it can be assumed that even when no longer slaves, the blacks will still be servants, cultivating the land for the benefit of white masters.

The assumption is not dissimilar to those made by British writers of the period about the lower orders in their own islands. In *The Hop-Garden*, Smart refers to 'Th'industrious vulgar', the Londoners who come to Kent for the hop-picking, in terms more extreme than anything Grainger says about Caribbean slaves. The hop-pickers are 'the tumultuous crew', 'the wild brutal crew', 'the mad pickers', 'the rebel rout', 'the mob/Irrational'. If Caribbean slaves are summoned from their beds by the bell or conch-shell, the hop-pickers are roused by the 'clam'rous bray' of a bugle; if the slaves have their drivers, the hop-pickers need a 'Severe dictator' even if it is admitted that sometimes female persuausion can have them 'tam'd to diligence' Dyer suggests in *The Fleece* that the 'village nymphs' who make a living from spinning will always have plenty of work to do and therefore should not complain

> [...] should the careful State, severely kind,
> In ev'ry province, to the house of toil
> Compel the vagrant, and each implement
> Of ruder art, the comb, the card, the wheel
> Teach their unwilling hands [...]

Dyer goes on to describe workhouses at length, 'Houses of labor, seats of kind constraint,' where the 'poor' and the 'children of affliction' may be 'compell'd/To happiness' through 'honest toil'; one such establishment is referred to as 'this delightful mansion'.[145]

Grainger's classical model is again relevant here. As Addison put it, a georgic 'is not to appear in the natural simplicity and nakedness of its subject, but in the pleasantest dress that Poetry can bestow on it.' One way of achieving this is selection and omission; the georgic is *'some part* of the science of husbandry put into a pleasing dress' (emphasis added). As Grainger was well aware, Roman poetry on rural themes did a good job of ignoring the fact that Italian agriculture in the classical period was based to a large extent on the labour, not of what Knox calls 'jolly Apulian swains', but of slaves. If the love-elegies of Tibullus, with their idealised (that is, falsified) tableaux of rural simplicity can be seen by a modern classical scholar as 'the poetry of a slave-holding upper class', the same is true of Virgil's *Georgics* (a fact which is brushed aside by some nineteenth-century British critics of Grainger, who appear to have felt that it was all right for Virgil to be reticent about slavery, while it was wrong for Grainger to acknowledge it frankly). We can see Grainger's imitation of Virgil, his 'West-India georgic', as being as much a form of translation as his *Poetical translation of the Elegies of Tibullus*; the importance of the form appears in a new light considered in terms of Lawrence Venuti's argument that 'fluent, domesticating translation' in this period 'remained affiliated with the British cultural elite.'[146] When Grainger's contemporaries in London or Paris praise what they see as his successful imitation of Virgil, they are celebrating more than a literary judgement. The 'West-India georgic' glorifies the domestication of classical culture by the British elite and also by the Caribbean elite, or at least by the elite planter of the Montano type or Eton-and-Oxford-educated Creoles like Junio. Such Creoles did exist: we can find them writing Latin poems celebrating the humanity of the slave trade in rescuing fortunate victims from a barbarous Africa given to cannibalism and human sacrifice.[147] Grainger's complaints that in fact most Creoles didn't read are irrelevant; what mattered to planters was not whether they were in fact (even by Eurocentric standards) culturally superior to their slaves, but simply that they claimed to be so. The mere existence of *The Sugar-Cane* supported that claim. In writing about the sugar-cane, Grainger was writing not just about any plant, but the plant around which the whole of Caribbean society was centred, the plant on which, for some, indeed, the whole of British commerce – the British Empire itself – depended. In writing a georgic, Grainger seeks to impose a European sense of order on the Caribbean landscape, and writes in support of the continuance of the colonial relationship from which the planters and their British allies benefited, a relationship which depended on the continuance of slavery. His claims on behalf of the colonies and the locally born elite into which he had married depend on the continuance of an empire dominated by the metropolitan partner, a Britain whose upper classes valued the kind of poem he is writing. Form and content are inseparable, and give *The Sugar-Cane* a unity and coherence, which has not always been apparent to critics who have assumed that imitation is a pointless exercise without exploring what Grainger actually does with his Virgilian and other models, and who have been led by Boswell into mistaken assumptions about what contemporaries actually thought of the poem.[148]

What appeal, then, can *The Sugar-Cane* have for the modern reader? If we are to read only those poets of previous generations whose morals and politics are in accordance with modern standards, we will not have much to read. At the time of the Peace of Utrecht, Pope expressed the hope 'Oh stretch thy Reign, fair Peace! from Shore to Shore,/Till Conquest cease, and Slav'ry be no more' (*Windsor-Forest*, ll. 407–8) but this did not stop both him and Swift investing in the South Sea Company in 1720, in the hope of profiting from the trade in slaves with the Spanish colonies which the Peace had made possible.[149] It is pointless to wish that Grainger had written a different poem, though the defence may wish to urge that its success may have persuaded readers to question their own assumptions about slavery precisely because it was not an abolitionist tract. While they are part of the poem's importance as a historical document, Grainger's acceptance of slavery and his aggrandisement of the slave-owning Creole elite disturb any attempt at dispassionate analysis. Perhaps the more we see the poem as skilled and successful in its own terms, the more disturbing these aspects become. In terms of modern postcolonial literary theory, Grainger does 'write back to the centre,' he does subvert his model by making his 'georgic' a 'West-India' one. From one point of view, it is not the 'swains', 'naiads' and 'dryads' which should catch our attention, but the 'Blacks', 'yams', 'cow-itch', 'stocks and millpoints', the canes themselves. The mere mention of such things in a work of 'polite literature' in the eighteenth century is an act of unprecedented boldness. While Grainger is imposing a European model on Caribbean reality, he is also to some extent doing the reverse: the Caribbean reality is being imposed on the European model, on a scale to which there is nothing earlier which is comparable in English. To the extent that it is a Caribbean poem, *The Sugar-Cane* is a poem of a Caribbean elite, but it is an early triumph of a process which eventually breaks the confines of race and class. By the mid-twentieth century, in his *Sandy Lane and other poems* (1945) Hilton Vaughan can make effective use of a formal sonnet to celebrate the sights and sounds of a Barbadian tuk-band. Less than 50 years afterwards, Brathwaite's *X/Self* (1987) and Walcott's *Omeros* (1990) show in their different ways the Caribbean's ability to reclaim and re-interpret the classical and European as well as other aspects of their cultural ancestry.[150]

## 5. A note on the text of the poem

[...] the fatigue of reading their explanatory comments was tenfold that which might suffice for understanding the original, and their works effectually increased our application, by professing to remove it [...]
(Oliver Goldsmith, *An Enquiry into the Present State of Polite Learning* (1759), on the rise of critics in the later Roman empire)

The text of *The Sugar-Cane* presented here is essentially that of the first edition (1764). The only surviving manuscript of *The Sugar-Cane* is that at Trinity College, Dublin, which is an unfinished draft. While Grainger was not satisfied with the text of the first edition,[151] we do not have anything better, as he died before he could produce a corrected edition, and none of the later editions has any independent authority. I have adopted a conservative approach to the 1764 text: while Grainger may write, for example, both 'Ethiop' and 'Æthiop', I have seen no reason to impose consistency for the sake of it. The only changes are as follows:

1. Corrections called for by the Errata to the 1764 edition have been made; details are given in the notes on the passages concerned.
2. Two further errors mentioned by Grainger in a letter to Percy (at III, 6, and IV, 253) have been corrected, as has one obvious error (at I, 22 n.). Errors in line numbering have also been corrected.
3. The long 's' has been modernised, and the use of drop capitals at

the beginning of each book and of large and small capitals for the first word of a verse paragraph has not been kept. Spacing between verse paragraphs has been eliminated.
4. The eighteenth-century practice of leaving a space before some marks of punctuation (especially colons and semi-colons) has not been retained. Punctuation is otherwise as in *1764*. It is somewhat eccentric, but it probably bears some resemblance to Grainger's own[152]; apparent difficulties will normally resolve themselves on reading the passage aloud.
5. Grainger's notes, originally given as footnotes, are printed as endnotes.

As *The Sugar-Cane* is a highly allusive poem, which makes extensive reference not only to its Caribbean surroundings but also to much earlier literature, I have preferred to err on the side of generosity in my own notes. I have endeavoured to identify all individuals mentioned by Grainger, to supply modern scientific names for plants, and to identify his literary borrowings and allusions (though I am well aware that some, which may be obvious to other readers, will have escaped me). As many works to which Grainger refers are not readily available outside larger libraries, I have often given parallel passages in full. Except where otherwise stated, translations are my own. While I have made some use of the TCD manuscript in my notes, I have not attempted to include all variant readings, which would have swelled the bulk of the notes out of all proportion to their possible interest to the majority of readers.

# Notes to Introduction

1 Testament Dative of Dr James Granger [sic], registered in Commissariat Record of Edinburgh, 8 April 1790; General Register Office for Scotland, Edinburgh, CC8/8/128/1. Grainger's daughter is referred to in this document as 'Helen Granger', but she was usually called Eleanora; Thomas Percy, who was her godfather, calls her Eleanora Catharine. She married Thomas Rowsell in 1798. Her elder sister, Louise Agnes (sometimes called Louisa) had died at school in 1774. See W. E. K. Anderson, *Percy Letters*, IX, 1, 74–5. One slight puzzle is posed by the fact that when the Testament Dative was registered, Grainger's widow may still have been living; however she appears to have been resident outside of Britain for many years and it is possible that her daughter was not in regular contact with her. Writing to Robert Anderson in 1801, General Robert Melville thought Grainger's widow had 'died about 6 years ago at Lille in Flanders' (Melville to Anderson, 3 December 1801; NLS Adv. MS. 22–4–10, ff. 20–1). There is a letter from her to Thomas Percy dated 'Near Bethun, in Flanders, July 19th, 1779' (printed in Nichols, *Illustrations*, VII, 296–9). Percy thought she had been 'obliged to retire to Lisle' [i.e., Lille] because she 'was unfortunately not a good Oeconomist' (W. E. K. Anderson, *Percy Letters*, IX, 81); this might mean she lived on the Continent because it was cheaper, or perhaps that she had fled Britain to escape her debts. He was unsure how long she had survived her husband, putting 'near 20 yr I believe, near 30 years' in a letter, before changing this to 'many years' (ibid., p. 74); the longer period would suggest she died sometime in the 1790s.

2 Letter printed in Nichols, *Illustrations*, VII, 293–5; original in the Hyde Collection. Grainger uses both 'St Christopher' and 'St Kitts' in his letters and in *The Sugar-Cane*; both forms are found in his note on I, 60.

3 W. E. K. Anderson, *Percy Letters*, IX, 182. The reference to the pig confirms it is the same letter, in which Grainger says he is sending 'a fat West India barrow, fed chiefly on sugar cane'.

4 William Cuming to Thomas Percy, 16 January 1775, NLS Adv. MS 22–4–10, ff. 14–17.

5 Nichols, *Illustrations*, VII, 230, note.

6 Nichols, *Illustrations*, VII, 230, note, quotes this, but erroneously gives the date as 'Dec. 14'.

7 Note in NLS Adv. MS. 22–4-10, f. 22, undated and unsigned, but identifiable from the following note (ibid., f. 23) in the same hand, which is endorsed in another hand as by 'Doctor Wright/Edinburgh' and which refers to the 'Linnæan Index' the writer supplied to the 1802 edition of Grainger's *Essay on the more common West-India Diseases*, as being by William Wright (1735–1819), for whom see *DNB*.

8 Personal communications, from Victoria Borg O'Flaherty, Archivist, National Archives of St Kitts and Nevis, 11 March 1997, and from Desmond V. Nicholson, Museum of Antigua and Barbuda, 25 April 1997.

There is a document called 'The Cayon Diary, St Kitts', printed in Oliver, *Caribbeana*, III, 100–13, 161–9, which has an entry (p. 108) 'Granger [sic], James, D$^r$, died in November 1767; fever.' However, the date is impossible in view of the fact that Grainger's will was proved in June 1767 (see below). The 'Diary' appears to be a later compilation from various sources, rather than a contemporary record; it is said (p. 100) to have been compiled by John Earle (1748–1807).

9 Recorded in St Christopher Deed Book G No. 2, National Archives, St. Kitts and Nevis. I am grateful to the Archivist, Ms O'Flaherty, for supplying me with a photocopy of this document.

10 W. E. K. Anderson, *Percy Letters*, IX, 178–9. Anderson says 'Some of his pieces are dated so early as 1739', though this is not true of any of his surviving poems (Anderson may have thought they were juvenilia unworthy of publication or preservation), and that 'two years after he seems to have been old enough to perform the duty of an army surgeon', but this almost certainly places the beginning of his army service too early.

11 Wright's note in NLS Adv. MS. 22–4-10, f. 22.

12 From 'The Life of Grainger' prefixed to Anderson's 1836 edition of Grainger's *Works* (I, v-xvi). The whole of this 'Life' is almost identical to that published in Anderson's *A Complete Edition of the Poets of Great Britain*, X, 891–4, which has a separate title-page for *The Poetical Works of James Grainger, M.D.* dated Edinburgh, 1794. This 'Life' is the ultimate source of many later summaries of Grainger's career. Anderson mentions having before him 'by the favour of Mrs. Grainger, his brother's relict,' a copy of Grainger's translation of Tibullus which he had given to his brother, and also mentions information from her in his correspondence with Percy; see W. E. K. Anderson, *Percy Letters*, IX, 88, 178.

13 Undated draft of letter to his brother-in-law, William Mathew Burt, in Nichols, *Illustrations*, VII, 271–5, at p. 272. This was printed by Nichols from a copy made in 1804 by Robert Anderson; this, or a similar copy, is now in the Osborn Collection, Beinecke Library, Yale.

14 W. E. K. Anderson, *Percy Letters*, IX, 75, 182. Percy added that Grainger 'might not think proper to instance this in his Letter to M<sup>r</sup> Burt' (which was a defence of Grainger's suitability as a husband). See also *Sugar-Cane*, III, 150–9.
15 W. E. K. Anderson, *Percy Letters*, IX, 87–8, 92; information from the General Register Office for Scotland, Edinburgh. It is just possible Grainger might have been baptised a Catholic, but the Catholic records for Duns go back only to 1874, with earlier ones under Haddington, but only from 1853. However, Grainger's writings as an adult sometimes show an anti-Catholic bias (see below).
16 Grainger's Scottishness was sometimes questioned in the nineteenth century; see, e.g., note on 'The Poet Grainger' signed 'G.', *Notes and Queries*, 3rd Series, Vol. VI, 19 November 1864. The latest *Oxford Dictionary of Quotations* (revised 4th edn., ed. Angela Partington) calls him an 'English physician and man of letters' (p. 314).
17 Grainger to Percy, 18 October 1758, Bod. MS Percy c. 10, ff. 16–17; *Sugar-Cane*, I, 517–18 and III, 150–9; William Cuming to Thomas Percy, 16 January 1775, NLS Adv. MS 22–4–10, ff. 14–17; note by William Wright, NLS Adv. MS 22–4–10, f. 22; General Robert Melville to Robert Anderson, 24 April 1801, NLS Adv. MS 22–3–11, ff. 15–16. Cuming's dates (1714–88) are given in W. E. K. Anderson, *Percy Letters*, IX, 124, note; in the same letter, Cuming said of Grainger that 'he was several years younger than me'. It is possible that the man Cuming thought was Grainger's 'uncle' was in fact his half-brother, who appears to have been significantly older than him. Melville may perhaps have been the original owner of a copy of *The Sugar-Cane* now in the British Library (classmark 1651/405) which bears the ownership signature 'Robert Melvill [sic] 1764'.
18 Robert Anderson, 'Life of Grainger' in 1836 edition of Grainger's *Works* (I, v-vi); Grainger to William Mathew Burt, in Nichols, *Illustrations*, VII, 271–5, at p. 272; personal communications from Mrs Jo Currie, Special Collections, Edinburgh University Library, 12 June and 25 June 1997; Pottle, *James Boswell: The Earlier Years*, p. 23. Gibbon matriculated at Oxford shortly before his fifteenth birthday: Reese, ed., *Gibbon's Autobiography*, p. 24. The Edinburgh Arts matriculations at this period have only a signature under the year in question, without supplying any additional information.
19 See Prebble, *Culloden*, and Black, *Culloden and the '45*.
20 After a number of changes of name, the 13th Foot became known as the Somerset Light Infantry; see Everett, *History of the Somerset Light*

*Infantry*, pp. 89–99, for the part played in the 'Forty-Five' by the 13th Foot, and what is known of the subsequent movements of the Regiment. The later regimental history by Popham offers much scantier information on this period.

21 Quoted (without indication of source) in Prebble, *Culloden* (Penguin edn.), pp. 60, 83, 89, 100, 111–113; this passage at p. 112.

22 For Grainger's rank as surgeon from 28 June 1746, see MS Army List for 1752 (with additions to 1757), Public Record Office, WO 64/11, p. 183; for his commission, Commission Book, PRO, WO 25/22, p. 27 and Notification Book, PRO, WO 25/136, p. 30. Everett, *History of the Somerset Light Infantry*, pp. 76–7, gives a list of the regiment's officers in 1715, including Hadzor as Surgeon. On the position of regimental surgeons at this period, see Johnston, *Roll of Commissioned Officers in the Medical Service*, pp. xxi, xxiv–xxv (the same work has a brief and not entirely accurate summary of Grainger's career at p. 17). Grainger stressed the significance of his commission in his letter to William Mathew Burt, in Nichols, *Illustrations*, VII, 271–5, at p. 272, where he says he was 'honoured with a commission in the army, where the King styled me Gentleman'; Grainger's commission was signed by King George II himself (some at this period were signed by the Duke of Cumberland). Grainger displayed a coat-of-arms on a bookplate (undated, but after he took his MD in 1753) described at pp. 75–6 of the (separately paginated) supplement on 'West Indian Bookplates' in Oliver, ed., *Caribbeana*, III, where the arms are given as 'Azure, a crescent between two mullets in pale Or' with crest, 'A hand holding a bow,' and motto 'Mente et Manu' (i.e., 'by mind and hand').

23 Grainger to William Mathew Burt, in Nichols, *Illustrations*, VII, 271–5, at p. 272; 'Three Elegies written from Italy,' in Robert Anderson, ed., *Poetical Works of James Grainger* (1836), II, 53–66; *Sugar-Cane*, II, 275–8, 476 (and note in this edition); review of anonymous English translation of Goldoni's comedies *The Father of a Family, and Pamela*, in *Monthly Review*, XVII, 47–50 (July 1757). On Grainger and the *Monthly Review*, see below. The Venetian Carlo Goldoni (1707–93) remains one of the best-known Italian writers of the eighteenth century. Grainger's review of *The Cadet: A Military Treatise, by an Officer*, in *Monthly Review*, XV, 402–7 (October 1756) also indicates at least some knowledge of Italian.

24 Quotation from Everett, *History of the Somerset Light Infantry*, p. 98. Grainger's notes on the soldier's wife are in Edinburgh University Library MS. La. III.186, a notebook consisting mainly of the draft of his later *Historia febris anomalae* (published 1753).

25 Read before the Edinburgh Medical Society, 3 May 1753, and published in Volume II (1756), pp. 257–63, of the Society's *Essays and Observations*.

26 Grainger, *Historia febris anomalae Batavae, annorum 1746, 47, 48, &c.* (the *Monita Siphylica* appended to this is a reprint of his MD dissertation), *DNB* entry on John Pringle (1707–82), and 'The Life of Grainger' by Alexander Chalmers, in his edition of Grainger's works in Chalmers, ed., *The Works of the English Poets* ... (1810), XIV, 467–511, at p. 469. Quotations from review in *Monthly Review*, IX, 429–32 (December 1753), identified by Nangle, *Monthly Review ... Indexes*, as by Sir Tanfield Leman (1714–62), physician and frequent reviewer of medical and miscellaneous works for the *Monthly Review*.

27 Grainger to William Mathew Burt, in Nichols, *Illustrations*, VII, 271–5, at p. 272; under 19 February 1754, the Notification Book in Public Record Office, WO 25/136, p. 360, specifically refers to St Clair's commission as being 'in the room of Surg$^n$. Granger [sic], who resigns'; St Clair's replacement of Grainger on this date is also referred to in the MS Army List for 1752 (with additions to 1757), PRO WO 64/11, pp. 183–4, and the MS 'Regimental List of Successions in the Army, from 1$^{st}$ January 1754, to 1$^{st}$ January 1764,' WO 25/209, at f. 97$^r$.

28 The 'few hundreds' are mentioned in Grainger to William Mathew Burt, in Nichols, *Illustrations*, VII, 271–5, at p. 272. For the College of Physicians, see Munk, *Roll of the Royal College of Physicians*, II, 219. On Bourryau as Grainger's 'pupil' in 1754, see William Cuming to Thomas Percy, 16 January 1775, NLS Adv. MS 22-4-10, ff. 14–17; see also Gilmore, 'Tibullus and the British Empire' and the article on 'Bourryau of St Kitts' in Oliver, ed., *Caribbeana*, III, 251–4. Grainger's references to Bourryau from his letters to Percy, 20 July 1758, in Nichols, *Illustrations*, VII, 260–1 (original in Hyde Collection), and undated (but late 1758 and possibly a continuation of that of 18 October 1758), Bod. MS Percy c.10, ff. 18–19. I have examined Grainger's contributions to the *Monthly Review*; for the identification of these and background to the periodical, see Nangle, *Monthly Review ... Indexes*. The title-page of Maitland's *History* mentioned its completion 'by another hand'; this is identified as Grainger in a letter from his friend George Paton (1721–1807) to the *Gentleman's Magazine*, LXI, pt. II, p. 614 (July 1791). On Paton, see Nichols, *Illustrations*, VII, 229; *DNB*; and W. E. K. Anderson, *Percy Letters*, IX, 5 and passim. In the same letter, Paton called Grainger 'my old and intimate acquaintance, who died at Antigua, Dec. 24, 1767' – the year at least is wrong.

29 On the history of Dodsley's *Collection*, see R. W. Chapman 'Dodsley's *Collection of Poems*, (collations, lists, and indexes)'. 'Solitude' appeared as 'By Dr Grainger' in (for example) the 1775 edition, IV, 229–39, and is in collected editions of his works, such as those by Anderson and Chalmers. For Johnson's quotation and comment, see Boswell's *Life* (World's Classics ed. by R. W. Chapman, p. 873).

30 These comments are drawn from Phillip B. Anderson's article, 'Mr. Young, Meet Mr. Pope: James Grainger's 'Solitude: An Ode',' who refers here to the poetry of William Collins (1721–59) and that of the brothers Joseph Warton (1722–1800) and Thomas Warton the younger (1728–90), and of Edward Young (1683–1765).

31 See Davis, *Thomas Percy*; for the introduction to Grainger, and those by him to Johnson and Goldsmith, ibid., pp. 37, 38, 56.

32 Grainger to Percy, 24 March 1757, Bod. MS Percy c.10, ff. 1–2.

33 *The Call of Aristippus, Epistle IV[,] To Mark Akenside, M.D.*, quoted in a review of the same, *Monthly Review*, XVIII, 167–70 (February 1758).

34 On the Tibullus translation, see below. For Percy and Grainger's translations from Ovid, see Bod. MS Percy e. 6–8; an edited version of Grainger's contributions is in Robert Anderson, ed., *Poetical Works of James Grainger* (1836), II, 91–115. *Ovid's Epistles, translated into English verse*, 'by St. Barrett, A.M.' (London, 1759), was given an uncomplimentary review in *Critical Review*, VII, 31–9 (January 1759), which echoed Smollett's complaints about excessive annotation in Grainger's translation of Tibullus. There were a number of earlier English translations of the *Epistles*, including a particularly well-known one by Dryden and others (1680).

35 For a more detailed discussion, see Gilmore, 'Tibullus and the British Empire.'

36 Lennox, ed., *Greek Theatre of Father Brumoy*, III, 441–51, 452–78. Grainger and Bourryau's contributions are identified on the unnumbered Advertisement leaf at the beginning of Volume III, where Grainger is described as 'author of the translation of Tibullus'; other contributors included Samuel Johnson. The work probably appeared about the middle of 1759: Mrs. Lennox's fulsome dedication to the Prince of Wales (the later George III) is dated on HRH's birthday, 4 June 1759.

*The Greek Theatre* was based on Pierre Brumoy, S. J., *Le Théatre des Grecs* (3 vols., Paris, 1730, and later editions).

37 Grainger to Percy, undated (but late 1758 and possibly a continuation of that of 18 October 1758), Bod. MS Percy c.10, ff. 18–19. In an earlier letter to Percy (14 April 1758; ibid., ff. 12–13), Grainger noted he had been unsuccessful in courting 'a physicians Daughter in the City' and his

reference to the problem being her family's demand for a 'Settlement' suggests they thought that financially speaking he was an unsuitable match.
38 Grainger to Percy, 9 April 1759, Bod. MS Percy c.10, ff. 25–6. Grainger's 'We shall, in a few Days, be plying in the Great Atlantic Ocean' suggests that he and Bourryau travelled together. While this is not explicitly stated, it also seems to be implied by a passage in a draft of *The Sugar-Cane*; see note on I, 19–20 in this edition. Bourryau was certainly in St Kitts later in the year, as he was sworn in as a member of the island's House of Assembly, 1 October 1759; see Minutes of St Kitts Council of that date, Public Record Office, CO 241/8.
39 Peter Robert Luard (John Bourryau's brother-in-law) to Percy, 30 October 1759, Bod. MS Percy c. 10, f. 48.
40 See Oliver, ed., *Caribbeana*, III, 134, and the same editor's *Registers of St Thomas, Middle Island* ..., pp. 29–30, for persons called Granger or Grainger in St Kitts. There were also Graingers in Barbados in the same period: *Caribbeana*, IV, 226, 243, 245, 246. In addition, a marriage bond, 2 August 1771, relating to the intended marriage of Susannah Grainger to Thomas Glasgo McShean is in St Christopher Marriage Bond Book, 1771–80 (photocopy of this document kindly supplied by Ms O'Flaherty). However, there is no mention in James Grainger's surviving correspondence of his having relatives in the Caribbean.
41 Grainger to Percy, 1 June 1760, NLS Adv. MS 22–3–11, ff. 1–2; pedigrees of Burt, Daniel and Mathew families in Oliver, *History of the Island of Antigua*, I, 87–91, 188–9; II, 251–8; III, 414; 'Burt of Nevis' in Oliver, ed., *Caribbeana*, V, 89–96; Henige, *Colonial Governors*, p. 131. The fragmentary baptismal record is printed in *Caribbeana*, V, 315; Daniel's sister Margaret was two years old when she was baptised in 1738 (ibid.). Daniel Mathew Burt's names deceived even Oliver; see *Caribbeana*, V, 92, where she is noted as witnessing the will of 'his sister.' William Mathew Burt resigned as a member of the St Kitts Council in 1755 because he had taken up residence in England: Public Record Office, CO 153/18, pp. 63–4, 66. The President of a British Caribbean colony was the senior member of the island's Council who administered the colony in the absence of a governor; as the Governor of the Leeward Islands normally resided in Antigua, the Presidents of St Kitts and Nevis were most of the time the persons responsible for the government of their respective islands.
42 Grainger to William Mathew Burt, in Nichols, *Illustrations*, VII, 271–5, at p. 273. The exact significance of 'pounds currency' in the British Caribbean varied with time and place, but it was always at a significant discount in relation to sterling.

43 Quotations from Grainger to Percy, 1 June 1760, NLS Adv. MS 22-3-11, ff. 1-2; his devotion is expressed in Grainger to Percy, 14 May 1764, NLS Adv. MS 22-4-10, ff. 1-2: 'I love, I idolize my family.' Several years after Grainger's death, an anonymous article in the English press claimed he had been driven into an early grave by his wife's infidelity and extravagance. Percy indignantly denied this, and the letters of Grainger's which he preserved do suggest a happy marriage. See W. E. K. Anderson, *Percy Letters*, IX, Appendix (pp. 326-8) and passim.
44 For the alleged quarrel, see Boswell's *Life of Johnson* (World's Classics ed. by R. W. Chapman, p. 700) and W. E. K. Anderson, *Percy Letters*, IX, 326. Grainger stayed with Spooner at 'Sunninge' in 1764 (Grainger to Percy, 22 January 1764, Nicholls, *Illustrations*, VII, 285-6) and the address identifies him as the Charles Spooner mentioned in Bourryau's will as his uncle – in 'Bourryau of St Kitts' in Oliver, ed., *Caribbeana*, III, 251-4 (the reference to Louisa Grainger is at p. 252). Charles Spooner married Mary Burt (Grainger's wife's sister) in St Kitts, 9 March 1761: Oliver, ed., *Caribbeana*, V, 92. Mrs. Grainger mentions the Spooners several times in her letters to Percy in NLS Adv. MS 22-4-10 and Bod. MS Percy c.10.
45 Peter Robert Luard to Percy, 30 October 1759, Bod. MS Percy c.10, f. 48. Luard's mention of '26 July the date I last heard from him' may be when Luard received Grainger's letter rather than when Grainger wrote it; Luard mentions the voyage out took Grainger six weeks, so if he had sailed from England as anticipated in early April and then written to Luard soon after his arrival, the letter could have reached England by the end of July. The delay in passing on the information to Percy can be explained by the fact that Luard's letter was written in anticipation of a visit to London by Percy. A pistole was 'a *French* or *Spanish* Piece of Gold, worth 17 s[hillings]' (Bailey); foreign coins were the usual circulating medium in the British Caribbean colonies at this period. The reference may possibly be to Grainger's expectations of his marriage rather than to professional income.
46 Grainger to Percy, 1 June 1760, NLS Adv. MS 22-3-11, ff. 1-2.
47 Population figures from PRO, CO 152/28, f. 172 (the total for white inhabitants is my own calculation, based on the assumption that the 888 'Men to bear Arms' are included in the 922 'Men'); Edwards quotations from his *History ... of the British West Indies*, I, 464; figures for St Kitts sugar production 1704-1943 are in Deerr, *History of Sugar* (I, 197); for prices see ibid., II, 530-1. The modern literature on the history of sugar and slavery in the Caribbean is enormous; for an introduction, see Beckles and Shepherd, *Caribbean Slave Society and Economy*.
48 Grainger to William Mathew Burt, in Nichols, *Illustrations*, VII,

271–5, at p. 274; Ramsay, *Essay*, p. 82; payment for attendance on prisoners authorised 31 January 1765, St Christopher Assembly Minutes 1761–9, p. 185 (I owe this reference to Ms. O'Flaherty). On Ramsay, see Shyllon, *James Ramsay: The Unknown Abolitionist*.

Somewhat later in the century, Bryan Edwards, *History ... of the British West Indies*, II, 166 (first published 1793) said that 'The usual recompence to the surgeon for attendance and medicines, is six shillings a head per annum for all the Negroes on the estate, whether sick or well. Amputations, difficult cases in midwifery, inoculation, &c. are paid for exclusively, and on a liberal scale.' If Edwards' figures were Jamaica currency, they would approximate to the sterling figures given by Ramsay. Edwards noted that a doctor's income from such sources was 'altogether independent of the profits of his practice with the Whites.'

49 For Crump, see Oliver, *History of the Island of Antigua*, I, 184–5; for Fraser, ibid., I, 259.

50 Notes by Wright in NLS Adv. MS 22–4–10, ff. 22, 23; Wright added fairly extensive 'practical notes' and a 'Linnæan Index' (giving the scientific names of plants mentioned) to the second edition of the *Essay* published in Edinburgh, 1802, and reprinted in Kingston, Jamaica, the same year. For medicine in the Caribbean at this period in general, see Sheridan, *Doctors and Slaves*, which discusses Grainger, pp. 28–32 and quotes frequently from the *Essay*.

51 Grainger to Percy, 1 June 1760, NLS Adv. 22–3–11, ff. 1–2; Grainger went on to say 'when the Reviews are no more! & their Memory has perished.' Presumably an allusion to his controversy with Smollett, this was heavily deleted, probably by Percy.

52 I owe this point to Kevan, 'Mid-eighteenth-century entomology and helminthology ...' (p. 194). *TCD* (37$^r$) refers only to 'the British Chief' but it is clear that Wolfe is meant from the comment 'So Heaven & Pitt ordain' – William Pitt the elder (1708–78, later first Earl of Chatham) was the effective head of the government (though the nominal prime minister was the Duke of Newcastle) and it was Pitt who had selected Wolfe to command the Quebec expedition. The version of this passage in *TCD* must have been written before Pitt resigned office in October 1761; Grainger later changed 'Pitt' to 'George' (referring to the King) which is what appears in *1764*, and it seems strange he did not then include any mention of Wolfe's death, which had as much of an impact on the British public as that of Nelson did two generations later.

53 Grainger to Percy, 5 June 1762, in Nichols, *Illustrations*, VII, 276–9, at pp. 278–9.

54 Percy to Grainger, 25 July 1762, Bod. MS Percy c. 10, ff. 28–9.
55 The manuscript is Trinity College, Dublin, MS 880, catalogued by Abbott, *Catalogue of the Manuscripts [...] of Trinity College, Dublin*, p. 153. Grainger's note to his nephews Benjamin Pym Markham and Benjamin William Hutchinson (also named in his will and there referred to as his nephews-in-law) is dated 27 September 1762. The dedication to Bute is f. 47ʳ, and he may have been named again in a draft of Book IV; see note on IV, 25. Bute was an acquaintance of Grainger's friend James White; see W. E. K. Anderson, *Percy Letters*, IX, 67–8, and *The Sugar-Cane*, III, 509, and additional note.
56 Grainger to Percy, 18 April 1763, Nicholls, *Illustrations*, VII, 282–4. Percy had in fact written to Grainger, 28 February 1763, to tell him of Shenstone's death, and an extract he copied from this letter is in British Library Add. MS 28221, ff. 107–8, and was published by Cleanth Brooks in *The Percy Letters*, VII, *The correspondence of Thomas Percy and William Shenstone* (New Haven and London, 1977), pp. 309–10. I owe this reference to Peter Jackson. In his will dated 17 July 1763 (for which see above) Grainger mentions 'Negroes' among his 'Real and Personal Estate' but there is no indication of their number.
57 Grainger to Percy, 30 November 1763, Nicholls, *Illustrations*, VII, 284. In May 1764, he told Percy he had been away from his family 'upward of eight months' which would place his departure from St Kitts sometime in September or early October of the preceding year; Grainger to Percy, NLS Adv. MS 22–4–10, ff. 1–2. Henry Home (1696–1782) was made a lord of session as Lord Kames, 1752.
58 Percy's journal, British Library, Add. MS 32,336, ff. 43ᵛ and 44ᵛ.
59 Grainger to Percy, 22 January 1764, Nicholls, *Illustrations*, VII, 285–6.
60 Grainger said in his letter to Percy of 22 January 1764 that he had planned to return to the Caribbean with 'Mʳ. Verchild' (printed by Nichols as 'Mr. Vershold'), presumably his wife's brother-in-law James Verchild, who sailed before Grainger's visit to Percy in December. In a later letter from St. Kitts (undated, but received by Percy 11 April 1765; NLS Adv. MS 22–4–10, ff. 3–4) Grainger said his main reason for going to Europe had been to see his older brother, referring to 'the long voyage I had undertaken chiefly to see Him.'
61 W. E. K. Anderson, *Percy Letters*, IX, 85, who notes of 'Bryan and Pereene' that 'Apart from Shenstone's 'Jemmy Dawson' this is the only contribution by a friend of Percy's (though he included other items by seventeenth- and eighteenth-century authors). For 'Bryan and Pereene', which is Grainger's only poem on a Caribbean theme apart from *The Sugar-Cane*, see Appendix II.

62 There had apparently been some discussion as to whether the notes should go at the foot of the page or the end of the poem; Grainger said 'The Notes do not disfigure the Page & therefore I have consented to let them remain where they desire them to be in my 300' – Grainger to Percy, 24 March 1764, Osborn Collection, Beinecke Library, Yale. On Robert Dodsley's hand-over to James, see Tierney, ed., *Correspondence of Robert Dodsley*, pp. 405–7. There are a few brief references to Grainger in this correspondence, but nothing later than 1759, and (unsurprisingly) no mention of *The Sugar-Cane*.

63 In his will he instructed it was to be offered to his nephews-in-law for £300 sterling, which he presumably considered a reasonable value. If they declined to pay this sum, it was to be sent to Scotland as a gift to the Hon. George Kinnaird, the Master of Kinnaird (a Scottish aristocrat whose connection with Grainger does not seem to be mentioned elsewhere). This did not include his manuscripts, which were to be sent to Percy, who was also left Grainger's copy of Johnson's Dictionary and a copy of 'Steven's Edition of the Greek Heroic Poets' (possibly the *Poetae Graeci principes* published in 1566 by the famous French printer Henri Estienne).

64 Grainger to Percy, 6 April and 30 April 1764, Nicholls, *Illustrations*, VII, 286–7; Grainger to Percy, 14 May 1764, Bod. MS Percy c. 10, f. 30 (part of a letter the rest of which is NLS Adv. MS 22–4–10, ff. 1–2); William Strahan's account book for printing work, 1739–68, British Library Add. MS 48800, f. 153$^v$; *Gentleman's Magazine*, XXXIV, 304 (June 1764), which also noted that *The Sugar-Cane* was priced at four shillings, and p. 342 (July 1764). Grainger referred to Strahan as the printer in his letter of 6 April 1764; he is mentioned several times in Grainger's correspondence and in an earlier letter Grainger calls him 'a particular Friend of mine' (Grainger to Percy, n.d., but dated February 1758 by Percy, Bod. MS Percy c.10, ff. 6–7). Strahan's account book is in Reel 1 of *Printing and Publishing History Series One: The Strahan Archive from the British Library*, published on microfilm by Research Publications.

65 Grainger to Percy (undated but received by Percy 11 April 1765), NLS Adv. MS 22–4–10, ff. 3–4. Percy later thought (W. E. K. Anderson, *Percy Letters*, IX, 82) the negligent manager was Mrs Grainger, which is possible, but not certain from Grainger's letter itself.

66 Grainger to Percy, 25 March 1765, Bod. MS Percy c.10, ff. 31–3; Grainger to Percy (undated but received by Percy September 1765), Nicholls, *Illustrations*, VII, 290–292. Quotation from Nichols.

67 Grainger to Percy (undated but marked by Percy 'Feb. 29. 1766' [sic, not a leap year], presumably approximating to date of receipt), Bod. MS Percy c.10, ff. 34–5.

68 Grainger to Percy, 4 December 1766, Nicholls, *Illustrations*, VII, 293–5.
69 Daniel Mathew Grainger to Thomas Percy, 27 January 1771, in Nicholls, *Illustrations*, VII, 295; W. E. K. Anderson, *Percy Letters*, IX, 38, 46 (Percy told Anderson 'I never saw nor heard of any portrait of him'); *Westminster Magazine*, 1773, as quoted in Nicholls, *Illustrations*, VII, 231–2 (see also W. E. K. Anderson, *Percy Letters*, IX, 326–8); William Cuming to Thomas Percy, 16 January 1775, NLS Adv. MS 22–4–10, ff. 14–17. The present writer enquired of the National Portrait Gallery, the National Portrait Gallery of Scotland, the Royal College of Physicians and the Wellcome Institute for the History of Medicine, but none of these possess a portrait of Grainger or could supply any information as to the whereabouts of such a portrait.
70 Boswell's *Life* (World's Classics ed. by R. W. Chapman, p. 699).
71 *Syphilis* was first published at Verona, 1530. There is a modern edition with translation by Geoffrey Eatough.
72 Sambrook, ed., *James Thomson: The Seasons and The Castle of Indolence*.
73 Grainger's review in *Monthly Review*, XVI, 328–40 (April 1757); quotations from Dyer, (*The Fleece*, Books III and IV; *Poems*, 1761, pp. 136, 183).
74 Grainger to Percy, 5 June 1762, in Nichols, *Illustrations*, VII, 276–9, at p. 278; Kevan, 'Mid-eighteenth-century entomology and helminthology in The West Indies: Dr James Grainger,' at p. 194.
75 On Manilius, see the Loeb edition by G. P. Goold.
76 Compare also the more modest pretensions of the young Christopher Smart, who claimed that he would have preferred to write epic if only he could:

> Had I such pow'r, no peasants toil, no hops
> Should e'er debase my lay: far nobler themes,
> The high atchievements of thy warrior kings
> Shou'd raise my thoughts, and dignify my song.
> But I, young rustic, dare not leave my cot,
> For so enlarg'd a sphere —
> (*Hop-Garden*, I, 22–7; Williamson, ed., p. 42)

77 Thomson is the only one not mentioned by name in *The Sugar-Cane*, but there is a direct quotation from *The Seasons* at III, 209, and a possible verbal reminiscence at III, 631. Grainger mentions his indebtedness to

'Shakespear, Milton, Philips, Thomson & others' in a draft of his Preface (*TCD*, f. 106ʳ).
78 Dix, ed., *The Poetical Works of Mark Akenside*, p. 89; Addison, 'An Essay on Virgil's Georgics,' in Guthkelch, ed., *Miscellaneous Works*, II, 11; Trapp, *Works of Virgil*, I, 93.
79 The phrase is that of Chalker (*English Georgic*, p. 1), who does show rather more of an understanding of the poem's subtleties than this statement might suggest.
80 I have relied mainly on the editions of the Georgics by R. D. Williams and R. F. Thomas, and on L. P. Wilkinson's study. The quotation from Dryden's translation is in Walker, ed., *Dryden*, p. 468; compare Dyer's 'What changes cannot toil,/ With patient art, effect?' (*The Fleece*, Book II; *Poems*, 1761, p. 98).
81 Addison, 'An Essay on Virgil's Georgics,' in Guthkelch, ed., *Miscellaneous Works*, II, 7–9; Warton as quoted by Wilkinson, *The Georgics of Virgil*, p. 300.
82 *Cyder*, I, 3, in Lloyd Thomas, *Poems of John Philips*, p. 44; for *The Splendid Shilling*, see ibid., pp. 3–8; Erasmus Darwin quoted by Deane, *Aspects of Eighteenth Century Nature Poetry*, p. 5. On the positive aspects of the diction, see Deane, esp. pp. 11–18, and Tillotson, 'Eighteenth-Century Poetic Diction.' Although unsympathetic to this kind of poetry in general and to Grainger in particular, Spate, 'The Muse of Mercantilism', is good on it as a 'game [...] played according to strict rules and a standard form'.
83 Dyer, *Poems* (1761), pp. 149, 152; *The Traveller*, ll. 387–8, in Mack, ed., *Oliver Goldsmith*, p. 42; *London*, l. 37, in Rudd, ed., *Johnson's Juvenal*, p. 2; Dobrée, 'Theme of Patriotism'; Dabydeen, 'Eighteenth-century English literature on commerce and slavery'; Colley, *Britons*.
84 Dryden's preface to his translation of the *Georgics*, quoted in Chalker, p. 26.
85 This was pointed out by Hugh Reid in *Notes and Queries*, CCXXXI, 518 (December 1986).
86 For an excellent detailed case-study of the artistic possibilities of imitation as the eighteenth century understood the term, see Rudd, ed., *Johnson's Juvenal*.
87 Anon., 'The Pleasures of Jamaica ...', *Gentleman's Magazine*, VIII, 158, 213–14 (March, April 1738). Reference in the poem to the Duke of Portland as Governor of Jamaica (an office he held 1722–6) suggests the poem was written much earlier than its appearance in the *Gentleman's Magazine*. Kamau Brathwaite in his 'Creative Literature ...' (*Roots*, p. 132)

quotes part of this poem, with slight variations, from a later source, the *Columbian Magazine* (Jamaica, 1798) where it was published with the title 'Of some portion of Jamaica and her beauties.'
88 Chalker, *English Georgic*, 56–60.
89 Weekes, *Barbados: A Poem*, pp. 60–1.
90 Life of Milton, in Johnson, *Lives of the English Poets* (Everyman edition, I, 110).
91 William Somervile, 'Epistle to Mr. Thomson, on the first Edition of his Seasons,' in Alexander Chalmers, ed., 'The Poems of William Somervile,' *Works of the English Poets*, XI, 147–240, at p. 201.
92 Review of Hughes's *Natural History of Barbados* in *Monthly Review*, July 1750, quoted in Dallett, 'Griffith Hughes dissected', at p. 23.
93 *Monthly Review*, XV, 402–7 (at p. 404, n.), 450–1 (October, November 1756). Both works reviewed were anonymous. *The Idea of Beauty* was published in Edinburgh.
94 Grainger to Percy, 5 June 1762, in Nichols, *Illustrations*, VII, 276–9, at p. 279.
95 In the course of a book-length study of the form called, we may note, *The English Georgic*, Chalker manages to avoid mentioning the Scottishness of either Grainger or Thomson.
96 Grainger to Percy, 18 October 1758, Bod. MS Percy c.10, ff. 16–17.
97 E.g., reviewing a book of continental travels [Sacheverell Stevens, *Miscellaneous Remarks* ...] (*Monthly Review*, XV, 451–66, November 1756), Grainger approves of Stevens's descriptions of what he (Grainger) calls 'popish priestcraft, and lay-bigotry' (at p. 466).
98 Boswell's *Life* (World's Classics ed. by R. W. Chapman, p. 876).
99 Quoted by Dabydeen, 'Eighteenth-century English literature on commerce and slavery', p. 28.
100 *The Patron* is in Vol. I of [Foote], *The Dramatic Works of Samuel Foote* ... (individual plays separately paginated; quotation from p. 10). *The West Indian* is in Lindsay, *The Beggar's Opera and other Eighteenth Century plays*, pp. 339–408; quotations from pp. 348–9.
101 See Crawford, *Devolving English Literature*, especially Ch. 2.
102 References in *The Sugar-Cane* to 'Britain' (I, 211, 464, 489; II, 24; III, 291, 458, 615; IV, 318, 676, 683), 'British' (I, 289; II, 175; III, 235, 289; IV, 682), 'Britons' (II, 81, 493) and 'Britannia' (II, 444; III, 365, 368; IV, 660) or to 'Albion' (II, 59, 483; III, 283, 508; IV, 353, 472, 630) greatly outnumber those to 'English' (III, 595; IV, 434), 'England' (III, 595, 596), or to 'Scotia' (III, 612; IV, 178) and 'Scotian' (IV, 437, 618). Compare how in *The Traveller*, the Irish Goldsmith, like the Scottish

Grainger, generally uses 'Britain' and 'Britons' rather than 'England.'
103 Grainger to Percy, (undated, but received by Percy 11 April 1765; NLS Adv. MS 22-4-10, ff. 3-4); the paper is damaged after the 'W' and 'World say' written above by Percy.
104 *London Chronicle*, XVI, 12, 20, 28 (3-5 July, 5-7 July, 7-10 July 1764).
105 See the 'Life of Dyer' in *Lives of the English Poets* (Everyman edition, II, 317-19), and Boswell's *Life* of Johnson (World's Classics ed. by R. W. Chapman, pp. 698-700).
106 Boswell's *Life* (World's Classics ed. by R. W. Chapman, p. 341); the remark about 'in jest' is from a cancelled passage not in the World's Classics ed., but is quoted from the Hill-Powell ed., in W. E. K. Anderson, *Percy Letters*, IX, 76; Percy's comment to Robert Anderson, ibid., Bertram H. Davis, *Thomas Percy*, pp. 122, 137 (who indicates that the manuscript is in the Hyde Collection). The manuscript is also referred to by 'J. B. N.' (i.e., J. B. Nichols) in *Gentleman's Magazine*, September 1847 (pt. II, pp. 251-2), where the opening paragraphs of the review (down to 'and how it is prepared') are printed as being in Johnson's writing.
W. E. K. Anderson (loc. cit., p. xiii) takes Percy's statement as showing 'that Percy (not, as is generally believed, Johnson) was mainly responsible for the review of *The Sugar Cane* which appeared in the *London Chronicle* and the *Critical Review*'; however, the review in the *Critical Review* (for which see below) is an entirely different piece from that in the *London Chronicle*. Courtney and Smith, *Bibliography of Samuel Johnson*, p. 103, describe the review in the *Critical Review* as 'attributed to Johnson' but simply state 'He also reviewed the poem in the *London Chronicle*', citing Nichols in *Gentleman's Magazine* (as above).
107 *Monthly Review*, XXXI, 105-18 (August 1764); attribution from Nangle, *Monthly Review ... Indexes*.
108 *Critical Review*, XVIII, 270-7 (October 1764) – the opening pages are misnumbered 170-2.
109 This presumably refers to the dance at IV, 582-605, though the review suggests it comes before the 'celebration of Rum'.
110 On La Condamine, see note on I, 44-5, n.
111 *Gazette Littéraire de l'Europe*, Vol. IV, No. 49 (5 December 1764), pp. 14-16. Quotations from this review are given as printed, without any attempt at modernising the French.
112 Grainger to Percy (undated, but received by Percy September 1765), in Nichols, *Illustrations*, VII, 290-2.
113 Grainger to Percy, 5 June 1762, in Nichols, *Illustrations*, VII, 276-9.

114 Grainger to Percy (undated, but received by Percy September 1765), in Nichols, *Illustrations*, VII, 290–2.
115 Grainger to Percy (undated, but received by Percy 11 April 1765), NLS Adv. MS 22–4–10, ff. 3–4. On literary production and printing and publishing in the Anglophone Caribbean in this period, see Brathwaite, 'Creative Literature of the British West Indies during the period of slavery' and Cave, *Printing and the Book Trade in the West Indies*.
116 Grainger to Percy, 25 March 1765, Bod. MS Percy c.10, ff. 31–3.
117 The copy of the 1764 edition in the Stanford University Libraries (shelfmark PR 3499.G7S8 1764) has on the title-page the signature 'Jn° Dovaston', the note 'Jamaica Aug$^t$ y$^e$ 10$^{th}$ 1764', a note of the price 'Pret$^m$ 0. 5. 0' and the later signature 'Jn°: Dovaston's 1768'. The corrections and annotations appear to be in the same hand, except for a note on the errata leaf, referring to the binding, 'Mr Dovaston ½ b$^d$: & Lett$^d$.' I am grateful to John E. Mustain of the Department of Special Collections at Stanford for photocopies of the relevant pages of this copy.
118 Singleton, *General Description of the West-Indian Islands*, pp. 36–7. Later editions of this poem appeared in London (1776, 1777) and Dublin (1776), but while the Dublin edition is a reprint of the Barbados one, there are substantial textual differences in the London editions; all, however, keep this passage on Grainger. For the identification of Singleton as a member of Lewis Hallam's troupe, see Wright, *Revels in Jamaica*, pp. 38, 40.
119 'Jamaica, A descriptive and didactic poem' occupies pp. 1–20 of *Poems, written chiefly in the West-Indies*. The 'Advertisement' is on an unnumbered page preceding the poem. Most, though not all, of the poems in the volume are by Bryan Edwards.
120 Chapman, *Barbadoes, and other poems*, p. vii.
121 Anon., *Jamaica, A Poem, in three parts*, pp. 18–19. There is also a passage, pp. 31–2, which invokes 'Freedom' in a manner reminiscent of *The Sugar-Cane*, IV, 232–43.
122 For details of the various editions, see Bibliography. The 'Speedily will be published [...]' announcement is from an unnumbered advertisement leaf (not present in all copies) at the end of a copy of the 1802 edition of Grainger's *Essay on the more common West-India Diseases* (Edinburgh University Library, Spec. Coll. 22/5). The 1804 reference is in W. E. K. Anderson, *Percy Letters*, IX, 141 – see this generally for details of the delays to publication.
123 Chalmers, 'The Life of Grainger' in *Works of the English Poets*, XIV, 469–474, at p. 474; on Ramsay, see Appendix IV; Davenport, 'The Life of

James Grainger' in *British Poets*, LIX, 6–16, at pp. 13–14; *The Poetical Works of Charles Mackay*, p. 13.
In his classic *Capitalism and Slavery* (1944), Eric Williams argued four main points: that black slavery was introduced into the Caribbean simply because it was profitable; that, at their peak, Caribbean slave plantations and the slave trade to the Caribbean were highly profitable; that these profits played a major part in financing the Industrial Revolution in Britain; and that the slave trade, and later slavery itself, were abolished in the British colonies because they had ceased to be profitable, and for no other reason. Half a century on, few would accept these conclusions without qualification, but they continue to stimulate argument and discussion. For the changing fortunes of sugar in the British Caribbean colonies in the nineteenth century, see Deerr, *History of Sugar*.
124 Wright, 'Advertisement' to 1802 edition of Grainger's *Essay on the more common West-India Diseases*, pp. v-viii, at p. v; Gilfillan, *Specimens*, III, 137–43, gives an inaccurate summary of Grainger's life and dismisses *The Sugar-Cane*, but prints part of 'Solitude' which receives qualified praise.
125 *Chambers' Eminent Scotsmen* (1875), II, 165–6. None of the following, for example, contain any mention of Grainger: Millar, *Literary History of Scotland*; Gregory Smith, *Scottish Literature*; MacQueen and Scott, *Oxford Book of Scottish Verse*; Watson, *Literature of Scotland*. Royle, *Macmillan Companion to Scottish Literature*, p. 125, has a brief and inaccurate account. In an essay on 'The Scottish Augustans' in Kinsley, ed., *Scottish Poetry*, pp. 119–49, A. M. Oliver has an unsympathetic passage (pp. 139–40) on Grainger, saying his Muse 'had achieved the *reductio ad absurdum* of didactic poetry.' Mary Jane Scott, 'James Thomson and the Anglo-Scots,' in Hook, ed., *History of Scottish Literature: Volume 2*, pp. 81–99, has no more than a few passing and not very complimentary references.
126 Gosse, *History of Eighteenth Century Literature*, pp. 310, 312.
127 Lewis and Lee, *Stuffed Owl*, pp. 77–81.
128 Published in Knox, *Literary Distractions*, pp. 98–108.
129 One would use a hoe to weed the soil between the rows of yams, but when ready, the yams would normally be dug up with a fork. Even in the eighteenth century, when hoes were frequently used for tasks (like cane-holing) which were later done with forks, it seems improbable that a hoe would have been used for lifting yams, as it would have been too likely to damage them.
130 Davison, *Eighteenth-Century English Verse*, pp. 184, 280–2; Lonsdale, *New Oxford Book of Eighteenth Century Verse*, pp. 519–21.

131 In *Journal of Commonwealth Literature*, No. 9 (July 1970), pp. 66–88.
132 Drayton, ibid., pp. 66–7, 78–9, 80–1. His quotations are from *The Sugar-Cane*, III, 98, 146.
133 In Brathwaite, *Roots*, pp. 127–170. This was first published in *Savacou*, Vol. 1, No. 1 (June 1970), pp. 46–73.
134 In *Nieuwe West-Indische Gids/New West Indian Guide*, LXI, 39–53 (1987).
135 See, e.g., Pope, *Essay on Criticism*, ll. 733–8; Chalmers, 'The Life of Grainger' in Chalmers, ed., *The Works of the English Poets* ... (1810), XIV, 467–74, at p. 474; Davenport, 'The Life of James Grainger' in *British Poets*, LIX, 6–16, at p. 15.
136 Sandiford, loc. cit., pp. 45–6, gives only partial line references, but III, 526–76, is clearly the passage meant. He says that 'humbler slave dwellings [...] are rated as "not delightful" ' whereas Grainger's line (III, 531) is '*Nor* not delightful are those reed-built huts,' (emphasis added).
137 David S. Shields, *Oracles of Empire: Poetry, Politics and Commerce in British America 1690–1750*, pp. 72–8.
Besides works previously discussed, we may note Wylie Sypher, *Guinea's Captive Kings*, pp. 168–75 (which is better on Grainger as 'drawn between commercial impulse and benevolism' than it is on *The Sugar-Cane* as literature), and Keith Ellis, 'Images of Sugar in English and Spanish Caribbean Poetry,' *Ariel*, Vol. 24, No. 1 (January 1993), pp. 149–59, which has only a passing mention of Grainger.
138 [Johnson], review of *The Sugar-Cane*, in *Critical Review*, XVIII, 270–7 (October 1764), at p. 277; Davenport, 'The Life of James Grainger' in *British Poets*, LIX, 6–16, at p. 15.
139 I owe this last point to Tobias Döring.
140 On the prevalence of slave resistance, see, e.g., Craton, *Testing the Chains*, and Gaspar, *Bondmen & Rebels*.
141 Ferguson, ed., *History of Mary Prince*, p. 84. Mary Prince's narrative was first published in London and Edinburgh in 1831.
142 Brown, *West Indian Poetry*, p. 20.
143 Grainger to Percy, 25 July 1762, Bod. MS Percy c. 10, ff. 28–9.
144 Grainger, *Essay on the more common West-India Diseases* (1764), pp. 41–2, 57.
145 *Hop-Garden*, II, 58, 82, 84, 91, 97, 151–2, 157–8 (Williamson, ed., pp. 56–7, 59); *The Fleece*, Book III (*Poems*, 1761, pp. 125–7, 134–7).
146 Quotations from Veyne, *Roman Erotic Elegy*, p. 144; Venuti, *The Translator's Invisibility*, pp. 64, 66. See also Gilmore, 'Tibullus and the British Empire'.

147 See the poem 'Assiento, sive Commercium Hispanicum' by the Barbadian, John Maynard, in *Academiæ Oxoniensis Comitia Philologica [...] Decimo Die Julii A.D. 1713. Celebrata [...]* (unpaginated).

148 The last person who appears to have read the contemporary reviews of *The Sugar-Cane* with much attention was Robert Anderson: several pages in his 'Life of Grainger' (*Poetical Works of James Grainger*, 1836, I, xi-xiv) are an unacknowledged paraphrase of passages from the *Monthly Review* and *Critical Review*. This 'Life' is virtually identical to the one Anderson published in his 1794 edition of Grainger. On Boswell's fatal influence on Grainger's reputation, see Appendix I.

149 Dabydeen, 'Eighteenth-century English literature on commerce and slavery', at pp. 44–5.

150 See Vaughan's sonnet, 'The Donkey' in *Sandy Lane* [1945], p. 39 – it is at p. 20 of the 2nd ed. (Barbados, 1985). Brathwaite's *X/Self* is the third of a trilogy, which begins with *Mother Poem* (1977) and *Sun Poem* (1982), and this in turn follows on from his first trilogy, *The Arrivants* (1975).

151 Grainger to Percy (undated, but c. February 1765, NLS Adv. MS. 22.4.10, ff. 3–4) complains of 'some very unpoetical Blunders of y$^e$ press' he had discovered in *1764*, but refers specifically only to the two mentioned below.

152 Grainger noted (*TCD*, f. 105$^r$) that he had 'presumed to innovate in pointing', but this is in a passage full of heavy cancellations, and I have not been able to make sense of whatever explanation he provided.

# SUGAR-CANE:

## A

# POEM.

### IN FOUR BOOKS.

### WITH NOTES.

*Agrediar primusque novis Helicona movere
Cantibus, et viridi nutantes vertice sylvas;
Hospita sacra ferens, nulli memorata priorum.* MANIL.

By JAMES GRAINGER, M. D. &c.

LONDON:
Printed for R. and J. DODSLEY, in Pall-mall.
MDCCLXIV.

# Preface

Soon after my arrival in the West-Indies, I conceived the design of writing a poem on the cultivation of the Sugar-Cane. My inducements to this arduous undertaking were, not only the importance and novelty of the subject, but more especially this consideration; that, as the face of this country was wholly different from that of Europe, so whatever hand copied its appearances, however rude, could not fail to enrich poetry with many new and picturesque images.

I cannot, indeed, say I have satisfied my own ideas in this particular: yet I must be permitted to recommend the precepts contained in this Poem. They are the children of Truth, not of Genius; the result of Experience, not the productions of Fancy. Thus, though I may not be able to please, I shall stand some chance of instructing the Reader; which, as it is the nobler end of all poetry, so should it be the principal aim of every writer who wishes to be thought a good man.

It must, however, be observed, that, though the general precepts are suited to every climate, where the Cane will grow; yet, the more minute rules are chiefly drawn from the practice of St. Christopher. Some selection was necessary; and I could adopt no modes of planting, with such propriety, as those I had seen practised in that island, where it has been my good fortune chiefly to reside since I came to the West-Indies.

I have often been astonished, that so little has been published on the cultivation of the Sugar-Cane, while the press has groaned under folios on every other branch of rural oeconomy. It were unjust to suppose planters were not solicitous for the improvement of their art, and injurious to assert they were incapable of obliging mankind with their improvements.

And yet, except some scattered hints in Pere Labat, and other French travellers in America; an Essay, by Colonel Martyn of Antigua, is the only piece on plantership I have seen deserving a perusal. That gentleman's pamphlet is, indeed, an excellent performance; and to it I own myself indebted.

It must be confessed, that terms of art look awkward in poetry, yet didactic compositions cannot wholly dispense with them.

Accordingly we find that Hesiod and Virgil, among the ancients, with Philips and Dyer, (not to mention some other poets now living in our own country); have been obliged to insert them in their poems. Their example is a sufficient apology for me, for in their steps I shall always be proud to tread.

> *Vos sequor, ô Graiae gentis decus, inque vestris nunc*
> *Fixa pedum pono pressis vestigia signis;*
> *Non ita certandi cupidus, quam propter amorem,*
> *Quod vos imitari aveo.* ——

Yet, like them too, I have generally preferred the way of description, wherever that could be done without hurting the subject.

Such words as are not common in Europe, I have briefly explained: because an obscure poem affords both less pleasure and profit to the reader. — For the same reason, some notes have been added, which, it is presumed, will not be disagreeable to those who have never been in the West-Indies.

In a West-India georgic, the mention of many indigenous remedies, as well as diseases, was unavoidable. The truth is, I have rather courted opportunities of this nature, than avoided them. Medicines of such amazing efficacy, as I have had occasion to make trials of in these islands, deserve to be universally known. And wherever, in the following poem, I recommend any such, I beg leave to be understood as a physician, and not as a poet.

*Basseterre, Jan.* 1763.

# THE
# SUGAR-CANE

## BOOK I.

### ARGUMENT.

*Subject proposed. Invocation and address. What soils the Cane grows best in. The grey light earth. Praise of St. Christopher. The red brick mould. Praise of Jamaica, and of Christopher Columbus. The black soil mixed with clay and gravel. Praise of Barbadoes, Nevis, and Mountserrat. Composts may improve other soils. Advantages and disadvantages of a level plantation. Of a mountain-estate. Of a midland one. Advantages of proper cultivation. Of fallowing. Of compost. Of leaving the Woura, and penning cattle on the distant Cane-pieces. Whether yams improve the soil. Whether dung should be buried in each hole, or scattered over the piece. Cane-lands may be holed at any time. The ridges should be open to the trade-wind. The beauty of holing regularly by a line. Alternate holing, and the wheel-plough recommended to trial. When to plant. Wet weather the best. Rain often falls in the West-Indies, almost without any previous signs. The signs of rainy weather. Of fogs round the high mountains. Planting described. Begin to plant mountain-land in July: the low ground in November, and the subsequent months, till May. The advantage of changing tops in planting. Whether the Moon has any influence over the Cane-plant. What quantity of mountain and of low Cane-land may be annually planted. The last Cane-piece should be cut off before the end of July. Of hedges. Of stone inclosures. Myrtle hedges recommended. Whether trees breed the blast. The character of a good planter. Of weeding. Of moulding. Of stripping.*

# THE SUGAR-CANE

## BOOK I.

What soil the Cane affects; what care demands;
Beneath what signs to plant; what ills await;
How the hot nectar best to christallize;
And Afric's sable progeny to treat:
5  A Muse, that long hath wander'd in the groves
Of myrtle-indolence, attempts to sing.
   Spirit of Inspiration, that did'st lead
Th'Ascrean Poet to the sacred Mount,
And taught'st him all the precepts of the swain;
10  Descend from Heaven, and guide my trembling steps
To Fame's eternal Dome, where Maro reigns;
Where pastoral Dyer, where Pomona's Bard,
And Smart and Sommerville in varying strains,
Their sylvan lore convey: O may I join
15  This choral band, and from their precepts learn
To deck my theme, which though to song unknown,
Is most momentous to my Country's weal!
   So shall my numbers win the Public ear;
And not displease Aurelius; him to whom,
20  Imperial George, the monarch of the main,
Hath given to wield the scepter of those isles,
Where first the Muse beheld the spiry Cane,
Supreme of Plants, rich subject of my song.
   Where'er the clouds relent in frequent rains,
25  And the Sun fiercely darts his Tropic beam,
The Cane will joint, ungenial tho' the soil.
But would'st thou see huge casks, in order due,
Roll'd numerous on the Bay, all fully fraught
With strong-grain'd muscovado, silvery-grey,
30  Joy of the planter; and if happy Fate

Permit a choice: avoid the rocky slope,
The clay-cold bottom, and the sandy beach.
But let thy biting ax with ceaseless stroke
The wild red cedar, the tough locust fell:
35 Nor let his nectar, nor his silken pods,
The sweet-smell'd cassia, or vast ceiba save.
Yet spare the guava, yet the guaiac spare;
A wholesome food the ripened guava yields,
Boast of the housewife; while the guaiac grows
40 A sovereign antidote, in wood, bark, gum,
To cause the lame his useless crutch forego,
And dry the sources of corrupted love.
Nor let thy bright impatient flames destroy
The golden shaddoc, the forbidden fruit,
45 The white acajou, and rich sabbaca:
For where these trees their leafy banners raise
Aloft in air, a grey deep earth abounds,
Fat, light; yet, when it feels the wounding hoe,
Rising in clods, which ripening suns and rain
50 Resolve to crumbles, yet not pulverize:
In this the soul of vegetation wakes,
Pleas'd at the planter's call, to burst on day.
    Thrice happy he, to whom such fields are given!
For him the Cane with little labour grows;
55 'Spite of the dog-star, shoots long yellow joints;
Concocts rich juice, tho' deluges descend.
What if an after-offspring it reject?
This land, for many a crop, will feed his mills;
Disdain supplies, nor ask from compost aid.
60     Such, green St. Christopher, thy happy soil! —
Not Grecian Tempé, where Arcadian Pan,
Knit with the Graces, tun'd his silvan pipe,
While mute Attention hush'd each charmed rill;
Not purple Enna, whose irriguous lap,
65 Strow'd with each fruit of taste, each flower of smell,
Sicilian Proserpine, delighted, sought;
Can vie, blest Isle, with thee. – Tho' no soft sound
Of pastoral stop thine echoes e'er awak'd;
Nor raptured poet, lost in holy trance,
70 Thy streams arrested with enchanting song:

Yet virgins, far more beautiful than she
Whom Pluto ravish'd, and more chaste, are thine:
Yet probity, from principle, not fear,
Actuates thy sons, bold, hospitable, free:
75 Yet a fertility, unknown of old,
To other climes denied, adorns thy hills;
Thy vales, thy dells adorns. – O might my strain
As far transcend the immortal songs of Greece,
As thou the partial subject of their praise!
80 Thy fame should float familiar thro' the world;
Each plant should own thy Cane her lawful lord;
Nor should old Time, song stops the flight of Time,
Obscure thy lustre with his shadowy wing.
    Scarce less impregnated, with every power
85 Of vegetation, is the red brick-mould,
That lies on marly beds. – The renter, this
Can scarce exhaust; how happy for the heir!
    Such the glad soil, from whence Jamaica's sons
Derive their opulence: thrice fertile land,
90 "The pride, the glory of the sea-girt isles,
"Which, like to rich and various gems, inlay
"The unadorned bosom of the deep,"
Which first Columbus' daring keel explor'd.
    Daughters of Heaven, with reverential awe,
95 Pause at that godlike name; for not your flights
Of happiest fancy, can outsoar his fame.
    Columbus, boast of science, boast of man!
Yet, by the great, the learned, and the wise,
Long held a visionary; who, like thee,
100 Could brook their scorn; wait seven long years at court,
A selfish, sullen, dilatory court;
Yet never from thy purpos'd plan decline?
No God, no Hero, of poetic times,
In Truth's fair annals, may compare with thee!
105 Each passion, weakness of mankind, thou knew'st,
Thine own concealing; firmest base of power:
Rich in expedients; what most adverse seem'd,
And least expected, most advanc'd thine aim.
    What storms, what monsters, what new forms of death,
110 In a vast ocean, never cut by keel,

And where the magnet first its aid declin'd;
Alone, unterrified, didst thou not view?
Wise Legislator, had the Iberian King
Thy plan adopted, murder had not drench'd
115 In blood vast kingdoms; nor had hell-born Zeal,
And hell-born Avarice, his arms disgrac'd.
Yet, for a world, discover'd and subdu'd,
What meed hads't thou? With toil, disease, worn out,
Thine age was spent solliciting the Prince,
120 To whom thou gavs't the sceptre of that world.
Yet, blessed spirit, where inthron'd thou sit'st,
Chief 'mid the friends of man, repine not thou:
Dear to the Nine, thy glory shall remain
While winged Commerce either ocean ploughs;
125 While its lov'd pole the magnet coyly shuns;
While weeps the guaiac, and while joints the Cane.
 Shall the Muse celebrate the dark deep mould,
With clay or gravel mix'd? —This soil the Cane
With partial fondness loves; and oft surveys
130 Its progeny with wonder. —Such rich veins
Are plenteous scatter'd o'er the Sugar-isles:
But chief that land, to which the bearded fig,
Prince of the forest, gave Barbadoes name:
Chief Nevis, justly for its hot baths fam'd:
135 And breezy Mountserrat, whose wonderous springs
Change, like Medusa's head, whate'er they touch,
To stony hardness; boast this fertile glebe.
 Tho' such the soils the Antillean Cane
Supremely loves; yet other soils abound,
140 Which art may tutor to obtain its smile.
Say, shall the experienc'd Muse that art recite?
How sand will fertilize stiff barren clay?
How clay unites the light, the porous mould,
Sport of each breeze? And how the torpid nymph
145 Of the rank pool, so noisome to the smell,
May be solicited, by wily ways,
To draw her humid train, and, prattling, run
Down the reviving slopes? Or shall she say
What glebes ungrateful to each other art,
150 Their genial treasures ope to fire alone?

Record the different composts; which the cold
To plastic gladness warm? The torrid, which
By soothing coolness win? The sharp saline,
Which best subdue? Which mollify the sour?
155     To thee, if Fate low level land assign,
Slightly cohering, and of sable hue,
Far from the hill; be parsimony thine.
For tho' this year when constant showers descend;
The speeding gale, thy sturdy numerous stock,
160 Scarcely suffice to grind thy mighty Canes:
Yet thou, with rueful eye, for many a year,
Shalt view thy plants burnt by the torch of day;
Hear their parch'd wan blades rustle in the air;
While their black sugars, doughy to the feel,
165 Will not ev'n pay the labour of thy swains.
    Or, if the mountain be thy happier lot,
Let prudent foresight still thy coffers guard.
For tho' the clouds relent in nightly rain,
Tho' thy rank Canes wave lofty in the gale:
170 Yet will the arrow, ornament of woe,
(Such monarchs oft-times give) their jointing stint;
Yet will winds lodge them, ravening rats destroy,
Or troops of monkeys thy rich harvest steal.
The earth must also wheel around the sun,
175 And half perform that circuit; ere the bill
Mow down thy sugars: and tho' all thy mills,
Crackling, o'erflow with a redundant juice;
Poor tastes the liquor; coction long demands,
And highest temper, ere it saccharize;
180 A meagre produce. Such is Virtue's meed,
Alas, too oft in these degenerate days.
Thy cattle likewise, as they drag the wain,
Charg'd from the beach; in spite of whips and shouts,
Will stop, will pant, will sink beneath the load;
185 A better fate deserving. ——
Besides, thy land itself is insecure:
For oft the glebe, and all its waving load,
Will journey, forc'd off by the mining rain;
And, with its faithless burden, disarrange
190 Thy neighbour's vale. So Markley-hill of old,

As sung thy bard, Pomona, (in these isles
Yet unador'd;) with all its spreading trees,
Full fraught with apples, chang'd its lofty site.
   But, as in life, the golden mean is best;
195 So happiest he whose green plantation lies
Not from the hill too far, nor from the shore.
   Planter, if thou with wonder wouldst survey
Redundant harvests load thy willing soil;
Let sun and rain mature thy deep-hoed land,
200 And old fat dung co-operate with these.
Be this great truth still present to thy mind;
The half well-cultur'd far exceeds the whole,
Which lust of gain, unconscious of its end,
Ungrateful vexes with unceasing toil.
205 As, not indulg'd, the richest lands grow poor;
And Liamuiga may, in future times,
If too much urg'd, her barrenness bewail:
So cultivation, on the shallowest soil,
O'erspread with rocky cliffs, will bid the Cane,
210 With spiry pomp, all bountifully rise.
   Thus Britain's flag, should discipline relent,
'Spite of the native courage of her sons,
Would to the lily strike: ah, very far,
Far be that woful day: the lily then
215 Will rule wide ocean with resistless sway;
And to old Gallia's haughty shore transport
The lessening crops of these delicious isles.
   Of composts shall the Muse descend to sing,
Nor soil her heavenly plumes? The sacred Muse
220 Nought sordid deems, but what is base; nought fair
Unless true Virtue stamp it with her seal.
Then, Planter, wouldst thou double thine estate;
Never, ah never, be asham'd to tread
Thy dung-heaps, where the refuse of thy mills,
225 With all the ashes, all thy coppers yield,
With weeds, mould, dung, and stale, a compost form,
Of force to fertilize the poorest soil.
   But, planter, if thy lands lie far remote
And of access are difficult; on these,
230 Leave the Cane's sapless foliage; and with pens

Wattled, (like those the Muse hath oft-times seen
When frolic fancy led her youthful steps,
In green Dorchestria's plains), the whole inclose:
There well thy stock with provender supply;
235 The well-fed stock will soon that food repay.
    Some of the skilful teach, and some deny,
That yams improve the soil. In meagre lands,
'Tis known the yam will ne'er to bigness swell;
And from each mould the vegetable tribes,
240 However frugal, nutriment derive:
Yet may their sheltering vines, their dropping leaves,
Their roots dividing the tenacious glebe,
More than refund the sustenance they draw.
    Whether the fattening compost, in each hole,
245 'Tis best to throw; or, on the surface spread;
Is undetermin'd: Trials must decide.
Unless kind rains and fostering dews descend,
To melt the compost's fertilising salts;
A stinted plant, deceitful of thy hopes,
250 Will from those beds slow spring where hot dung lies:
But, if 'tis scatter'd generously o'er all,
The Cane will better bear the solar blaze;
Less rain demand; and, by repeated crops,
Thy land improv'd, its gratitude will show.
255     Enough of composts, Muse; of soils, enough:
When best to dig, and when inhume the Cane;
A task how arduous! next demands thy song.
    It not imports beneath what sign thy hoes
The deep trough sink, and ridge alternate raise:
260 If this from washes guard thy gemmy tops;
And that arrest the moisture these require.
    Yet, should the site of thine estate permit,
Let the trade-wind thy ridges ventilate;
So shall a greener, loftier Cane arise,
265 And richest nectar in thy coppers foam.
    As art transforms the savage face of things,
And order captivates the harmonious mind;
Let not thy Blacks irregularly hoe:
But, aided by the line, consult the site
270 Of thy demesnes; and beautify the whole.

So when a monarch rushes to the war,
To drive invasion from his frighted realm;
Some delegated chief the frontier views,
And to each squadron, and brigade, assigns
275 Their order'd station: Soon the tented field
Brigade and squadron, whiten on the sight;
And fill spectators with an awful joy.
    Planter, improvement is the child of time;
What your sires knew not, ye their offspring know:
280 But hath your art receiv'd Perfection's stamp?
Thou can'st not say. —Unprejudic'd, then learn
Of ancient modes to doubt, and new to try:
And if Philosophy, with Wisdom, deign
Thee to enlighten with her useful lore;
285 Fair Fame and riches will reward thy toil.
    Then say, ye swains, whom wealth and fame inspire,
Might not the plough, that rolls on rapid wheels,
Save no small labour to the hoe-arm'd gang?
Might not the culture taught the British hinds,
290 By Ceres' son, unfailing crops secure;
Tho' neither dung nor fallowing lent their aid?
    The cultur'd land recalls the devious Muse;
Propitious to the planter be the call:
For much, my friend, it thee imports to know
295 The meetest season to commit thy tops,
With best advantage, to the well-dug mould.
The task how difficult, to cull the best
From thwarting sentiments; and best adorn
What Wisdom chuses, in poetic garb!
300 Yet, Inspiration, come: the theme unsung,
Whence never poet cropt one bloomy wreath;
Its vast importance to my native land,
Whose sweet idea rushes on my mind,
And makes me 'mid this paradise repine;
305 Urge me to pluck, from Fancy's soaring wing,
A plume to deck Experience' hoary brow.
    Attend. —The son of Time and Truth declares;
Unless the low-hung clouds drop fatness down,
No bunching plants of vivid green will spring,
310 In goodly ranks, to fill the planter's eye.

>    Let then Sagacity, with curious ken,
>    Remark the various signs of future rain.
>    The signs of rain, the Mantuan Bard hath sung
>    In loftiest numbers; friendly to thy swains,
> 315 Once fertile Italy: but other marks
>    Portend the approaching shower, in these hot climes.
>    Short sudden rains, from Ocean's ruffled bed,
>    Driven by some momentary squalls, will oft
>    With frequent heavy bubbling drops, down-fall;
> 320 While yet the Sun, in cloudless lustre, shines:
>    And draw their humid train o'er half the isle.
>    Unhappy he! who journeys then from home,
>    No shade to screen him. His untimely fate
>    His wife, his babes, his friends, will soon deplore;
> 325 Unless hot wines, dry cloaths, and friction's aid,
>    His fleeting spirits stay. Yet not even these,
>    Nor all Apollo's arts, will always bribe
>    The insidious tyrant death, thrice tyrant here:
>    Else good Amyntor, him the graces lov'd
> 330 Wisdom caress'd, and Themis call'd her own,
>    Had liv'd by all admir'd, had now perus'd
>    "These lines, with all the malice of a friend."
>    Yet future rains the careful may foretell:
>    Mosquitos, sand-flies, seek the shelter'd roof,
> 335 And with fell rage the stranger-guest assail,
>    Nor spare the sportive child; from their retreats
>    Cockroaches crawl displeasingly abroad:
>    These without pity, let thy slaves destroy;
>    (Like Harpies, they defile whate'er they touch:)
> 340 While those, the smother of combustion quells.
>    The speckled lizard to its hole retreats,
>    And black crabs travel from the mountain down;
>    Thy ducks their feathers prune; thy doves return,
>    In faithful flocks, and, on the neighbouring roof,
> 345 Perch frequent; where, with pleas'd attention, they
>    Behold the deepening congregated clouds,
>    With sadness, blot the azure vault of heaven.
>        Now, while the shower depends, and rattle loud
>    Your doors and windows, haste ye housewives, place
> 350 Your spouts and pails; ye Negroes, seek the shade,

Save those who open with the ready hoe
The enriching water-course: for see, the drops,
Which fell with slight aspersion, now descend
In streams continuous on the laughing land.
355 The coyest Naiads quit their rocky caves,
And, with delight, run brawling to the main;
While those, who love still visible to glad
The thirsty plains from never-ceasing urns,
Assume more awful majesty, and pour,
360 With force resistless, down the channel'd rocks.
The rocks, or split, or hurried from their base,
With trees, are whirl'd impetuous to the sea:
Fluctuates the forest; the torn mountains roar:
The main itself recoils for many a league,
365 While its green face is chang'd to sordid brown.
A grateful freshness every sense pervades;
While beats the heart with unaccustom'd joy:
Her stores fugacious Memory now recalls;
And Fancy prunes her wings for loftiest flights.
370 The mute creation share the enlivening hour;
Bounds the brisk kid, and wanton plays the lamb.
The drooping plants revive; ten thousand blooms,
Which, with their fragrant scents, perfume the air,
Burst into being; while the Canes put on
375 Glad Nature's liveliest robe, the vivid green.
  But chief, let fix'd Attention cast his eye
On the capt mountain, whose high rocky verge
The wild fig canopies, (vast woodland king,
Beneath thy branching shade a banner'd host
380 May lie in ambush!) and whose shaggy sides,
Trees shade, of endless green, enormous size,
Wondrous in shape, to botany unknown,
Old as the deluge. —There, in secret haunts,
The watery spirits ope their liquid court;
385 There, with the wood-nymphs, link'd in festal band,
(Soft airs and Phoebus wing them to their arms)
Hold amorous dalliance. Ah, may none profane,
With fire, or steel, their mystic privacy:
For there their fluent offspring first see day,
390 Coy infants sporting; silver-footed dew

>     To bathe by night thy sprouts in genial balm;
>     The green-stol'd Naiad of the tinkling rill,
>     Whose brow the fern-tree shades; the power of rain
>     To glad the thirsty soil on which, arrang'd,
> 395 The gemmy summits of the Cane await
>     Thy Negroe-train, (in linen lightly wrapt,)
>     Who now that painted Iris girds the sky,
>     (Aerial arch, which Fancy loves to stride!)
>     Disperse, all-jocund, o'er the long-hoed land.
> 400   The bundles some untie; the withered leaves
>     Others strip artful off, and careful lay,
>     Twice one junk, distant in the amplest bed:
>     O'er these, with hasty hoe, some lightly spread
>     The mounded interval; and smooth the trench:
> 405 Well-pleas'd, the master-swain reviews their toil;
>     And rolls, in fancy, many a full-fraught cask.
>     So, when the shield was forg'd for Peleus' Son;
>     The swarthy Cyclops shar'd the important task:
>     With bellows, some reviv'd the seeds of fire;
> 410 Some, gold, and brass, and steel, together fus'd
>     In the vast furnace; while a chosen few,
>     In equal measures lifting their bare arms,
>     Inform the mass; and hissing in the wave,
>     Temper the glowing orb: their sire beholds,
> 415 Amaz'd, the wonders of his fusile art.
>       While Procyon reigns yet fervid in the sky;
>     While yet the fiery Sun in Leo rides;
>     And the Sun's child, the mail'd anana, yields
>     His regal apple to the ravish'd taste;
> 420 And thou green avocato, charm of sense,
>     Thy ripened marrow liberally bestow'st;
>     Begin the distant mountain-land to plant:
>     So shall thy Canes defy November's cold,
>     Ungenial to the upland young; so best,
> 425 Unstinted by the arrow's deadening power,
>     Long yellow joints shall flow with generous juice.
>       But, till the lemon, orange, and the lime,
>     Amid their verdant umbrage, countless glow
>     With fragrant fruit of vegetable gold;
> 430 'Till yellow plantanes bend the unstain'd bough

With crooked clusters, prodigally full;
'Till Capricorn command the cloudy sky;
And moist Aquarius melt in daily showers,
Friend to the Cane-isles; trust not thou thy tops,
435  Thy future riches, to the low-land plain:
And if kind Heaven, in pity to thy prayers,
Shed genial influence; as the earth absolves
Her annual circuit, thy rich ripened Canes
Shall load thy waggons, mules, and Negroe-train.
440     But chief thee, Planter, it imports to mark
(Whether thou breathe the mountain's humid air,
Or pant with heat continual on the plain;)
What months relent, and which from rain are free.
    In different islands of the ocean-stream,
445  Even in the different parts of the same isle,
The seasons vary; yet attention soon
Will give thee each variety to know.
This once observ'd; at such a time inhume
Thy plants, that, when they joint, (important age,
450  Like youth just stepping into life) the clouds
May constantly bedew them: so shall they
Avoid those ails, which else their manhood kill.
    Six times the changeful moon must blunt her horns,
And fill with borrowed light her silvery urn;
455  Ere thy tops, trusted to the mountain-land,
Commence their jointing: but four moons suffice
To bring to puberty the low-land Cane.
    In plants, in beasts, in man's imperial race,
An alien mixture meliorates the breed;
460  Hence Canes, that sickened dwarfish on the plain,
Will shoot with giant-vigour on the hill.
Thus all depends on all; so God ordains.
Then let not man for little selfish ends,
(Britain, remember this important truth;)
465  Presume the principle to counteract
Of universal love; for God is love,
And wide creation shares alike his care.
    'Tis said by some, and not unletter'd they,
That chief the Planter, if he wealth desire,
470  Should note the phases of the fickle moon.

On thee, sweet empress of the night, depend
The tides; stern Neptune pays his court to thee;
The winds, obedient at thy bidding shift,
And tempests rise or fall; even lordly man
475 Thine energy controls. —Not so the Cane;
The Cane its independency may boast,
Tho' some less noble plants thine influence own.
   Of mountain-lands oeconomy permits
A third, in Canes of mighty growth to rise:
480 But, in the low-land plain, the half will yield
Tho' not so lofty, yet a richer Cane,
For many a crop; if seasons glad the soil.
   While rolls the Sun from Aries to the Bull,
And till the Virgin his hot beams inflame;
485 The Cane, with richest, most redundant juice,
Thy spacious coppers fills. Then manage so,
By planting in succession; that thy crops
The wondering daughters of the main may waft
To Britain's shore, ere Libra weigh the year:
490 So shall thy merchant chearful credit grant,
And well-earned opulence thy cares repay.
   Thy fields thus planted; to secure the Canes
From the Goat's baneful tooth; the churning boar;
From thieves; from fire or casual or design'd;
495 Unfailing herbage to thy toiling herds
Woulds't thou afford; and the spectators charm
With beauteous prospects: let the frequent hedge
Thy green plantation, regular, divide.
   With limes, with lemons, let thy fences glow,
500 Grateful to sense; now children of this clime:
And here and there let oranges erect
Their shapely beauties, and perfume the sky.
Nor less delightful blooms the logwood-hedge,
Whose wood to coction yields a precious balm,
505 Specific in the flux: Endemial ail,
Much cause have I to weep thy fatal sway. —
But God is just, and man must not repine.
Nor shall the ricinus unnoted pass;
Yet, if the cholic's deathful pangs thou dread'st,
510 Taste not its luscious nut. The acassee,

With which the sons of Jewry, stiff-neck'd race,
Conjecture says, our God-Messiah crown'd;
Soon shoots a think impenetrable fence,
Whose scent perfumes the night and morning sky,
515 Tho' baneful be its root. The privet too,
Whose white flowers rival the first drifts of snow
On Grampia's piny hills; (O might the muse
Tread, flush'd with health, the Grampian hills again!)
Emblem of innocence shall grace my song.
520 Boast of the shrubby tribe, carnation fair,
Nor thou repine, tho' late the muse record
Thy bloomy honours. Tipt with burnish'd gold,
And with imperial purple crested high,
More gorgeous than the train of Juno's bird,
525 Thy bloomy honours oft the curious muse
Hath seen transported: seen the humming bird,
Whose burnish'd neck bright glows with verdant gold;
Least of the winged vagrants of the sky,
Yet dauntless as the strong-pounc'd bird of Jove;
530 With fluttering vehemence attack thy cups,
To rob them of their nectar's luscious store.
    But if with stones thy meagre lands are spread;
Be these collected, they will pay thy toil:
And let Vitruvius, aided by the line,
535 Fence thy plantations with a thick-built wall.
On this lay cuttings of the prickly pear;
They soon a formidable fence will shoot:
Wild liquorice here its red beads loves to hang,
Whilst scandent blossoms, yellow, purple, blue,
540 Unhurt, wind round its shield-like leaf and spears.
Nor is its fruit inelegant of taste,
Tho' more its colour charms the ravish'd eye;
Vermeil, as youthful beauty's roseat hue;
As thine, fair Christobelle: ah, when will fate,
545 That long hath scowl'd relentless on the bard,
Give him some small plantation to inclose,
Which he may call his own? Not wealth he craves,
But independance: yet if thou, sweet maid,
In health and virtue bloom; tho' worse betide,
550 Thy smile will smoothe adversity's rough brow.

In Italy's green bounds, the myrtle shoots
A fragrant fence, and blossoms in the sun.
Here, on the rockiest verge of these blest isles,
With little care, the plant of love would grow.
555 Then to the citron join the plant of love,
And with their scent and shade enrich your isles.
Yet some pretend, and not unspecious they,
The wood-nymphs foster the contagious blast.
Foes to the Dryads, they remorseless fell
560 Each shrub of shade, each tree of spreading root,
That woo the first glad fannings of the breeze.
Far from the muse be such inhuman thoughts;
Far better recks she of the woodland tribes,
Earth's eldest birth, and earth's best ornament.
565 Ask him, whom rude necessity compels
To dare the noontide fervor, in this clime,
Ah, most intensely hot; how much he longs
For cooling vast impenetrable shade?
The muse, alas, th'experienc'd muse can tell:
570 Oft hath she travell'd, while solstitial beams,
Shot yellow deaths on the devoted land;
Oft, oft hath she their ill-judg'd avarice blam'd,
Who, to the stranger, to their slaves and herds,
Denied this best of joys, the breezy shade.
575 And are there none, whom generous pity warms,
Friends to the woodland reign; whom shades delight?
Who, round their green domains, plant hedge-row trees;
And with cool cedars, screen the public way?
Yes, good Montano; friend of man was he:
580 Him persecution, virtue's deadliest foe,
Drove, a lorn exile, from his native shore;
From his green hills, where many a fleecy flock,
Where many a heifer cropt their wholesome food;
And many a swain, obedient to his rule,
585 Him their lov'd master, their protector, own'd.
Yet, from that paradise, to Indian wilds,
To tropic suns, to fell barbaric hinds,
A poor outcast, an alien, did he roam;
His wife, the partner of his better hours,
590 And one sweet infant, chear'd his dismal way.

Unus'd to labour; yet the orient sun,
Yet western Phœbus, saw him wield the hoe.
At first a garden all his wants supplied,
(For Temperance sat chearful at his board,)
595 With yams, cassada, and the food of strength,
Thrice-wholesome tanies: while a neighbouring dell,
(Which nature to the soursop had resign'd,)
With ginger, and with Raleigh's pungent plant,
Gave wealth; and gold bought better land and slaves.
600 Heaven bless'd his labour: now the cotton-shrub,
Grac'd with broad yellow flowers, unhurt by worms,
O'er many an acre shed its whitest down:
The power of rain, in genial moisture bath'd
His cacao-walk, which teem'd with marrowy pods;
605 His coffee bath'd, that glow'd with berries, red
As Danae's lip, or Theodosia, thine,
Yet countless as the pebbles on the shore;
Oft, while drought kill'd his impious neighbour's grove.
In time, a numerous gang of sturdy slaves,
610 Well-fed, well-cloath'd, all emulous to gain
Their master's smile, who treated them like men;
Blacken'd his Cane-lands: which with vast increase,
Beyond the wish of avarice, paid his toil.
No cramps, with sudden death, surpriz'd his mules;
615 No glander-pest his airy stables thinn'd:
And, if disorder seiz'd his Negroe-train,
Celsus was call'd, and pining Illness flew.
His gate stood wide to all; but chief the poor,
The unfriended stranger, and the sickly, shar'd
620 His prompt munificence: No surly dog,
Nor surlier Ethiop, their approach debarr'd.
The Muse, that pays this tribute to his fame,
Oft hath escap'd the sun's meridian blaze,
Beneath yon tamarind-vista, which his hands
625 Planted; and which, impervious to the sun,
His latter days beheld. —One noon he sat
Beneath its breezy shade, what time the sun
His sultry vengeance from the Lion pour'd;
And calmly thus his eldest hope addrest.
630     "Be pious, be industrious, be humane;

"From proud oppression guard the labouring hind.
"Whate'er their creed, God is the Sire of man,
"His image they; then dare not thou, my son,
"To bar the gates of mercy on mankind.
635 "Your foes forgive, for merit must make foes;
"And in each virtue far surpass your sire.
"Your means are ample, Heaven a heart bestow!
"So health and peace shall be your portion here;
"And yon bright sky, to which my soul aspires,
640 "Shall bless you with eternity of joy."
    He spoke, and ere the swift-wing'd zumbadore
The mountain-desert startl'd with his hum;
Ere fire-flies trimm'd their vital lamps; and ere
Dun Evening trod on rapid Twilight's heel:
645 His knell was rung; ——
And all the Cane-lands wept their father lost.
    Muse, yet awhile indulge my rapid course;
And I'll unharness, soon, the foaming steeds.
    If Jove descend, propitious to thy vows,
650 In frequent floods of rain; successive crops
Of weeds will spring. Nor venture to repine,
Tho' oft their toil thy little gang renew;
Their toil tenfold the melting heavens repay:
For soon thy plants will magnitude acquire,
655 To crush all undergrowth; before the sun,
The planets thus withdraw their puny fires.
And tho' untutor'd, then, thy Canes will shoot:
Care meliorates their growth. The trenches fill
With their collateral mold; as in a town
660 Which foes have long beleaguer'd, unawares
A strong detachment sallies from each gate,
And levels all the labours of the plain.
    And now thy Cane's first blades their verdure lose,
And hang their idle heads. Be these stript off;
665 So shall fresh sportive airs their joints embrace,
And by their dalliance give the sap to rise.
But, O beware, let no unskilful hand
The vivid foliage tear: Their channel'd spouts,
Well-pleas'd, the watery nutriment convey,
670 With filial duty, to the thirsty stem;

And, spreading wide their reverential arms,
Defend their parent from solstitial skies.

[The END of BOOK I.]

# THE
# SUGAR-CANE

## BOOK II.

### ADVERTISEMENT to BOOK II.

The following Book having been originally addressed to WILLIAM SHENSTONE, Esq; and by him approved of; the Author should deem it a kind of poetical sacrilege, now, to address it to any other. To his memory, therefore, be it sacred; as a small but sincere testimony of the high opinion the Author entertained of that Gentleman's genius and manners; and as the only return now, alas! in his power to make, for the friendship wherewith Mr. SHENSTONE had condescended to honour him.

### ARGUMENT.

*Subject proposed. Address to William Shenstone, Esq. Of monkeys. Of rats and other vermin. Of weeds. Of the yellow fly. Of the greasy fly. Of the blast. A hurricane described. Of calms and earthquakes. A tale.*

# THE
# SUGAR-CANE

## BOOK II.

    Enough of culture. —A less pleasing theme,
What ills await the ripening Cane, demands
My serious numbers: these, the thoughtful Muse
Hath oft beheld, deep-pierc'd with generous woe.
5  For she, poor exile! boasts no waving crops;
For her no circling mules press dulcet streams;
No Negro-band huge foaming coppers skim;
Nor fermentation (wine's dread fire) for her,
With Vulcan's aid, from Cane a spirit draws,
10 Potent to quell the madness of despair.
Yet, oft, the range she walks, at shut of eve;
Oft sees red lightning at the midnight-hour,
When nod the watches, stream along the sky;
Not innocent, as what the learned call
15 The Boreal morn, which, through the azure air,
Flashes its tremulous rays, in painted streaks,
While o'er night's veil her lucid tresses flow:
Nor quits the Muse her walk, immers'd in thought,
How she the planter, haply, may advise;
20 Till tardy morn unbar the gates of light,
And, opening on the main with sultry beam,
To burnish'd silver turns the blue-green wave.
    Say, will my SHENSTONE lend a patient ear,
And weep at woes unknown to Britain's Isle?
25 Yes, thou wilt weep; for pity chose thy breast,
With taste and science, for their soft abode:
Yes, thou wilt weep: thine own distress thou bear'st
Undaunted; but another's melts thy soul.
    "O were my pipe as soft, my dittied song"
30 As smooth as thine, my too too distant friend,

SHENSTONE; my soft pipe, and my dittied song
Should hush the hurricanes tremendous roar,
And from each evil guard the ripening Cane!
   Destructive, on the upland sugar-groves
35 The monkey-nation preys: from rocky heights,
In silent parties, they descend by night,
And posting watchful sentinels, to warn
When hostile steps approach; with gambols, they
Pour o'er the Cane-grove. Luckless he to whom
40 That land pertains! in evil hour, perhaps,
And thoughtless of to-morrow, on a die
He hazards millions; or, perhaps, reclines
On Luxury's soft lap, the pest of wealth;
And, inconsiderate, deems his Indian crops
45 Will amply her insatiate wants supply.
   From these insidious droles (peculiar pest
Of Liamuiga's hills) would'st thou defend
Thy waving wealth; in traps put not thy trust,
However baited: Treble every watch,
50 And well with arms provide them; faithful dogs,
Of nose sagacious, on their footsteps wait.
With these attack the predatory bands;
Quickly the unequal conflict they decline,
And, chattering, fling their ill-got spoils away.
55 So when, of late, innumerous Gallic hosts
Fierce, wanton, cruel, did by stealth invade
The peaceable American's domains,
While desolation mark'd their faithless rout;
No sooner Albion's martial sons advanc'd,
60 Than the gay dastards to their forests fled,
And left their spoils and tomahawks behind.
   Nor with less waste the whisker'd vermine-race,
A countless clan, despoil the low-land Cane.
These to destroy, while commerce hoists the sail,
65 Loose rocks abound, or tangling bushes bloom,
What Planter knows? —Yet prudence may reduce.
Encourage then the breed of savage cats,
Nor kill the winding snake, thy foes they eat.
Thus, on the mangrove-banks of Guayaquil,
70 Child of the rocky desert, sea-like stream,

With studious care, the American preserves
The gallinazo, else that sea-like stream
(Whence traffic pours her bounties on mankind)
Dread alligators would alone possess.
75 Thy foes, the teeth-fil'd Ibbos also love;
Nor thou their wayward appetite restrain.
   Some place decoys, nor will they not avail,
Replete with roasted crabs, in every grove
These fell marauders gnaw; and pay their slaves
80 Some small reward for every captive foe.
So practise Gallia's sons; but Britons trust
In other wiles; and surer their success.
   With Misnian arsenic, deleterious bane,
Pound up the ripe cassada's well-rasp'd root,
85 And form in pellets; these profusely spread
Round the Cane-groves, where sculk the vermin-breed:
They, greedy, and unweeting of the bait,
Crowd to the inviting cates, and swift devour
Their palatable Death; for soon they seek
90 The neighbouring spring; and drink, and swell, and die.
But dare not thou, if life deserve thy care,
The infected rivulet taste; nor let thy herds
Graze its polluted brinks, till rolling time
Have fin'd the water, and destroyed the bane.
95 'Tis safer then to mingle nightshade's juice
With flour, and throw it liberal 'mong thy Canes:
They touch not this; its deadly scent they fly,
And sudden colonize some distant vale.
   Shall the muse deign to sing of humble weeds,
100 That check the progress of the imperial cane?
   In every soil, unnumber'd weeds will spring;
Nor fewest in the best: (thus oft we find
Enormous vices taint the noblest souls!)
These let thy little gang, with skilful hand,
105 Oft as they spread abroad, and oft they spread;
Careful pluck up, to swell thy growing heap
Of rich manure. And yet some weeds arise,
Of aspect mean, with wondrous virtues fraught:
(And doth not oft uncommon merit dwell
110 In men of vulgar looks, and trivial air?)

Such, planter, be not thou asham'd to save
From foul pollution, and unseemly rot;
Much will they benefit thy house and thee.
But chief the yellow thistle thou select,
115 Whose seed the stomach frees from nauseous loads;
And, if the music of the mountain-dove
Delight thy pensive ear, sweet friend to thought!
This prompts their cooing, and enflames their love.
Nor let rude hands the knotted grass profane,
120 Whose juices worms fly: Ah, dire endemial ill!
How many fathers, fathers now no more;
How many orphans, now lament thy rage?
The cow-itch also save; but let thick gloves
Thine hands defend, or thou wilt sadly rue
125 Thy rash imprudence, when ten thousand darts
Sharp as the bee-sting, fasten in thy flesh,
And give thee up to torture. But, unhurt,
Planter, thou mays't the humble chickweed cull;
And that, which coyly flies the astonish'd grasp.
130 Not the confection nam'd from Pontus' King;
Not the bless'd apple Median climes produce,
Tho' lofty Maro (whose immortal muse
Distant I follow, and, submiss, adore)
Hath sung its properties, to counteract
135 Dire spells, slow-mutter'd o'er the baneful bowl,
Where cruel stepdames poisonous drugs have brewed;
Can vie with these low tenants of the vale,
In driving poisons from the infected frame:
For here, alas! (ye sons of luxury mark!)
140 The sea, tho' on its bosom Halcyons sleep,
Abounds with poison'd fish; whose crimson fins,
Whose eyes, whose scales, bedropt with azure, gold,
Purple, and green, in all gay Summer's pride,
Amuse the sight; whose taste the palate charms;
145 Yet death, in ambush, on the banquet waits,
Unless these antidotes be timely given.
But, say what strains, what numbers can recite,
Thy praises, vervain; or wild liquorice, thine?
For not the costly root, the gift of God,
150 Gather'd by those, who drink the Volga's wave,

(Prince of Europa's streams, itself a sea)
Equals your potency! Did planters know
But half your virtues; not the Cane itself,
Would they with greater, fonder pains preserve!
155     Still other maladies infest the Cane,
And worse to be subdu'd. The insect-tribe
That, fluttering, spread their pinions to the sun,
Recal the muse: nor shall their many eyes,
Tho' edg'd with gold, their many-colour'd down,
160 From Death preserve them. In what distant clime,
In what recesses are the plunderers hatch'd?
Say, are they wafted in the living gale,
From distant islands? Thus, the locust-breed,
In winged caravans, that blot the sky,
165 Descend from far, and, ere bright morning dawn,
Astonish'd Afric sees her crop devour'd.
Or, doth the Cane a proper nest afford,
And food adapted to the yellow fly? —
The skill'd in Nature's mystic lore observe,
170 Each tree, each plant, that drinks the golden day,
Some reptile life sustains: Thus cochinille
Feeds on the Indian fig; and, should it harm
The foster plant, its worth that harm repays:
But YE, base insects! no bright scarlet yield,
175 To deck the British Wolf; who now, perhaps,
(So Heaven and George ordain) in triumph mounts
Some strong-built fortress, won from haughty Gaul!
And tho' no plant such luscious nectar yields,
As yields the Cane-plant; yet, vile paricides!
180 Ungrateful ye! the Parent-cane destroy.
    Muse! say, what remedy hath skill devis'd
To quell this noxious foe? Thy Blacks send forth,
A strong detachment! ere the encreasing pest
Have made too firm a lodgment; and, with care,
185 Wipe every tainted blade, and liberal lave
With sacred Neptune's purifying stream.
But this Augæan toil long time demands,
Which thou to more advantage mays't employ:
If vows for rain thou ever dids't prefer,
190 Planter, prefer them now: the rattling shower,

Pour'd down in constant streams, for days and nights,
Not only swells, with nectar sweet, thy Canes;
But, in the deluge, drowns thy plundering foe.
When may the planter idly fold his arms,
195 And say, "My soul take rest?" Superior ills,
Ills which no care nor wisdom can avert,
In black succession rise. Ye men of Kent,
When nipping Eurus, with the brutal force
Of Boreas, join'd in ruffian league, assail
200 Your ripen'd hop-grounds; tell me what you feel,
And pity the poor planter; when the blast,
Fell plague of Heaven! perdition of the isles!
Attacks his waving gold. Tho' well-manur'd;
A richness tho' thy fields from nature boast;
205 Though seasons pour; this pestilence invades:
Too oft it seizes the glad infant-throng,
Nor pities their green nonage: Their broad blades
Of which the graceful wood-nymphs erst compos'd
The greenest garlands to adorn their brows,
210 First pallid, sickly, dry, and withered show;
Unseemly stains succeed; which, nearer viewed
By microscopic arts, small eggs appear,
Dire fraught with reptile-life; alas, too soon
They burst their filmy jail, and crawl abroad,
215 Bugs of uncommon shape; thrice hideous show!
Innumerous as the painted shells, that load
The wave-worn margin of the Virgin-isles!
Innumerous as the leaves the plumb-tree sheds,
When, proud of her fæcundity, she shows,
220 Naked, her gold fruit to the God of noon.
Remorseless to its youth; what pity, say,
Can the Cane's age expect? In vain, its pith
With juice nectarious flows; to pungent sour,
Foe to the bowels, soon its nectar turns:
225 Vain every joint a gemmy embryo bears,
Alternate rang'd; from these no filial young
Shall grateful spring, to bless the planter's eye. —
With bugs confederate, in destructive league,
The ants' republic joins; a villain crew,
230 As the waves, countless, that plough up the deep,

(Where Eurus reigns vicegerent of the sky,
Whom Rhea bore to the bright God of day)
When furious Auster dire commotions stirs:
These wind, by subtle sap, their secret way,
235 Pernicious pioneers! while those invest,
More firmly daring, in the face of Heaven,
And win, by regular approach, the Cane.
 'Gainst such ferocious, such unnumber'd bands,
What arts, what arms shall sage experience use?
240 Some bid the planter load the favouring gale,
With pitch, and sulphur's suffocating steam: —
Useless the vapour o'er the Cane-grove flies,
In curling volumes lost; such feeble arms,
To man tho' fatal, not the blast subdue.
245 Others again, and better their success,
Command their slaves each tainted blade to pick
With care, and burn them in vindictive flames.
Labour immense! and yet, if small the pest;
If numerous, if industrious be thy gang;
250 At length, thou may'st the victory obtain.
But, if the living taint be far diffus'd,
Bootless this toil; nor will it then avail
(Tho' ashes lend their suffocating aid)
To bare the broad roots, and the mining swarms
255 Expose, remorseless, to the burning noon.
Ah! must then ruin desolate the plain?
Must the lost planter other climes explore?
Howe'er reluctant, let the hoe uproot
The infected Cane-piece; and, with eager flames,
260 The hostile myriads thou to embers turn:
Far better, thus, a mighty loss sustain,
Which happier years and prudence may retrieve;
Than risque thine all. As when an adverse storm,
Impetuous, thunders on some luckless ship,
265 From green St. Christopher, or Cathäy bound:
Each nautic art the reeling seamen try:
The storm redoubles: death rides every wave:
Down by the board the cracking masts they hew;
And heave their precious cargo in the main.
270 Say, can the Muse, the pencil in her hand,

## The Sugar Cane, Book II

The all-wasting hurricane observant ride?
Can she, undazzled, view the lightning's glare,
That fires the welkin? Can she, unappall'd,
When all the flood-gates of the sky are ope,
275 The shoreless deluge stem? The Muse hath seen
The pillar'd flame, whose top hath reach'd the stars;
Seen rocky, molten fragments, flung in air
From Ætna's vext abyss; seen burning streams
Pour down its channel'd sides; tremendous scenes! —
280 Yet not vext Ætna's pillar'd flames, that strike
The stars; nor molten mountains hurl'd on high;
Nor ponderous rapid deluges, that burn
Its deeply-channel'd sides: cause such dismay,
Such desolation, Hurricane! as thou;
285 When the Almighty gives thy rage to blow,
And all the battles of thy winds engage.
    Soon as the Virgin's charms ingross the Sun;
And till his weaker flame the Scorpion feels;
But, chief, while Libra weighs the unsteddy year:
290 Planter, with mighty props thy dome support;
Each flaw repair; and well, with massy bars,
Thy doors and windows guard; securely lodge
Thy stocks and mill-points. —Then, or calms obtain;
Breathless the royal palm-tree's airiest van;
295 While, o'er the panting isle, the dæmon Heat
High hurls his flaming brand; vast, distant waves
The main drives furious in, and heaps the shore
With strange productions: Or, the blue serene
Assumes a louring aspect, as the clouds
300 Fly, wild-careering, thro' the vault of heaven;
The transient birds, of various kinds, frequent
Each stagnant pool; some hover o'er thy roof;
Then Eurus reigns no more; but each bold wind,
By turns, usurps the empire of the air
305 With quick inconstancy;
Thy herds, as sapient of the coming storm,
(For beasts partake some portion of the sky,)
In troops associate; and, in cold sweats bath'd,
Wild-bellowing, eye the pole. Ye seamen, now,
310 Ply to the southward, if the changeful moon,

Or, in her interlunar palace hid,
Shuns night; or, full-orb'd, in Night's forehead glows:
For, see! the mists, that late involv'd the hill,
Disperse; the midday-sun looks red; strange burs
315 Surround the stars, which vaster fill the eye.
A horrid stench the pools, the main emits;
Fearful the genius of the forest sighs;
The mountains moan; deep groans the cavern'd cliff.
A night of vapour, closing fast around,
320 Snatches the golden noon. —Each wind appeas'd,
The North flies forth, and hurls the frighted air:
Not all the brazen engineries of man,
At once exploded, the wild burst surpass.
Yet thunder, yok'd with lightning and with rain,
325 Water with fire, increase the infernal din:
Canes, shrubs, trees, huts, are whirl'd aloft in air. —
The wind is spent; and "all the isle below
"Is hush as death."
Soon issues forth the West, with sudden burst;
330 And blasts more rapid, more resistless drives:
Rushes the headlong sky; the city rocks;
The good man throws him on the trembling ground;
And dies the murderer in his inmost soul. —
Sullen the West withdraws his eager storms. ——
335 Will not the tempest now his furies chain?
Ah, no! as when in Indian forests, wild,
Barbaric armies suddenly retire
After some furious onset, and, behind
Vast rocks and trees, their horrid forms conceal,
340 Brooding on slaughter, not repuls'd; for soon
Their growing yell the affrighted welkin rends,
And bloodier carnage mows th'ensanguin'd plain:
So the South, sallying from his iron caves
With mightier force, renews the aerial war;
345 Sleep, frighted, flies; and, see! yon lofty palm,
Fair nature's triumph, pride of Indian groves,
Cleft by the sulphurous bolt! See yonder dome,
Where grandeur with propriety combin'd,
And Theodorus with devotion dwelt;
350 Involv'd in smouldering flames. —From every rock,

Dashes the turbid torrent; thro' each street
A river foams, which sweeps, with untam'd might,
Men, oxen, Cane-lands to the billowy main. —
Pauses the wind. — Anon the savage East
355 Bids his wing'd tempests more relentless rave;
Now brighter, vaster corruscations flash;
Deepens the deluge; nearer thunders roll;
Earth trembles; ocean reels; and, in her fangs,
Grim Desolation tears the shrieking isle,
360 Ere rosy Morn possess the ethereal plain,
To pour on darkness the full flood of day. —
Nor does the hurricane's all-wasting wrath
Alone bring ruin on its sounding wing:
Even calms are dreadful, and the fiery South
365 Oft reigns a tyrant in these fervid isles:
For, from its burning furnace, when it breathes,
Europe and Asia's vegetable sons,
Touch'd by its tainting vapour, shrivel'd, die.
The hardiest children of the rocks repine:
370 And all the upland Tropic-plants hang down
Their drooping heads; shew arid, coil'd, adust. —
The main itself seems parted into streams,
Clear as a mirror; and, with deadly scents,
Annoys the rower; who, heart-fainting, eyes
375 The sails hang idly, noiseless, from the mast.
Thrice hapless he, whom thus the hand of fate
Compels to risque the insufferable beam!
A fiend, the worst the angry skies ordain
To punish sinful man, shall fatal seize
380 His wretched life, and to the tomb consign.
  When such the ravage of the burning calm,
On the stout, sunny children of the hill;
What must thy Cane-lands feel? Thy late green sprouts
Nor bunch, nor joint; but sapless, arid, pine:
385 Those, who have manhood reach'd, of yellow hue,
(Symptom of health and strength) soon ruddy show;
While the rich juice that circled in their veins,
Acescent, watery, poor, unwholesome tastes.
  Nor only, planter, are thy Cane-groves burnt;
390 Thy life is threatened. Muse, the manner sing.

Then earthquakes, nature's agonizing pangs,
Oft shake the astonied isles: The solfaterre
Or sends forth thick, blue, suffocating steams;
Or shoots to temporary flame. A din,
395 Wild, thro' the mountain's quivering rocky caves,
Like the dread crash of tumbling planets, roars.
When tremble thus the pillars of the globe,
Like the tall coco by the fierce North blown;
Can the poor, brittle, tenements of man
400 Withstand the dread convulsion? Their dear homes,
(Which shaking, tottering, crashing, bursting, fall,)
The boldest fly; and, on the open plain
Appal'd, in agony the moment wait,
When, with disrupture vast, the waving earth
405 Shall whelm them in her sea-disgorging womb.
    Nor less affrighted are the bestial kind.
The bold steed quivers in each panting vein,
And staggers, bath'd in deluges of sweat:
Thy lowing herds forsake their grassy food,
410 And send forth frighted, woful, hollow sounds:
The dog, thy trusty centinel of night,
Deserts his post assign'd; and, piteous, howls. ——
Wide ocean feels: ——
The mountain-waves, passing their custom'd bounds,
415 Make direful, loud incursions on the land,
All-overwhelming: Sudden they retreat,
With their whole troubled waters; but, anon,
Sudden return, with louder, mightier force;
(The black rocks whiten, the vext shores resound;)
420 And yet, more rapid, distant they retire.
Vast coruscations lighten all the sky,
With volum'd flames; while thunder's awful voice,
From forth his shrine, by night and horror girt,
Astounds the guilty, and appals the good:
425 For oft the best, smote by the bolt of heaven,
Wrapt in ethereal flame, forget to live:
Else, fair Theana. —Muse, her fate deplore.
    Soon as young reason dawn'd in Junio's breast,
His father sent him from these genial isles,
430 To where old Thames with conscious pride surveys

Green Eton, soft abode of every Muse.
Each classic beauty soon he made his own;
And soon fam'd Isis saw him woo the Nine,
On her inspiring banks: Love tun'd his song;
435 For fair Theana was his only theme,
Acasto's daughter, whom, in early youth,
He oft distinguish'd; and for whom he oft
Had climb'd the bending coco's airy height,
To rob it of its nectar; which the maid,
440 When he presented, more nectarious deem'd. —
The sweetest sappadillas oft he brought;
From him more sweet ripe sappadillas seem'd. —
Nor had long absence yet effac'd her form;
Her charms still triumph'd o'er Britannia's fair.
445 One morn he met her in Sheen's royal walks;
Nor knew, till then, sweet Sheen contain'd his all.
His taste mature approv'd his infant choice.
In colour, form, expression, and in grace,
She shone all-perfect; while each pleasing art,
450 And each soft virtue that the sex adorns,
Adorn'd the woman. My imperfect strain,
Which Percy's happier pencil would demand,
Can ill describe the transports Junio felt
At this discovery: He declar'd his love;
455 She own'd his merit, nor refus'd his hand.
    And shall not Hymen light his brightest torch,
For this delighted pair? Ah, Junio knew,
His sire detested his Theana's House! —
Thus duty, reverence, gratitude, conspir'd
460 To check their happy union. He resolv'd
(And many a sigh that resolution cost)
To pass the time, till death his sire remov'd,
In visiting old Europe's letter'd climes:
While she (and many a tear that parting drew)
465 Embark'd, reluctant, for her native isle.
    Tho' learned, curious, and tho' nobly bent,
With each rare talent to adorn his mind,
His native land to serve; no joys he found. —
Yet sprightly Gaul; yet Belgium, Saturn's reign;
470 Yet Greece, of old the seat of every Muse,

Of freedom, courage; yet Ausonia's clime,
His steps explor'd; where painting, music's strains,
Where arts, where laws, (philosophy's best child),
With rival beauties, his attention claim'd.
475 To his just-judging, his instructed eye,
The all-perfect Medicean Venus seem'd
A perfect semblance of his Indian fair:
But, when she spoke of love, her voice surpass'd
The harmonious warblings of Italian song.
480 Twice one long year elaps'd, when letters came,
Which briefly told him of his father's death.
Afflicted, filial, yet to Heaven resign'd,
Soon he reach'd Albion, and as soon embark'd,
Eager to clasp the object of his love.
485 Blow, prosperous breezes; swiftly sail, thou Po:
Swift sail'd the Po, and happy breezes blew.
In Biscay's stormy seas an armed ship,
Of force superiour, from loud Charente's wave
Clapt them on board. The frighted flying crew
490 Their colours strike; when dauntless Junio, fir'd
With noble indignation, kill'd the chief,
Who on the bloody deck dealt slaughter round.
The Gauls retreat; the Britons loud huzza;
And touch'd with shame, with emulation stung,
495 So plied their cannon, plied their missil fires,
That soon in air the hapless Thunderer blew.
Blow prosperous breezes, swiftly sail thou Po,
May no more dangerous fights retard thy way!
Soon Porto Santo's rocky heights they spy,
500 Like clouds dim rising in the distant air.
Glad Eurus whistles; laugh the sportive crew;
Each sail is set to catch the favouring gale,
While on the yard-arm the harpooner sits,
Strikes the boneta, or the shark insnares.
505 The fring'd urtica spreads her purple form
To catch the gale, and dances o'er the waves:
Small winged fishes on the shrouds alight;
And beauteous dolphins gently played around.
Tho' faster than the Tropic-bird they flew,
510 Oft Junio cried, ah! when shall we see land?

Soon land they made: and now in thought he claspt
His Indian bride, and deem'd his toils o'erpaid.
She, no less amorous, every evening walk'd
On the cool margin of the purple main,
515 Intent her Junio's vessel to descry.
One eve, (faint calms for many a day had rag'd,)
The winged dæmons of the tempest rose:
Thunder, and rain, and lightning's awful power.
She fled: could innocence, could beauty claim
520 Exemption from the grave; the æthereal Bolt,
That stretch'd her speechless, o'er her lovely head
Had innocently roll'd.
Mean while, impatient Junio lept ashore,
Regardless of the Dæmons of the storm.
525 Ah youth! what woes, too great for man to bear,
Are ready to burst on thee? Urge not so
Thy flying courser. Soon Theana's porch
Receiv'd him: at his sight, the antient slaves
Affrighted shriek, and to the chamber point: —
530 Confounded, yet unknowing what they meant,
He entered hasty ——
Ah! what a sight for one who lov'd so well!
All pale and cold, in every feature death,
Theana lay; and yet a glimpse of joy
535 Played on her face, while with faint, faultering voice,
She thus addrest the youth, whom yet she knew.
"Welcome, my Junio, to thy native shore!
"Thy sight repays this summons of my fate:
"Live, and live happy; sometimes think of me:
540 "By night, by day, you still engag'd my care;
"And next to God, you now my thoughts employ:
"Accept of this —— My little all I give;
"Would it were larger" —— Nature could no more;
She look'd, embrac'd him, with a groan expir'd.
545   But say, what strains, what language can express
The thousand pangs, which tore the lover's breast?
Upon her breathless corse himself he threw,
And to her clay-cold lips, with trembling haste,
Ten thousand kisses gave. He strove to speak;
550 Nor words he found: he claspt her in his arms;

He sigh'd, he swoon'd, look'd up, and died away.
One grave contains this hapless, faithful pair;
And still the Cane-isles tell their matchless love!

[The END of BOOK II.]

# THE
# SUGAR-CANE

## BOOK III.

### ARGUMENT.

*Hymn to the month of January, when crop begins. Address. Planters have employment all the year round. Planters should be pious. A ripe Cane-piece on fire at midnight. Crop begun. Cane cutting described. Effects of music. Great care requisite in feeding the mill. Humanity towards the maimed recommended. The tainted Canes should not be ground. Their use. How to preserve the laths and mill-points from sudden squalls. Address to the Sun, and praise of Antigua. A cattle-mill described. Care of mules, &c. Diseases to which they are subject. A water-mill the least liable to interruption. Common in Guadaloupe and Martinico. Praise of Lord Romney. The necessity of a strong, clear fire, in boiling. Planters should always have a spare set of vessels, because the iron furnaces are apt to crack, and copper vessels to melt. The danger of throwing cold water into a thorough-heated furnace. Cleanliness, and skimming well, recommended. A boiling-house should be lofty, and open at top, to the leeward. Constituent parts of vegetables. Sugar an essential salt. What retards its granulation. How to forward it. Dumb Cane. Effects of it. Bristol-lime the best temper. Various uses of Bristol lime. Good muscovado described. Bermudas-lime recommended. The Negroes should not be hindered from drinking the hot liquor. The chearfulness and healthiness of the Negroes in crop-time. Boilers to be encouraged. They should neither boil the Sugar too little, nor too much. When the Sugar is of too loose a grain, and about to boil over the teache, or last copper, a little grease settles it, and makes it boil closer. The French often mix sand with their Sugars. This practice not followed by the English. A character. Of the skimmings. Their various uses. Of rum. Its praise. A West-India prospect, when crop is finished. An address to the Creoles, to live more upon their estates than they do. The reasons.*

# THE
# SUGAR-CANE

## BOOK III.

    From scenes of deep distress, the heavenly Muse,
Emerging joyous, claps her dewy wings.
As when a pilgrim, in the howling waste,
Hath long time wandered, fearful at each step,
5  Of tumbling cliffs, fell serpents, whelming bogs;
At last, from some lone eminence, descries
Fair haunts of social life; wide-cultur'd plains,
O'er which glad reapers pour; he chearly sings:
So she to sprightlier notes her pipe attunes,
10  Than e'er these mountains heard; to gratulate,
With duteous carols, the beginning year.
    Hail, eldest birth of Time! in other climes,
In the old world, with tempests usher'd in;
While rifled nature thine appearance wails,
15  And savage winter wields his iron mace:
But not the rockiest verge of these green isles,
Tho' mountains heapt on mountains brave the sky,
Dares winter, by his residence, prophane.
At time the ruffian, wrapt in murky state,
20  Inroads will, sly, attempt; but soon the sun,
Benign protector of the Cane-land isles,
Repells the invader, and his rude mace breaks.
Here, every mountain, every winding dell,
(Haunt of the Dryads; where, beneath the shade
25  Of broad-leaf'd china, idly they repose,
Charm'd with the murmur of the tinkling rill;
Charm'd with the hummings of the neighbouring hive;)
Welcome thy glad approach: but chief the Cane,
Whose juice now longs to murmur down the spout,
30  Hails thy lov'd coming; January, hail!

O M * * *! thou, whose polish'd mind contains
Each science useful to thy native isle!
Philosopher, without the hermit's spleen!
Polite, yet learned; and, tho' solid, gay!
35 Critic, whose head each beauty, fond, admires;
Whose heart each error flings in friendly shade!
Planter, whose youth sage cultivation taught
Each secret lesson of her sylvan school:
To thee the Muse a grateful tribute pays;
40 She owes to thee the precepts of her song:
Nor wilt thou, sour, refuse; tho' other cares,
The public welfare, claim thy busy hour;
With her to roam (thrice pleasing devious walk)
The ripened cane-piece; and, with her, to taste
45 (Delicious draught!) the nectar of the mill!
  The planter's labour in a round revolves;
Ends with the year, and with the year begins.
  Ye swains, to Heaven bend low in grateful prayer,
Worship the Almighty; whose kind-fostering hand
50 Hath blest your labour, and hath given the cane
To rise superior to each menac'd ill.
  Nor less, ye planters, in devotion, sue,
That nor the heavenly bolt, nor casual spark,
Nor hand of malice may the crop destroy.
55   Ah me! what numerous, deafning bells, resound?
What cries of horror startle the dull sleep?
What gleaming brightness makes, at midnight, day?
By its portentuous glare, too well I see
Palæmon's fate; the virtuous, and the wise!
60 Where were ye, watches, when the flame burst forth?
A little care had then the hydra quell'd:
But, now, what clouds of white smoke load the sky!
How strong, how rapid the combustion pours!
Aid not, ye winds! with your destroying breath,
65 The spreading vengeance. —They contemn my prayer.
  Rous'd by the deafning bells, the cries, the blaze;
From every quarter, in tumultuous bands,
The Negroes rush; and, 'mid the crackling flames,
Plunge, dæmon-like! All, all, urge every nerve:
70 This way, tear up those Canes; dash the fire out,

Which sweeps, with serpent-error, o'er the ground.
There, hew these down; their topmost branches burn:
And here bid all thy watery engines play;
For here the wind the burning deluge drives.
75     In vain. —More wide the blazing torrent rolls;
More loud it roars, more bright it fires the pole!
And toward thy mansion, see, it bends its way.
Haste! far, O far, your infant-throng remove:
Quick from your stables drag your steeds and mules:
80 With well-wet blankets guard your cypress-roofs;
And where thy dried Canes in large stacks are pil'd. —
    Efforts but serve to irritate the flames:
Naught but thy ruin can their wrath appease.
Ah, my Palæmon! what avail'd thy care,
85 Oft to prevent the earliest dawn of day,
And walk thy ranges, at the noon of night?
What tho' no ills assail'd thy bunching sprouts,
And seasons pour'd obedient to thy will:
All, all must perish; nor shalt thou preserve
90 Wherewith to feed thy little orphan-throng.
    Oh, may the Cane-isles know few nights, like this!
For now the sail-clad points, impatient, wait
The hour of sweet release, to court the gale.
The late-hung coppers wish to feel the warmth,
95 Which well-dried fewel from the Cane imparts:
The Negroe-train, with placid looks, survey
Thy fields, which full perfection have attain'd,
And pant to wield the bill: (no surly watch
Dare now deprive them of the luscious Cane:)
100 Nor thou, my friend, their willing ardour check;
Encourage rather; cheerful toil is light.
So from no field, shall slow-pac'd oxen draw
More frequent loaded wanes; which many a day,
And many a night shall feed thy crackling mills
105 With richest offerings: while thy far seen flames,
Bursting thro' many a chimney, bright emblaze
The Æthiop-brow of night. And see, they pour
(Ere Phosphor his pale circlet yet withdraws,
What time grey dawn stands tip-toe on the hill,)
110 O'er the rich Cane-grove: Muse, their labour sing.

## The Sugar Cane, Book III

      Some bending, of their sapless burden ease
The yellow jointed canes, (whose height exceeds
A mounted trooper, and whose clammy round
Measures two inches full;) and near the root
115 Lop the stem off, which quivers in their hand
With fond impatience: soon it's branchy spires,
(Food to thy cattle) it resigns; and soon
It's tender prickly tops, with eyes thick set,
To load with future crops thy long-hoed land.
120 These with their green, their pliant branches bound,
(For not a part of this amazing plant,
But serves some useful purpose) charge the young:
Not laziness declines this easy toil;
Even lameness from it's leafy pallet crawls,
125 To join the favoured gang. What of the Cane
Remains, and much the largest part remains,
Cut into junks a yard in length, and tied
In small light bundles; load the broad-wheel'd wane,
The mules crook-harnest, and the sturdier crew,
130 With sweet abundance. As on Lincoln-plains,
(Ye plains of Lincoln sound your Dyer's praise!)
When the lav'd snow-white flocks are numerous penn'd;
The senior swains, with sharpen'd shears, cut off
The fleecy vestment; others stir the tar;
135 And some impress, upon their captives sides,
Their master's cypher; while the infant throng
Strive by the horns to hold the struggling ram,
Proud of their prowess. Nor meanwhile the jest
Light-bandied round, but innocent of ill;
140 Nor choral song are wanting: eccho rings.
      Nor need the driver, Æthiop authoriz'd,
Thence more inhuman, crack his horrid whip;
From such dire sounds the indignant muse averts
Her virgin-ear, where musick loves to dwell:
145 'Tis malice now, 'tis wantonness of power
To lash the laughing, labouring, singing throng.
      What cannot song? all nature feels its power:
The hind's blithe whistle, as thro' stubborn soils
He drives the shining share; more than the goad,
150 His tardy steers impells. —The muse hath seen,

When health danc'd frolic in her youthful veins,
And vacant gambols wing'd the laughing hours;
The muse hath seen on Annan's pastoral hills,
Of theft and slaughter erst the fell retreat,
155 But now the shepherd's best-beloved walk:
Hath seen the shepherd, with his sylvan pipe,
Lead on his flock o'er crags, thro' bogs, and streams,
A tedious journey; yet not weary they,
Drawn by the enchantment of his artless song.
160 What cannot musick? —When brown Ceres asks
The reapers sickle; what like magic sound,
Puff'd from sonorous bellows by the squeeze
Of tuneful artist, can the rage disarm
Of the swart dog-star, and make harvest light?
165 And now thy mills dance eager in the gale;
Feed well their eagerness: but O beware;
Nor trust, between the steel-cas'd cylinders,
The hand incautious: off the member snapt
Thou'lt ever rue; sad spectacle of woe!
170 Are there, the muse can scarce believe the tale;
Are there, who lost to every feeling sense,
To reason, interest lost; their slaves desert,
And manumit them, generous boon! to starve
Maim'd by imprudence, or the hand of Heaven?
175 The good man feeds his blind, his aged steed,
That in his service spent his vigorous prime:
And dares a mortal to his fellow man,
(For spite of vanity, thy slaves are men)
Deny protection? Muse suppress the tale.
180 Ye! who in bundles bind the lopt-off Canes;
But chiefly ye! who feed the tight-brac'd mill;
In separate parcels, far, the infected fling:
Of bad Cane-juice the least admixture spoils
The richest, soundest; thus, in pastoral walks,
185 One tainted sheep contaminates the fold.
Nor yet to dung-heaps thou resign the canes,
Which or the sun hath burnt, or rats have gnaw'd.
These, to small junks reduc'd, and in huge casks
Steept, where no cool winds blow; do thou ferment:—
190 Then, when from his entanglements inlarg'd

Th'evasive spirit mounts; by Vulcan's aid,
(Nor Amphitryte will her help deny,)
Do thou through all his winding ways pursue
The runaway; till in thy sparkling bowl
195 Confin'd, he dances; more a friend to life,
And joy, than that Nepenthe fam'd of yore,
Which Polydamna, Thone's imperial queen,
Taught Jove-born Helen on the banks of Nile.
  As on old ocean, when the wind blows high,
200 The cautious mariner contracts his sail;
So here, when squaly bursts the speeding gale,
If thou from ruin would'st thy points preserve,
Less-bellying canvas to the storm oppose.
  Yet the faint breeze oft flags on listless wings,
205 Nor tremulates the coco's airiest arch,
While the red sun darts deluges of fire;
And soon (if on the gale thy crop depend,)
Will all thy hopes of opulence defeat.
  "Informer of the planetary train!"
210 Source undiminished of all-cheering light,
Of roseat beauty, and heart-gladning joy!
Fountain of being, on whose water broods
The organic spirit, principle of life!
Lord of the seasons! who in courtly pomp
215 Lacquay thy presence, and with glad dispatch,
Pour at thy bidding, o'er the land and sea!
Parent of vegetation, whose fond grasp
The Sugar-cane displays; and whose green car
Soft-stealing dews, with liquid pearls adorn'd,
220 Fat-fostering rains, and buxom genial airs
Attend triumphant! Why, ah why so oft,
Why hath Antigua, sweetly social isle,
Nurse of each art; where science yet finds friends
Amid this waste of waters; wept thy rage?
225   Then trust not, planter, to the unsteddy gale;
But in Tobago's endless forests fell
The tall tough hiccory, or calaba.
Of this, be forc'd two pillars in the ground,
Four paces distant, and two cubits high:
230 Other two pillars raise; the wood the same,

Of equal size and height. The Calaba
Than steel more durable, contemns the rain,
And sun's intensest beam; the worm, that pest
Of mariners, which winds its fatal way
235 Through heart of British oak, reluctant leaves
The closer calaba. —By transverse beams
Secure the whole; and in the pillar'd frame,
Sink, artist, the vast bridge-tree's mortis'd form
Of ponderous hiccory; hiccory time defies:
240 To this be nail'd three polish'd iron plates;
Whereon, three steel Capouces, turn with ease,
Of three long rollers, twice-nine inches round,
With iron cas'd, and jagg'd with many a cogg.
The central Cylinder exceeds the rest
245 In portly size, thence aptly Captain nam'd.
To this be rivetted th'extended sweeps;
And harness to each sweep two seasoned mules:
They pacing round, give motion to the whole.
The close brac'd cylinders with ease revolve
250 On their greas'd axle; and with ease reduce
To trash, the Canes thy negroes throw between.
Fast flows the liquor through the lead-lin'd spouts;
And depurated by opposing wires,
In the receiver floats a limpid stream.
255 So twice five casks, with muscovado fill'd,
Shall from thy staunchions drip, ere Day's bright god
Hath in the Atlantic six times cool'd his wheels.
   Wouldst thou against calamity provide?
Let a well shingled roof, from Raleigh's land,
260 Defend thy stock from noon's inclement blaze,
And from night-dews; for night no respite knows.
   Nor, when their destin'd labour is perform'd,
Be thou asham'd to lead the panting mules
(The muse, soft parent of each social grace,
265 With eyes of love God's whole creation views)
To the warm pen; where copious forage strowed,
And strenuous rubbing, renovate their strength.
So, fewer ails, (alas, how prone to ails!)
Their days shall shorten; ah, too short at best!
270    For not, even then, my friend, art thou secure

## The Sugar Cane, Book III

From fortune: spite of all thy steady care,
What ills, that laugh to scorn Machaon's art,
Await thy cattle! farcy's tabid form,
Joint-racking spasms, and cholic's pungent pang,
275 Need the muse tell? which, in one luckless moon,
Thy sheds dispeople; when perhaps thy groves,
To full perfection shot, by day, by night,
Indesinent demand their vigorous toil.
Then happiest he, for whom the Naiads pour,
280 From rocky urns, the never-ceasing stream,
To turn his rollers with unbought dispatch.
In Karukera's rich well-water'd isle!
In Matanina! boast of Albion's arms,
The brawling Naiads for the planters toil,
285 Howe'er unworthy; and, through solemn scenes,
Romantic, cool, with rocks and woods between,
Enchant the senses! but, among thy swains,
Sweet Liamuiga! who such bliss can boast?
Yes, Romney, thou mays't boast; of British heart,
290 Of courtly manners, join'd to antient worth:
Friend to thy Britain's every blood-earn'd right,
From tyrants wrung, the many or the few.
By wealth, by titles, by ambition's lure,
Not to be tempted from fair honour's path:
295 While others, falsely flattering their Prince,
Bold disapprov'd, or by oblique surmise
Their terror hinted, of the people arm'd;
Indignant, in the senate, he uprose,
And, with the well-urg'd energy of zeal,
300 Their specious, subtle sophistry disprov'd;
The importance, the necessity display'd,
Of civil armies, freedom's surest guard!
Nor in the senate didst thou only win
The palm of eloquence, securely bold;
305 But rear'd'st thy banners, fluttering in the wind:
Kent, from each hamlet, pour'd her marshal'd swains,
To hurl defiance on the threatening Gaul.

Thy foaming coppers well with fewel feed;
For a clear, strong, continued fire improves
310 Thy muscovado's colour, and its grain.—

Yet vehement heat, protracted, will consume
Thy vessels, whether from the martial mine,
Or from thine ore, bright Venus, they are drawn;
Or hammer, or hot fusion, give them form.
315 If prudence guides thee then, thy stores shall hold
Of well-siz'd vessels a complete supply:
For every hour, thy boilers cease to skim,
(Now Cancer reddens with the solar ray,)
Defeats thy honest purposes of gain.
320 Nor small the risque, (when piety, or chance,
Force thee from boiling to desist) to lave
Thy heated furnace, with the gelid stream.
The chemist knows, when all-dissolving fire
Bids the metalline ore abruptly flow;
325 What dread explosions, and what dire effects,
A few cold drops of water will produce,
Uncautious, on the novel fluid thrown.
    For grain and colour, wouldst thou win, my friend,
At every curious mart, the constant palm?
330 O'er all thy works let cleanliness preside,
Child of frugality; and, as the skum
Thick mantles o'er the boiling wave, do thou
The skum that mantles carefully remove.
    From bloating dropsy, from pulmonic ails,
335 Wouldst thou defend thy boilers, (prime of slaves,)
For days, for nights, for weeks, for months, involv'd
In the warm vapour's all-relaxing steam;
Thy boiling-house be lofty: all atop
Open, and pervious to the tropic breeze;
340 Whose cool perflation, wooed through many a grate,
Dispells the steam, and gives the lungs to play.
    The skill'd in chemia, boast of modern arts,
Know from experiment, the fire of truth,
In many a plant that oil, and acid juice,
345 And ropy mucilage, by nature live:
These, envious, stop the much desir'd embrace
Of the essential salts, tho' coction bid
The aqueous particles to mount in air.
    'Mong salts essential, sugar wins the palm,
350 For taste, for colour, and for various use:

## The Sugar Cane, Book III

And, in the nectar of the yellowest Cane,
Much acor, oil, and mucilage abound:
But in the less mature, from mountain-land,
These harsh intruders so redundant float,
355   Muster so strong, as scarce to be subdued.
    Muse, sing the ways to quell them. Some use Cane,
That Cane, whose juices to the tongue apply'd,
In silence lock it, sudden, and constrain'd,
(Death to Xantippe,) with distorting pain.
360   Nor is it not effectual: But wouldst thou
Have rival brokers for thy cades contend;
Superior arts remain. —Small casks provide,
Replete with lime-stone thoroughly calcin'd,
And from the air secur'd: This Bristol sends,
365   Bristol, Britannia's second mart and eye!
    Nor "to thy waters only trust for fame,"
Bristol; nor to thy beamy diamonds trust:
Tho' these oft deck Britannia's lovely fair;
And those oft save the guardians of her realm.
370   Thy marble-quarries claim the voice of praise,
Which rich incrusts thy Avon's banks, sweet banks!
Tho' not to you young Shakespear, Fancy's child,
All-rudely warbled his first woodland notes;
Tho, not your caves, while terror stalk'd around,
375   Saw him essay to clutch the ideal sword,
With drops of blood distain'd: yet, lovely banks,
On you reclin'd, another tun'd his pipe;
Whom all the Muses emulously love,
And in whose strains your praises shall endure,
380   While to Sabrina speeds your healing stream.
    Bristol, without thy marble, by the flame
Calcin'd to whiteness, vain the stately reed
Would swell with juice mellifluent; heat would soon
The strongest, best-hung furnaces, consume.
385   Without its aid the cool-imprison'd stream,
Seldom allow'd to view the face of day,
Tho' late it roam'd a denizen of air;
Would steal from its involuntary bounds,
And, by sly windings, set itself at large.
390   But chief thy lime the experienc'd boiler loves,

Nor loves ill-founded; when no other art
Can bribe to union the coy floating salts,
A proper portion of this precious dust,
Cast in the wave, (so showers alone of gold
395 Could win fair Danae to the God's embrace;)
With nectar'd muscovado soon will charge
Thy shelving coolers, which, severely press'd
Between the fingers, not resolves; and which
Rings in the cask; and or a light-brown hue,
400 Or thine, more precious silvery-grey, assumes.
    The fam'd Bermuda's ever-healthy isles,
More fam'd by gentle Waller's deathless strains,
Than for their cedars, which, insulting, fly
O'er the wide ocean; 'mid their rocks contain
405 A stone, which, when calcin'd, (experience says,)
Is only second to Sabrina's lime.
    While flows the juice mellifluent from the Cane,
Grudge not, my friend, to let thy slaves, each morn,
But chief the sick and young, at setting day,
410 Themselves regale with oft-repeated draughts
Of tepid Nectar; so shall health and strength
Confirm thy Negroes, and make labour light.
    While flame thy chimneys, while thy coppers foam,
How blithe, how jocund, the plantation smiles!
415 By day, by night, resounds the choral song
Of glad barbarity; serene, the sun
Shines not intensely hot; the trade-wind blows:
How sweet, how silken, is its noontide breath?
While to far climes the fell destroyer, Death,
420 Wings his dark flight. Then seldom pray for rain:
Rather for cloudless days thy prayers prefer;
For, if the skies too frequently relent,
Crude flows the Cane-juice, and will long elude
The boiler's wariest skill: thy Canes will spring
425 To an unthrifty loftiness; or, weigh'd
Down by their load, (Ambition's curse,) decay.
    Encourage thou thy boilers; much depends
On their skill'd efforts. If too soon they strike,
E'er all the watery particles have fled;
430 Or lime sufficient granulate the juice:

In vain the thickning liquor is effus'd;
An heterogeneous, an uncertain mass,
And never in thy coolers to condense.
　　Or, planter, if the coction they prolong
435　Beyond its stated time; the viscous wave
Will in huge flinty masses chrystalize,
Which forceful fingers scarce can crumble down;
And which with its melasses ne'er will part:
Yet this, fast-dripping in nectarious drops,
440　Not only betters what remains, but when
With art fermented, yields a noble wine,
Than which nor Gallia, nor the Indian clime,
Where rolls the Ganges, can a nobler show.
So misers in their coffers lock that gold;
445　Which, if allowed at liberty to roam,
Would better them, and benefit mankind.
　　In the last coppers, when the embrowning wave
With sudden fury swells; some grease immix'd,
The foaming tumult sudden will compose,
450　And force to union the divided grain.
So when two swarms in airy battle join,
The winged heroes heap the bloody field;
Until some dust, thrown upward in the sky,
Quell the wild conflict, and sweet peace restore.
455　　False Gallia's sons, that hoe the ocean-isles,
Mix with their Sugar, loads of worthless sand,
Fraudful, their weight of sugar to increase.
Far be such guile from Britain's honest swains.
Such arts, awhile, the unwary may surprise,
460　And benefit the Impostor; but, ere long,
The skilful buyer will the fraud detect,
And, with abhorrence, reprobate the name.
　　Fortune had crown'd Avaro's younger years,
With a vast tract of land, on which the cane
465　Delighted grew, nor ask'd the toil of art.
The Sugar-bakers deem'd themselves secure,
Of mighty profit, could they buy his cades;
For, whiteness, hardness, to the leeward-crop,
His muscovado gave. But, not content
470　With this pre-eminence of honest gain,

He baser sugars started in his casks;
His own, by mixing sordid things, debas'd.
One year the fraud succeeded; wealth immense
Flowed in upon him, and he blest his wiles:
475 The next, the brokers spurn'd the adulterate mass,
Both on the Avon and the banks of Thame.
   Be thrifty, planter, even thy skimmings save:
For, planter, know, the refuse of the Cane
Serves needful purposes. Are barbecues
480 The cates thou lov'st? What like rich skimmings feed
The grunting, bristly kind? Your labouring mules
They soon invigorate: Give old Baynard these,
Untir'd he trudges in his destin'd round;
Nor need the driver crack his horrid lash.
485 Yet, with small quantities indulge the steed,
Whom skimmings ne'er have fatten'd: else, too fond,
So gluttons use, he'll eat intemperate meals;
And, staggering, fall the prey of ravening sharks.
   But say, ye boon companions, in what strains,
490 What grateful strains, shall I record the praise
Of their best produce, heart-recruiting rum?
Thrice wholesome spirit! well-matur'd with age,
Thrice grateful to the palate! when, with thirst,
With heat, with labour, and wan care opprest,
495 I quaff thy bowl, where fruit my hands have cull'd,
Round, golden fruit; where water from the spring,
Which dripping coolness spreads her umbrage round;
With hardest, whitest sugar, thrice refin'd;
Dilates my soul with genuine joy; low care
500 I spurn indignant; toil a pleasure seems.
For not Marne's flowery banks, nor Tille's green bounds,
Where Ceres with the God of vintage reigns,
In happiest union; not Vigornian hills,
Pomona's lov'd abode, afford to man
505 Goblets more priz'd, or laudable of taste,
To slake parch'd thirst, and mitigate the clime.
   Yet, 'mid this blest ebriety, some tears,
For friends I left in Albion's distant isle,
For Johnson, Percy, White, escape mine eyes:
510 For her, fair Auth'ress! whom first Calpe's rocks

A sportive infant saw; and whose green years
True genius blest with her benignest gifts
Of happiest fancy. O, were ye all here,
O, were ye here; with him, my Pæon's son!
515 Long-known, of worth approv'd, thrice candid soul!
How would your converse charm the lonely hour?
Your converse, where mild wisdom tempers mirth;
And charity, the petulance of wit;
How would your converse polish my rude lays,
520 With what new, noble images adorn?
Then should I scarce regret the banks of Thames,
All as we sat beneath that sand-box shade;
Whence the delighted eye expatiates wide
O'er the fair landscape; where in loveliest forms,
525 Green cultivation hath array'd the land.
    See! there, what mills, like giants raise their arms,
To quell the speeding gale! what smoke ascends
From every boiling house! What structures rise,
Neat tho' not lofty, pervious to the breeze;
530 With galleries, porches, or piazzas grac'd!
Nor not delightful are those reed-built huts,
On yonder hill, that front the rising sun;
With plantanes, with banana's bosom'd deep,
That flutter in the wind: where frolick goats,
535 Butt the young negroes, while their swarthy sires,
With ardent gladness wield the bill; and hark,
The crop is finish'd, how they rend the sky! —
    Nor, beauteous only shows the cultured soil,
From this cool station. No less charms the eye
540 That wild interminable waste of waves:
While on the horizon's farthest verge are seen
Islands of different shape, and different size;
While sail-clad ships, with their sweet produce fraught,
Swell on the straining sight; while near yon rock,
545 On which ten thousand wings with ceaseless clang
Their airies build, a water spout descends,
And shakes mid ocean; and while there below,
That town, embowered in the different shade
Of tamarinds, panspans, and papaws, o'er which
550 A double Iris throws her painted arch,

Shows commerce toiling in each crowded street,
And each throng'd street with limpid currents lav'd.
  What tho' no bird of song, here charms the sense
With her wild minstrelsy; far, far beyond,
555 The unnatural quavers of Hesperian throats!
Tho' the chaste poet of the vernal woods,
That shuns rude folly's din, delight not here
The listening eve; and tho' no herald-lark
Here leave his couch, high-towering to descry
560 The approach of dawn, and hail her with his song:
Yet not unmusical the tinkling lapse
Of yon cool argent rill, which Phœbus gilds
With his first orient rays; yet musical,
Those buxom airs that through the plantanes play,
565 And tear with wantonness their leafy scrolls;
Yet not unmusical the waves hoarse sound,
That dashes, sullen, on the distant shore;
Yet musical those little insects hum,
That hover round us, and to reason's ear,
570 Deep, moral truths convey; while every beam
Flings on them transient tints, which vary when
They wave their purple plumes; yet musical
The love-lorn cooing of the mountain-dove,
That woos to pleasing thoughtfulness the soul;
575 But chief the breeze, that murmurs through yon canes,
Enchants the ear with tunable delight.
  While such fair scenes adorn these blissful isles;
Why will their sons, ungrateful, roam abroad?
Why spend their opulence in other climes?
580   Say, is pre-eminence your partial aim? —
Distinction courts you here; the senate calls.
Here, crouching slaves, attendant wait your nod:
While there, unnoted, but for folly's garb,
For folly's jargon; your dull hours ye pass,
585 Eclips'd by titles, and superior wealth.
  Does martial ardour fire your generous veins?
Fly to your native isles: Bellona, there,
Hath long time rear'd her bloody flag; these isles
Your strenuous arms demand; for ye are brave!
590 Nor longer to the lute and taber's sound

Weave antic measures. O, could my weak song,
O could my song, like his, heaven-favoured bard,
Who led desponding Sparta's oft-beat hosts,
To victory, to glory; fire your souls
595 With English ardor! for now England's swains,
(The Man of Norfolk, swains of England, thank;)
All emulous, to Freedom's standard fly,
And drive invasion from their native shore:
How would my soul exult with conscious pride;
600 Nor grudge those wreaths Tyrtæus gain'd of yore.
    Or are ye fond of rich luxurious cates? —
Can aught in Europe emulate the pine,
Or fruit forbidden, native of your isles?
Sons of Apicius, say, can Europe's seas,
605 Can aught the edible creation yields,
Compare with turtle, boast of land and wave?
Can Europe's seas, in all their finny realms,
Aught so delicious as the Jew-fish show?
Tell me what viands, land or streams produce,
610 The large, black, female, moulting crab excel?
A richer flavour not wild Cambria's hills,
Nor Scotia's rocks with heath and thyme o'erspread,
Give to their flocks; than, lone Barbuda, you,
Than you, Anguilla, to your sheep impart.
615 Even Britain's vintage, here, improv'd, we quaff;
Even Lusitanian, even Hesperian wines.
Those from the Rhine's imperial banks (poor Rhine!
How have thy banks been died with brother-blood?
Unnatural warfare!) strength and flavour gain
620 In this delicious clime. Besides, the Cane
Wafted to every quarter of the globe,
Makes the vast produce of the world your own.
    Or rather, doth the love of nature charm;
Its mighty love your chief attention claim?
625 Leave Europe; there, through all her coyest ways,
Her secret mazes, nature is pursued:
But here, with savage loneliness, she reigns
On yonder peak, whence giddy fancy looks,
Affrighted, on the labouring main below.
630 Heavens! what stupendous, what unnumbered trees,

"Stage above stage, in various verdure drest,"
Unprofitable shag its airy cliffs!
Heavens! what new shrubs, what herbs with useless bloom,
Adorn its channel'd sides; and, in its caves
635 What sulphurs, ores, what earths and stones abound!
There let philosophy conduct thy steps,
"For naught is useless made:" With candid search,
Examine all the properties of things;
Immense discoveries soon will crown your toil,
640 Your time will soon repay. Ah, when will cares,
The cares of Fortune, less my minutes claim?
Then, with what joy, what energy of soul,
Will I not climb yon mountain's airiest brow!
The dawn, the burning noon, the setting sun,
645 The midnight-hour, shall hear my constant vows
To Nature; see me prostrate at her shrine!
And, O, if haply I may aught invent
Of use to mortal man, life to prolong,
To soften, or adorn; what genuine joy,
650 What exultation of supreme delight,
Will swell my raptured bosom. Then, when death
Shall call me hence, I'll unrepining go;
Nor envy conquerors their storied tombs,
Tho' not a stone point out my humble grave.

[The END of BOOK III.]

# THE
# SUGAR-CANE

## BOOK IV.

### ARGUMENT.

*Invocation to the Genius of Africa. Address. Negroes when bought should be young, and strong. The Congo-negroes are fitter for the house and trades, than for the field. The Gold-Coast, but especially the Papaw-negroes, make the best fieldnegroes: but even these, if advanced in years, should not be purchased. The marks of a sound negroe at a negroe sale. Where the men do nothing but hunt, fish or fight, and all field drudgery is left to the women; these are to be preferred to their husbands. The Minnahs make good tradesmen, but addicted to suicide. The Mundingos, in particular, subject to worms; and the Congas, to dropsical disorders. How salt-water, or new negroes should be seasoned. Some negroes eat dirt. Negroes should be habituated by gentle degrees to field labour. This labour, when compared to that in lead-mines, or of those who work in the gold and silver mines of South America, is not only less toilsome, but far more healthy. Negroes should always be treated with humanity. Praise of freedom. Of the dracunculus, or dragon-worm. Of chigres. Of the yaws. Might not this disease be imparted by inoculation? Of worms, and their multiform appearance. Praise of commerce. Of the imaginary disorders of negroes, especially those caused by their conjurers or Obia-men. The composition and supposed virtues of a magicphiol. Field-negroes should not begin to work before six in the morning, and should leave off between eleven and twelve; and beginning again at two, should finish before sunset. Of the weekly allowance of negroes. The young, the old, the sickly, and even the lazy, must have their victuals prepared for them. Of negroeground, and its various productions. To be fenced in, and watched. Of an American garden. Of the situation of the negroe-huts. How best defended from fire. The great negroe-dance described. Drumming, and intoxicating spirits not to be allowed. Negroes should be made to marry in their masters plantation. Inconveniences arising from the contrary practice. Negroes to be cloathed once a year, and before Christmas. Praise of Lewis XIV. for the Code Noir. A body of laws of this kind recommended to the English sugar colonies. Praise of the river Thames. A moon-light landscape and vision.*

# THE
# SUGAR-CANE

## BOOK IV.

    Genius of Africk! whether thou bestrid'st
The castled elephant; or at the source,
(While howls the desart fearfully around,)
Of thine own Niger, sadly thou reclin'st
5  Thy temples shaded by the tremulous palm,
Or quick papaw, whose top is necklac'd round
With numerous rows of party-colour'd fruit:
Or hear'st thou rather from the rocky banks
Of Rio Grandê, or black Sanaga?
10  Where dauntless thou the headlong torrent brav'st
In search of gold, to brede thy wooly locks,
Or with bright ringlets ornament thine ears,
Thine arms, and ankles: O attend my song.
A muse that pities thy distressful state;
15  Who sees, with grief, thy sons in fetters bound;
Who wishes freedom to the race of man;
Thy nod assenting craves: dread Genius, come!
    Yet vain thy presence, vain thy favouring nod;
Unless once more the muses; that erewhile
20  Upheld me fainting in my past career,
Through Caribbe's cane-isles; kind condescend
To guide my footsteps, through parch'd Libya's wilds;
And bind my sun-burnt brow with other bays,
Than ever deck'd the Sylvan bard before.
25     Say, will my Melvil, from the public care,
Withdraw one moment, to the muses shrine?
Who smit with thy fair fame, industrious cull
An Indian wreath to mingle with thy bays,
And deck the hero, and the scholar's brow!
30  Wilt thou, whose mildness smooths the face of war,

## The Sugar Cane, Book IV

Who round the victor-blade the myrtle twin'st,
And mak'st subjection loyal and sincere;
O wilt thou gracious hear the unartful strain,
Whose mild instructions teach, no trivial theme,
35    What care the jetty African requires?
Yes, thou wilt deign to hear; a man thou art
Who deem'st nought foreign that belongs to man.
    In mind, and aptitude for useful toil,
The negroes differ: muse that difference sing.
40    Whether to wield the hoe, or guide the plane;
Or for domestic uses thou intend'st
The sunny Libyan: from what clime they spring,
It not imports; if strength and youth be theirs.
    Yet those from Congo's wide extended plains,
45    Through which the long Zaire winds with chrystal stream,
Where lavish Nature sends indulgent forth
Fruits of high flavour, and spontaneous seeds
Of bland nutritious quality, ill bear
The toilsome field; but boast a docile mind,
50    And happiness of features. These, with care,
Be taught each nice mechanic art: or train'd
To houshold offices: their ductile souls
Will all thy care, and all thy gold repay.
    But, if the labours of the field demand
55    Thy chief attention; and the ambrosial cane
Thou long'st to see, with spiry frequence, shade
Many an acre: planter, chuse the slave,
Who sails from barren climes; where want alone,
Offspring of rude necessity, compells
60    The sturdy native, or to plant the soil,
Or stem vast rivers for his daily food.
    Such are the children of the Golden Coast;
Such the Papaws, of negroes far the best:
And such the numerous tribes, that skirt the shore,
65    From rapid Volta to the distant Rey.
    But, planter, from what coast soe'er they sail,
Buy not the old: they ever sullen prove;
With heart-felt anguish, they lament their home;
They will not, cannot work; they never learn
70    Thy native language; they are prone to ails;

And oft by suicide their being end.—
Must thou from Africk reinforce thy gang?—
Let health and youth their every sinew firm;
Clear roll their ample eye; their tongue be red;
75   Broad swell their chest; their shoulders wide expand;
Not prominent their belly; clean and strong
Their thighs and legs, in just proportion rise.
Such soon will brave the fervours of the clime;
And free from ails, that kill thy negroe-train,
80   A useful servitude will long support.
Yet, if thine own, thy childrens life, be dear;
Buy not a Cormantee, tho' healthy, young.
Of breed too generous for the servile field;
They, born to freedom in their native land,
85   Chuse death before dishonourable bonds:
Or, fir'd with vengeance, at the midnight hour,
Sudden they seize thine unsuspecting watch,
And thine own poinard bury in thy breast.
At home, the men, in many a sylvan realm,
90   Their rank tobacco, charm of sauntering minds,
From clayey tubes inhale; or, vacant, beat
For prey the forest; or, in war's dread ranks,
Their country's foes affront: while, in the field,
Their wives plant rice, or yams, or lofty maize,
95   Fell hunger to repel. Be these thy choice:
They, hardy, with the labours of the Cane
Soon grow familiar; while unusual toil,
And new severities their husbands kill.
The slaves from Minnah are of stubborn breed:
100  But, when the bill, or hammer, they affect;
They soon perfection reach. But fly, with care,
The Moco-nation; they themselves destroy.
Worms lurk in all: yet, pronest they to worms,
Who from Mundingo sail. When therefore such
105  Thou buy'st, for sturdy and laborious they,
Straight let some learned leach strong medicines give,
Till food and climate both familiar grow.
Thus, tho' from rise to set, in Phœbus' eye,
They toil, unceasing; yet, at night, they'll sleep,
110  Lap'd in Elysium; and, each day, at dawn,

Spring from their couch, as blythsome as the sun.
One precept more, it much imports to know.—
The Blacks, who drink the Quanza's lucid stream,
Fed by ten thousand springs, are prone to bloat,
115 Whether at home or in these ocean-isles:
And tho' nice art the water may subdue,
Yet many die; and few, for many a year,
Just strength attain to labour for their lord.
Would'st thou secure thine Ethiop from those ails,
120 Which change of climate, change of waters breed,
And food unusual? let Machaon draw
From each some blood, as age and sex require;
And well with vervain, well with sempre-vive,
Unload their bowels. —These, in every hedge,
125 Spontaneous grow. —Nor will it not conduce
To give what chemists, in mysterious phrase,
Term the white eagle; deadly foe to worms.
But chief do thou, my friend, with hearty food,
Yet easy of digestion, likest that
130 Which they at home regal'd on; renovate
Their sea-worn appetites. Let gentle work,
Or rather playful exercise, amuse
The novel gang: and far be angry words;
Far ponderous chains; and far disheartning blows. —
135 From fruits restrain their eagerness; yet if
The acajou, haply, in thy garden bloom,
With cherries, or of white or purple hue,
Thrice wholesome fruit in this relaxing clime!
Safely thou may'st their appetite indulge.
140 Their arid skins will plump, their features shine:
No rheums, no dysenteric ails torment:
The thirsty hydrops flies. — 'Tis even averr'd,
(Ah, did experience sanctify the fact;
How many Lybians now would dig the soil,
145 Who pine in hourly agonies away!)
This pleasing fruit, if turtle join its aid,
Removes that worst of ails, disgrace of art,
The loathsome leprosy's infectious bane.
There are, the muse hath oft abhorrent seen,
150 Who swallow dirt; (so the chlorotic fair

   Oft chalk prefer to the most poignant cates:)
   Such, dropsy bloats, and to sure death consigns;
   Unless restrain'd from this unwholesome food,
   By soothing words, by menaces, by blows:
155 Nor yet will threats, or blows, or soothing words,
   Perfect their cure; unless thou, Pæan, deign'st
   By medicine's power their cravings to subdue.
    To easy labour first inure thy slaves;
   Extremes are dangerous. With industrious search,
160 Let them fit grassy provender collect
   For thy keen stomach'd herds. —But when the earth
   Hath made her annual progress round the sun,
   What time the conch or bell resounds, they may
   All to the Cane-ground, with thy gang, repair.
165  Nor, Negroe, at thy destiny repine,
   Tho' doom'd to toil from dawn to setting sun.
   How far more pleasant is thy rural task,
   Than theirs who sweat, sequester'd from the day,
   In dark tartarean caves, sunk far beneath
170 The earth's dark surface; where sulphureous flames,
   Oft from their vapoury prisons bursting wild,
   To dire explosion give the cavern'd deep,
   And in dread ruin all its inmates whelm? —
   Nor fateful only is the bursting flame;
175 The exhalations of the deep-dug mine,
   Tho' slow, shake from their wings as sure a death.
   With what intense severity of pain
   Hath the afflicted muse, in Scotia seen
   The miners rack'd, who toil for fatal lead?
180 What cramps, what palsies shake their feeble limbs,
   Who on the margin of the rocky Drave,
   Trace silver's fluent ore? Yet white men these!
    How far more happy ye, than those poor slaves,
   Who, whilom, under native, gracious chiefs,
185 Incas and emperors, long time enjoy'd
   Mild government, with every sweet of life,
   In blissful climates? See them dragg'd in chains,
   By proud insulting tyrants, to the mines
   Which once they call'd their own, and then despis'd!
190 See, in the mineral bosom of their land,

How hard they toil! how soon their youthful limbs
Feel the decrepitude of age! how soon
Their teeth desert their sockets! and how soon
Shaking paralysis unstrings their frame!
195 Yet scarce, even then, are they allow'd to view
The glorious God of day, of whom they beg,
With earnest hourly supplications, death;
Yet death slow comes, to torture them the more!
    With these compar'd, ye sons of Afric, say,
200 How far more happy is your lot? Bland health,
Of ardent eye, and limb robust, attends
Your custom'd labour; and, should sickness seize,
With what solicitude are ye not nurs'd! —
Ye Negroes, then, your pleasing task pursue;
205 And, by your toil, deserve your master's care.
    When first your Blacks are novel to the hoe;
Study their humours: Some, soft-soothing words;
Some, presents; and some, menaces subdue;
And some I've known, so stubborn is their kind,
210 Whom blows, alas! could win alone to toil.
    Yet, planter, let humanity prevail. —
Perhaps thy Negroe, in his native land,
Possest large fertile plains, and slaves, and herds:
Perhaps, whene'er he deign'd to walk abroad,
215 The richest silks, from where the Indus rolls,
His limbs invested in their gorgeous pleats:
Perhaps he wails his wife, his children, left
To struggle with adversity: Perhaps
Fortune, in battle for his country fought,
220 Gave him a captive to his deadliest foe:
Perhaps, incautious, in his native fields,
(On pleasurable scenes his mind intent)
All as he wandered; from the neighbouring grove,
Fell ambush dragg'd him to the hated main. —
225 Were they even sold for crimes; ye polish'd, say!
Ye, to whom Learning opes her amplest page!
Ye, whom the knowledge of a living God
Should lead to virtue! Are ye free from crimes?
Ah pity, then, these uninstructed swains;
230 And still let mercy soften the decrees

Of rigid justice, with her lenient hand.
  Oh, did the tender muse possess the power,
Which monarchs have, and monarchs oft abuse:
'Twould be the fond ambition of her soul,
235 To quell tyrannic sway; knock off the chains
Of heart-debasing slavery; give to man,
Of every colour and of every clime,
Freedom, which stamps him image of his God.
Then laws, Oppression's scourge, fair Virtue's prop,
240 Offspring of Wisdom! should impartial reign,
To knit the whole in well-accorded strife:
Servants, not slaves; of choice, and not compell'd;
The Blacks should cultivate the Cane-land isles.
  Say, shall the muse the various ills recount,
245 Which Negroe-nations feel? Shall she describe
The worm that subtly winds into their flesh,
All as they bathe them in their native streams?
There, with fell increment, it soon attains
A direful length of harm. Yet, if due skill,
250 And proper circumspection are employed,
It may be won its volumes to wind round
A leaden cylinder: But, O, beware,
No rashness practise; else 'twill surly snap,
And suddenly, retreating, dire produce
255 An annual lameness to the tortured Moor.
  Nor only is the dragon worm to dread:
Fell, winged insects, which the visual ray
Scarcely discerns, their sable feet and hands
Oft penetrate; and, in the fleshy nest,
260 Myriads of young produce; which soon destroy
The parts they breed in; if assiduous care,
With art, extract not the prolific foe.
  Or, shall she sing, and not debase her lay,
The pest peculiar to the Æthiop-kind,
265 The yaw's infectious bane? —The infected far
In huts, to leeward, lodge; or near the main.
With heartning food, with turtle, and conchs;
The flowers of sulphur, and hard niccars burnt,
The lurking evil from the blood expel,
270 And throw it on the surface: There in spots

## The Sugar Cane, Book IV

     Which cause no pain, and scanty ichor yield,
     It chiefly breaks about the arms and hips,
     A virulent contagion! — When no more
     Round knobby spots deform, but the disease
275  Seems at a pause: then let the learned leach
     Give, in due dose, live-silver from the mine;
     Till copious spitting the whole taint exhaust. —
     Nor thou repine, tho' half-way round the sun,
     This globe, her annual progress shall absolve;
280  Ere, clear'd, thy slave from all infection shine.
     Nor then be confident; successive crops
     Of defœdations oft will spot the skin:
     These thou, with turpentine and guaiac pods,
     Reduc'd by coction to a wholesome draught,
285  Total remove, and give the blood its balm.
        Say, as this malady but once infests
     The sons of Guinea, might not skill ingraft
     (Thus, the small-pox are happily convey'd;)
     This ailment early to thy Negroe-train?
290    Yet, of the ills which torture Libya's sons,
     Worms tyrannize the worst. They, Proteus-like,
     Each symptom of each malady assume;
     And, under every mask, the assassins kill.
     Now, in the guise of horrid spasms, they writhe
295  The tortured body, and all sense o'er-power.
     Sometimes, like Mania, with her head downcast,
     They cause the wretch in solitude to pine;
     Or frantic, bursting from the strongest chains,
     To frown with look terrific, not his own.
300  Sometimes like Ague, with a shivering mien,
     The teeth gnash fearful, and the blood runs chill:
     Anon the ferment maddens in the veins,
     And a false vigour animates the frame.
     Again, the dropsy's bloated mask they steal;
305  Or, "melt with minings of the hectic fire."
        Say, to such various mimic forms of death;
     What remedies shall puzzled art oppose?—
     Thanks to the Almighty, in each path-way hedge,
     Rank cow-itch grows, whose sharp unnumber'd stings,
310  Sheath'd in Melasses, from their dens expell,

Fell dens of death, the reptile lurking foe.—
A powerful vermifuge, in skilful hands,
The worm-grass proves; yet, even in hands of skill,
Sudden, I've known it dim the visual ray
315 For a whole day and night. There are who use
(And sage Experience justifies the use)
The mineral product of the Cornish mine;
Which in old times, ere Britain laws enjoyed,
The polish'd Tyrians, monarchs of the main,
320 In their swift ships convey'd to foreign realms:
The sun by day, by night the northern star,
Their course conducted. —Mighty commerce, hail!
By thee the sons of Attic's sterile land,
A scanty number, laws impos'd on Greece:
325 Nor aw'd they Greece alone; vast Asia's King,
Tho' girt by rich arm'd myriads, at their frown
Felt his heart wither on his farthest throne.
Perennial source of population thou!
While scanty peasants plough the flowery plains
330 Of purple Enna; from the Belgian fens,
What swarms of useful citizens spring up,
Hatch'd by thy fostering wing. Ah where is flown
The dauntless free-born spirit, which of old,
Taught them to shake off the tyrannic yoke
335 Of Spains insulting King; on whose wide realms
The sun still shone with undiminished beam?
Parent of wealth! in vain, coy nature hoards
Her gold and diamonds; toil, thy firm compeer,
And industry of unremitting nerve,
340 Scale the cleft mountain, the loud torrent brave,
Plunge to the center, and thro' Nature's wiles,
(Led on by skill of penetrative soul)
Her following close, her secret treasures find,
To pour them plenteous on the laughing world.
345 On thee Sylvanus, thee each rural god,
On thee chief Ceres, with unfailing love
And fond distinction, emulously gaze.
In vain hath nature pour'd vast seas between
Far-distant kingdoms; endless storms in vain
350 With double night brood o'er them; thou dost throw

O'er far-divided nature's realms, a chain
To bind in sweet society mankind.
By thee white Albion, once a barbarous clime,
Grew fam'd for arms, for wisdom, and for laws;
355   By thee she holds the balance of the world,
Acknowledg'd now sole empress of the main.
Coy though thou art, and mutable of love,
There may'st thou ever fix thy wandering steps;
While Eurus rules the wide atlantic foam!
360   By thee, thy favourite, great Columbus found
That world, where now thy praises I rehearse
To the resounding main and palmy shore;
And Lusitania's chiefs those realms explor'd,
Whence negroes spring, the subject of my song.
365      Nor pine the Blacks, alone, with real ills,
That baffle oft the wisest rules of art:
They likewise feel imaginary woes;
Woes no less deadly. Luckless he who owns
The slave, who thinks himself bewitch'd; and whom,
370   In wrath, a conjurer's snake-mark'd staff hath struck!
They mope, love silence, every friend avoid;
They inly pine; all aliment reject;
Or insufficient for nutrition take:
Their features droop; a sickly yellowish hue
375   Their skin deforms; their strength and beauty fly.
Then comes the feverish fiend, with firy eyes,
Whom drowth, convulsions, and whom death surround,
Fatal attendants! if some subtle slave
(Such, Obia-men are stil'd) do not engage,
380   To save the wretch by antidote or spell.
   In magic spells, in Obia, all the sons
Of sable Africk trust:— Ye, sacred nine!
(For ye each hidden preparation know)
Transpierce the gloom, which ignorance and fraud
385   Have render'd awful; tell the laughing world
Of what these wonder-working charms are made.
   Fern root cut small, and tied with many a knot;
Old teeth extracted from a white man's skull;
A lizard's skeleton; a serpent's head:
390   These mix'd with salt, and water from the spring,

  Are in a phial pour'd; o'er these the leach
Mutters strange jargon, and wild circles forms.
  Of this possest, each negroe deems himself
Secure from poison; for to poison they
395 Are infamously prone: and arm'd with this,
Their sable country dæmons they defy,
Who fearful haunt them at the midnight hour,
To work them mischief. This, diseases fly;
Diseases follow: such its wondrous power!
400 This o'er the threshold of their cottage hung,
No thieves break in; or, if they dare to steal,
Their feet in blotches, which admit no cure,
Burst loathsome out: but should its owner filch,
As slaves were ever of the pilfering kind,
405 This from detection screens; — so conjurers swear.
  'Till morning dawn, and Lucifer withdraw
His beamy chariot; let not the loud bell
Call forth thy negroes from their rushy couch:
And ere the sun with mid-day fervour glow,
410 When every broom-bush opes her yellow flower;
Let thy black labourers from their toil desist:
Nor till the broom her every petal lock,
Let the loud bell recall them to the hoe.
But when the jalap her bright tint displays,
415 When the solanum fills her cup with dew,
And crickets, snakes and lizards 'gin their coil;
Let them find shelter in their cane-thatch'd huts:
Or, if constrain'd unusual hours to toil,
(For even the best must sometimes urge their gang)
420 With double nutriment reward their pains.
  Howe'er insensate some may deem their slaves,
Nor 'bove the bestial rank; far other thoughts
The muse, soft daughter of humanity!
Will ever entertain.— The Ethiop knows,
425 The Ethiop feels, when treated like a man;
Nor grudges, should necessity compell,
By day, by night, to labour for his lord.
  Not less inhuman, than unthrifty those;
Who, half the year's rotation round the sun,
430 Deny subsistence to their labouring slaves.

## The Sugar Cane, Book IV 157

But would'st thou see thy negroe-train encrease,
Free from disorders; and thine acres clad
With groves of sugar: every week dispense
Or English beans, or Carolinian rice;
435 Iërne's beef, or Pensilvanian flour;
Newfoundland cod, or herrings from the main
That howls tempestuous round the Scotian isles!
Yet some there are so lazily inclin'd,
And so neglectful of their food, that thou,
440 Would'st thou preserve them from the jaws of death;
Daily, their wholesome viands must prepare:
With these let all the young, and childless old,
And all the morbid share; — so heaven will bless,
With manifold encrease, thy costly care.
445    Suffice not this; to every slave assign
Some mountain-ground: or, if waste broken land
To thee belong, that broken land divide.
This let them cultivate, one day, each week;
And there raise yams, and there cassada's root:
450 From a good dæmon's staff cassada sprang,
Tradition says, and Caribbees believe;
Which into three the white-rob'd genius broke,
And bade them plant, their hunger to repel.
There let angola's bloomy bush supply,
455 For many a year, with wholesome pulse their board.
There let the bonavist, his fringed pods
Throw liberal o'er the prop; while ochra bears
Aloft his slimy pulp, and help disdains.
There let potatos mantle o'er the ground;
460 Sweet as the cane-juice is the root they bear.
There too let eddas spring in order meet,
With Indian cale and foodful calaloo:
While mint, thyme, balm, and Europe's coyer herbs,
Shoot gladsome forth, nor reprobate the clime.
465    This tract secure, with hedges or of limes,
Or bushy citrons, or the shapely tree
That glows at once with aromatic blooms,
And golden fruit mature. To these be join'd,
In comely neighbourhood, the cotton shrub;
470 In this delicious clime the cotton bursts

On rocky soils. — The coffee also plant;
White as the skin of Albion's lovely fair,
Are the thick snowy fragrant blooms it boasts:
Nor wilt thou, cocô, thy rich pods refuse;
475 Tho' years, and heat, and moisture they require,
Ere the stone grind them to the food of health.
Of thee, perhaps, and of thy various sorts,
And that kind sheltering tree, thy mother nam'd,
With crimson flowerets prodigally grac'd;
480 In future times, the enraptur'd muse may sing:
If public favour crown her present lay.
But let some antient, faithful slave erect
His sheltered mansion near; and with his dog,
His loaded gun, and cutlass, guard the whole:
485 Else negro-fugitives, who skulk 'mid rocks
And shrubby wilds, in bands will soon destroy
Thy labourer's honest wealth; their loss and yours.
Perhaps, of Indian gardens I could sing,
Beyond what bloom'd on blest Phæacia's isle,
490 Or eastern climes admir'd in days of yore:
How Europe's foodful, culinary plants;
How gay Pomona's ruby-tinctured births;
And gawdy Flora's various-vested train;
Might be instructed to unlearn their clime,
495 And by due discipline adopt the sun.
The muse might tell what culture will entice
The ripened melon, to perfume each month;
And with the anana load the fragrant board.
The muse might tell, what trees will best exclude
500 ("Insuperable height of airiest shade")
With their vast umbrage the noon's fervent ray.
Thee, verdant mammey, first, her song should praise:
Thee, the first natives of these Ocean-isles,
Fell anthropophagi, still sacred held;
505 And from thy large high-flavour'd fruit abstain'd,
With pious awe; for thine high-flavoured fruit,
The airy phantoms of their friends deceas'd
Joy'd to regale on. —— Such their simple creed.
The tamarind likewise should adorn her theme,
510 With whose tart fruit the sweltering fever loves

*The Sugar Cane, Book IV* 159

      To quench his thirst, whose breezy umbrage soon
Shades the pleas'd planter, shades his children long.
Nor, lofty cassia, should she not recount
Thy woodland honours! See, what yellow flowers
515  Dance in the gale, and scent the ambient air;
While thy long pods, full-fraught with nectar'd sweets,
Relieve the bowels from their lagging load.
Nor chirimoia, though these torrid isles
Boast not thy fruit, to which the anana yields
520  In taste and flavour, wilt thou coy refuse
Thy fragrant shade to beautify the scene.
But, chief of palms, and pride of Indian-groves,
Thee, fair palmeto, should her song resound:
What swelling columns, form'd by Jones or Wren,
525  Or great Palladio, may with thee compare?
Not nice-proportion'd, but of size immense,
Swells the wild fig-tree, and should claim her lay:
For, from its numerous bearded twigs proceed
A filial train, stupendous as their sire,
530  In quick succession; and, o'er many a rood,
Extend their uncouth limbs; which not the bolt
Of heaven can scathe; nor yet the all-wasting rage
Of Typhon, or of hurricane, destroy.
Nor should, tho' small, the anata not be sung:
535  Thy purple dye, the silk and cotton fleece
Delighted drink; thy purple dye the tribes
Of Northern-Ind, a fierce and wily race,
Carouse, assembled; and with it they paint
Their manly make in many a horrid form,
540  To add new terrors to the face of war.
The muse might teach to twine the verdant arch,
And the cool alcove's lofty roof adorn,
With ponderous granadillas, and the fruit
Call'd water-lemon; grateful to the taste:
545  Nor should she not pursue the mountain-streams,
But pleas'd decoy them from their shady haunts,
In rills, to visit every tree and herb;
Or fall o'er fern-clad cliffs, with foaming rage;
Or in huge basons float, a fair expanse;
550  Or, bound in chains of artificial force,

Arise thro' sculptured stone, or breathing brass. —
But I'm in haste to furl my wind-worn sails,
And anchor my tir'd vessel on the shore.
It much imports to build thy Negroe-huts,
555 Or on the sounding margin of the main,
Or on some dry hill's gently-sloping sides,
In streets, at distance due. —— When near the beach,
Let frequent coco cast its wavy shade;
'Tis Neptune's tree; and, nourish'd by the spray,
560 Soon round the bending stem's aerial height,
Clusters of mighty nuts, with milk and fruit
Delicious fraught, hang clattering in the sky.
There let the bay-grape, too, its crooked limbs
Project enormous; of impurpled hue
565 Its frequent clusters glow. And there, if thou
Would'st make the sand yield salutary food,
Let Indian millet rear its corny reed,
Like arm'd battalions in array of war.
But, round the upland huts, bananas plant;
570 A wholesome nutriment bananas yield,
And sun-burnt labour loves its breezy shade.
Their graceful screen let kindred plantanes join,
And with their broad vans shiver in the breeze;
So flames design'd, or by imprudence caught,
575 Shall spread no ruin to the neighbouring roof.
 Yet not the sounding margin of the main,
Nor gently sloping side of breezy hill,
Nor streets, at distance due, imbower'd in trees;
Will half the health, or half the pleasure yield,
580 Unless some pitying naiad deign to lave,
With an unceasing stream, thy thirsty bounds.
 On festal days; or when their work is done;
Permit thy slaves to lead the choral dance,
To the wild banshaw's melancholy sound.
585 Responsive to the sound, head feet and frame
Move aukwardly harmonious; hand in hand
Now lock'd, the gay troop circularly wheels,
And frisks and capers with intemperate joy.
Halts the vast circle, all clap hands and sing;
590 While those distinguish'd for their heels and air,

Bound in the center, and fantastic twine.
Meanwhile some stripling, from the choral ring,
Trips forth; and not, ungallantly, bestows
On her who nimblest hath the greensward beat,
595 And whose flush'd beauties have inthrall'd his soul,
A silver token of his fond applause.
Anon they form in ranks; nor inexpert
A thousand tuneful intricacies weave,
Shaking their sable limbs; and oft a kiss
600 Steal from their partners; who, with neck reclin'd,
And semblant scorn, resent the ravish'd bliss.
But let not thou the drum their mirth inspire;
Nor vinous spirits: else, to madness fir'd,
(What will not bacchanalian frenzy dare?)
605 Fell acts of blood, and vengeance they pursue.
 Compel by threats, or win by soothing arts,
Thy slaves to wed their fellow slaves at home;
So shall they not their vigorous prime destroy,
By distant journeys, at untimely hours,
610 When muffled midnight decks her raven-hair
With the white plumage of the prickly vine.
 Would'st thou from countless ails preserve thy gang;
To every Negroe, as the candle-weed
Expands his blossoms to the cloudy sky,
615 And moist Aquarius melts in daily showers;
A wooly vestment give, (this Wiltshire weaves)
Warm to repel chill Night's unwholesome dews:
While strong coarse linen, from the Scotian loom,
Wards off the fervours of the burning day.
620  The truly great, tho' from a hostile clime,
The sacred Nine embalm; then, Muses, chant,
In grateful numbers, Gallic Lewis' praise:
For private murder quell'd; for laurel'd arts,
Invented, cherish'd in his native realm;
625 For rapine punish'd; for grim famine fed;
For sly chicane expell'd the wrangling bar;
And rightful Themis seated on her throne:
But, chief, for those mild laws his wisdom fram'd,
To guard the Æthiop from tyrannic sway!
630  Did such, in these green isles which Albion claims,

Did such obtain; the muse, at midnight-hour,
This last brain-racking study had not ply'd:
But, sunk in slumbers of immortal bliss,
To bards had listned on a fancied Thames!
635   All hail, old father Thames! tho' not from far
Thy springing waters roll; nor countless streams,
Of name conspicuous, swell thy watery store;
Tho' thou, no Plata, to the sea devolve
Vast humid offerings; thou art king of streams:
640   Delighted Commerce broods upon thy wave;
And every quarter of this sea-girt globe
To thee due tribute pays; but chief the world
By great Columbus found, where now the muse
Beholds, transported, slow vast fleecy clouds,
645   Alps pil'd on Alps romantically high,
Which charm the sight with many a pleasing form.
The moon, in virgin-glory, gilds the pole,
And tips yon tamarinds, tips yon Cane-crown'd vale,
With fluent silver; while unnumbered stars
650   Gild the vast concave with their lively beams.
The main, a moving burnish'd mirror, shines;
No noise is heard, save when the distant surge
With drouzy murmurings breaks upon the shore! —
Ah me, what thunders roll! the sky's on fire!
655   Now sudden darkness muffles up the pole!
Heavens! what wild scenes, before the affrighted sense,
Imperfect swim! — See! in that flaming scroll,
Which Time unfolds, the future germs bud forth,
Of mighty empires! independent realms! ——
660   And must Britannia, Neptune's favourite queen,
Protect'ress of true science, freedom, arts;
Must she, ah! must she, to her offspring crouch?
Ah, must my Thames, old Ocean's favourite son,
Resign his trident to barbaric streams;
665   His banks neglected, and his waves unsought,
No bards to sing them, and no fleets to grace? ——
Again the fleecy clouds amuse the eye,
And sparkling stars the vast horizon gild —
She shall not crouch; if Wisdom guide the helm,
670   Wisdom that bade loud Fame, with justest praise,

Record her triumphs! bade the lacquaying winds
Transport, to every quarter of the globe,
Her winged navies! bade the scepter'd sons
Of earth acknowledge her pre-eminence! —
675 She shall not crouch; if these Cane ocean-isles,
Isles which on Britain for their all depend,
And must for ever; still indulgent share
Her fostering smile: and other isles be given,
From vanquish'd foes. — And see, another race!
680 A golden æra dazzles my fond sight!
That other race, that long'd-for æra, hail!
THE BRITISH GEORGE NOW REIGNS, THE PATRIOT KING!
BRITAIN SHALL EVER TRIUMPH O'ER THE MAIN.

[The END of BOOK IV.]

# Grainger's Notes to The Sugar-Cane

## [Book I]

VER. 22. *the spiry Cane*,] The botanical name of the Cane is *Saccharum*. The Greeks and Romans seem to have known very little of this most useful and beautiful plant. Lucan and Pliny are the only Authors among the latter who mention it; and, so far as I can find, Arrian is the only Greek. The first of these Writers, in enumerating Pompey's Eastern auxiliaries, describes a nation who made use of the Cane-juice as a drink:

*Dulces bibebant ex arundine succos.*

The industrious Naturalist says, *Saccharum et Arabia fert, sed laudatius India*; and the Greek Historian, in his περιπλους of the Red-sea, tells us of a neighbouring nation who drank it also; his words are, μελι το καλαμινον το λεγομενον σακχαρι. The Cane, however, as it was a native of the East, so has it been probably cultivated there time immemorial. The raw juice was doubtless first made use of; they afterwards boiled it into a syrup; and, in process of time, an inebriating spirit was prepared therefrom by fermentation. This conjecture is confirmed by the etymology, for the Arabic word סכר is evidently derived from the Hebrew שכר, which signifies an *intoxicating liquor*. When the Indians began to make the Cane-juice into sugar, I cannot discover; probably, it soon found its way into Europe in that form, first by the Red-sea, and afterwards through Persia, by the Black-sea and Caspian; but the plant itself was not known to Europe, till the Arabians introduced it into the southern parts of Spain, Sicily, and those provinces of France which border on the Pyrenean mountains. It was also successfully cultivated in Egypt, and in many places on the Barbary-coast. From the Mediterranean, the Spaniards and Portuguese transported the Cane to the Azores, the Madeiras, the Canary and the Cape-Verd islands, soon after they had been discovered in the fifteenth century: and, in most of these, particularly Madeira, it throve exceedingly. Whether the Cane is a native of either the Great or Less Antilles cannot now be determined, for their discoverers were so wholly employed in searching after imaginary gold-mines, that they took little or no notice of the natural productions. Indeed the wars, wherein they wantonly engaged themselves with the natives, was another hindrance to physical investigation. But whether the Cane was a production of the West-Indies or not, it is probable, the Spaniards and Portuguese did not begin to cultivate it either there on in South America (where it certainly was found), till some years after their discovery. It is also equally uncertain whether Sugar was first made in the Islands or on the Continent, and whether the Spaniards or Portuguese were the first planters in the new world: it is indeed most likely that the latter erected the first sugar-works in Brazil, as they are more lively and enterprizing than the Spaniards. However they had not long the start of the latter; for, in 1506, Ferdinand the Catholic ordered the Cane to be carried from the Canaries to St. Domingo, in which island one Pedro de Atenca soon after built an *Ingenio de açucar*, for so the Spaniards call a Sugar-work. But, though they began thus early to turn their thoughts to sugar, the Portuguese far outstripped them in that trade; for Lisbon soon supplied most of Europe with that commodity; and, notwithstanding the English then paid the Portuguese at the rate of 4 *l. per C.* wt. for muscovado, yet that price, great as it may now appear, was probably much less than what the Sugar from the East-Indies had commonly been sold for. Indeed, so intent was the Crown of Portugal on extending their Brazil-trade, that that of the East-Indies began to be neglected, and soon after suffered a manifest decay. However, their sugar made them ample amends, in which trade they continued almost without a rival for upwards of a century. At last the Dutch, in 1623, drove the Portuguese out of all the northern part of Brazil; and, during the one and twenty years they kept that conquest, those industrious republicans learned the art of making sugar. This probably inspired the English with a desire of coming in for a share of the sugar-trade; accordingly they, renouncing their chimerical search after gold mines in Florida and Guiana, settled themselves soon after at the mouth of the river Surinam, where they cultivated the Cane with such success, that when the colony was ceded to the Dutch by the treaty of Breda, it maintained not less than 40,000 Whites, half that number of slaves, and employed one year with another 15,000 ton of shipping. This cession was a severe blow to the English-trade, which it did not recover for several years, though many of the Surinam Planters carried their art and Negroes to the Leeward Islands and Jamaica, which then began to be the object of political consideration in England.

Sugar is twice mentioned by Chaucer, who flourished in the fourteenth century; and succeeding poets, down to the middle of the last, use the epithet *Sugar'd*, whenever they would express any thing uncommonly pleasing: since that time, the more elegant writers seldom admit of that adjective in a metaphorical sense; but herein perhaps they are affectedly squeamish.

VER. 29. *Muscovado,*] The Cane-juice being brought to the consistence of syrup, and, by subsequent coction, granulated, is then called *muscovado* (a Spanish word probably, though not to be found in Pineda) vulgarly brown Sugar; the French term it *sucre brut*.

VER. 34. *wild red Cedar*] There are two species of Cedar commonly to be met with in the West-Indies, the white and red, which differ from the cedars cultivated in the Bermudas: both are lofty, shady, and of quick growth. The white succeeds in any soil, and produces a flower which, infused like tea, is useful against fish poison. The red requires a better mould, and always emits a disagreeable smell before rain. The wood of both are highly useful for many mechanical purposes, and but too little planted.

VER. 34. *Locust*] This is also a lofty tree. It is of quick growth and handsome, and produces a not disagreeable fruit in a flat pod or legumen, about three inches long. It is a serviceable wood. In botanical books, I find three different names for the locust-tree; that meant here is the *Siliqua edulis*.

VER. 36. *or vast ceiba save.*] Canoes have been scooped out of this tree, capable of holding upwards of a hundred people; and many hundreds, as authors relate, have been at once sheltered by its shade. Its pods contain a very soft short cotton, like silk: hence the English call the tree the Silk-cotton-tree; and the Spaniards name its cotton *Lana de ceiba*. It has been wrought into stockings; but its commonest use is to stuff pillows and mattrasses. It might be made an article of commerce, as the tree grows without trouble, and is yearly covered with pods. An infusion of the leaves is a gentle diaphoretic, and much recommended in the small-pox. The botanical name of the ceiba is *Bombax*; and the French call it *Fromager*.

There are two species; the stem of the one being prickly, and that of the other smooth.

VER. 37. *Yet spare the guava,*] The Spaniards call this tree *guayava*. It bears a fruit as large, and of much the same shape as a golden pippen. This is of three species, the yellow, the amazon, and the white; the last is the most delicate, but the second sort the largest: All are equally wholesome, when stewed or made into jelly, or marmalade. When raw, they are supposed to generate worms. Strangers do not always at first like their flavour, which is peculiarly strong. This, however, goes off by use, and they become exceedingly agreeable. Acosta says the Peruvian guavas surpass those of any other part of America. The bark of the tree is an astringent, and tanns leather as well as that of oak. The French call the tree *Goyavier*.

VER. 37. – *yet the guaiac spare*;] The lignum-vitæ, or pockwood-tree. The virtues of every part of this truly medical tree are too well known to be enumerated here. The hardness and incorruptibility of its timber make abundant amends for the great slowness of its growth, for of it are formed the best posts for houses against hurricanes, and it is no less usefully employed in building wind-mills and cattle-mills.

VER. 44. *The golden shaddoc,*] This is the largest and finest kind of orange. It is not a native of America, but was brought to the islands, from the East-Indies, by an Englishman, whose name it bears. It is of three kinds, the sweet, the sour, and the bitter; the juice of all of them is wholesome, and the rind medical. In flavour and wholesomeness, the sweet shaddoc excels the other two, and indeed every other kind of orange, except the forbidden fruit, which scarce yields to any known fruit in the four quarters of the world.

VER. 45. *sabbaca:*] This is the Indian name of the avocato, avocado, avigato, or, as the English corruptly call it, alligator-pear. The Spaniards in South-America name it *aguacate*, and under that name it is described by Ulloa. However, in Peru and Mexico, it is better known by the appellation of *palta* or *palto*. It is a sightly tree, of two species; the one bearing a green fruit, which is the most delicate, and the other a red, which is less esteemed, and grows chiefly in Mexico. When ripe, the skin peels easily off, and discovers a butyraceous, or rather a marrowy like substance, with greenish veins interspersed. Being eat with salt and pepper, or sugar and lime-juice, it is not only agreeable, but highly nourishing; hence Sir Hans Sloane used to stile it Vegetable marrow. The fruit is of the size and shape of the pear named Lady's-thighs, and contains a large stone, from whence the tree is propagated. These trees bear fruit but once a year. Few strangers care for it; but, by use, soon become fond of it. The juice of the kernel marks linen with a violet-colour. Its wood is soft, and consequently of little use. The French call it *Bois d'anise*, and the tree *Avocat:* the botanical name is *Persea*.

VER. 60. *green St. Christopher*,] This beautiful and fertile island, and which, in Shakespear's words, may justly be stiled

"A precious stone set in the silver sea,"

lies in the seventeenth degree N. L. It was discovered by the great Christopher Columbus, in his second voyage, 1493, who was so pleased with its appearance, that he honoured it with his Christian-name. Though others pretend, that appellation was given it from an imaginary resemblance between a high mountain in its centre, now called Mount Misery, to the fabulous legend of the Devil's carrying St. Christopher on his shoulders. But, be this as it will, the Spaniards soon after settled it, and lived in tolerable harmony with the natives for many years; and, as their fleets commonly called in there to and from America for provision and water, the settlers, no doubt, reaped some advantage from their situation. By Templeman's Survey, it contains eighty square miles, and is about seventy miles in circumference. It is of an irregular oblong figure, and has a chain of mountains, that run South and North almost from the one end of it to the other, formerly covered with wood, but now the Cane-plantations reach almost to their summits, and extend all the way, down their easy declining sides, to the sea. From these mountains some rivers take their rise, which never dry up; and there are many others which, after rain, run into the sea, but which, at other times, are lost before they reach it. Hence, as this island consists of mountain-land and valley, it must always make a midling crop; for when the low grounds fail, the uplands supply that deficiency; and, when the mountain canes are lodged (or become watery from too much rain) those in the plains yield surprisingly. Nor are the plantations here only seasonable, their Sugar sells for more than the Sugar of any other of his Majesty's islands; as their produce cannot be refined to the best advantage, without a mixture of St. Kitts' muscovado. In the barren part of the island, which runs out towards Nevis, are several ponds, which in dry weather crystallize into good salt; and below Mount Misery is a small Solfaterre and collection of fresh water, where fugitive Negroes often take shelter, and escape their pursuers. Not far below is a large plain which affords good pasture, water, and wood; and, if the approaches thereto were fortified, which might be done at a moderate expence, it would be rendered inaccessible. The English, repulsing the few natives and Spaniards, who opposed them, began to plant tobacco here *A. D.* 1623. Two years after, the French landed in St. Christopher on the same day that the English-settlers received a considerable reinforcement from their mother-country; and, the chiefs of both nations, being men of sound policy, entered into an agreement to divide the island between them: the French retaining both extremities, and the English possessing themselves of the middle parts of the island. Some time after both nations erected sugar-works, but there were more tobacco, indigo, coffee, and cotton-plantations, than Sugar ones, as these require a much greater fund to carry them on, than those other. All the planters, however, lived easy in their circumstances; for, though the Spaniards, who could not bear to be spectators of their thriving condition, did repossess themselves of the island, yet they were soon obliged to retire, and the colony succeeded better than ever. One reason for this was, that it had been agreed between the two nations, that they should here remain neutral whatever wars their mother-countries might wage against each other in Europe. This was a wise regulation for an infant settlement; but, when King James abdicated the British throne, the French suddenly rose, and drove out the unprepared English by force of arms. The French colonists of St., Christopher had soon reason, however, to repent their impolitic breach of faith; for the expelled planters, being assisted by their countrymen from the neighbouring isles, and supported by a formidable fleet, soon recovered, not only their lost plantations, but obliged the French totally to abandon the island. After the treaty of Ryswick, indeed, some few of those among them, who had not obtained settlements in Martinico and Hispaniola, returned to St. Christopher: but the war of the partition soon after breaking out, they were finally expelled, and the whole island was ceded in Sovereignty to the crown of Great Britain, by the treaty of Utrecht. Since that time, St. Christopher has gradually improved, and it is

# Grainger's Notes to The Sugar-Cane. Book I 171

now at the height of perfection. The Indian name of St. Christopher is *Liamuiga*, or the Fertile Island.

VER. 71. *yet virgins, far more beautiful*] The inhabitants of St. Christopher look whiter, are less sallow, and enjoy finer complexions, than any of the dwellers on the other islands. *Sloane.*

VER. 111. *and where the magnet*] The declension of the needle was discovered, A. D. 1492, by Columbus, in his first voyage to America; and would have been highly alarming to any, but one of his undaunted and philosophical turn of mind.

This century will always make a distinguished figure in the history of the human mind; for, during that period, printing was invented, Greek-learning took refuge in Italy, the Reformation began, and America was discovered.

The island of Jamaica was bestowed on Columbus, as some compensation for his discovery of the new world; accordingly his son James settled, and planted it, early [*A. D.* 1509] the following century. What improvements the Spaniards made therein is no where mentioned; but, had their industry been equal to their opportunities, their improvements should have been considerable; for they continued in the undisturbed possession of it till the year 1596, when Sir Anthony Shirley, with a single man of war, took and plundered St. Jago de la Vega, which then consisted of 2000 houses. In the year 1635, St. Jago de la Vega was a second time plundered by 500 English from the Leeward islands, tho' that capital, and the fort, (which they also took) were defended by four times their number of Spaniards. One and twenty years afterwards, the whole island was reduced by the forces sent thither by Oliver Cromwell, and has ever since belonged to England. It is by far the largest island possessed by the English in the West Indies. Sir Thomas Modyford, a rich and eminent planter of Barbadoes, removed to Jamaica *A. D.* 1660, to the great advantage of that island, for he instructed the young English settlers to cultivate the Sugar-cane; for which, and other great improvements which he then made them acquainted with, King Charles, three years afterwards, appointed him Governour thereof, in which honourable employment he continued till the year 1669.

VER. 132. *the bearded Fig*] This wonderful tree, by the Indians called the *Banian-tree*, and by the botanists *Ficus Indica*, or *Bengaliensis*, is exactly described by Q. Curtius, and beautifully by Milton in the following lines:

"The Fig-tree, not that kind renown'd for fruit,
"But such as at this day to Indians known,
"In Malabar and Decan spreads her arms;
"Branching so broad and long, that in the ground,
"The bended twigs take root, and daughters grow
"About the mother-tree, a pillar'd shade,
"High over-arch'd, and echoing walks between.
"There oft the Indian herdsman, shunning heat,
"Shelters in cool, and tends his pasturing herds
"At Loop-holes cut through thickest shade."—

What year the Spaniards first discovered Barbadoes is not certainly known; this however is certain, that they never settled there, but only made use of it as a stock-island in their voyages to and from South-America, and the Islands; accordingly we are told, when the English first landed there, which was about the end of the sixteenth or beginning of the seventeenth century, they found in it an excellent breed of wild hogs, but no inhabitants. In the year 1627, Barbadoes, with most of the other Caribbee-islands, were granted by Charles I. to the Earl of Carlisle, that nobleman agreeing to pay to the Earl of Marlborough, and his heirs, a perpetual annuity of 300 *l. per annum*, for his waving his claim to Barbadoes, which he had obtained, by patent, in the preceding reign. The adventurers to whom that nobleman parcelled out this island, at first cultivated tobacco; but, that not turning out to their advantage, they applied, with better success, to cotton, indigo, and ginger. At last, some cavaliers of good fortune transporting themselves thither, and introducing the Sugar-cane [*A. D.* 1647] probably from Brazil, in ten years time the island was peopled with upwards of 30,000 Whites, and twice that number of Negroes, and sent yearly very considerable quantities of sugar to the mother-country. At the Restoration, King Charles II. bought off the claim of the Carlisle-family; and, in consideration of its then becoming a royal instead of a proprietary government, the planters gave the Crown $4\frac{1}{2}$ *per cent.* on their sugars; which duty still continues, although the island is said to be less able to pay it now than it was a hundred years ago. It is upwards of 20 miles long, and in some places almost 14 broad.

VER. 134. *Chief Nevis,*] This island, which does not contain many fewer square miles than St. Christopher, is more rocky, and

## Grainger's Notes to The Sugar-Cane. Book I 173

almost of a circular figure. It is separated from that island by a channel not above one mile and an half over, and lies to windward. Its warm bath possesses all the medical properties of the hot well at Bristol, and its water, being properly bottled, keeps as well at sea, and is no less agreeable to the palate. It was for many years the capital of the Leeward Island government; and, at that period, contained both more Whites and Blacks than it does at present, often mustering 3000 men. The English first settled there A. D. 1628. Sixty-two years afterwards, the chief town was almost wholly destroyed by an earthquake; and, in 1706, the planters were wellnigh ruined by the French, who carried off their slaves contrary to capitulation. It must have been discovered in Columbus's second voyage, A. D. 1493.

VER. 135. *And breezy Mountserrat,*] This island, which lies about 30 miles to the south-west of Antigua, is not less famous for its solfaterre (or volcano), and hot petrifying spring, than for the goodness of its sugars. Being almost circular in its shape, it cannot contain much less land than either Nevis or St. Christopher. It is naturally strong, so that when the French made descents thereon, in K. William and Q. Anne's time, they were always repulsed with considerable loss. It was settled by that great adventurer Sir Thomas Warner, A. D. 1632, who sent thither some of his people from St. Christopher, for that purpose. In the beginning of the reign of Charles II. the French took it, but it was restored, A. D. 1667, by the treaty of Breda. In this island, the Roman-catholics, who behaved well when our enemies attempted to conquer it, have many privileges, and of course are more numerous there, than in any other of the English Caribbee-islands. Its capital is called Plymouth. Columbus discovered it in his second voyage.

VER. 170. *Yet will the arrow,*] That part of the Cane which shoots up into the fructification, is called by the planters its Arrow, having been probably used for that purpose by the Indians. Till the arrow drops, all additional jointing in the Cane is supposed to be stopped.

VER. 179. *And highest temper,*] Shell, or rather marble quicklime, is so called by the planters: Without this, the juice of the Cane cannot be concreted into sugar, at least to advantage. See Book III. With quick-lime the French join ashes as a temper, and this mixture they call *Enyvrage*. It is hoped the Reader will pardon the introduction of the verb *saccharize*, as no other so emphatically expressed the Author's meaning; for some chemists define sugar to be a native salt, and others a soap.

VER. 206. *And Liamuiga,*] The Caribbean name of St. Christopher.

VER. 237. *That yams improve the soil.*] The botanical name of this plant is *Dioscoria*. Its leaves, like those of the water-melon, or gourd, soon mantle over the ground where it is planted. It takes about eight months to come to perfection, and then is a wholesome root, either boiled or roasted. They will sometimes weigh one and an half, or two pounds, but their commonest size is from six ounces to nine. They cannot be kept good above half a year. They are a native of South-America, the West-Indies, and of most parts of Guinea.

VER. 260. *gemmy tops*;] The summit of the Cane being smaller-jointed as well as softer, and consequently having more gems, from whence the young sprouts shoot, is properer for planting than any other part of it. From one to four junks, each about a foot long, are put in every hole. Where too many junks are planted in one hole, the Canes may be numerous, but can neither become vigorous, nor yield such a quantity of rich liquor as they otherwise would. In case the young shoots do not appear above ground in four or five weeks, the deficiencies must be supplied with new tops.

VER. 290. *By Ceres' son,*] Jethro Tull, Esq; the greatest improver in modern husbandry.

VER. 334. *Mosquitos,*] This is a Spanish word, signifying a Gnat, or Fly. They are very troublesome, especially to strangers, whom they bite unmercifully, causing a yellow coloured tumour, attended with excessive itching. Ugly ulcers have often been occasioned by scratching those swellings, in persons of a bad habit of body. Though natives of the West-Indies, they are not less common in the coldest of regions; for Mr. Maupertuis takes notice how troublesome they were to him and his attendants on the snowy summit of certain mountains within the arctic circle. They, however, chiefly love shady, moist, and warm places. Accordingly they are commonest to be met with in the corners of rooms, towards evening, and before rain. They are so light, as not to be felt when they pitch on the skin; and, as soon as they have darted in their proboscis, fly off, so that the first intimation one has of being bit by them, is the itching tumour. Warm lime-juice is its remedy. The Mosquito makes a humming noise, especially in the night-time.

VER. 334. *sand-flies*,] This insect the Spaniards call *Mosquitilla*, being much smaller than the Mosquito. Its bite is like a spark of fire, falling on the skin, which it raises into a small tumour accompanied with itching. But if the sand-fly causes a sharper and more sudden pain than the Mosquito, yet it is a more honourable enemy, for remaining upon the skin after the puncture, it may easily be killed. Its colour is grey and black, striped. Lemon-juice or first runnings cure its bite.

VER. 337. *Cockroaches crawl*] This is a large species of the chafer, or scaribæus, and is a most disagreeable as well as destructive insect. There is scarce any thing which it will not devour, and wherever it has remained for any time, it leaves a nauseous smell behind it. Though better than an inch long, their thickness is no ways correspondent, so that they can insinuate themselves almost through any crevise, *&c.* into cabinets, drawers, *&c.* The smell of cedar is said to frighten them away, but this is a popular mistake, for I have often killed them in presses of that wood. There is a species of Cockroach, which, on account of a beating noise which it makes, especially in the night, is called the Drummer. Though larger, it is neither of so burnished a colour, nor so quick in its motions as the common sort, than which it is also less frequent, and not so pernicious; yet both will nibble peoples toe-ends, especially if not well washed, and have sometimes occasioned uneasy sores there. They are natives of a warm climate. The French call them *Ravets*.

VER. 341. *the speckled lizard*] This is meant of the ground-lizard, and not of the tree-lizard, which is of a fine green colour. There are many kinds of ground-lizards, which, as they are common in the hot parts of Europe, I shall not describe. All of them are perfectly innocent. The Caribbeans used to eat them; they are not inferiour to snakes as a medicated food. Snuff forced into their mouth soon convulses them. They change colour, and become torpid; but, in a few hours, recover. The guana, or rather Iguana, is the largest sort of lizard. This, when irritated, will fly at one. It lives mostly upon fruit. It has a saw-like appearance, which ranges from its head all along its back, to its tail. The flesh of it is esteemed a great delicacy. The first writers on the *Lues Venerea*, forbid its use, to those who labour under that disease. It is a very ugly animal. In some parts of South-America, the alligator is called *Iguana*.

VER. 342. *And black crabs*] Black land-crabs are excellent eating; but as they sometimes will occasion a most violent *cholera morbus*, (owing, say planters, to their feeding on the mahoe-berry) they should never be dressed till they have fed for some weeks in a crab-house, after being caught by the Negroes. When they moult, they are most delicate; and then, it is believed, never poison. This however, is certain, that at that time they have no gall, but, in its stead, the petrifaction called a Crabs-eye is found. As I have frequently observed their great claws (with which they severely bite the unwary) of very unequal sizes, it is probable, these regenerate when broke off by accident, or otherwise.

VER. 393. *Whose brow the fern-tree*] This only grows in mountainous situations. Its stem shoots up to a considerable height, but it does not divide into branches, till near the summit, where it shoots out horizontally, like an umbrella, into leaves, which resemble those of the common fern. I know of no medical uses, whereto this singularly beautiful tree has been applied, and indeed its wood, being spungy, is seldom used to oeconomical purposes. It, however, serves well enough for building mountain-huts, and temporary fences for cattle.

VER. 418. *the mail'd anana*] This is the pine-apple, and needs no description; the cherimoya, a South-American fruit, is by all, who have tasted both, allowed to surpass the pine, and is even said to be more wholesome. The botanical name of the pine-apple is *bromelia*. Of the wild pine-apple, or ananas bravo, hedges are made in South-America. It produces an inferior sort of fruit.

VER. 482. *if seasons glad the soil.*] Long-continued and violent rains are called *Seasons* in the West-Indies.

VER. 500. *Now children of this clime:*] It is supposed that oranges, lemons, and limes were introduced into America by the Spaniards; but I am more inclined to believe they are natural to the climate. The Spaniards themselves probably had the two first from the Saracens, for the Spanish noun *Naranja*, whence the English word *Orange*, is plainly Arabic.

VER. 503. *the logwood-hedge.*] Linnæus's name for this useful tree is *Hæmotoxylon*, but it is better known to physicians by that of *Lignum campechense*. Its virtues, as a medicine, and properties as an ingredient in dying, need not to be enumerated in this place. It makes a no less strong than beautiful hedge in the West-Indies, where it rises to a considerable height.

VER. 508. *Nor shall the ricinus*] This shrub is commonly called the physic-nut. It is generally divided into three kinds, the com-

## Grainger's Notes to The Sugar-Cane. Book I 177

mon, the French, and the Spanish, which differ from each other in their leaves and flowers, if not in their fruit or seeds. The plant from which the castor-oil is extracted is also called *Ricinus*, though it has no resemblance to any of the former, in leaves, flowers, or seeds. In one particular they all agree, *viz.* in their yielding to coction or expression a purgative or emetic oil. The Spaniards name these nuts *Avellanas purgativas*; hence Ray terms them *Avellanæ purgatrices novi orbis*. By roasting they are supposed to lose part of their virulency, which is wholly destroyed, say some people, by taking out a leaf-like substance that is to be found between the lobes. The nut exceeds a walnut, or even an almond, in sweetness, and yet three or four of them will operate briskly both up and down. The French call this useful shrub *Medecinier*. That species of it which bears red coral-like flowers is named *Bellyach* by the Barbadians; and its ripe seeds are supposed to be specific against melancholy.

VER. 510. *the acassee,*] *Acacia*. This is a species of thorn; the juice of the root is supposed to be poisonous. Its seeds are contained in a pod or ligumen. It is of the class of the syngenesia. No astringent juice is extracted from it. Its trivial name is *Cashaw*. Tournefort describes it in his voyage to the Levant. Some call it the Holy Thorn, and others Sweet Brier. The half-ripe pod affords a strong cement; and the main stem, being wounded, produces a transparent gum, like the Arabic, to which this tree bears a strong resemblance.

VER. 515. *the privet*] *Ligustrum*. This shrub is sufficiently known. Its leaves and flowers make a good gargle in the aphthæ, and ulcered throat.

VER. 520. *carnation fair.*] This is indeed a most beautiful flowering shrub. It is a native of the West-Indies, and called, from a French governor, named Depoinci, *Poinciana*. If permitted, it will grow twenty feet high; but in order to make it a good fence, it should be kept low. It is always in blossom. Tho' not purgative, it is of the senna kind. Its leaves and flowers are stomachic, carminative, and emmenagogue. Some authors name it *Cauda pavonis*, on account of its inimitable beauty; the flowers have a physicky smell. How it came to be called *Doodle-doo* I know not; the Barbadians more properly term it *Flower Fence*. This plant grows also in Guinea.

VER. 526. *seen the humming bird,*] The humming bird is called *Picaflore* by the Spaniards, on account of its hovering over flowers, and sucking their juices, without lacerating, or even so much as discomposing their petals. Its Indian name, says Ulloa, is *Guinde*, though it is also known by the appellation of *Rabilargo* and *Lizongero*. By the Caribbeans it was called *Collobree*. It is common in all the warm parts of America. There are various species of them, all exceeding small, beautiful and bold. The crested one, though not so frequent, is yet more beautiful than the others. It is chiefly to be found in the woody parts of the mountains. Edwards has described a very beautiful humming bird, with a long tail, which is a native of Surinam, but which I never saw in these islands. They are easily caught in rainy weather.

VER. 536. *prickly pear;*] The botanical name of this plant is *Opuntia*; it will grow in the barrenest soils, and on the tops of walls, if a small portion of earth be added. There are two sorts of it, one whose fruit is roundish and sweet, the other, which has more the shape of a fig, is sour. The former is sometimes eaten, but the other seldom. The French call them *Pomme de Raquette*. Both fruit and leaves are guarded with sharp prickles, and, even in the interior part of the fruit, there is one which must be removed before it is eaten. The leaves, which are half an inch thick, having a sort of pulp interposed between their surfaces, being deprived of their spines, and softened by the fire, make no bad poultice for inflammations. The juice of the fruit is an innocent fucus, and is often used to tinge guava jellies. The opuntia, upon which the cochineal insect breeds, has no spines, and is cultivated with care in South-America, where it also grows wild. The prickly pear makes a strong fence, and is easily trimmed with a scymitar. It grows naturally in some parts of Spain.

VER. 538. *wild liquorice*] This is a scandent plant, from which the Negroes gather what they call *Jumbee Beeds*. These are about the size of pigeon-peas, almost round, of a red colour, with a black speck on one extremity. They act as an emetic, but, being violent in their operation, great caution should be observed in using them. The leaves make a good pectoral drink in disorders of the breast. By the French it is named *Petit Panacoco*, to distinguish it from a large tree, which bears seeds of the same colours, only much bigger. This tree is a species of black ebony.

VER. 558. *contagious blast.*] So a particular species of blight is called in the West-Indies. See its description in the second book.

VER. 571. *yellow deaths*] The yellow fever, to which Europeans of a sanguine habit of body, and who exceed in drinking or exercise, are liable on their arrival in the West Indies. The French call it *Maladie de Siame*, or more properly, *La Fievre des Matelots*. Those who have lived any time in the islands are no more liable to this disease than the Creoles, whence, however, some physicians have too hastily concluded, that it was of foreign extraction.

VER. 595. *cassada*,] Cassavi, cassava, is called *Jatropha* by botanists. Its meal makes a wholesome and well-tasted bread, although its juice be poisonous. There is a species of cassada which may be eat with safety, without expressing the juice; this the French call *Camagnoc*. The colour of its root is white, like a parsnip; that of the common kind is of a brownish red, before it is scraped. By coction the cassada-juice becomes an excellent sauce for fish; and the Indians prepare many wholesome dishes from it. I have given it internally mixed with flour without any bad consequences; it did not however produce any of the salutary effects I expected. A good starch is made from it. The stem is knotty, and, being cut into small junks and planted, young sprouts shoot up from each knob. Horses have been poisoned by eating its leaves. The French name it *Manihot*, *Magnoc*, and *Manioc*, and the Spaniards *Mandiocha*. It is pretended that all creatures but man eat the raw root of the cassada with impunity; and, when dried, that it is a sovereign antidote against venomous bites. A wholesome drink is prepared from this root by the Indians, Spaniards, and Portuguese, according to Pineda. There is one species of this plant which the Indians only use, and is by them called *Baccacoua*.

VER. 596. *tanies:*] This wholesome root, in some of the islands, is called *Edda:* Its botanical name is *Arum maximum Ægyptiacum*. There are three species of tanies, the blue, the scratching, and that which is commonly roasted. The blossoms of all three are very fragrant, in a morning or evening. The young leaves, as well as the spiral stalks which support the flower, are eaten by Negroes as a salad. The root makes a good broth in dysenteric complaints. They are seldom so large as the yam, but most people think them preferable in point of taste.

VER. 597. *to the soursop*] The true Indian name of this tree is *Suirsaak*. It grows in the barrenest places to a considerable height. Its fruit will often weigh two pounds. Its skin is green, and somewhat prickly. The pulp is not disagreeable to the palate, being cool, and having its sweetness tempered with some degree of an acid. It is one of the *Anonas*, as are also the custard, star, and sugar-apples. The leaves of the soursop are very shining and green. The fruit is wholesome, but seldom admitted to the tables of the elegant. The seeds are dispersed through the pulp like the guava. It has a peculiar flavour. It grows in the East as well as the West-Indies. The botanical name is *Guanabanus*. The French call it *Petit Corosol*, or *Cœur de bœuf*, to which the fruit bears a resemblance. The root, being reduced to a powder, and snuffed up the nose, produces the same effect as tobacco. Taken by the mouth, the Indians pretend it is a specific in the epilepsy.

VER. 600. *cotton*] The fine down, which this shrub produces to invelope its seeds, is sufficiently known. The English, Italian, and French names, evidently are derived from the Arabic *Algodon*, as the Spaniards at this day call it. It was first brought by the Arabians into the Levant, where it is now cultivated with great success. Authors mention four species of cotton, but they confound the silk-cotton tree, or *Ceiba*, among them. The flower of the West-India cotton-shrub is yellow, and campanulated. It produces twice every year. That of Cayenne is the best of any that comes from America. This plant is very apt to be destroyed by a grub within a short time; bating that, it is a profitable production. Pliny mentions *Gossipium*, which is the common botanical name of cotton. It is likewise called *Zylon*. Martinus, in his Philological Lexicon, derives cotton from the Hebrew word קטן *Katon*, (or, as pronounced by the German-Jews, *Kotoun*.)

VER. 604. *cacao-walk*] It is also called *Cocao* and *Cocô*. It is a native of some of the provinces of South-America, and a drink made from it was the common food of the Indians before the Spaniards came among them, who were some time in those countries ere they could be prevailed upon to taste it; and it must be confessed that the Indian Chocolate had not a tempting aspect; yet I much doubt whether the Europeans have greatly improved its wholesomeness, by the addition of vanellas and other hot ingredients. The tree often grows fifteen or twenty feet high, and is streight and handsome. The pods, which seldom contain less than thirty nuts of the size of a flatted olive, grow upon the stem and principal branches. The tree loves a moist, rich and shaded soil: Hence those who plant cacao-walks, sometimes screen them by a hardier tree, which the Spaniards aptly term *Madre de Cacao*. They may be planted fifteen or twenty feet distant, though some advise to plant them much nearer, and perhaps wisely; for it is an easy matter to thin them, when they are past the danger of being destroyed by dry weather, &c. Some recommend planting cassada, or bananas, in the intervals, when the cacao-trees are young, to destroy weeds, from which the walk cannot be kept too free. It is generally three years before they produce good pods; but, in six years, they are in highest perfection. The pods are commonly of the size and shape of a large cucumber. There are three or four sorts of cacao, which differ from one another in the colour and goodness of their nuts. That from the Caraccas is certainly the best. None of the species grow in Peru. Its alimentary, as well as physical properties, are sufficiently known. This word is Indian.

VER. 605. *his coffee*] This is certainly of Arabic derivation; and has been used in the East, as a drink, time immemorial. The inhabitants about the mouth of the Red-Sea were taught the use of it by the Persians, say authors, in the fifteenth century; and the coffee-shrub was gradually introduced into Arabia Felix, whence it passed into Egypt, Syria, and lastly Constantinople. The Turks, though so excessively fond of coffee, have not known it much above one hundred and fifty years; whereas the English have been acquainted therewith for upwards of an hundred, one Pasqua, a Greek, having opened a coffee-house in London about the middle of the last century. The famous traveller, Thevenot, introduced coffee into France. This plant is cultivated in the West-Indies, particularly by the French, with great success, but the berry from thence is not equal to that from Mocha. It is a species of Arabian jasmine; the flower is particularly redolent, and from it a pleasant cordial water is distilled. It produces fruit twice every year; but the shrub must be three years old before any can be gathered. It should not be allowed to grow above six foot high. It is very apt to be destroyed by a large fly, which the French call *Mouche a caffe*; as well as by the white grub, which they name *Puceron*. Its medical and alimentary qualities are as generally known as those of tea.

VER. 624. *tamarind-vista,*] This large, shady, and beautiful tree grows fast even in the driest soils, and lasts long; and yet its wood is hard, and very fit for mechanical uses. The leaves are smaller than those of senna, and pennated: they taste sourish, as does the pulp, which is contained in pods four or five inches long. They bear once a year. An excellent vinegar may be made from the fruit; but the Creoles chiefly preserve it with sugar, as the Spaniards with salt. A pleasant syrup may be made from it. The name is, in Arabic, *Tamara*. The Antients were not acquainted therewith; for the Arabians first introduced tamarinds into physic; it is a native of the East as well as of the West-Indies and South-America, where different provinces call it by different names. Its cathartic qualities are well known. It is good in sea-sickness. The botanical name is *Tamarindus*.

VER. 641. *and ere the swift-wing'd zumbadore*,] This bird, which is one of the largest and swiftest known, is only seen at night, or rather heard; for it makes a hideous humming noise (whence its name) on the desert tops of the Andes. See Ulloa's Voyage to South-America. It is also called *Condor*. Its wings, when expanded, have been known to exceed sixteen feet from tip to tip. See *Phil. Trans.* N° 208.

VER. 643. *Ere fire-flies*] This surprising insect is frequent in Guadaloupe, &c. and all the warmer parts of America. There are none of them in the English Caribbee, or Virgin-Islands.

VER. 644. *on rapid Twilight's heel:*] There is little or no twilight in the West-Indies. All the year round it is dark before eight at night. The dawn is equally short.

*[Book II]*

VER. 46. *peculiar pest*] The monkeys which are now so numerous in the mountainous parts of St. Christopher, were brought thither by the French when they possessed half that island. This circumstance we learn from *Pere Labat*, who further tells us, that they are a most delicate food. The English-Negroes are very fond of them, but the White-inhabitants do not eat them. They do a great deal of mischief in St. Kitts, destroying many thousand pounds *Sterling*'s worth of Canes every year.

VER. 64. *These to destroy*] Rats, *&c.* are not natives of America, but came by shipping from Europe. They breed in the ground, under loose rocks and bushes. Durante, a Roman, who was physician to Pope Sixtus Quintus, and who wrote a Latin poem on the preservation of health, enumerates domestic rats among animals that may be eaten with safety. But if these are wholesome, cane-rats must be much more delicate, as well as more nourishing. Accordingly we find most field Negroes fond of them, and I have heard that straps of cane-rats are publicly sold in the markets of Jamaica.

VER. 69. *mangrove-banks*] This tree, which botanists call *Rizophora*, grows in marshy soils, and on the sides of rivers; and, as the branches take root, they frequently render narrow streams impassable to boats. Oysters often adhere to their roots, *&c.* The French name of this strange water-shrub is *Paltuvier*. The species meant here is the red mangrove.

VER. 74. *Dread alligators*] This dreadful animal is amphibious, and seldom lays fewer than 100 eggs. These she carefully covers with sand. But, notwithstanding this precaution, the gallinazo (a large species of carrion-crow) conceals itself among the thick boughs of the neighbouring trees, and thus often discovers the hoard of the alligator, which she no sooner leaves, than the gallinazo souses down upon it, and greedily scraping off the sand, regales on its contents. Nor is the male alligator less an enemy to the increase of his own horrid brood, than these useful birds; for, when Instinct prompts the female to let her young fry out by breaking the eggs, he never fails to accompany her, and to devour as many of them as he can: So that the mother scarce ever escapes into the river with more than five out of all her hundred. Thus providence doubly prevents the otherwise immense propagation of that voracious animal, on the banks of the river Guayaquil; for the gallinazo is not always found, where alligators are. *Ulloa*.

VER. 75. *teeth-fil'd Ibbos*] Or *Ebbos*, as they are more commonly called, are a numerous nation. Many of them have their teeth filed, and blackened in an extraordinary manner. They make good slaves when bought young; but are, in general, foul feeders, many of them greedily devouring the raw guts of fowls: They also feed on dead mules and horses; whose carcasses, therefore, should be buried deep, that the Negroes may not come at them. But the surest way is to burn them; otherwise, they will be apt, privily, to kill those useful animals, in order to feast on them.

VER. 76. *Nor thou their wayward*] Pere Labat says that Cane-rats give those Negroes who eat them pulmonic disorders, but the good Jesuit was no physician. I have been told by those who have eat them, that they are very delicate food.

VER. 95. *'Tis safer then to mingle nightshade's juice*] See the article *Solanum* in Newman's Chemistry published by Dr. Lewis. There is a species of East-India animal, called a *Mungoes*, which bears a natural antipathy to rats. Its introduction into the Sugar-Islands would, probably, effectuate the extirpation of this destructive vermin.

VER. 114. *the yellow thistle*] The seeds of this plant are an excellent emetic; and almost as useful in dysenteric complaints as ipecacuan. It grows every where.

VER. 119. *Nor let rude hands the knotted grass profane,*] This is truly a powerful vermifuge; but, uncautiously administered, has often proved mortal. The juice of it clarified, is sometimes given; but a decoction of it is greatly preferable. Its botanical name is *Spigelia*.

VER. 123. *The cow-itch also save*;] This extraordinary vine should not be permitted to grow in a Cane-piece; for Negroes have been known to fire the Canes, to save themselves from the torture which attends working in grounds where it has abounded. Mixed with melasses, it is a safe and excellent vermifuge. Its seeds, which resemble blackish small beans, are purgative. Its flower is purple; and its pods, on which the stinging brown *Setæ* are found, are as large as a full-grown English field-pea.

VER. 128. *Planter, thou mayst the humble chickweed*] There are two kinds of chickweed, which grow spontaneously in the Caribbees, and both possess very considerable virtues, particularly that which botanists call *Cajacia*, and which the Spaniards emphatically name *Erudos Cobres*, or Snakeweed, on account of its remarkable qualities against poisonous bites. It is really of use against fish-poison; as is also the sensitive plant, which the Spaniards prettily call the *Vergonzoza*, the Bashful, and *La Donzella*, or the Maiden. There are many kinds of this extraordinary plant, which grow every where in the Islands and South-America. The botanical name of the former is *Alsine*, and that of the latter *Mimosa*.

VER. 130. *Not the confection*] This medicine is called *Mithridatium*, in honour of Mithridates king of Pontus; who, by using it constantly, had secured himself from the effects of poison, in such a manner, that, when he actually attempted to put an end to his life, by that means, he failed in his purpose. So, at least, Pliny informs us. But we happily are not obliged to believe, implicitly, whatever that elaborate compiler has told us. When poisons immediately operate on the nervous system, and their effects are to be expelled by the skin, this electuary is no contemptible antidote. But how many poisons do we know at present, which produce their

## Grainger's Notes to The Sugar-Cane. Book II

effects in a different manner? and, from the accounts of authors, we have reason to be persuaded, that the antients were not much behind us in their variety of poisons. If, therefore, the King of Pontus had really intended to have destroyed himself, he could have been at no loss for the means, notwithstanding the daily use of this antidote.

VER. 131. *Not the bless'd apple*] Authors are not agreed what the apple is, to which Virgil attributes such remarkable virtues, nor is it indeed possible they ever should. However, we have this comfort on our side, that our not knowing it is of no detriment to us; for as spells cannot affect us, we are at no loss for antidotes to guard against them.

VER. 149. *For not the costly root,*] Some medical writers have bestowed the high appellation of *Donum Dei* on rhubarb.

VER. 171. *Thus cochinille*] This is a Spanish word. For the manner of propagating this useful insect, see Sir Hans Sloane's Natural History of Jamaica. It was long believed in Europe to be a seed, or vegetable production. The botanical name of the plant on which the cochinille feeds, is *Opuntia maxima, folio oblongo, majore, spinulis obtusis, mollibus et innocentibus obsito, flore, striis variegato.* Sloane.

VER. 205. *Tho' seasons*] Without a rainy season, the Sugar-cane could not be cultivated to any advantage: For what Pliny the Elder writes of another plant may be applied to this, *Gaudet irriguis, et toto anno bibere amat.*

VER. 205. *this pestilence*] It must, however, be confessed, that the blast is less frequent in lands naturally rich, or such as are made so by well-rotted manure.

VER. 218. *the plumb-tree sheds,*] This is the Jamaica plumb tree. When covered with fruit, it has no leaves upon it. The fruit is wholesome. In like manner, the panspan is destitute of foliage when covered with flowers. The latter is a species of jessamine, and grows as large as an apple-tree.

VER. 231. *Eurus reigns*] The East is the centre of the trade-wind in the West-Indies, which veers a few points to the North or South. What Homer says of the West-wind, in his islands of the blessed, may more aptly be applied to the trade-winds.

VER. 265. *Catháy*] An old name for China.

VER. 293. *stocks and mill-points:*] The sails are fastened to the mill-points, as those are to the stocks. They should always be taken down before the hurricane-season.

VER. 314. *strange burs*] These are astral halos. Columbus soon made himself master of the signs that precede a hurricane in the West-Indies, by which means he saved his own squadron; while another large fleet, whose commander despised his prognostics, put to sea, and was wrecked.

VER. 392. *solfaterre*] Volcanos are called *sulphurs, or solfaterres*, in the West-Indies. There are few mountainous islands in that part of the globe without them, and those probably will destroy them in time. I saw much sulphur and alum in the solfaterre at Mountserrat. The stream that runs through it, is almost as hot as boiling water, and its steams soon blacken silver, *&c.*

VER. 438. *the bending coco's*] The coco-nut tree is of the palm genus; there are several species of them, which grow naturally in the Torrid Zone. The coco-nut tree is, by no means, so useful as travellers have represented it. The wood is of little or no service, being spungy, and the brown covering of the nuts is of too rough a texture to serve as apparel. The shell of the nut receives a good polish; and, having a handle put to it, is commonly used to drink water out of. The milk, or water of the nut, is cooling and pleasant; but if drunk too freely, will frequently occasion a pain in the stomach. A salutary oil may be extracted from the kernel; which, if old, and eaten too plentifully, is apt to produce a shortness of breathing. A species of arrack is made from this tree, in the East-Indies. The largest coco-nut trees grow on the banks of the river Oronoko. They thrive best near the sea, and look beautiful at a distance. They afford no great shade. Ripe nuts have been produced from them in three years after planting. The nuts should be macerated in water, before they are put in the ground. Coco is an Indian name; the Spaniards call it also *palma de las Indias*; as the smallest kind, whose nuts are less than walnuts, is termed by them *Coquillo*. This grows in Chili, and the nuts are esteemed more delicate than those of a larger size. In the Maldivy Islands, it is pretended, they not only build houses of the coco-nut tree, but also vessels, with all their rigging; nay, and load them too with wine, oil, vinegar, black sugar, fruit, and strong water, from the same tree. If this be true, the Maldivian coco-nut trees must differ widely from those that grow in the West-Indies. The coco must not be confounded with the coco-nut tree. That shrub grows in the hottest and moistest vales of the Andes. Its leaf, which is gathered two or three times a year, is much coveted by the natives of South-America, who will travel great journeys upon a single handful of the leaves, which they do not swallow, but only chew. It is of an unpleasant taste, but, by use, soon grows agreeable. Some authors have also confounded the coco-nut palm, with the coco, or chocolate tree. The French call the coco-nut tree, *Cocotier*. Its stem, which is very lofty, is always bent; for which reason it looks better in an orchard than in a regular garden. As one limb fades, another shoots up in the center, like a pike. The botanical name is *Palma indica, coccifera, angulosa*.

VER. 441. *sappadillas*] This is a pleasant-tasted fruit, somewhat resembling a bergamot-pear, in shape and colour. The tree which produces it, is large and shady. Its leaves are of a shining green; but the flowers, which are monopetalous, are of a palish white. The fruit is coronated when ripe, and contains, in its pulp, several longish black seeds. It is wholesome. Antigua produces the best sappadillas I ever tasted. The trivial name is Spanish. Botanists call it *Cainito*.

VER. 499. *Porto Santo*] This is one of the Madeira islands, and of course subject to the King of Portugal. It lies in 32.33 degrees of N. latitude. It is neither so fruitful nor so large as Madeira Proper, and is chiefly peopled by convicts, *&c*.

VER. 504. *The boneta*] This fish, which is equal in size to the largest salmon, is only to be found in the warm latitudes. It is not a delicate food, but those who have lived for any length of time on salt meats at sea, do not dislike it. Sir Hans Sloane, in his voyage to Jamaica, describes the method of striking them.

VER. 504. *Or the shark*] This voracious fish needs no description; I have seen them from 15 to 20 foot long. Some naturalists call it *Canis Carharias*. They have been known to follow a slave-ship from Guinea to the West Indies. They swim with incredible celerity, and are found in some of the warmer seas of Europe, as well as between the tropics.

VER. 505. *urtica*] This fish the seaman call a Portuguese man of war. It makes a most beautiful appearance on the water.

VER. 507. *winged fishes*] This extraordinary species of fish is only found in the warm latitudes. Being pursued in the water by a fish of prey called Albacores, they betake themselves in shoals to flight, and in the air are often snapt up by the Garayio, a sea fowl. They sometimes fall on the shrouds or decks of ships. They are well tasted, and commonly sold at Barbadoes.

VER. 508. *Dolphins*] This is a most beautiful fish, when first taken out of the sea; but its beauty vanishes, almost as soon as it is dead.

VER. 509. *Tropic-bird*] The French call this bird Fregate, on account of its swift flying. It is only to be met with in the warm latitudes.

*[Book III]*

VER. 17. *Tho' mountains heapt on mountains*] This more particularly alludes to St. Kitts; where one of the highest ridges of that chain of mountains, which run through its center, from one end of it to the other, bears upon it another mountain, which, somewhat resembling the legendary prints of the devil's carrying on his shoulders St. Christopher; or, as others write, of a giant, of that appellation, carrying our Saviour, in the form of a child, in the same manner, through a deep sea; gave name, to this island.

VER. 25. *Of broad-leaf'd china,*] The leaves of this medicinal tree are so large, that the Negroes commonly use them to cover the water, which they bring in pails from the mountain, where it chiefly grows. The roots of this tree were introduced into European practice, soon after the venereal disease; but, unless they are fresh, it must be confessed they possess fewer virtues than either sarsaparilla or lignum vitæ. It also grows in China, and many parts of the East-Indies, where it is greatly recommended in the gout, palsy, sciatica, obstructions, and obstinate headachs: but it can surely not effect the removal of these terrible disorders; since, in China, the people eat the fresh root, boiled with their meat, as we do turnips; and the better sort, there, use a water distilled from it. The Spaniards call it *Palo de China*. The botanical name is *Smilax*.

VER. 81. *And where thy dried Canes*] The Cane-stalks which have been ground, are called *Magoss*; probably a corruption of the French word *Bagasse*, which signifies the same thing. They make an excellent fewel.

VER. 168. *Off the member snapt*] This accident will sometimes happen, especially in the night: and the unfortunate wretch must fall a victim to his imprudence or sleepiness, if a hatchet do not immediately strike off the entangled member; or the mill be not instantly put out of the wind.

Pere Labat says, he was informed the English were wont, as a punishment, thus to grind their negroes to death. But one may venture to affirm this punishment never had the sanction of law; and if any Englishman ever did grind his negroes to death, I will take upon me to aver, he was universally detested by his countrymen.

Indeed the bare suspicion of such a piece of barbarity leaves a stain: and therefore authors cannot be too cautious of admitting into their writings, any insinuation that bears hard on the humanity of a people.

Daily observation affords but too many proofs, where domestic slavery does not obtain, of the fatal consequences of indulged passion and revenge; but where one man is the absolute property of another, those passions may perhaps receive additional activity: planters, therefore, cannot be too much on their guard against the first sallies of passion; as by indulgence, passion, like a favourite, will at last grow independently powerful.

Ver. 192. *Amphitryte*] A mixture of sea water, is a real improvement in the distillation of rum.

VER. 222. *Why hath Antigua*] This beautiful island lies in 16 degrees and 14 min. N. lat. It was long uninhabited on account of its wanting fresh-water rivers; but is now more fully peopled, and as well cultivated as any of the leeward islands. In a seasonable year, it has made 30,000 hogsheads of sugar. It has no very high mountains. The soil is, in general, clayey. The water of the body-ponds may be used for every purpose of life. Antigua is well fortified, and has a good militia.

VER. 227. *Hiccory*] This is a lofty spreading tree, of very hard wood, excellently adapted to the purposes of the mill-wright. The nut, whose shell is thick, hard, and roughish, contains an agreeable and wholesome kernel. It grows in great abundance in St. Croix, Crab island, and Tobago.

VER. 227. *Calaba*] This lofty tree is commonly called Mastic: it is a hard wood, and is found in the places where the Hiccory grows. The flowers are yellow, and are succeeded by a fruit, which bears a distant resemblance to a shrub.

VER. 259. *Raleigh's land*] Sir Walter Raleigh gave the name of Virginia, in honour of Q. Elizabeth, to the whole of the north-east of North America, which Sebastian Cabot, a native of Bristol, (though others call him a Venetian,) first discovered, *A. D.* 1497, in the time of King Henry VII. by whom he was employed; but no advantages could be reaped from this discovery, on account of the various disturbances that ensued in England during the succeeding reigns, till about the year 1584, Q. Elizabeth gave Sir Walter Raleigh a patent for all such land, from 33. to 40. N. lat. as he should chuse to settle with English, reserving only to the crown a fifth part of all the gold and silver which should therein be discovered, in lieu of all services. Accordingly several imbarkations were fitted out from England, but all to no purpose. Some farther attempts, however, were made to settle this part of the country in the succeeding reign; but it was not till the year 1620, that a regular form of government took place. Then was tobacco planted, and negroes imported into Virginia. Since that time it has gradually improved, and does not now contain fewer than 100,000 white people of better condition, besides twice as many servants and slaves. The best shingles come from Egg Harbour.

VER. 282. *Karukera*] The Indian name of Guadaloupe.

VER. 283. *Matanina*] The Caribbean name of Martinico. The Havannah had not then been taken.

VER. 312. *Thy vessels,*] The vessels, wherein the Cane-juice is reduced to Sugar by coction, are either made of iron or of copper. Each sort hath its advantages and disadvantages. The teache, or smallest vessel from whence the Sugar is laved into the cooler, is generally copper. When it melts, it can be patched; but, when the large sort of vessels, called iron-furnaces, crack, which they are too apt to do, no further use can be made of them.

VER. 339. *Open, and pervious*] This also assists the christallization of the Sugar.

VER. 350. *For taste, for colour, and for various use:*] It were impossible, in the short limits of a note, to enumerate the various uses of Sugar; and, indeed, as these are in general so well known, it is needless. A few properties of it, however, wherewith the learned are not commonly acquainted, I shall mention. In some places of the East-Indies, an excellent arrack is made from the Sugar-Cane: And, in South-America, Sugar is used as an antidote against one of the most sudden, as well as fatal poisons in the world. Taken by mouth, *pocula morte carent,* this poison is quite innocent; but the slightest wound made by an arrow, whose point is tinged therewith, proves immediate death; for, by driving all the blood of the body immediately to the heart, it forthwith bursts it. The fish and birds killed by these poisoned arrows (in the use of which the Indians are astonishingly expert) are perfectly wholesome to feed on. See Ulloa and De la Condamine's account of the great river of Amazon. It is a vegetable production.

VER. 357. *That Cane*] This, by the natives, is emphatically called the *Dumb Cane*; for a small quantity of its juice being rubbed on the brim of a drinking vessel, whoever drinks out of it, soon after will have his lips and tongue enormously swelled. A physician, however, who wrote a short account of the diseases of Jamaica, in Charles II.'s time, recommends it both by the mouth and externally, in dropsical and other cases: But I cannot say, I have had any experience of its efficacy in these disorders. It grows wild in the mountains; and, by its use in Sugar-making, should seem to be somewhat of an alcalescent nature. It grows to four feet high, having, at the top, two green shining leaves, about nine inches long; and, between these, a small spire emerges.

VER. 428. *If too soon they strike,*] When the Cane-juice is granulated sufficiently, which is known by the Sugar's sticking to the ladle, and roping like a syrup, but breaking off from its edges; it is poured into a cooler, where, its surface being smoothed, the christallization is soon completed. This is called *striking*. The general precept is to temper high, and strike low. When the Muscovado is of a proper consistence, it is dug out of the cooler, and put into hogsheads; this is called *potting*. The casks being placed upon staunchions, the melasses drips from them into a cistern, made on purpose, below them, to receive it. The Sugar is sufficiently cured, when the hogshead rings upon being struck with a stick; and when the two canes, which are put into every cask, shew no melasses upon them, when drawn out of it.

VER. 501. *Marne's flowery banks, nor Tille's*] Two rivers in France, along whose banks the best Burgundy and Champagne-grapes grow.

VER. 510. *For her, fair Auth'ress!*] Mrs. Lennox.

VER. 522. *sand-box*] So called, from the pericarpium's being often made use of for containing sand; when the seeds, which are a violent emetic, are taken out. This is a fine shady tree, especially when young; and its leaves are efficaciously applied in headachs to the temples, which they sweat. It grows fast; but loses much of its beauty by age. Its wood is brittle, and when cut emits a milky juice, which is not caustic. The sand-box thrives best in warm shady places. The sun often splits the pericarpium, which then cracks like a pistol. It is round, flatted both above and below, and divided into a great number of regular compartments, each of which contains one seed flatted ovularly. The botanical name is *Hura*.

VER. 549. *panspans*] See the notes on Book II.

VER. 549. *papaws*] This singular tree, whose fruits surround its summit immediately under the branches and leaves, like a necklace; grows quicker than almost any other in the West Indies. The wood is of no use, being spungy, hollow, and herbacious; however, the blossoms and fruit make excellent sweet-meats; but above all, the juice of the fruit being rubbed upon a spit, will intenerate new killed fowls, *&c.* a circumstance of great consequence in a climate, where the warmth soon renders whatever meats are attempted to be made tender by keeping, unfit for culinary purposes. Nor, will it only intenerate fresh meat; but, being boiled with salted beef, will render it easily digestible. Its milky juice is sometimes used to cure ringworms. It is said, that the guts of hogs would in time be lacerated, were they to feed on the ripe, unpeeled fruit. Its seed is said to be anthelmintic. The botanical name is *Papaya*.

VER. 596. *The Man of Norfolk,*] The Honourable General George Townshend.

VER. 608. *Jew-fish*] This, tho' a very large, is one of the most delicate fishes that swim; being preferable to caramaw, king-fish, or camaree: some even chuse it before turtle. The Jew-fish is often met with at Antigua, which enjoys the happiness of having on its coast few, if any, poisoned fishes.

VER. 613. *Barbuda,*] This is a low, and not large stock-island, belonging to the Codrington family. Part of this island, as also two plantations in Barbadoes, were left by Colonel Christopher Codrington, for building a college in Barbadoes, and converting Negroes to the Christian religion.

VER. 614. *Anguilla,*] This island is about thirty miles long and ten broad. Though not mountainous, it is rocky, and abounds in strong passes; so that a few of its inhabitants, who are indeed expert in the use of fire-arms, repulsed, with great slaughter, a considerable detachment of French, who made a descent thereon in the war preceding the last. Cotton and cattle are its chief commodities. Many of the inhabitants are rich; the captain-general of the Leeward-Islands nominates the governor and council. They have no assembly.

## [Book IV]

VER. 137. *cherries,*] The tree which produces this wholesome fruit is tall, shady, and of quick growth. Its Indian name is *Acajou*; hence corruptly called *Cashew* by the English. The fruit has no resemblance to a cherry, either in shape or size; and bears, at its lower extremity, a nut (which the Spaniards name *Anacardo*, and physicians *Anacardium*) that resembles a large kidney-bean. Its kernel is as grateful as an almond, and more easy of digestion. Between its rinds is contained a highly caustic oil; which, being held to a candle, emits bright salient sparkles, in which the American fortune-tellers pretended they saw spirits who gave answers to whatever questions were put to them by their ignorant followers. This oil is used as a cosmetic by the ladies, to remove freckles and sun-burning; but the pain they necessarily suffer makes its use not very frequent. The tree also produces a gum not inferior to Gum-Arabic; and its bark is an approved astringent. The juice of the cherry stains exceedingly. The long citron, or amber-coloured, is the best. The cashew-nuts, when unripe, are of a green colour; but, ripe, they assume that of a pale olive. This tree bears fruit but once a year.

VER. 163. *the conch*] Plantations that have no bells, assemble their Negroes by sounding a conch-shell.

VER. 181. *rocky Drave,*] A river in Hungary, on whose banks are found mines of quicksilver.

VER. 257. *winged insects*] These, by the English, are called *Chigoes* or *Chigres*. They chiefly perforate the toes, and sometimes the fingers; occasioning an itching, which some people think not unpleasing, and are at pains to get, by going to the copper-holes, or mill-round, where chigres most abound. They lay their eggs in a bag, about the size of a small pea, and are partly contained therein themselves. This the Negroes extract without bursting, by means of a needle, and filling up the place with a little snuff; it soon heals, if the person has a good constitution. One species of them is supposed to be poisonous; but, I believe, unjustly. When they bury themselves near a tendon, especially if the person is in a bad habit of body, they occasion troublesome sores. The South-Americans call them *Miguas*.

VER. 268. *niccars*] The botanical name of this medicinal shrub is called *Guilandina*. The fruit resembles marbles, though not so round. Their shell is hard and smooth, and contains a farinaceous nut, of admirable use in seminal weaknesses. They are also given to throw out the yaws.

VER. 309. *Cow-itch*] See notes in Book II.

VER. 317. *The mineral product of the Cornish mine*] Tin-filings are a better vermifuge than tin in powder. The western parts of Britain, and the neighbouring isles, have been famous for this useful metal from the remotest antiquity; for we find from Strabo, that the Phænicians made frequent voyages to those parts (which they called *Cassiterides* from Κασσιτερον, stannum) in quest of that commodity, which turned out so beneficial to them, that a pilot of that nation stranded his vessel, rather than show a Roman ship, that watched him, the way to those mines. For this public spirited action, he was amply rewarded, says that accurate writer, upon his return to his country. The Romans, however, soon made themselves masters of the secret, and shared with them in the profit of that merchandize.

VER. 370. *snake-mark'd*] The negroe-conjurers, or Obia-men, as they are called, carry about them a staff, which is marked with frogs, snakes, *&c*. The blacks imagine that its blow, if not mortal, will at least occasion long and troublesome disorders. A belief in magic is inseparable from human nature, but those nations are most addicted thereto, among whom learning, and of course, philosophy have least obtained. As in all other countries, so in Guinea, the conjurers, as they have more understanding, so are they almost always more wicked than the common herd of their deluded countrymen; and as the negroe-magicians can do mischief, so they can also do good on a plantation, provided they are kept by the white people in proper subordination.

VER. 410. *broom-bush*] This small plant, which grows in every pasture, may, with propriety, be termed an American clock; for it begins every forenoon at eleven to open its yellow flowers, which about one are fully expanded, and at two closed. The jalap, or marvel of Peru, unfolds its petals between five and six in the evening, which shut again as soon as night comes on, to open again in the cool of the morning. This plant is called four o'clock by the natives, and bears either a yellow or purple-coloured flower.

VER. 415. *solanum*] So some authors name the fire-weed, which grows every where, and is the *datura* of Linnæus; whose virtues Dr. Stork, at Vienna, has greatly extolled in a late publication. It bears a white monopetalous flower, which opens always about sun-set.

VER. 449. *cassada*] To an antient Caribbean, bemoaning the savage uncomfortable life of his countrymen, a deity clad in white apparel appeared, and told him, he would have come sooner to have taught him the ways of civil life, had he been addressed before. He then showed him sharp-cutting stones to fell trees and build houses; and bade him cover them with the palm leaves. Then he broke his staff in three; which, being planted, soon after produced cassada. See Ogilvy's America.

VER. 454. *angola*] This is called *Pidgeon-pea*, and grows on a sturdy shrub, that will last for years. It is justly reckoned among the most wholesome legumens. The juice of the leaves, dropt into the eye, will remove incipient films. The botanic name is *Cytisus*.

VER. 456. *bonavist*] This is the Spanish name of a plant, which produces an excellent bean. It is a parasitical plant. There are five sorts of bonavist, the green, the white, the moon-shine, the small or common; and, lastly, the black and red. The flowers of all are white and papilionaceous; except the last, whose blossoms are purple. They commonly bear in six weeks. Their pulse is wholesome, though somewhat flatulent; especially those from the black and red. The pods are flattish, two or three inches long; and contain from three to five seeds in partitional cells.

VER. 457. *Ochra*] Or *Ockro*. This shrub, which will last for years, produces a not less agreeable, than wholesome pod. It bears all the year round. Being of a slimy and balsamic nature, it becomes a truly medicinal aliment in dysenteric complaints. It is of the *Malva* species. It rises to about four or five feet high, bearing, on and near the summit, many yellow flowers; succeeded by green, conic, fleshy pods, channelled into several grooves. There are as many cells filled with small round seeds, as there are channels.

VER. 459. *potatos*] I cannot positively say, whether these vines are of Indian original or not; but as in their fructification, they differ from potatos at home, they probably are not European. They are sweet. There are four kinds, the red, the white, the long, and round: The juice of each may be made into a pleasant cool drink; and, being distilled, yield an excellent spirit.

VER. 461. *eddas*] See notes on Book I. The French call this plant *Tayove*. It produces eatable roots every four months, for one year only.

VER. 462. *Indian cale*] This green, which is a native of the New World, equals any of the greens in the Old.

VER. 462. *calaloo*] Another species of Indian pot-herb, no less wholesome than the preceding. These, with mezamby, and the Jamaica prickle-weed, yield to no esculent plants in Europe. This is an Indian name.

VER. 466. *the shapely tree*] The orange tree.

VER. 478. *thy mother nam'd*] See Book I. p. 43.

VER. 502. *mammey*] This is a lofty, shady, and beautiful tree. Its fruit is as large as the largest melon, and of an exquisite smell, greatly superior to it in point of taste. Within the fruit are contained one or two large stones, which when distilled, give to spirits a ratafia flavour, and therefore the French call them *Les apricots de St. Domingue:* accordingly, the *l'eaux des noiaux*, one of the best West-Indian cordials, is made from them. The fruit, eaten raw, is of an aperient quality; and made into sweet-meats, *&c.* is truly exquisite. This tree, contrary to most others in the New World, shoots up to a pyramidal figure: the leaves are uncommonly green; and it produces fruit, but once a year. The name is Indian. The English commonly call it *Mammey-sapota*. There are two species of it, the sweet, and the tart. The botanical name is *Achras*.

VER. 509. *tamarind*] See Book I. p. 44.

VER. 513. *cassia*,] Both this tree and its mild purgative pulp are sufficiently known.

VER. 523. *palmeto*,] This being the most beautiful of palms, nay, perhaps, superior to any other known tree in the world, has with propriety obtained the name of *Royal*. The botanical name is *Palma Maxima*. It will shoot up perpendicularly to an hundred feet and more. The stem is perfectly circular; only towards the root, and immediately under the branches at top, it bulges out. The bark is smooth, and of an ash-brown colour, except at the top where it is green. It grows very fast, and the seed from whence it springs is not bigger than an acorn. In this, as in all the palm-genus, what the natives call *Cabbage* is found; but it resembles in taste an almond, and is in fact the pith of the upper, or greenish part of the stem. But it would be the most unpardonable luxury to cut down so lovely a tree, for so mean a gratification; especially as the wild, or mountain cabbage tree, sufficiently supplies the table with that esculent. I never ride past the charming vista of royal palms on the Cayon-estate of Daniel Mathew, Esq; in St. Christopher, without being put in mind of the pillars of the Temple of the Sun at Palmyra. This tree grows on the tops of hills, as well as in valleys; its hard cortical part makes very durable laths for houses. There is a smaller species not quite so beautiful.

VER. 534. *anata*,] Or *Anotto*, or *Arnotta*; thence corruptly called *Indian Otter*, by the English. The tree is about the size of an ordinary apple-tree. The French call it *Rocou*; and send the farina home as a paint, *&c.* for which purpose the tree is cultivated by them in their islands. The flower is pentapetalous, of a bluish and spoon-like appearance. The yellow filaments are tipped with purplish apices. The style proves the rudiment of the succeeding pod, which is of a conic shape, an inch and a half long. This is divided into many cells, which contain a great number of small seeds, covered with a red farina.

VER. 543. *granadilla*] This is the Spanish name, and is a species of the *passiflora*, or passion-flower, called by Linnæus *Musa*. The seeds and pulp, through which the seeds are dispersed, are cooling, and grateful to the palate. This, as well as the water-lemon, bell-apple, or honeysuckle, as it is named, being parasitical plants, are easily formed into cooling arbors, than which nothing can be more grateful in warm climates. Both fruits are wholesome. The granadilla is commonly eat with sugar, on account of its tartness, and yet the pulp is viscid. Plumier calls it *Granadilla, latefolia, fructu maliformi*. It grows best in shady places. The unripe fruit makes an excellent pickle.

VER. 563. *bay-grape*] Or sea-side grape, as it is more commonly called. This is a large, crooked, and shady tree, (the leaves being broad, thick, and almost circular;) and succeeds best in sandy places. It bears large clusters of grapes once a year; which, when ripe, are not disagreeable. The stones, seeds, or *acini*, contained in them, are large in proportion; and, being reduced to a powder, are an excellent astringent. The bark of the tree has the same property. The grapes, steept in water and fermented with sugar, make an agreeable wine.

VER. 567. *Indian millet*] Or maise. This is commonly called *Guinea-corn*, to distinguish it from the great or Indian corn, that grows in the southern parts of North-America. It soon shoots up to a great height, often twenty feet high, and will ratoon like the other; but its blades are not so nourishing to horses as those of the great corn, although its seeds are more so, and rather more agreeable to the taste. The Indians, Negroes, and poor white people, make many (not unsavoury) dishes with them. It is also called

*Turkey wheat.* The turpentine tree will also grow in the sand, and is most useful upon a plantation.

VER. 584. *banshaw*] This is a sort of rude guitar, invented by the Negroes. It produces a wild pleasing melancholy sound.

VER. 611. *prickly vine*] This beautiful white rosaceous flower is as large as the crown of one's hat, and only blows at midnight. The plant, which is prickly and attaches itself firmly to the sides of houses, trees, *&c.* produces a fruit, which some call *Wythe Apple*, and others with more propriety, *Mountain strawberry*. But though it resembles the large Chili-strawberry in looks and size; yet being inelegant of taste, it is seldom eaten. The botanical name is *Cereus scandens minor*. The rind of the fruit is here and there studded with tufts of small sharp prickles.

VER. 613. *candle-weed*] This shrub, which produces a yellow flower somewhat resembling a narcissus, makes a beautiful hedge, and blows about November. It grows wild every where. It is said to be diuretic, but this I do not know from experience.

VER. 638. *no Plata*,] One of the largest rivers of South America.

# Appendix I
## 'Great Homer deignd to sing of little Mice'

After what is II, 33 in *1764*, *TCD* (ff. 28r–29r) has the following passage (later replaced by what is II, 62–3):

>     Where shall the Muse the Muster-roll begin?
>     Where breathless end? say shall she sing of mice? —
>     Critic forbear thy supercilious Smile:
>     Great Homer deignd to sing of little Mice:
> 5   And do not faithful Chronicles relate:
>     How Famine, worst of Heavens relentless Ills
>     Hath ghastly trod their desolating Steps?
>     Nor by the planter are unfelt the Woes
>     The puny whisker'd vermine-race produce.
> 10  With these associate shall the numerous Clan
>     Of Rats be joind? an unrelenting Crew!
>     Whatever Canes these fell marauders gnaw,
>     Fall prostrate, snapt off by the slightest Breeze!

  8  Woes] written above 'Ills' deleted.
10  With] first three letters double underlined (perhaps intended to indicate a new paragraph).
these] inserted above line.
numerous] written above 'plundering' deleted.
12  these fell marauders] '& many a Cane the plunderers' written above the line as an alternative (though this would give the line too many syllables). It also appears that 'these' has been altered to 'the'.

This transcript differs in several points from those published by G. S. Alleman in a letter to the editor, *Times Literary Supplement*, 13 August 1938 and by Anon., 'Dr. Grainger's "Sugar Cane",' *Times*

*Literary Supplement*, 16 February 1951. Much of this is due to the fact that while Grainger's writing is usually legible, he makes little distinction between capital and small forms of several letters; the editor's choice is often, perforce, an arbitrary one.

This passage, or a later version of it, appears to be the basis of the well-known anecdote in Boswell's *Life of Johnson* (World's Classics ed. by R. W. Chapman, pp. 698–9), where the phrase 'Now, Muse, let's sing of rats' is said to 'have made all the assembled wits burst into a laugh' when the poem was read in manuscript at the house of Sir Joshua Reynolds. Three points are worth noting: (a) Boswell records this anecdote about a dozen years later, with reference to a conversation with Johnson, 21 March 1776; (b) he had got the anecdote not from Johnson but another acquaintance; and (c) it is not absolutely certain Grainger himself was 'the reader' as 'the poet began a new paragraph' is ambiguous – it may be Grainger had sent someone a copy, perhaps even before his return to Britain, and it was read in his absence. The evidence that 'Now, Muse, let's sing of rats' ever appeared in any version of the poem in exactly that form is, in my view, less than compelling: it sounds like a variation of 'say shall she sing of mice?' either half-remembered or deliberately heightened for the sake of a joke.

Percy came to Grainger's defence with a version which Boswell printed, suggesting that Grainger's intention was deliberately mock-heroic, and intended as a parody of the *Battle of the Frogs and the Mice*, an ancient mock-heroic poem popular in the eighteenth century, which ascribed it to Homer. More recently, Chalker (*English Georgic*, pp. 58–9) suggested that

Now muse let's sing of rats

would be broadly comic, burlesque, in its effect, but

Nor with less waste the whisker'd vermin race

is far more delicate in its methods. It avoids the rather crude contrast of *Muse* and *rats* yet maintains the contrast obliquely. The Bishop of Dromore's evidence is valuable because it suggests that the effect is calculated, that Grainger is not (as the original anecdote suggests)) simply striving for the dignified only to achieve the bathetic, but is deliberately cultivating a mock-heroic attitude towards his subject.

However, the version in *TCD* does not appear intended as mock-heroic at all. 'Great Homer' is indeed invoked to lend dignity to the subject, but it is clear Grainger feels that, whatever the 'Critic' with his 'supercilious Smile' may think, both the 'little Mice' and the 'numerous Clan/Of Rats' have a real importance because of their effect on the 'imperial cane' (II, 100). Creatures which, like the monkeys, destroy 'many thousand pounds *Sterling*'s worth of Canes every year' (II, 46 n.) are not to be laughed at – though it is possible Grainger did alter the passage because he found a British audience less able than a Caribbean one to appreciate this fact.

For a more obviously tongue-in-cheek reference to the *Battle of the Frogs and the Mice*, compare Cowper, *The Task*, Book III, 452–6 (Sambrook, ed., *William Cowper: The Task and Selected Other Poems*, pp. 125–6).

Many more people have read Boswell's *Life of Johnson* than have ever read contemporary criticism of Grainger. This makes it possible to suggest that *The Sugar-Cane* 'struck Johnson and others as a ludicrous imitation of Homer and Virgil' (Brown, *West Indian Poetry*, p. 20) or that the poem 'was ridiculed mercilessly by the critics in London' (Royle, *Macmillan Companion to Scottish Literature*, p. 125). The evidence of the contemporary reviews, presented in the Introduction to the present work, makes clear that these suggestions are simply untrue.

# *Appendix II*
# *Bryan and Pereene*

Grainger's only other poem on a Caribbean subject, this was first published in his friend Thomas Percy's collection of *Reliques of Ancient English Poetry*. This may seem an odd place for it, but Percy explained in his Preface (I, x) that 'To atone for the rudeness of the more obsolete poems, each volume concludes with a few modern attempts in the same kind of writing.' In his introduction to the poem, Percy claimed that 'Bryan and Pereene' was 'founded on a real fact, that happened in the island of St. Christophers [sic] about two years ago', i.e., about 1763, and that Grainger 'was in the island when this tragical incident happened.' The text given here is from the first edition (1765) of Percy's *Reliques*, I, 313–16. Percy's introductory comments (mostly on Grainger's 'Solitude: An Ode') are omitted.

BRYAN AND PEREENE,
A WEST-INDIAN BALLAD

The north-east wind did briskly blow,
  The ship was safely moor'd,
Young Bryan thought the boat's-crew slow,
  And so leapt over-board.

Pereene, the pride of Indian dames,    5
  His heart long held in thrall,
And whoso his impatience blames,
  I wot, ne'er lov'd at all.

A long long year, one month and day,
  He dwelt on English land,    10
Nor once in thought or deed would stray,
  Tho' ladies sought his hand.

## Appendix II

For Bryan he was tall and strong,
    Right blythsome roll'd his een,
Sweet was his voice whene'er he sung,    15
    He scant had twenty seen.

But who the countless charms can draw,
    That grac'd his mistress true;
Such charms the old world seldom saw,
    Nor oft I ween the new.    20

Her raven hair plays round her neck,
    Like tendrils of the vine;
Her cheeks red dewy rose buds deck,
    Her eyes like diamonds shine.

Soon as his well-known ship she spied,    25
    She cast her weeds away,
And to the palmy shore she hied,
    All in her best array.

In sea-green silk so neatly clad,
    She there impatient stood;    30
The crew with wonder saw the lad
    Repell the foaming flood.

Her hands a handkerchief display'd,
    Which he at parting gave;
Well pleas'd the token he survey'd,    35
    And manlier beat the wave.

Her fair companions one and all,
    Rejoicing crowd the strand;
For now her lover swam in call,
    And almost touch'd the land.    40

Then through the white surf did she haste,
    To clasp her lovely swain;
When, ah! a shark bit through his waste:
    His heart's blood dy'd the main!

He shriek'd! his half sprang from the wave,    45
    Streaming with purple gore,
And soon it found a living grave,
    And ah! was seen no more.

> Now haste, now haste, ye maids, I pray,
>     Fetch water from the spring:  50
> She falls, she swoons, she dyes away,
>     And soon her knell they ring.
>
> Now each May morning round her tomb
>     Ye fair, fresh flow'rets strew,
> So may your lovers scape his doom,  55
>     Her hapless fate scape you.

# Appendix III
# Colonel Martin's directions for planting and sugar-making

The following extracts are taken from Samuel Martin, *An Essay upon Plantership [...]* (4th ed., Antigua printed, London reprinted, 1765), a work known to Grainger in one of its earlier editions. They provide a good summary of mid-eighteenth-century practice in the Leeward Islands, though Martin gives much additional detail which is here omitted for reasons of space. The instructions for planting depend on the fact that the creole cane (the only variety known at the time) required more than a year to reach maturity; it was therefore essential for the planter to stagger the planting of new canes, so that there would be a constant supply of ripe ones for grinding during the crop-season.

\*\*\*

In stiff soils where canes require most age, half the quantity of land intended for the crop should be planted in September: but in hot loose soils in October and November: and the whole planting-season conclude with the month of January or February, when the tops of the first canes cut, may furnish the last pieces planted. By strict observance of this method, the canes will be at full maturity in the proper season for yielding most sugar, which is from the first of January (if the weather permits) to the 29th of July. But by grinding later, we hazard not only the destruction of our wind-mills by hurricanes, but make bad sugar, at infinite expence of time and labor, both of negroes and cattle, when the juice of canes becomes weak and waterish. There is not therefore a greater error in the whole practice of plantership, than to make sugar, or to plant canes at improper seasons of the year; for, by mismanagements of this kind every succeeding crop is put out of regular order, tho' a plantation ought to be considered as a well-constructed machine, compounded of various wheels, turning different ways, and yet all contributing to the great end proposed: but if any one part runs too fast or too slow in proportion to the rest, the main purpose is defeated. [pp. 36–7]

In making good sugar there is a great variety of incidents, of which, if any one fails, the end is absolutely frustrated; the wise planter therefore must be very attentive to every minute step throughout the whole process. It must be his first care to keep his mill in perfect good order, so that common accidents may not retard his crop in the season, when canes yield the most and best sugar; every part of his works must be very clean, and his coppers hung so judiciously, as to boil perfectly well with little fewel; for nothing contributes more to the making of good sugar, than quick boiling, after the cane-juice is well clarified. To this end therefore the great coppers, or first clarifiers, should be hung singly, or to separate fires, and pinned about ten or twelve inches from the bottom; that the scum may be separated by slow degrees, and kept floating upon the surface long enough to be taken off perfectly: for, if the liquor be suffered to boil with violence, the scum will incorporate again with it, and never after be separable but by the refining pan: and thus dark foul sugar is made of that cane-juice which might have produced, by good management, fine bright sugar of much greater value at the market. This is a point of great importance to every planter, whose profit depends much upon the goodness of his sugar: for, the worst pays the same freight, duty, and charges as the very best.

The cane-juice therefore, after being strained at the mill thro' a brass wire sieve, ought to run down to the boiling-house in spouts lined with lead, to preserve it from tainting; and being let into the first clarifier, must be there boiled over a moderate fire until perfectly freed from all scum: afterwards it must be strained thro' a thick coarse blanket, and then boiled to sugar with all possible celerity. But let the coppers be ever so judiciously hung, the liquor cannot be boiled with due quickness, unless the manager takes peculiar care to provide great plenty of *dry fewel*, or mill-trash: a material circumstance in which there is a most absurd and general remissness [...]

The judicious boiler's next care is to provide quick-lime of the best sort to temper his liquor; for, otherwise the sugar will be clammy, than which it cannot have a worse quality. That defect in sugar arises from two very different causes; for, slow boiling, and bad temper-lime have the very same effect [...]

It is impossible to prescribe exactly the quantity of lime necessary for every sort of cane-juice. Experience only can teach this art [...]

After duly tempering the cane-juice with the strongest quicklime, clarifying it over a moderate fire, and straining it as before described, let it be boiled with the utmost quickness to a middling sugar-height, which will give it a large grain, and a fair color, never-failing qualities to procure the best price at market. This art of boiling sugar, tho' of the greatest importance to every planter, is (I know not by what means) generally least understood, either by overseers, or their masters; but that point of greatest consequence is trusted wholly to the skill of negro-boilers, who indeed arrive by long habit to some degree of judgement by *the eye only* [...]

The method of boiling muscovado-sugar I have said is below loaf-height, and if then it is cooled with quickness in a broad superficies, and in a wooden cooler, the sugar will be of larger grain than if cooled in a deep or copper vessel, as experience evinces. But if the sugar is intended to be cured in pots or earthen moulds, it must be cooled in copper, or deep wooden coolers, that it may be conveyed from thence into the pots, while in the state of a thick liquid. [pp. 43–50]

# Appendix IV
# Ramsay's account of a plantation day

There are many accounts of slave life in the eighteenth-century Caribbean which could be contrasted with Grainger's carefully selective view. These extracts, from the Rev. James Ramsay, *An Essay on the Treatment and Conversion of African Slaves in the British Sugar Colonies* (London, 1784), have been chosen partly because they are based on Ramsay's experience in St. Kitts during the years 1762 to 1781. They have the further advantage that they are not taken from some later piece of anti-slavery propaganda which is anxious to emphasise the horrors of the system as much as possible: Ramsay's *Essay* does not demand emancipation – which is described as something 'that we may rather wish for, than expect for some time to see' (pp. 127–8) – but asks only that the slaves should be better treated than they generally were. The grim picture he presents is not one of occasional atrocities, though he mentions the existence of these elsewhere (e.g., pp. 85–6), but of routine brutality.

Ramsay (1733–89) was a Scot who had been trained as a physician, and had spent six years as a naval surgeon before he first arrived in St. Kitts, where some friends hoped to set him up in a medical practice. By then, however, he had already decided to take orders. He married the daughter of a Kittitian planter, and had himself owned slaves. See the biography by Folarin Shyllon (1977) for a full account of Ramsay's career.

\*\*\*

The discipline of a sugar plantation is as exact as that of a regiment: at four o'clock in the morning the plantation bell rings to call the slaves into the field. Their work is to manure, dig, and hoe, plow the ground, to plant, weed, and cut the cane, to bring it to the mill, to have the juice expressed, and boiled into sugar. About nine o'clock, they have half an hour for breakfast, which they take in the field. Again they fall to work, and, according to the custom of the plantation, continue until eleven o'clock, or noon; the bell then rings, and the slaves are dispersed in the neighbourhood, to pick up about the fences, in the mountains, and fallow or waste grounds, natural grass and weeds for the horses and cattle. The time allotted for this branch of work, and preparation of dinner, varies from an hour and an half, to near three hours. In collecting pile by pile their little bundles of grass, the slaves of low land plantations, frequently burnt up by the sun, must wander in their neighbours [sic] grounds, perhaps more than two miles from home. In their return, often some lazy fellow, of the intermediate plantation, with the view of saving himself the trouble of picking his own grass, seizes on them, and pretends to insist on carrying them to his master, for picking grass, or being found in his grounds; a crime that forfeits the bundle, and subjects the offender to twenty lashes of a long cart whip, of twisted leathern thongs. The wretch, rather than be carried to judgment in another man's plantation, is fain to escape with the loss of his bundle, and often to put up quietly with a good drubbing from the robber into the bargain. The hour of delivering in his grass, and renewing his task, approaches, while hunger importunately solicits him to remember its call; but he must renew the irksome toil, and search out some green, shady, unfrequented spot, from which to repair his loss.

At one, or in some plantations, at two o'clock, the bell summons them to deliver in the tale of their grass, and assemble to their field work. If the overseer thinks their bundles too small, or if they come too late with them, they are punished with a number of stripes from four to ten. Some masters, under a fit of carefulness for their cattle, have gone as far as fifty stripes, which effectually disable the culprit for weeks. If a slave has no grass to deliver in, he keeps away out of fear, skulks about in the mountains, and is absent from his work often for months; an aggravation of his crime, which, when he is caught, he is made to remember.

About half an hour before sun set, they may be found scattered again over the land, like the Israelites in Egypt, to cull, blade by blade, from among the weeds, their scanty parcels of grass. About seven o'clock in the evening, or later, according to the season of the year, when the overseer can find leisure, they are called over by list, to deliver in their second bundles of grass; and the same punishment, as at noon, is inflicted on the delinquents. They then separate, to pick up, in their way to their huts, (if they have not done it, as they generally do, while gathering grass) a little brush wood, or dry cow-dung, to prepare some simple mess for supper, and tomorrow's breakfast. This employs them till near midnight, and then they go to sleep, till the bell calls them in the morning. [pp. 69–72]

The work here mentioned, is considered as the field duty of slaves, that may be insisted on without reproach to the manager, of unusual severity, and which the white and black overseers stand over them to see executed; the transgression against which, is quickly followed with the smart of the cart whip. This instrument, in the hands of a skilful driver, cuts out flakes of skin and flesh with every stroke; and the wretch, in this mangled condition, is turned out to work in dry or wet weather, which last, now and then, brings on the cramp, and ends his sufferings and slavery together.

In crop-time, which may be when reckoned altogether on a plantation, from five to six months; the cane tops, by supplying the cattle with food, gives the slaves some little relaxation in picking grass. But some pretendedly industrious planters, men of much bustle, and no method, will, especially in moon-light, keep their people till ten o'clock at night, carrying wowra, the decayed leaves of the cane, to boil off the cane juice. A considerable number of slaves is kept to attend in turn the mill and boiling house all night. They sleep over their work; the sugar is ill tempered, burnt in the boiler, and improperly struck; while the mill every now-and-then grinds off an hand, or an arm, of those drowsy worn down creatures that feed it. Still the process of making sugar is carried on in many plantations, for months, without any other interruption, than during some part of day light on Sundays. In some plantations it is the custom, during crop-time, to keep the whole gang employed as above, from morning to night, and alternately one half throughout the night, to supply the mill with canes, and the boiling house with wowra.

This labour is more or less moderated, in proportion to the method and good sense of the manager. In some plantations the young children and worn out slaves are set apart to pick grass, and bring cane tops from the field for the cattle, and do no other work. Sometimes the field gangs bring both their bundles of grass at once, being allowed for that purpose a little extra time, during the meridian heat; which saves them an unnecessary repetition of wandering in the evening three or four miles to search for it, and enables the manager to employ the cool part of the afternoon in the common

## Appendix IV

labour of the plantation. Sometimes they are dismissed for grass before the usual hour; or if they be hoe-ploughing land, frequently none is required from them. In some plantations, they are not punished for coming late into the field, if they appear there about sunrise. In most well-ordered plantations, they leave off grinding and boiling before midnight, and begin not again till about dawn: it having been found, that the quantity of sugar made in the night, is not in proportion to the time; that it not only suffers in quality, but also lies open to pilferage; and that the mules, particularly the most tractable, and easily harnessed, are injured by being worked indiscriminately, in the dark, out of their turn; another valuable consequence, this of their being confusedly huddled together in that inclosed dung-heap, the pen: for the danger of grinding off a drowsy negroe's arm, or harrassing him to death, is a consideration which without these other circumstances, would hardly interrupt the grand work of sugar-making. [pp. 74–7]

# *Additional Notes to* The Sugar-Cane

### *Title-page*

The epigraph is from the *Astronomica* (I, 4–6) of Manilius (early 1st century AD), and may be translated: '... and I am the first to attempt to stir with new songs Helicon and its green-topped, nodding woods, bringing strange mysteries, proclaimed by none before me.' (See Introduction.)

### *Preface*

'Pere Labat' was Jean-Baptiste Labat (1663–1738), a Dominican friar who spent several years in the Caribbean and who was the author of a well-known, if not entirely reliable, travel account, the *Nouveau Voyage aux Iles de l'Amérique* (first published 1722); see Marcel Chatillon, *Le Père Labat à travers ses manuscrits*.

'Colonel Martyn' was Colonel Samuel Martin (c. 1690–1776), author of *An Essay upon Plantership [...]* (4th ed., Antigua printed, London reprinted, 1765). This was first printed in Antigua in 1750, and went through eight or nine editions (most of them printed in Antigua) between then and 1802, when the Jamaican printer Alexander Aikman included it in *Three Tracts on West-Indian Agriculture*, together with Grainger's *Sugar-Cane* and (under a different title) *Essay on the more common West-India Diseases* (see Bibliography, and Swan, *The Caribbean Area*, pp. 21–2).

Janet Schaw met Colonel Martin in 1774 and described him as 'the loved and revered father of Antigua, to whom it owes a thousand advantages [...] This is one of the oldest families on the Island, has for many generations enjoyed great power and riches, of which they have made the best use, living on their Estates, which are cultivated to the height by a large troop of healthy Negroes, who cheerfully perform the labour imposed on them by a kind and beneficent master, not a harsh and unreasonable Tyrant. Well fed, well supported, they appear the subjects of a good prince, not the slaves of a planter.' See Andrews, *Journal of a Lady of Quality*, pp. 103–4, and Appendix II, pp. 259–73.

Hesiod was a Greek poet of the eighth century BC, and the presumed

214   The Poetics of Empire

author of *Works and Days*, a poem on the relationship of man to nature and the labours of the farmer, which was a major influence on Virgil's *Georgics*.

Virgil (Publius Virgilius Maro, 70–19 BC), the most famous of Latin poets, wrote the *Eclogues* (pastoral poems giving an idealised picture of the shepherd's life), the *Georgics* (a poem in four books which is, like Hesiod's *Works and Days*, superficially about agriculture, but which is much broader in its concerns), and the *Aeneid*, an epic about the wanderings of the Trojan hero Aeneas and the founding of Rome.

John Philips (1676–1709), English poet, best known as the author of *Cyder* (1708), the first of the modern English georgic poems.

John Dyer (?1700–57), English poet, author of *The Fleece* (1757), another important poem in the English georgic tradition, reviewed by Grainger in *Monthly Review*, XVI, 328–340 (April 1757).

The Latin quotation is adapted from the poem *De Rerum Natura* ('On the Nature of Things', III, 2–6) by Lucretius (Titus Lucretius Carus, 1st century BC), and may be translated 'I follow you, o ornament of the Greek race, and plant my footsteps in the tracks you have made, not out of any wish to compete with you, but on account of love, because I want to be like you' (the Latin *imitari* does not necessarily have the negative connotations of the English 'to imitate'). Grainger has altered the Latin to make plural the references to 'you' which were singular in the original (referring to the philosopher Epicurus), thus transforming the passage into a tribute to all of the poetic predecessors he has just mentioned.

The same quotation (unaltered) was used by Alexander Pope (1688–1744) as the epigraph to his translation of the *Iliad*, so that it invoked Homer himself. Many of Grainger's readers would have known this, as Pope's *Iliad* (first published 1715–20) was one of the best-known poems of the eighteenth century, and Grainger's use of it is a further indication of the loftiness of his poetic claims.

Basseterre   The capital of St Kitts.

## Book I

Argument   The 'Woura' is 'the Cane's sapless foliage' (I, 230), known as trash or cane-trash in modern Caribbean English. Grainger does not use the word again, and may have decided it was too foreign for incorporation into English poetic diction. James Ramsay (*Essay*, p. 75) refers to 'wowra, the decayed leaves of the cane,' as fuel.

*Additional Notes to* The Sugar-Cane. *Book I* 215

In a note in *TCD* (f. 51ᵛ – not used in *1764*) on a passage in Book III, Grainger says 'The dryed leaves of yᵉ Cane are called Woula [sic], & yᵉ dried Stalkes Magoss. Both are used as Fuel in the Boiling House & Stillhouse.' This may be a slip of the pen rather than a genuine alternative. (On 'Magoss', see III, 81, Grainger's note, and the note below.)

The origin of the word is obscure; it does not appear in Allsopp, *Dictionary of Caribbean English Usage*, or Cassidy and Le Page, *Dictionary of Jamaican English*, though it may possibly be connected with Jamaican English 'were-were', the meanings of which include 'anything ragged' and for which Twi and Yoruba parallels have been suggested (Cassidy and Le Page, s.v.).

1–6   The opening passage is ultimately based on *G*, I, 1–5):

> Quid faciat laetas segetes, quo sidere terram
> vertere, Maecenas, ulmisque adiungere vitis
> conveniat, quae cura boum, qui cultus habendo
> sit pecori, apibus quanta experentia parcis,
> hinc canere incipiam.

> What makes a plenteous harvest, when to turn
> The fruitful soil, and when to sow the corn;
> The care of sheep, of oxen, and of kine,
> And how to raise on elms the teeming vine;
> The birth and genius of the frugal bee,
> I sing, Maecenas, and I sing to thee.
>         (Dryden's translation, in Keith Walker,
>                     ed., *John Dryden*, p. 463)

Just as Virgil summarises the subject-matter of the four books of his poem, so does Grainger; the parallel is a close one, and, ominously, 'How [...] Afric's sable progeny to treat' echoes the *cura boum* ('care of cattle') and the other references to farm livestock.

A more immediate influence is the opening of Philips' *Cyder* (I, 1–6):

> What Soil the Apple loves, what Care is due
> To Orchats, timeliest when to press the Fruits,
> Thy Gift, *Pomona*, in *Miltonian* Verse
> Adventrous I presume to sing; of Verse
> Nor skill'd, nor studious: But my Native Soil
> Invites me, and the Theme as yet unsung.
>         (Lloyd Thomas, *Poems of John Philips*, p. 44)

Smart's *Hop-Garden* begins in a similar manner (Williamson, ed., p. 42). The myrtle to which Grainger refers is a Mediterranean evergreen shrub, *Myrtus communis*, which in classical mythology was sacred to Venus. As Grainger later points out (I, 551–4), he did not find it in the Caribbean, though he thought it 'would grow' there; related species occur elsewhere in the world, including parts of South America. Often when Grainger talks about his muse, it is simply a periphrasis for himself; the reference to 'myrtle-indolence' perhaps suggests that he had been devoting his time to love rather than poetry (alluding to his marriage, for which see introduction), or it may simply be pointing out the very different character of his previous major work, the translation of Tibullus, much of which consists of love-poetry.

4   'Afric' (also at II, 166; IV, 199) or 'Africk' (IV, 1, 72, 382) used instead of 'Africa' which, with its initial stressed syllable followed by two unstressed ones, will not fit the iambic metre of Grainger's blank verse.

8–13   The 'Ascrean Poet' is Hesiod, whose alleged birthplace, Ascra, was a village near Mount Helicon, 'the sacred Mount' which was the traditional home of the Muses; Maro is Virgil; 'Pomona's Bard' is John Philips, the author of *Cyder* (Pomona was the Roman goddess of fruit and fruit-trees); on these and 'pastoral Dyer' (so called in reference to his authorship of *The Fleece*), see notes on Grainger's Preface.

Virgil mentions *Ascraeum ... carmen*, 'Ascraean song', in the sense of didactic poetry on agriculture in a passage (*G*, II, 173–6) imitated by Smart (*Hop-Garden*, I, 156–63; Williamson, ed., p. 46), who refers to 'th'Ascræan muse.'

Christopher Smart (1722–70), English poet, is now best remembered for his *Song to David* (1763), but is invoked here as the author of *The Hop-Garden* (begun by 1743, but first published 1752).

'Sommerville' is William Somerville (1675–1742), English poet, author of *The Chace* (1735), a long poem on hunting which has some of the characteristics of the georgic tradition.

Grainger invokes these names as a deliberate statement that he is placing his own poem in the well-established tradition of georgic poetry; for a fuller discussion of this, see Introduction.

11   Here, and elsewhere (II, 290; II, 347), Grainger uses 'Dome' in the sense of 'house' (Latin *domus*). Dyer uses the word with reference to an English workhouse (*The Fleece*, Book III; *Poems*, 1761, p. 135) and it

appears in other contexts in *The Fleece* (ibid., pp 54, 92, 119). In *The School-Mistress* (version in Dodsley's *Collection*), Shenstone (see note below on the Advertisement to Book II) refers both to the 'little dome' of the village schoolmistress (also called a 'lowly shed') and to 'the pompous dome of kesar or of king.'

16   Grainger's insistence on the novelty of his subject also appears in his Preface, and at I, 67–70; I, 300–301 and IV, 23–24.

This is a more or less standard feature of eighteenth-century didactic poetry, echoing Virgil's *primus ego* (G, III, 10: 'I first ... '); compare how John Armstrong ends his invocation to Hygeia at the opening of *The Art of Preserving Health*, I, 50–52 (1744 ed., p. 4):

> Yet with thy aid the secret wilds I trace
> Of nature, and with daring steps proceed
> Thro' paths the muses never trod before.

Compare also Dyer's introduction to the passage at the end of *The Fleece*, Book IV (*Poems*, 1761, pp. 178–188) in which he describes British commerce with the Americas:

> Now to the other hemisphere, my muse,
> A new world found, extend thy daring wing.
> Be thou the first of the harmonious Nine
> From high Parnassus, the unweary'd toils
> Of industry and valour, in that world
> Triumphant, to reward with tuneful song.

19–20   'Aurelius' is George Thomas (c. 1694–1774), Governor of the Leeward Islands, 1753–66. He was a member of a prominent Antiguan family: his father had been a Member of the House of Assembly of Antigua, and his grandfather had been a member of the island's Council, while his mother was the grand-daughter of a previous governor of Antigua. George Thomas had earlier been governor of Pennsylvania (1738–1747) and was created a baronet on his retirement from the Leewards. See Oliver, *History of Antigua*, I, 269, and III, 128–35, and *Caribbeana*, II, 337. Thomas was also the dedicatee of Martin's *Essay upon Plantership*.

'Imperial George' is the British king, George III (reigned 1760–1820). *TCD* (f. 4$^r$) has

> So shall my Numbers win the public Ear;
> And not displease my Bourryau; with whom,
> Leaving Augusta's Joys, (what cannot Friends?)
> I voyag'd first the vast Atlantic Deep;
> First wondering saw the Charibbean Cane [...]

Grainger later deleted 'Bourryau' and substituted 'Memmius,' the name of the person to whom Lucretius dedicated his *De rerum natura*. On John Bourryau, see introduction. 'Augusta' was a conventional poetic name for London, though it is not used by Grainger in the published version of the poem. A draft of the 'Aurelius' version of this passage is on *TCD*, f. 3ᵛ.

22, n. *1764* has 'Lucan and Pliny are the only Authors among the former' which is an obvious error after mention of 'The Greeks and Romans' in that order. *1764* also has 'the Great or Lesser Antilles' but the *Errata* say 'for *lesser* read *less*.' This change is followed by both Chalmers (1810) and Anderson (1836) in their editions. Modern Caribbean English usage refers to the Greater Antilles (Cuba, Hispaniola, Puerto Rico and Jamaica) and the Lesser Antilles (the remaining, smaller islands of the region).

For Grainger's use of the word 'Indian', see note on I, 586, below.

Grainger's quotation ('they drank sweet juices from a reed') from Lucan (Marcus Annaeus Lucanus, Roman poet, 39–65 AD) is presumably from memory, as it is inaccurate and will not fit the scansion of Latin verse. Lucan (*Pharsalia*, III, 237) has *quique bibunt tenera dulces ab harundine sucos* ('who drank sweet juices from a soft reed'); see Loeb trs. by J. D. Duff, p. 133.

'The industrious Naturalist' is Gaius Plinius Secundus (Pliny the Elder, Roman writer, 23–79 AD), whose statement that 'Arabia also produces cane-sugar, but that grown in India is more esteemed' is at Book XII (xvii, 32) of his *Natural History*; see Loeb trs. by Rackham et al., IV, 22–3.

Arrian (Greek historian, first to second century AD) is no longer regarded as the author of the 'περιπλους of the Red-sea', now generally referred to as *The Periplus of the Erythraean Sea*, a work of unknown authorship of the late first or early second century AD. A periplus is a sailing-guide. See Huntingford's translation, where the passage cited by Grainger ('honey-cane called sakkhari') is at p. 29.

Geoffrey Chaucer (c. 1340–1400) mentions 'sugre' twice in *The Canterbury Tales* (Squire's Tale, l. 614; Tale of Sir Thopas, l. 856) and uses 'sucred' and 'sucre' in *Troilus and Criseyde* (II, 384; III, 1194).

## Additional Notes to The Sugar-Cane. Book I    219

29, n.  Grainger refers to *A New Dictionary, Spanish and English and English and Spanish [...]* (London, 1740) by Peter Pineda (or Pedro Pineda, as his name is given on a facing title-page with all details in Spanish), which he mentions again, I, 595, n. Pineda has no entry for 'muscovado' but the word is indeed of Spanish origin. Nearly all the sugar exported from the Caribbean was muscovado; most of it was further refined in Europe before being sold to the consumer.

30  'Planter' was, from the seventeenth century, the usual word in the English-speaking Caribbean for the owner of any reasonably extensive area of land cultivated in export crops (a 'plantation'), and may be found in this sense in, for example, Richard Ligon, *A True & Exact History of the Island of Barbadoes* (2nd ed., 1673), p. 42. Grainger uses the word frequently and naturally in its Caribbean sense, but he may have been encouraged to do so by the fact that it appears in earlier English poetry in other senses: Philips (*Cyder*, I, 41; Lloyd Thomas, *Poems of John Philips*, p. 45) uses it to refer to a farmer who plants apple-trees for cider, and Smart (*Hop-Garden*, II, 74, 101; II, 236; Williamson, ed., pp. 57, 63) uses it for the hop-grower.

31   Here, and later, the description of specific types of soil echoes *G*, II, 177–258.

34–7  Grainger's 'wild red cedar' is probably *Tabebuia heterophylla*; the locust is *Hymenæa courbaril*; the cassia is *Cassia fistula* (see also IV, 513–17 and note on IV, 513, n.); the ceiba or silk-cotton tree is *Ceiba pentandra*; the guava (*Psidium guajava*) is a fruit widely popular in the Caribbean and South America, and which in the late twentieth century is beginning to appear in British supermarkets; the guaiac or lignum-vitae (Latin = 'wood of life') tree is *Guaiacum officinale*, the resin of which was until the late eighteenth century widely considered to be a cure for venereal disease (hence Grainger's reference to 'corrupted love').

'Acosta' is probably José de Acosta (?1539–1600), author of a *Historia natural y moral de las Indias* (Seville, 1590). An English translation was published in 1604.

44–5, n.  The shaddoc (more usually shaddock, sometimes called pummelo) is *Citrus grandis*, a fruit similar to the grapefruit. It is a native of the Malaysian archipelago, but was being grown in the Caribbean by the seventeenth century. The story, to which Grainger refers in his note, that it is called after a Captain Shaddock who brought it to the Caribbean, is derived from Sloane, *A Voyage to the Islands*, I, 41, but cannot be proved. 'Forbidden fruit' was a common name for the grapefruit, *Citrus paradisii*, which may have originated in Barbados. The 'white acajou' is probably *Anacardium occidentale*, while the sabbaca is, as Grainger identifies it in his note, the avocado pear, *Persea americana*.

The brothers Jorge Juan de Ulloa and Antonio de Ulloa were sent as Spanish representatives on the French expedition of Charles Marie de la Condamine and others which left Paris in 1735 and travelled in South America for several years as part of a project for the exact measurement of an arc of the earth's surface. The Ulloas' account, first published in Madrid, 1748, appeared in English as *A Voyage to South America [...] Translated from the Original Spanish* (2nd. ed., 2 vols., London, 1760). The name 'aguacate' is used in the translation (I, 301–2). Grainger refers to the Ulloas again (I, 526, n.; I, 641, n.; II, 74, n.; III, 350, n.) and also cites La Condamine's account (III, 350, n.).

Sloane, *A Voyage to the Islands [...]*, II, 132–3, describes the avocado, but does not use the expression 'vegetable marrow' either there or in his *Catalogus Plantarum*.

55   The two 'Dog Stars' are prominent in the night-sky during the 'Dog Days' in the heat of summer (July and August). See also I, 416 and III, 164.

57   The 'after-offspring' are ratoon-canes, i.e., those allowed to grow from the stumps of canes cut the previous crop, as distinct from plant-canes, which were those freshly planted for the new season, as was the usual practice in St Kitts. See Edwards, *History ... of the British West Indies*, I, 465.

60–83   The praise of St Kitts echoes, in tone rather than in specific detail, the *Laudes Italiae* ('Praises of Italy', *G*, II, 136–76), one of the most famous passages in Virgil.

60, n.   The Shakespeare reference is to *The Tragedy of King Richard the Second*, II, i, from the famous lines spoken by John of Gaunt in which he praises England as 'This other Eden, demi-paradise'.

The area of St Kitts is given from Thomas Templeman, *A New Survey of the Globe ...* (London, n.d., c. 1729), in which Plate 28 is a table giving the dimensions and locations of the 'Islands of America.' The area is more correctly 63 square miles; Templeman's figures were derived from measur-

## Additional Notes to The Sugar-Cane. Book I 221

ing existing maps and globes, and not from actual surveys. The statement that the island 'lies in the seventeenth degree N[orth] L[atitude]' is accurate enough; the capital Basseterre is 17° 18' N, 62° 44' W. The figures Grainger gives for the dimensions of Barbados (I, 132, n.) and the latitude of Antigua (III, 222, n.) do not accord with Templeman's.

Martin, *Essay upon Plantership*, p. 15 describes the soil of St Kitts as 'the best in the known world for producing sugar in great quantity, and of the best quality.'

61 Tempé (or Tempe) was a valley in northern Greece proverbial among classical authors for its beauty, e.g. *G*, II, 469; IV, 317. Arcadia is an area in Greece which even in classical times was celebrated for the primitive simplicity of its inhabitants, so that 'Arcadian' has become synonymous with idealised images of the shepherd's life. One of the chief deities of Arcadia was Pan, a god of shepherds, flocks and woodlands, usually shown with the ears, horns and legs of a goat, and playing 'his silvan pipe'.

Akenside mentions 'Fair Tempe! haunt belov'd of sylvan powers' in connection with Pan (*The Pleasures of Imagination*, I, 299–302; ed. Dix, p.100).

64–72 Enna was a city in Sicily particularly associated with the legend of Proserpine or Proserpina (the Latinised form of the Greek Persephone), who in classical mythology was the daughter of Zeus and the earth-goddess Demeter (identified by the Romans with their goddess of grain and harvests, Ceres, who is mentioned by name by Grainger below, I, 290; III, 160, 502; IV, 346). She was carried off to the underworld by Pluto (also known as Dis or Hades), but was later permitted to return to earth for part of each year because her mother would otherwise have prevented the crops growing. Enna is mentioned again (IV, 330).

Grainger is almost certainly influenced here by Milton's description (*Paradise Lost*, IV, 268–72) of how nothing could exceed the beauties of the Garden of Eden:

> Not that fair field
> Of Enna, where Proserpine gathering flowers
> Her self a fairer flower by gloomie Dis
> Was gathered, which cost Ceres all that pain
> To seek her through the world [...]

A little earlier (IV, 254–5), Milton refers to how in Eden 'the flowery lap/Of some irriguous valley spread her store.' There is also a hint of Virgil's description (*G*, IV, 30–2) of ideal conditions for bees:

> haec circum casiae virides et olentia late
> serpylla et graviter spirantis copia thymbrae
> floreat, iriguumque bibant violaria fontem.

(Around these let green cassias flourish, and wild-thyme that spreads its perfume far and wide, and an abundance of heavy-scented savory, and let banks of violets drink from the flowing spring.)

Tibullus (II, i, 44) has 'tunc bibit irriguas fertilis hortus aquas', which Grainger translated as 'While through the thirsty Ground meandring Runnels flow'd' (*Poetical Translation of the Elegies of Tibullus*, II, 21). Compare also Akenside, 'th' irriguous lawn', *The Pleasures of Imagination*, II, 642 (ed. Dix, p. 129) and Dyer, 'th' irriguous vales', (*The Fleece*, Book I; *Poems*, 1761, p. 84).

Bryan Edwards uses 'th'irriguous valley deep below' in 'Jamaica, A descriptive and didactic poem', *Poems, written chiefly in the West-Indies*, p. 11.

71, n.  The reference is to Sloane, *A Voyage to the Islands [...]*, I, 46.

90–2  Adapted from Milton, *Comus*, ll. 21–3, which refers to Neptune having

> Imperial rule of all the sea-girt isles
> That like to rich, and various gems inlay
> The unadorned bosom of the deep [...]

94  The 'Daughters of Heaven' are the Muses.

97–126  Praise of Columbus was frequent in poetry in the centuries after his death. A near contemporary example is in *The Sea-Piece* (1750) by another medically qualified poet, James Kirkpatrick (d. 1770):

> Bold was the Man, who dar'd at first to shew
> From an Old World the Passage to a new;
> Who greatly went in Quest of Lands unknown,
> And for uncertain Regions left his own;
> Who o'er extensive Seas a Journey taught,
> Seas as extensive as a Poet's Thought!

– and so on for nearly a hundred lines (pp. 108–13). Grainger certainly knew the Renaissance Latin poem *Syphilis* (1530) by Girolamo Fracastoro (see Introduction).

## Additional Notes to The Sugar-Cane. Book I

In the 'Advertisement' to his unfinished 'Jamaica, A descriptive and didactic poem', in *Poems, written chiefly in the West-Indies*, Bryan Edwards lists 'the first voyage and discoveries of Columbus' among the topics which 'afford rich materials for a Poem, that might prove at once original, instructive, pathetic, and sublime.'

The 'Iberian King' (l. 113) and 'the Prince,/To whom thou gavs't the sceptre of that world' (ll. 119–20) are both Ferdinand, King of Aragon (reigned 1479–1516), who was with his wife Isabella, Queen of Castile (reigned 1474–1504), the patron of Columbus' voyages. The 'Nine' are the Muses.

See also IV, 360.

128   The *Errata* say 'for *elay* read *clay*', but the copies of *1764* I have seen have 'clay' in this line.

132–3 n.   The name of Barbados was (and is) widely supposed to be derived from the bearded fig-tree (modern scientific name *Ficus citrifolia*), but this is debatable. See entry 'Barbados (Name)' in Fraser, et al., *A-Z of Barbadian Heritage* and P. F. Campbell, 'Barbados: The Early Years,' *Journal of the Barbados Museum and Historical Society*, XXXV, No. 3 (1977), pp. 157–77. Barbados is approximately 21 miles long by 14 broad.

Grainger appears to have known his Milton well, but he may have been reminded of the passage he quotes (*Paradise Lost*, IX, 1101–10) by its appearance in Hughes, *Natural History of Barbados* (1750), p. 176, where he could also have found the reference to what the Roman writer Quintus Curtius Rufus (1st century AD), said in his *History of Alexander the Great*, IX, i, , 9–10 (Loeb trs. by J. C. Rolfe, II, 367). The Curtius reference is also in Sloane, *A Voyage to the Islands*, II, 139.

Bryan Edwards mentions 'yon mightier fig' in his 'Jamaica, A descriptive and didactic poem', *Poems, written chiefly in the West-Indies*, pp. 13–14 and note, quoting the same passage of Milton.

In a similar context, Chapman also quotes the same passage of Milton (*Barbadoes, and other poems*, note, pp. 87–8).

134, n.   Nevis is 50 square miles; the channel separating it from St Kitts is about two miles at its narrowest point.

In his *Essay on the more common West-India Diseases* (1764, p. 44), Grainger claimed 'the waters of the hot-bath at Nevis' were 'more powerful in all cases of relaxation than that of Bristol.' See also note on III, 366–80.

135, n.  Montserrat is about 25 miles southwest of Antigua, and 39½ square miles.

166  Possibly an echo of Philips, *Cyder*, I, 91: 'If a penurious Clay should be thy Lot,' (Lloyd Thomas, *Poems of John Philips*, p. 47).

172–3  Rats, monkeys and other pests of the cane are described in more detail in Book II.

175  The bill (or bill-hook), often known in the Caribbean as a cane-bill, is 'an edged Tool used by Husbandmen in lopping Trees, &c.' (Bailey). It has a broad blade with a wide, straight or slightly curved end without a point, but usually with a hook on the side opposite the cutting edge; the hook is used for stripping the trash (dried leaves) from the cane-stalk after it has been cut.

185  This line is short (seven syllables instead of the usual ten). There are a number of these short lines in *The Sugar-Cane* (see also I, 645; II, 305, 328, 413, 522, 531), probably in conscious imitation of the lines which were left short in the *Aeneid* because Virgil died before he was able to finish revising it. This affectation seems to have first been adopted in English poetry by Abraham Cowley (1618–67) in his *Davideis*; see Johnson, *Lives of the English Poets* (Everyman edition, I, 43).

186–93  If Grainger had not actually seen such land-slips in the Caribbean, or heard first-hand accounts of them, he could have found several examples in Hughes, *Natural History of Barbados*, pp. 21–2. John Philips ('thy bard, Pomona'; see note on ll. 8–13 above) refers to one at Marcley Hill in Herefordshire in 1571 (hence Grainger's 'of old') – see Lloyd Thomas, *Poems of John Philips*, pp. 46–7, 100.

198  *1764* has a comma after 'harvests'; the *Errata* call for its removal. Chalmers (1810) keeps the comma, while Anderson (1836) removes it. There is no comma in *TCD* (f. 14ʳ).

206, n.  Grainger uses 'Liamuiga' for St Kitts again (II, 47; III, 288); see also his note on I, 60. He does not use the word 'Caribbean' in the poem itself; in his notes (here and at I, 341, 526; III, 283; IV, 449), he consistently uses it to mean 'Amerindian.' Ogilby, *America* (cited by Grainger at IV, 449, n.) uses 'the Caribbeeans' [sic] to refer to the indigenous inhabitants of the Lesser Antilles (e.g., pp. 357, 359). See also note on I, 586, below.

213 The 'lily' refers to the flag of pre-Revolutionary France: three gold fleurs-de-lys on a white ground.

216 Here and elsewhere, Grainger uses the classical Latin name Gallia (II, 81; III, 442, 455) or its anglicised version, Gaul (II, 177, 469) for France. The French are also referred to as 'the Gaul' (III, 307) or Gauls (II, 493), and the adjective Gallic (II, 55; IV, 622) is also used. This is a normal feature of eighteenth-century poetic diction; compare, e.g., Thomson, *The Seasons* (Summer, l. 430): 'Gallia's humbled coast'.

218-27 Grainger of course has the example of Virgil (*G*, I, 79-81) for the introduction of dung into poetry:

> sed tamen alternis facilis labor, arida tantum
> ne saturare fimo pingui pudeat sola neve
> effetos cinerem immundum iactare per agros.

However alternating crops makes the task easy, provided you are not ashamed to glut the dried earth with rich dung, or to scatter filthy ashes over the worn-out fields.

There is also a passage on compost in Philips, *Cyder*, I, 119-25 (Lloyd Thomas, *Poems of John Philips*, p. 48). On the other hand, while Smart has eight lines on the use of lime to improve the soil, and says 'But now to plant, to dig, to dung, to weed;/Tasks how indelicate? demand the muse', in fact he mentions dung and compost only briefly and in passing (*Hop-Garden*, I, 87, 130-7, 255-6, 288; Williamson, ed., pp. 44, 45, 49, 50). For the problem of whether this is suitable material for a poet, see Introduction.

Both St Kitts and Nevis had a reputation for high yields of sugar to the acre, and this was generally attributed to a more careful attention to manuring and a more lavish use of manure than was the case in Jamaica and other islands – see Merrill, *Historical Geography of St. Kitts and Nevis*, pp. 75-9. Janet Schaw commented in 1775 that

> tho' perhaps there is no such rich land in the world as this Island, they use manure in great abundance, and would be as glad of the rakes of

Edinburgh streets as the Lothian farmers. No planter is above attending to this grand article, which is hoarded up with the utmost care, and I every where saw large dunghills of compound manure, composed of the ashes from the boiling kettle, the bruised canes, the spilt leaves of the cane, the cleanings of the houses and dung of the stables. These are turned up and kept till proper for use, and no infant cane is placed in its pit without a very sufficient quantity of this to bed and nurse it up.

(Andrews, *Journal of a Lady of Quality*, p. 127)

For a mock-heroic parallel, compare Cowper's description of how to grow cucumbers under glass (*The Task*, Book III, 463–5):

> The stable yields a stercorarious heap,
> Impregnated with quick fermenting salts,
> And potent to resist the freezing blast.
> (Sambrook, ed., *William Cowper: The Task and Selected Other Poems*, p. 126)

230   See note on the Argument to Book I.

233   Dorchestria is the Latinised name of the English county of Dorset. Dyer refers to 'Dorcestrian fields' (*The Fleece*, Book I; *Poems*, 1761, p. 53) Grainger spent 'about 6 or 8 weeks' in Dorchester, the county town, with his pupil John Bourryau in 1754 (William Cuming to Thomas Percy, 16 January 1775, NLS Adv. MS 22-4-10, ff. 14–17).

237   Yams (*Dioscorea var species*) are a root vegetable still popular in many parts of the Caribbean.

260 n.   Junks are here (and at I, 402) the cut pieces of cane which are planted for new canes to grow from them (as distinct from ratoons, which are new growth from the roots of canes which have been cut). The word is still current in Jamaica in this sense; in other parts of the Caribbean they are referred to as plant-canes or cane-butts. Perhaps originally a sailors' word; Bailey has only 'JUNK (among *Sailors*) Pieces of old cable.' See also I, 595 n. (referring to pieces of cassava), III, 127, 188. *OED* quotes Grainger under definition of junk as 'A piece or lump of anything; a chunk.'

262–5   This hint is derived from Martin (*Essay upon Plantership*, p. 32) but it also echoes Philips' suggestions on suitable locations for the farmer to plant apple-trees:

> But to the West
> Let him free Entrance grant, let *Zephyrs* bland
> Administer their tepid genial Airs;
> Naught fear he from the West, whose gentle Warmth
> Discloses well the Earth's all-teeming Womb,
> Invigorating tender Seeds
> [...]
> with the fertile Moisture chear'd,
> The Orchats smile; joyous the Farmers see
> Their thriving Plants, and bless the heav'nly Dew.
> (*Cyder*, I, 26–40; Lloyd Thomas,
> *Poems of John Philips*, p. 45)

266–77 Compare *G*, II, 277–87, where the ordered planting of trees which will be used to support vines is compared to an army drawn up in battle array. Grainger only hints (ll. 262–5) at what Virgil makes explicit – that such patterns are of practical as well as aesthetic value. Note how the chiasmic repetition of 'squadron, and brigade, [...] Brigade and squadron' emphasises the idea of 'Their order'd station.' The simile is a reminder of Grainger's own military career, and line 272 suggests the anti-Jacobite campaign of 1746 in which he took part. Smart (*Hop-Garden*, I, 350–357; Williamson, ed., p. 52) compares the 'comely order' of hop-poles to the 'neat arrangement' in which 'the men of Kent [...] Intrepid march'd' to confront William the Conqueror.

One of the effects of having slaves dig cane-holes with hoes instead of spades was that it was possible to maintain a much stricter discipline. This was described by a slightly later writer on Jamaica, William Beckford (d. 1799, not to be confused with his relative and more famous namesake, the author of the orientalist fantasy *Vathek*) in a 1788 publication:

> Their different instruments of husbandry, particularly their gleaming hoes, when uplifted to the sun, and which, particularly when they are digging cane-holes, they frequently raise all together, and in as exact time as can be observed, in a well-conducted orchestra, in the bowing of the fiddles, occasion the light to break in momentary flashes around them.

(quoted in Hogg, *Slavery: The Afro-American Experience*, pp. 42–44). Grainger's question about whether the plough might offer a better method (ll. 286–8) was asked by many others, but even after the end of slavery, the continued availability of cheap labour kept the hoe in use well into the twentieth century on sugar plantations in a number of Caribbean territories.

290 n.  On Ceres, see note on I, 64–72 above. Jethro Tull (1674–1741), English writer on agriculture, was famous for *The Horse-hoing Husbandry* (London, 1733).

301  Compare Akenside, *The Pleasures of Imagination*, I, 55: 'Where never poet gain'd a wreath before.' (ed. Dix, p. 92).

308  Philips (*Cyder*, II, 158; Lloyd Thomas, *Poems of John Philips*, p. 73) has 'The Clouds dropt Fatness'. Compare also Grainger's 'Fat-fostering rains' (III, 220) and Psalm lxv, 12, in the *Book of Common Prayer*: 'Thou crownest the year with thy goodness: and thy clouds drop fatness.'

311  TCD (f. 19$^r$) has 'Let Observation then with curious Ken'. The change removes not only the jingling effect of having 'then' and 'Ken' so close to each other, but also the reminiscence of the opening line of Johnson's *The Vanity of Human Wishes* (1749): 'Let Observation with extensive view'.

313  The 'Mantuan Bard' is Virgil, who was born in Mantua; his discussion of 'The signs of rain' is in *G*, I, 351–92, a passage imitated by Smart (*Hop-Garden*, II, 106–148; Williamson, ed., pp. 58–9). Grainger's discussion of weather-signs is generally inspired by Virgil although, as he says (ll. 315–16), his specific details are chosen with a view to local circumstances.

327  Apollo is the classical god of healing, hence 'Apollo's arts' here simply means medicine.

329–30  Amyntor comes from a Greek word meaning 'defender,' and is the name of a minor character in Homer (*Iliad*, IX, 448; X, 266), also mentioned in Ovid's *Metamorphoses*. The reference to Themis (classical goddess of justice) and the context suggests that Grainger had in mind some Caribbean lawyer of his acquaintance who had met an 'untimely fate'. The passage appears in a slightly different form in *TCD* (f. 20$^r$), where the pseudonym was first Aurelius, later changed to Themistius; a note opposite (f. 19$^v$) gives the identification 'The Hon[ble] Ralph Payne Esq[re] Chief Judge of y[e] Isl[d] of S[t] Christopher' and presumably this was still meant to apply to Amyntor. Ralph Payne died in 1762, and was the father of another Ralph Payne (1737–1807), later Lord Lavington and twice governor of the Leeward Islands – see Mrs Lanaghan, *Antigua and the Antiguans*, II, 347, and *DNB*.

332   Adapted from Edward Young, *The Universal Passion. Satire III. To the Right Honourable Mr. Dodington* (1725), p. 1:

> Tho' prone to like, yet cautious to commend,
> You read with all the malice of a friend.

Young published seven separate satires with the title *The Universal Passion* (1725–28) which were collected as *Love of Fame, The Universal Passion* (2nd ed., London, 1728). Although eclipsed by Pope's satires, *Love of Fame* remained popular throughout the eighteenth century and was often reprinted, both on its own and as part of collected editions of the works of Young (1683–1765), who achieved renewed fame as the author of *The Complaint, or, Night-Thoughts on Life, Death and Immortality* (London, 1742–46).

The phrase 'with all the malice of a friend' may have become proverbial; Percy uses it (without any indication of its being a quotation or allusion) in an 1802 letter to Robert Anderson (W. E. K. Anderson, *Percy Letters*, IX, 109).

334, n.   Grainger implies that the word mosquito would not have been familiar to his British readers, though it appears in English literature from the sixteenth century. Bailey has 'MOSCHETTO, a stinging Gnat, very troublesome in the *West Indies*.' Pierre Louis Moreau de Maupertuis (1698–1759), French mathematician and astronomer, headed an expedition sent by Louis XV to Lapland in 1736 to measure the length of a degree of the meridian.

The mosquitos referred to are *Anopheles* spp., *Aedes* spp., or both; while the 'sand-flies' are *Phlebotomus* spp. or *Culicoides* spp. For this, and much other information on insects and worms in subsequent notes, I am indebted to the article by Kevan, 'Mid-eighteenth-century entomology and helminthology in The West Indies: Dr James Grainger' (see Bibliography).

337, n.   Cockroaches are a common feature of Caribbean life; they are less common in poetry, but 'The obscene roaches gather from their holes' as one of the portents of a hurricane in Chapman, *Barbadoes, and other poems*, p. 70.

Grainger's 'common sort' of cockroach is *Periplaneta americana*, while his 'Drummer' is *Blaberus* sp.

339   In classical mythology, the Harpies (from a Greek word meaning the Snatchers) were originally personified spirits of storms, but Grainger's reference is to their later depiction as creatures part-bird and part-woman, who torment Phineus in the version of the story of the voyage of the Argo in Apollodorus (Greek writer, perhaps 2nd century AD): as a divine punishment, whenever food is put in front of Phineus, the Harpies swoop down to snatch it away, and whatever fragments they leave behind are tainted by their foul smell; see Ireland, ed., *Apollodorus: The Argonauts & Herakles*, p. 21. The Harpies are described in similar terms in *Aeneid*, III.

341, n.   The 'speckled lizard' identified as a 'ground-lizard' is probably *Ameiva* sp. The 'tree-lizard ... of a fine green colour' could be any of several species; there are also several species of iguana. *Lues Venerea* is Latin for venereal disease.

342, n.   Black crabs are referred to again as a delicacy at III, 610. Compare the section 'On the Abundance of Land Crabs and Fish in Jamaica, and Negro Methods of catching them' in Barclay, *Practical View*, pp. 313–20, where it is claimed that of the two varieties of crab eaten in Jamaica in the early nineteenth century, 'The black is the finest, and has ever been esteemed one of the greatest delicacies in the West Indies, not excepting even the turtle' (p. 314). Barclay also said 'Almost every estate has a negro employed as a fisherman, and generally another, an old man, as a crab-catcher' (p. 319). Landcrabs of various species are still eaten in parts of the Caribbean, but they appear to be both less common and less esteemed than they were when Grainger or Barclay wrote. The species referred to by Grainger is identified by Wright in Anderson (1836) as *Cancer ruricula*; this is possibly the black land-crab whose modern scientific name is *Gecarcinus lateralis* or, alternatively, *Cardiosoma* sp.

Grainger refers to 'roasted crabs' as bait for rat-traps at II, 78.

The mahoe-berry is probably the fruit of the seaside mahoe (*Thespesia populnea*) also known as the hibiscus-tree or tulip-tree, which is found on the sea-shore in much of the Caribbean and which has a fruit about 3 cm in diameter.

355   In classical mythology, naiads are water-nymphs, and hence used here and elsewhere (I, 392; III, 279, 284; IV, 580) by Grainger as a poeti-

cal expression for streams, in a manner conventional among British poets of the period. Compare, for example, Matthew Green, *The Spleen* (1737), ll. 684–7:

> And silver streams through meadows stray,
> And Naiads on the margin play,
> And lesser nymphs on side of hills
> From plaything urns pour down the rills.
> (Fausset, ed., *Minor Poets*, p. 226)

Armstrong, *Art of Preserving Health* (II, 352–3; 1744 ed., p. 45) and Dyer (*The Fleece*, Book III; *Poems*, 1761, p. 151) mention naiads in a similar manner.

Grainger may also have known (see on IV, 317, below) Akenside's *Hymn to the Naiads* (ed. Dix, pp. 360–78), first published in Dodsley's *Collection* in 1758.

376–94   There may be an influence here from Milton, *Il Penseroso*:

> [...] me Goddess bring
> To arched walks of twilight groves,
> And shadows brown that *Sylvan* loves
> Of Pine, or monumental Oake,
> Where the rude Ax with heaved stroke,
> Was never heard the Nymphs to daunt,
> Or fright them from their hallow'd haunt [...]

Grainger's recognition of the importance of woodland in ensuring adequate rainfall is interesting in view of the planter's traditional hostility to trees (compare I, 558–69). It is echoed by Chapman, *Barbadoes, and other poems*, pp. 39–40. Dyer, on the other hand, claimed that trees 'rob the lawns', i.e., damage the sheep's pasture (*The Fleece*, Book I; *Poems*, 1761, p. 56).

In the mid-nineteenth century, one observer claimed 'a Barbadian planter hates a tree as a bull does a red rag' – Gilmore, ed., *Chester's Barbados*, p. 15.

386   Phoebus is Apollo, as the sun-god (also at I, 592; III, 562; IV, 108).

393, n.   The 'fern-tree,' or tree-fern, is *Cyathea arborea*.

397   Iris (also at III, 550) is the goddess of the rainbow in classical mythology.

399 'all-jocund' – Thomas Gray, in one of the best-known poems of the eighteenth century (*Elegy Written in a Country Church-Yard*, l. 27), refers to English agricultural labourers in a similar way: 'How jocund did they drive their team afield!' (Lonsdale, ed., *Thomas Gray and William Collins: Poetical Works*, p. 35). Grainger quotes from Gray's poem below (I, 634) and he referred to it explicitly in his *Letter to Tobias Smollet* (London,1759), p. 10.

Grainger also uses 'jocund' (III, 414) in a passage describing the happiness of crop-time on the plantation, which may echo Smart's picture of summer work pruning hop-vines in England (*Hop-Garden*, I, 331-2; Williamson, ed., p. 51): 'When smiling June in jocund dance leads on/Long days and happy hours.' In *L'Allegro*, Milton refers to 'jocond rebecks' in the context of country festivities.

Compare Chapman, *Barbadoes, and other poems* (p. 10):

> [...] at the loud command,
> From their embowered huts come forth in throngs
> The sable race, and wake their joyful songs:
> They come to labour, but they come with joy,
> While themes of happiness their minds employ.

Chapman has a similar passage on the 'mirth unwearied' of the slaves at p. 13, and prose notes on the same theme (pp. 89-90, 92-3). He insists that the slaves in Barbados would be quite happy, were it not for the interference of English abolitionists (pp. 40-2, 54-6, 78-9; notes, pp. 99-100, 101-2, 107-8).

Bryan Edwards refers to the 'jocund toil' of slaves, though this is in a passage describing 'Lybian maidens' enjoying a swim in the river during a break from their labours: 'Jamaica, A descriptive and didactic poem', *Poems, written chiefly in the West-Indies*, pp. 6-7.

402 See note on I, 260 n.

407-15 Closely based on *G*, IV, 170-175, where the labours of bees are compared to those of the Cyclopes:

> ac veluti lentis Cyclopes fulmina massis
> cum properant, alii taurinis follibus auras
> accipiunt redduntque, alii stridentia tingunt
> aera lacu; gemit impositis incudibus Ætna;
> illi inter sese magna vi bracchia tollunt
> in numerum, versantque tenaci forcipe ferrum:

# Additional Notes to The Sugar-Cane. Book I 233

Just as when the Cyclopes hasten to make thunderbolts from molten masses [of metal], some with ox-hide bellows take in air and send it out again, others temper the sounding brass in the lake; Ætna groans with anvils placed in it; they [the Cyclopes] with great force raise their arms in rhythmic alternation, and turn the iron with grasping forceps [...]

Virgil adapts these lines in *Aeneid*, VIII, 449–53, where it forms part of a description of Vulcan and the Cyclopes making arms for the hero Aeneas. However, 'Peleus' Son' is Achilles; Grainger has conflated his Virgilian sources with *Iliad*, XVIII, 468–613, where Homer describes Hephaestus (the Greek equivalent of Vulcan) making arms for Achilles, without any assistance. The effect is to compare the planter ('the master swain') with Vulcan, and the slaves with the Cyclopes, and while Virgil half apologises for the comparison of the bees with the Cyclopes, saying *si parva licet componere magnis* ('if it is permissible to compare small things with great'; *G*, IV, 176), Grainger does nothing of the sort. See also note on II, 275–84.

Compare Smart's reference to charcoal-burners as 'The sable priests of Vulcan' (*Hop-Garden*, II, 200; Williamson, ed., p. 62).

415   Bailey defines 'fusile' as 'that may be melted or cast.' Philips refers to melted glass as 'a fusil Sea' (*Cyder*, II, 336; Lloyd Thomas, *Poems of John Philips*, p. 78), and Milton, *Paradise Lost*, XI, 572–3, has 'what might else be wrought/Fusile or graven in metal.'

416   Procyon is one of the two 'Dog Stars' – see note on I, 55.

417   Here and elsewhere (I, 432–3, 483–4, 489, 628; II, 287–9; III, 318; IV, 615), Grainger uses the signs of the zodiac, rather than the names of the months, to indicate the time of the year; a common convention in eighteenth-century poetry. Compare, for example, Philips, *Cyder*, I, 128 (Lloyd Thomas, *Poems of John Philips*, p. 48), 'when the Sun in *Leo* rides' or Smart, *Hop-Garden*, I, 281 (Williamson, ed., p. 50), 'When Phœbus looks thro' Aries on the spring'.

Leo is 'a Lion, the Name of one of the 12 signs of the Zodiac, which the Sun enters in *July*' (Bailey). Also referred to as 'the Lion' at I, 628.

418, n.   'mail'd' in the sense of 'armoured.' Compare John Armstrong, *Art of Preserving Health*, II, 334–5: 'in horrid mail/The soft Ananas wraps its tender sweets' (1744 ed., p. 44).

Chapman, *Barbadoes, and other poems*, p. 11, refers to 'The mailed anana' and in his note (p. 90) acknowledges that 'This epithet is applied to the pine by Grainger.'

Grainger refers to the pineapple again as 'anana' at IV, 498, 519. The modern scientific name is *Anana comosus*. The 'wild pine-apple' is perhaps *Bromelia plumieri*, also known as pingwing or monkey banana in the Anglophone Caribbean.

The Spanish name cherimoya (more correctly, chirimoya) can be applied to more than one species of fruit; see note on IV, 518.

426   Philips refers to the 'gen'rous Juice' of apples (*Cyder*, I, 273; Lloyd Thomas, *Poems of John Philips*, p. 52).

430   Widely popular in the Caribbean, the plantain (*Musa paradisiaca*) is a fruit similar to the banana, but normally (though not invariably) eaten cooked.

432–3   The signs of the zodiac are used for December (Capricorn) and January (Aquarius); see also note on I, 417.

Compare Philips, *Cyder*, I, 188–9: '*Aquarius* had not shed/His wonted Show'rs' (Lloyd Thomas, *Poems of John Philips*, p. 50).

472   Neptune is the Roman god of the sea.

482, n.   Compare the definition in Cassidy and Le Page, *Dictionary of Jamaican English* ('A period of rainfall lasting one or more days that makes the ground fit to plant in') which is supported by a quotation from Sloane. Note also these lines from Anon., 'The Pleasures of Jamaica' (published 1738):

> Oh! may the seasons never fail again,
> Nor heav'n deny the kind refreshing rain,
> To bless the soil, and fill the growing cane [...]

483–4   Aries is 'the first Sign of the *Zodiack*, into which the Sun enters in the Beginning of *March*', while 'the Bull' is Taurus, 'the 2d Sign of the Zodiack, which the Sun enters in *April*.' The 'Virgin' is the zodiacal sign Virgo, 'which the Sun enters in *August*' (Bailey). See also note on I, 417, above.

488 'The wondering daughters of the main' are ships. One might be tempted to correct this to 'wandering' but the *1764* reading is also that of *TCD* (f. 25ʳ). The ships are presumably envisaged as being astonished at the large quantity of sugar the fortunate planter is able to send to Britain.

489 The zodiacal sign Libra is here used to indicate September. See also note on I, 417, above.

503, n. Logwood (*Hæmatoxylum campechianum*) was used to produce a red dye, and in the treatment of 'the flux' (i.e., dysentery), an all-too-common and frequently fatal complaint in the period. Linnæus is the Latinised name of the famous Swedish botanist Carl von Linné (1707–1778), whose pioneering work on botanical classification, *Systema naturae*, was first published 1735.

508, n. Grainger here refers to several different plants. His common physic-nut is *Jatropha curcas*, the French physic-nut is *Jatropha multifida*, while the bellyache bush or wild physic-nut is *Jatropha gossypifolia*. What he means by the Spanish physic-nut is unclear. The castor-oil plant is *Ricinus communis*, formerly called *Ricinus Americanus*; the name ricinus got applied to the unrelated physic-nut species because they all have, as Grainger says, purgative properties. The Spanish name mentioned by Grainger means 'purgative hazelnuts', while the Latin one cited from the famous English naturalist John Ray (1627–1705) means 'purgative hazelnuts of the New World.' Grainger could have got his reference to bellyache bush as the Barbadian name from Hughes, *Natural History of Barbados*, pp. 152–3.

510 The acassee is *Acacia tortuosa*, one of whose common names still in use in the Caribbean is casha; also known as cassie or cassie-bush. The suggestion that this was the plant used for Jesus' Crown of Thorns is implausible, as it is not an Old World plant, and the reference Grainger gives to the eminent French botanist Joseph Pitton de Tournefort (1656–1708) and his *Relation d'un voyage du Levant* (posthumously published, 1717) almost certainly alludes to a different species.

515, n. The privet to which Grainger refers is probably *Clerodendrum aculeatum* (still sometimes called privet in the Caribbean and still sometimes planted as a hedge), though he appears to confuse it with the common European privet, *Ligustrum vulgare*; both species were believed to have medicinal properties. The aphthae is the disease, thrush.

517–8 The Grampian Mountains are in central Scotland, and divide the Highlands from the Lowlands.

520–31 The carnation or flower fence is the *Caesalpinia pulcherrima*, sometimes also known as the Pride of Barbados. The name poinciana is now usually applied to the flamboyant (*Delonix regia*), though *Caesalpinia pulcherrima* is occasionally called dwarf poinciana. Philippe de Longvilliers de Poincy was the French governor of St Kitts, 1639–60, who built himself a magnificent château in the hills above Basseterre and imported exotic plants for its garden. Sloane, *A Voyage to the Islands*, II, 49–50, describes the plant and gives Latin names used by various authors, including *cauda pavonis* ('Peacock's tail'); the peacock was associated with Juno, queen of heaven in Roman mythology (see l. 524). In his *Catalogus Plantarum*, p. 149, Sloane gives the names '*Flour* [sic] *fence of Barbados. Wild sena* [sic] *or Spanish Carnations.*' Grainger could also have found 'Flower Fence' in Hughes, *Natural History of Barbados*, p. 79, where the plant is also referred to as 'Spanish Carnation' and 'Ponciana'. Where he got 'Doodle-doo' from is a matter of conjecture; this name seems to be no longer current. Before he relegated it to the note, Grainger had 'fair Doodle-Doo' in a draft of this passage (*TCD*, f. 16$^r$). He had briefly visited Barbados ('y$^t$ [that] large & populous Island'), according to a reference in *TCD*, f. 103$^v$.

Many different species of hummingbird are found throughout the Caribbean. Grainger gets the names picaflore ('flower-pecker'), rabilargo ('long-tail') and lizongero ('flatterer') from Ulloa (*A Voyage to South America [...]*, I, 458), which has (both here and in the Spanish original) 'quinde' rather than Grainger's 'Guinde', though this may be a printer's error. The Edwards referred to in Grainger's note on l. 526 is not Bryan Edwards (1743–1800), the well-known historian of the British West Indies and author of most of the poems in *Poems, written chiefly in the West-Indies* (1792), but George Edwards (1694–1773), librarian of the Royal College of Physicians from 1733 and author of *A Natural History of Uncommon Birds* ... (London, four parts, 1743–51). In Part I, originally published as *A Natural History of Birds* (London, 1743), Plates 32–8 inclusive are of humming-birds, though the only one which fits Grainger's description is what Edwards calls 'The Long-Tail'd Red Huming-Bird' [sic] in Plate 32, which is indeed said to be from Suriname.

'Juno's bird' (l. 524) is the peacock, while 'the strong-pounc'd bird of Jove' (l. 529) is the eagle. Compare Bailey: 'POUNCE [in *Falconry*] the Talon or Claw of a Bird of Prey. *Strong* POUNCED *Eagle*, an Eagle having strong Talons or Claws.'

# Additional Notes to The Sugar-Cane. Book I 237

Bryan Edwards does refer to 'Barbados pride' in his 'Jamaica, A descriptive and didactic poem', *Poems, written chiefly in the West-Indies*, p. 12 and note, but there is no verbal resemblance.
Chapman, *Barbadoes, and other poems*, p. 7, describes a humming-bird feeding from flowers, but apart from his using Grainger's spelling of 'collobree', there are no similarities of detail. The name colibri or coulibri is still used in Caribbean French Creole (and in those parts of the Anglophone Caribbean which have been influenced by it) for various species of hummingbird.

534   The original Vitruvius was a Roman architect, Marcus Vitruvius Pollio (1st century BC), and author of a work on architecture, *De architectura*, which enjoyed a renewed influence from the Renaissance onward. Grainger is simply using his name as an elegant way of saying 'a builder.'

536, n.   The prickly pear (*Opuntia dillenii*) is widespread throughout the Eastern Caribbean. Describing Antigua in 1774, Janet Schaw refers to its use for fences (Andrews, *Journal of a Lady of Quality*, p. 91).

538, n.   The wild liquorice (also mentioned at II, 148) is *Abrus precatorius*. The term jumbie-beads for the seeds of this plant is still common in Caribbean English; a jumbie is an evil spirit, particularly that of a dead person.

542–50   These lines are probably a tribute to Grainger's wife, whose masculine-sounding Christian name (Daniel – the name of one of the prominent Leeward Islands families to whom she was related) would have seemed inappropriate in poetry; in accordance with a convention going back to classical love poetry, her poetic pseudonym has the same metrical value as her real name. Grainger seems to have called her Danny – he refers to 'my poor Dany' [sic] in a letter to Percy (14 May 1764, NLS Adv. MS 22-4-10, ff. 1–2) – but this would have been even less appropriate. However, it is just possible that it is she who is complimented at I, 606, under the name of Danae (in classical mythology, the name of a royal virgin who was loved by Zeus in the form of a shower of gold, and who became the mother of the hero Perseus). Danae is mentioned again, III, 395. The version in *TCD* (f. 18r) has 'my lov'd Louise' (i.e. Grainger's first daughter) rather than 'fair Christobelle'.
Note the implied comment on the poet's financial status and ambitions; compare II, 5–10.

551   On the myrtle, see note on ll. 1–6 above.

554   This line is misnumbered 555 in *1764*, and all subsequent numbering in Book I is out by one line accordingly; this has been corrected in this edition.

558   On the 'blast,' see note on II, 194.

559   In classical mythology, dryads (also at III, 24) are wood-nymphs. Smart (*Hop-Garden*, I, 306; Williamson, ed., p. 50) mentions 'weeping dryads' in connection with the felling of trees.

570   Grainger is thinking of the middle of the year, when the sun is at its hottest, and the young canes are growing, but the reference to the summer solstice (the longest day of the year in northern climates) is inappropriate in the tropics. There is a reference to 'Heat/Solstitial' in Philips, *Cyder*, I, 189–90, and Philips also describes (*Cyder*, I, 137–166) men seeking shade from summer heat in Britain and how this heat can bring 'grim Death, in different Shapes' (Lloyd Thomas, *Poems of John Philips*, pp. 48–9, 50.)

The 'yellow deaths' are, as is made clear in Grainger's note, yellow fever. That this was in some way connected with mosquitos was first suggested (1807) after Grainger's time, and the importance of the *Aedes aegypti* mosquito as the vector for the disease was not conclusively demonstrated until the beginning of the twentieth century.

575–8   Martin, *Essay upon Plantership*, pp. 10–12, recommends the planting of shade-trees along roadsides.

The phrase 'the woodland reign' is also used by Bryan Edwards in his 'Jamaica, A descriptive and didactic poem', *Poems, written chiefly in the West-Indies*, p. 13.

579   The whole Montano passage is in some ways reminiscent of Virgil's description of the old man of Tarentum (*G*, IV, 125–46), with the important difference that, while Virgil's old man is happy through the satisfaction of extremely modest wants, Montano is happy in the enjoyment of great wealth legitimately acquired by hard work and upright conduct.

If Grainger in fact meant any particular individual by Montano (and ll. 622–6 hint a claim to personal acquaintance), his identity is now obscure. The reference to 'persecution' (l. 580) might, in view of Grainger's prejudices against Catholic France, suggest that he was a French Huguenot, a number of whom ended up in the British Caribbean colonies, especially after Louis XIV's revocation of the Edict of Nantes in 1685 made their position untenable in their own country – the most famous example was Lewis Galdy (d. 1739), who enjoyed a providential escape from the Port Royal earthquake (1692) in Jamaica. The family of Grainger's patron, John Bourryau, may have been of Huguenot origin: see the record (in French) of the marriage of Claude Petreau and Anne Bourriau, whose parents were 'de l'Isle de Ré en Aunis', from the Wandsworth Parish Register, London, printed in Oliver, *Caribbeana*, III, 253–4.

Sypher, *Guinea's Captive Kings*, p. 172, suggests that Montano was 'David [sic, i.e. Daniel] Mathew to whom the *Essay* is dedicated', but this seems unlikely, as Mathew was still alive; see note on III, 31, below.

Dyer (*The Fleece*, Book III; *Poems*, 1761, p. 141) refers to 'wrong'd/Brethren, by impious persecution driven' in the context of English colonisation. Thomson also refers to British colonies as 'the better Home/Of Those whom *Bigots* chase from foreign Lands' in *Liberty, A Poem* (1735–6), V, 640–641 (ed. Sambrook, p. 144) – I owe this reference to Dobrée, 'Theme of Patriotism,' p. 57.

Deliberately or otherwise, Grainger's description of Montano's career echoes the historical progress of British colonisation in the Caribbean: he begins with subsistence agriculture, experiments with a number of export crops (ginger, tobacco, cotton, cocoa, and coffee), and eventually has accumulated enough capital to move into sugar, which proves to be the source of 'vast increase,/Beyond the wish of avarice'.

586   Grainger uses the word 'Indian' (here and at II, 44, 172, 336, 346, 477, 512; III, 442–3; IV, 28, 462, 488, 522, 567) in an entirely normal eighteenth-century manner to mean 'of the Indies', referring to either the West or East Indies. In fact, only at III, 442–3 ('the Indian clime,/Where rolls the Ganges') does the word refer to the East Indies; elsewhere it refers to the Americas. At II, 172, the reference to cochinille and 'the Indian fig' suggests Mexico, while II, 336, appears to refer to North America. All the other references in the poem itself are to the Caribbean, with the word being used virtually as a synonym for 'West Indian.' See also note on II, 477.

'Indian' is used in Grainger's notes (at I, 22, 45, 60, 132, 170, 526, 595, 597, 604; II, 438; III, 282, 350; IV, 137, 459, 462, 502, 534, 567) with a similar range of meanings, though it is often used with reference to Amerindian names for islands, plants, etc. Grainger also uses 'Caribbean' in his notes to mean Amerindian; see his notes to III, 282 and 283, where first 'Indian' and then 'Caribbean' is used in this sense. See also note on I, 206, above.

587   Possibly an echo of the 'foul, barbarian hands' in Akenside, *The Pleasures of Imagination*, II, 16 (ed. Dix, p. 111).

591–2   On Phoebus, see note on l. 386 above; these lines simply mean that Montano worked from sunrise ('the orient sun') until the sun set in the west ('western Phœbus').

595, n.   Both sweet and poison cassavas are *Manihot esculenta*. See also note on I, 260 n.

Under 'Mandiocha', Pineda, *A New Dictionary, Spanish and English [...]*(1740), mentions 'a very wholesome Liquor to drink' made by the Indians and the Portuguese in Brazil, and also says 'All Creatures but Man eat these Roots raw, and yet the Juice of them press'd out is rank Poison.' Grainger's reference to '*Baccacoua*' comes from some other source.

596, n.   In Caribbean English, 'eddo' and 'tannia' (Grainger's 'Edda' and 'tanies'; see also IV, 461, n.) are both used as common names for the plant whose scientific name is *Colocasia esculenta*, which is of East Indian origin. 'Tannia' is also used for *Xanthosoma sagittifolium*, a member of a tropical American genus of nearly forty species. A number of different species of eddoes, tannias and yams (*Dioscorea spp.*), all root vegetables still widely cultivated in St Kitts in the mid-twentieth century, are discussed in Merrill, *Historical Geography of St. Kitts and Nevis*, pp. 117–18, who comments that

> It is interesting that while yams and sweet potatoes have won a place in the diet of the white folk, the tannia, dasheen, and eddo are considered to be Negro food, and do not generally find a place on the table of the white folk. Similarly, the cassava, which was quite important to the early European settlers, has failed to gain a lasting recognition among the whites as an unprocessed food. Cassava is hardly a staple in the Negro diet in these islands. It is used as a vegetable in the cooking pot, but it is not widely used as flour.

597, n.   The soursop is *Annona muricata*, while custard-apple is *Annona reticulata*, and the sugar-apple is *Annona squamosa*. If the star-apple is the

### Additional Notes to The Sugar-Cane. Book I 241

same as the fruit now generally known in the Caribbean by that name, it is *Chrysophyllum cainito*, though this is a member of a different family. The French name *cœur de bœuf* is also applied to *Annona reticulata*. See also note on IV, 518.

598   Ginger is *Zingiber officinale*; 'Raleigh's pungent plant' is tobacco (*Nicotiana tabaccum*), so called because Sir Walter Raleigh (?1552–1618; mentioned again at III, 259 and note) was credited with having popularised its use in England.

600, n.   Cotton (*Gossypium barbadense*) was grown extensively in St Kitts and other Caribbean islands at different periods, though it was never as important as sugar. The 'worms' or 'grub' mentioned as a pest is the West Indian cotton-worm (*Alabama agrillacea*).

In his *Natural History*, Pliny mentions *gossipinum* (XII, xxii, 39) and *gossypion* (XIX, ii, 14), describing what appears to be cotton (Rackham et al., IV, 28–9; V, 428–9).

'Martinus' appears to be a reference to Matthias Martinius (1572–1630), in whose *Lexicon Philologicum* (Bremen, 1623) the article 'Gossipium' (column 1042) provides philological information similar to that used here by Grainger (though, while it gives Arabic and Syriac derivations, this edition does not mention Hebrew). Later editions (Frankfurt am Main, 1655; Amsterdam, 1701; Amsterdam, 1703) give the article word for word; there was also a Utrecht, 1711, edition which I have not seen.

603   Philips has 'genial Moisture' (*Cyder*, I, 380; Lloyd Thomas, *Poems of John Philips*, p. 55).

604, n.   Cocoa (the source of the raw material for the manufacture of chocolate) is *Theobroma cacao*. Grainger's reference to the Madre de Cacao (*Gliricidia sepium*) seems like a piece of book-learning; if he had encountered it on his travels, it is strange he does not mention the value of its seeds and leaves as rat-poison. 'That from the Caraccas is certainly the best' is not a reference to Caracas in Venezuela, but an erroneous reading of Sloane, *A Voyage to the Islands*, II, 17: 'The best Sort of Cacao Nuts are call'd *Caraccas*, a Word corrupted from the Name of the Province of *Nicaragua*, whence they are brought.'

Grainger's note also marks the first appearance of the banana, not mentioned in the poem itself until III, 533.

605, n.   In Grainger's time, the world's major producer of coffee (*Coffea arabica*) was the French Caribbean colony of St.-Domingue.

In Grainger's note, *1764* has 'The Turks [...] have not known it much above eighty years' but the *Errata* say 'for *eighty*, read *one hundred and fifty*'; the correction is more in accordance with historical fact (though coffee-houses may have been established in Constantinople as early as the mid-sixteenth century) but it makes nonsense of the following 'whereas' and suggests that whoever revised the proofs of *1764* did so in haste: this was probably Grainger himself, who certainly saw at least some of the poem in proof form (Grainger to Percy, 24 March 1764, in Nichols, *Illustrations*, VII, 286). Chalmers (1810) and Anderson (1836) both follow the *Errata*.

Pasqua is remembered only for his coffee-house, but Jean de Thévenot (1633–67) was a distinguished French linguist and traveller in the Levant and Persia; his accounts of his travels were first published 1665–84 and an English translation appeared in 1687.

Kevan discusses various possibilities for the insect pests of coffee mentioned in Grainger's note, and suggests that the 'large fly' is most probably the Coffee borer, *Xyleutes (Psychonoctua) lillianae*, while the 'white grub' is probably the Citrus mealy-bug, *Planococcus citri*.

606   Who Grainger was complimenting here under the names of Danae and Theodosia is obscure, but see note on ll. 542–50 above.

613   The modern reader may here recall Samuel Johnson's comment about the sale of Thrale's brewery as the sale of 'the potentiality of growing rich, beyond the dreams of avarice', but this was not until 1781. However, the phrase 'rich beyond the dreams of avarice' appears in a play, *The Gamester* (London, 1753), by Edward Moore (1712–57).

617   The name of Celsus, a well-known Roman physician and medical writer (Aurelius Cornelius Celsus, 1st century AD), is here used simply to mean a doctor. It is used in a similar fashion by Armstrong, *Art of Preserving Health* (III, 509; 1744 ed., p. 91). Compare also, e.g., Pope, *The First Satire of the Second Book of Horace Imitated*, l. 19.

621   'Ethiop' (also at IV, 119, 424, 425) or 'Æthiop' (III, 141; IV, 629) to refer to a person of African descent in general, in the same way that 'African' (IV, 35) includes Afro-Caribbean people. Grainger also uses 'Æthiop-kind' (IV, 264) for black people in general, and refers to the

### Additional Notes to The Sugar-Cane. Book I    243

'Æthiop-brow of night' (III, 107). 'Ethiop' and its variants are poetic diction; Grainger does not use them in his notes.

624, n.   The Tamarind-tree is *Tamarindus indica*.

628    On 'the Lion', see note on I, 417.

634    Lifted from Thomas Gray, *Elegy Written in a Country Church-Yard*, l. 68: 'And shut the gates of mercy on mankind' (Lonsdale, ed., *Thomas Gray and William Collins: Poetical Works*, p. 36). Grainger first introduces the line, in quotation marks, in an addition to Montano's speech in *TCD*, f. 45$^v$ (where the whole Montano episode is at the end of Book II, not Book I). It is possible that the quotation marks got lost when a fair copy was made, as the whole speech was put in quotation marks; in any case, Grainger can hardly have intended to deceive anybody, as Gray's poem was so well known that most of his readers would have recognised the quotation.

641, n.    As Grainger makes clear in his note, the zumbadore or condor has simply been dragged in from the very distant 'desert tops of the Andes.' The details are mainly from Ulloa, *A Voyage to South America [...]*, I, 457, though that about the wing-span is from Sloane's article, 'An Account of a prodigiously large feather of the Bird *Cuntur*, brought from *Chili*, and supposed to be a kind of Vultur [...]' in No. 208 (February 169$\frac{3}{4}$) of *Philosophical Transactions: Giving some Accompt of the present Undertakings, Studies, and Labours of the Ingenious in many considerable parts of the World* (XVII, 61–4), a periodical usually known as the *Philosophical Transactions, of the Royal Society of London* (the title adopted from 1776 onwards).

643, n.    Fireflies (probably *Photinus* sp., rather than *Pyrophorus* sp., are meant) are more widespread in the Caribbean than Grainger's note suggests. However, distribution may have changed in historic times; see Kevan (p. 198, and p. 215, n. 6).

647–8    These lines echo Virgil's ending at *G*, II, 541–2:

> Sed nos immensum spatiis confecimus aequor,
> et iam tempus equum fumantia solvere colla.

But we have traversed a plain enormous in extent, and it is now time to free the horses' steaming necks.

649   Jove, or Jupiter, the king of the gods in Roman mythology, was particularly associated with rain (Jupiter Pluvius).

652   The 'little gang' consisted of children employed to weed the fields, gather grass as animal fodder and perform other tasks around the plantation which were considered to be within their capacity; under the name of the 'third gang' or 'weeding gang,' this practice continued in parts of the Caribbean until the twentieth century. See also II, 104.

659–62   Another use of military metaphor.

672   See note on I, 570, above.

## Book II

Advertisement   Grainger's friend William Shenstone (1714–63) was the author of many poems first collected after his death (1764–9) and reprinted into the nineteenth century. Most of his work is now forgotten, but *The School-Mistress* still makes an appearance in anthologies; described as 'A Poem, in imitation of Spenser,' its humour depends on the contrast between the elevated style and the mundane or even coarse subject matter (a village school and the deeds of the children as well as the schoolmistress) rather in the manner of the Miltonic parody in John Phillips, *The Splendid Shilling* (1701). See the original version of *The School-Mistress* published in 1737 and reprinted in Lonsdale, *Eighteenth Century Verse*, pp. 305–7; later versions (e.g., in Dodsley's *Collection*) were revised, expanded, and toned down.

Shenstone was also a celebrated landscape-gardener, which may have given him some sympathy with the subject matter of *The Sugar-Cane*.

2   Philips describes birds, swine, snails and wasps as pests of apples (*Cyder*, I, 393–436; Lloyd Thomas, *Poems of John Philips*, pp. 56–7), while Dyer, speaking of 'the new-dropt lamb', warns the shepherd to guard him from 'Th'innum'rous ills, that rush around his life' and which are then described at length (*The Fleece*, Book I; *Poems*, 1761, pp. 70–2).

'What ills await the ripening Cane' are paralleled by the description of diseases of slaves in Book IV.

5–10   Grainger himself never owned a plantation, though he clearly hoped to do so; compare I, 544–7.

## Additional Notes to The Sugar-Cane. Book II

9   Vulcan is the classical god of fire (compare III, 191); the reference here is to the distillation of rum from fermented cane-juice or molasses.

15   The 'Boreal morn' is the *aurora borealis*, or Northern Lights.

20–2   Based on Shakespeare, *A Midsummer Night's Dream* (III, ii, 391–3):

> Even till the eastern gate, all fiery red,
> Opening on Neptune with fair blessed beams,
> Turns into yellow gold his salt green streams.

Grainger copied this passage opposite his own version in *TCD* (ff. 27$^v$-28$^r$), and his own line was 'Turns into burnishd Gold the Salt-green-Waves' in inverted commas, before he changed it to 'To burnishd silver turns y$^e$ salt-green Waves'.

29   Adapted from Milton, *Comus*, l. 86, 'Who with his soft pipe, and smooth-dittied song'.

34–54   The monkey to which Grainger refers is the 'green monkey' or vervet (*Cercopithecus aethiops*), an African species introduced by man into the Caribbean in the seventeenth century. It is found only in St Kitts, Nevis and Barbados, though a related species (*Cercopithecus mona*) is found in Grenada. See Woodrow W. Denham, *West Indian Green Monkeys*.

Chapman, like Grainger, refers to monkeys (*Barbadoes, and other poems*, p. 6, and note on p. 88), but because he believed (incorrectly) that they were extinct in Barbados, he can wax sentimental about them:

> Man drove him first from his ancestral wood,
> Then, cruel tyrant! thirsted for his blood.
> [...]
> The cunning miniature of man is gone,
> Slain in the empire which was once his own!

44   See note on I, 586.

46   The 'insidious droles' are 'insidious Drolls' (as Grainger wrote in *TCD*, f. 31$^r$), i.e., clowns. Their 'gambols' (l. 38) may be amusing, but the destruction they produce is very real.

46, n. Labat describes going on a monkey hunt during a visit to St Kitts in 1700, and (once he had overcome his initial reluctance) his enjoyment of monkey meat: *Nouveau Voyage aux Isles de l'Amerique* (1724), II, 183–4.

51 Chalker (*English Georgic*, 57) sees 'a mock-element' here. This may be so, but it is possible that Grainger is sincere in his attempt to make the struggle between dog and monkey as heroic as possible in view of the extent and financial importance of the damage caused to canes by monkeys; see Grainger's note on II, 46. 'Sagacious' is used in the sense of 'having a keen sense of smell'; in *Paradise Lost*, X, 281, Milton describes Death as 'Sagacious of his quarry from so far'. Compare also Pope's 'hound sagacious' (*Essay on Man*, I, 214).

55–61 The 'Gallic hosts' and their 'tomahawks' are a topical reference to the use by both the British and the French of American Indian allies in the Seven Years War (1756–63, known in North America as the French and Indian War) which led to the final British conquest of Canada in 1760. Compare Macaulay's famous comment on the far-flung consequences of Frederick the Great's ambitions: 'In order that he might rob a neighbour whom he had promised to defend, black men fought on the coast of Coromandel, and red men scalped each other by the Great Lakes of America.'

Janet Schaw, a fellow Scot who shared Grainger's anti-French prejudices, described St Kitts monkeys in similar terms in 1775, suggesting that they were the reincarnations of the island's earlier French settlers, and saying that

> When pursued, they fly to the mountain and laugh at their pursuers, as they are as little ashamed of a defeat as a French admiral or general. In short they are the torment of the planters; they destroy whole cane-pieces in a few hours, and come in troops from the mountain, whose trees afford them shelter. No method to get the better of them has yet been found out. I should think strong English dogs the best; as the English is your only animal to humble your French monkey and settle his frolicks.

See Andrews, *Journal of a Lady of Quality*, pp. 131–2.

59 'Albion' (also at II, 483; III, 283, 508; IV, 353, 472, 630), defined by Bailey as 'the ancient Name of *Great Britain*, so called from its white Rocks', is frequently used in the poetry of the period.

## Additional Notes to The Sugar-Cane. Book II           247

62   On Grainger, rats, and Boswell's *Life of Johnson*, see Appendix I.
The cane-piece rat was not the Black or Ship rat (*Rattus rattus*), but a distinct species (*Oryzomys antillarum*).

64, n.   Sixtus V was pope from 1585 to 1590; Durante is an obscure figure (not mentioned, e.g., in IJsewijn's comprehensive *Companion to Neo-Latin Studies*), but Grainger's contributions to the *Monthly Review* show that he had an extensive acquaintance with modern Latin literature. An earlier version of the note (*TCD*, f. 28$^v$) refers to Castor Durante and 'his eleg[an]t poem on the preservation of Health.' Castor Durante Da Gualdo, 'Physician and Citizen of Rome,' was the author of *A Treasure of Health*, translated by John Chamberlayne (London, 1686), but this was a prose treatise in Italian rather than a Latin poem and (at least in Chamberlayne's version) contains no mention of rats.

Peter Jackson (personal communication) informs me that Castore Durante (1529–90) was the author of *Tesoro della sanità* (Venice, 1586), which discusses edible dormice ('Ghiri', i.e., *Glis glis*), and also of a *Herbario nuovo* (Rome, 1585).

The detail about rats for sale as food in Jamaica may have come from Sloane, *A Voyage to the Islands*, I, xxv, rather than from any more recent information.

68   A number of different species of snake are found in various Caribbean islands; it is unclear whether Grainger has any particular one in mind.

69   The red mangrove is *Rhizophora mangle*.

74, n.   'Souses down upon it' is a Scotticism; the definitions of 'souse' in Warrack, *Chambers Scots Dictionary*, include 'to fall of a heap; to sit down suddenly with a bump; to let fall heavily, drop.' On the other hand, the word was also found in literary usage south of the Border, e.g., 'The Diræ sowse from Heaven', Dryden's *Aeneid* (VIII, 931).

Grainger sets this scene specifically in South America (Guayaquil is in modern Ecuador) and notes that his information is taken from Ulloa. In *A Voyage to South America [...]*, the gallinazo is described at I, 56–7, and its attacks on alligator eggs at I, 194–6. Grainger follows this quite closely, paraphrasing rather than copying exactly. While he has 'Dread alligators', Ulloa says 'they avoid a man.' Also, while Ulloa notes the birds' usefulness, both as destroyers of alligator eggs and as garbage collectors in Cartagena, there is nothing which corresponds to Grainger's 'the American preserves/The gallinazo.'

In turn, in his 'Jamaica, A descriptive and didactic poem', Bryan Edwards has a passage probably based on this part of *The Sugar-Cane*, in which 'The rav'ning Gallinazo [...] riots on the embryo young' of the crocodile – *Poems, written chiefly in the West-Indies*, pp. 15–16. Edwards has a footnote describing the gallinazo as 'The Turkey vulture, vulgarly called the carrion-crow' which suggests he might be identifying it with the Jamaican bird known since the nineteenth century as the John Crow (scientific name *Cathartes aura*). The South American bird might be *Corvus brachyrhyncos* or *Cathartes aura* (often called the Turkey vulture).

A species of crocodile (*Crocodylus acutus*, popularly called alligator in the island) is found in Jamaica, but there would have been none for Grainger to see in St Kitts.

75, n. Perhaps a reference to the Igbo people of what is now Nigeria, but the efforts of eighteenth-century writers in the Caribbean to distinguish between different African peoples, and the confident assumptions they made about differing national characteristics, need to be treated with some degree of scepticism (a well-known example is Edwards, *History ... of the British West Indies*, II, 70–106). The victims of the slave trade were often brought considerable distances before they arrived at the ports from which they were shipped to the Americas; European traders in Africa, and planters and merchants in the Caribbean (who very seldom had any knowledge of any African language) tended to assume that all slaves from a given port were of the same national origin.

76, n. Grainger is in error in describing Labat as a Jesuit: he was a Dominican friar; see note on Grainger's Preface. Labat lays considerable stress on the destructiveness of rats and the importance of having a rat-catcher on the estate, though he says care should be taken to stop the slaves eating rats, as they are a 'mauvaise nourriture' ('bad eating') and 'l'usage trop fréquent des rats, des serpens & des lezards, subtilise tellement le sang qu'il fait à la fin tomber en phtisie' ('eating rats, snakes and lizards too often thins the blood so much that eventually it leads to consumption [i.e. tuberculosis]'). Unlike Grainger, Labat claims that cats are useless as rat-catchers in the Caribbean, and that dogs are much to be preferred for the purpose. See *Nouveau Voyage aux Isles de l'Amerique* (1724), I, 237–8.

83 'Misnian' is a Latinised adjective from Meissen in Germany; the silver-mines at Freiberg, which were well-known as a place where native

arsenic was found in association with silver ore, were in the margravate of Meissen, which formed part of the kingdom of Saxony.

88   'Cates' are victuals. Elsewhere (III, 480, 601; IV, 151), Grainger uses the word only with reference to human consumption.

95, n.   Grainger may refer not to the European Deadly Nightshade (*Atropa belladonna*), but to one or more of a number of *Datura* and *Solanum* species found in the Caribbean, such as *Solanum americanum*. Although this last is used in folk medicines and its leaves are employed as a substitute for spinach (in callalou soup), the fruit is poisonous when unripe and the plant contains chemical compounds which have been known to cause death in children. See also IV, 415, and note below.

The mongoose (*Herpestes auropunctatus auropunctatus*) was introduced into Jamaica from India in 1872, and did indeed exterminate the cane-piece rat. As a result it was subsequently imported into the other sugar-producing islands.

Grainger perhaps refers to William Lewis (1714–72), a well-known chemist of the period, but a search of the English Short Title Catalogue failed to identify 'Newman's Chemistry.'

104   For the 'little gang,' see note on I, 652.

114   The 'yellow thistle' is *Argemone mexicana*, still used as a folk medicine in the Caribbean, although it is potentially poisonous.

116   The 'mountain-dove' (also at III, 573) is *Zenaida aurita*, known as a pea-dove in Jamaica and a wood-dove in Barbados.

119   The 'knotted grass' is *Spigelia anthelmia*; as Grainger notes, it is effective against worms (it is sometimes known as 'worm bush' or 'worm grass' in parts of the Caribbean; compare IV, 313) and also potentially poisonous.

123, n.   The cow-itch is *Mucuna pruriens*. *Setæ* (or *saetae*) are hairs or bristles (Latin).

128, n.   The chickweed is *Drymaria cordata*, while 'that, which coyly flies the astonish'd grasp' is *Mimosa pudica*, which is found throughout the Eastern Caribbean and is a purgative and emetic.

129  *Errata* say 'for *eoily* read *coily*' but *1764* has 'coyly', as do Chalmers (1810) and Anderson (1836).

130, n.  Mithridates VI (king of Pontus in northern Anatolia,120–63 BC) and his antidote are referred to by several classical writers (e.g., Pliny, *Natural History*, XXV, iii, 5–7; see Rackham et al., VII, 138–41) and mentioned in medical dictionaries into the nineteenth century.

131  The reference is to *G*, II, 126–130:

> Media fert tristis sucos tardumque saporem
> felicis mali, quo non praesentius ullum,
> pocula si quando saevae infecere novercae,
> [miscueruntque herbas et non innoxia verba,]
> auxilium venit ac membris agit atra venena.

Media [i.e. an area more or less equivalent to modern Azerbaijan, though the name was loosely used in antiquity for Persia, Assyria and other countries to the east of the Roman Empire] brings the sour juices and lingering taste of the health-giving citron, than which nothing provides a swifter antidote and drives the black poison from the limbs if cruel stepmothers have poisoned cups and mixed in herbs and harmful spells.

*Malum*, 'citron', which Grainger translates as 'apple,' could refer to a wide range of different fruits. The line in brackets is considered by modern editors an interpolation in this passage (from *G*, III, 283).

Compare Dryden's translation (Keith Walker, ed., *John Dryden*, p. 484):

> Sharp-tasted citrons Median climes produce,
> (Bitter the rind, but generous is the juice,)
> A cordial fruit, a present antidote
> Against the direful stepdame's deadly draught,
> Who, mixing wicked weeds with words impure,
> The fate of envied orphans would procure.

There is a similar passage in Tibullus, I, ii; in the notes to his translation of this (*A poetical translation of the Elegies of Tibullus*, I, 30–35), Grainger cites numerous other classical references and comments: 'However disso-

# Additional Notes to The Sugar-Cane. Book II

nant to sound Sense and Philosophy, magical Descriptions may be, yet they have an excellent Effect in Poetry, where Admiration is to be excited.' Compare the description of obeah in IV, 381 ff.

140 In other words, the sea is calm. The Halcyon was 'a Bird called a King's-Fisher, which breeds on the Sea-Shore about the Winter Solstice; and for about fourteen Days the Eggs are hatching there is no Tempest or Storm' (Bailey). It was long a matter of popular belief that these birds actually built their nests on the surface of the sea during this period of calm, hence the expression 'Halcyon days' meaning 'quiet or peacable Times, pleasant Days, fair Weather' (Bailey).

141 In Part III, Chapter II, 'Of Spinous Fishes in general' of *An History of the Earth, and Animated Nature* (1774), Goldsmith refers to 'the poisonous qualities which many of them are found to possess' and goes on to say: 'The fact of their being poisonous when eaten, is equally notorious; and the cause equally inscrutable. My poor worthy friend Dr Grainger, who resided for many years at St Christopher's, assured me, that of the fish caught, of the same kind, at one end of the island, some were the best and most wholesome in the world; while others taken at a different end, were always dangerous, and most commonly fatal' (VI, 348-9).

In an appendix to his article on Grainger's entomology, Kevan suggests a number of Caribbean fish species which can be toxic. However, Grainger is almost certainly referring to ciguaterra (or ciguatera) poisoning which is caused by eating fish which have consumed a certain type of algae (*Gambierdiscus* or *Ostreopsis*), which in the Caribbean is particularly associated with barracuda (Sphyraenidae). As well as producing unpleasant digestive symptoms, ciguaterra also affects the muscles, and in some instances can lead to death from respiratory paralysis. Grainger's observation that some fish can be perfectly safe, while others of the same species caught only a few miles away are potentially fatal, is consonant with ciguaterra.

Grainger mentions 'Fish poison' in similar terms in his *Essay on the more common West-India Diseases* (1764, p. 38), and correctly suggests that it 'can [..] be ascribed to the submarine vegetables whereon they feed.'

149 The 'gift of God' translates the Latin name for rhubarb, *Donum Dei*, referred to in Grainger's note. The rhubarb which was particularly valued as a purgative in the eighteenth century was a costly drug brought from China by way of Russia; the rhubarb cultivated for the table is

another species, originally from the Volga basin, and was sometimes used as a substitute for the Chinese rhubarb. Grainger's reference to the plant's being 'Gather'd by those, who drink the Volga's wave' could imply either species, though it is also influenced by the fact that *Rhaponticum*, another name for rhubarb, referred to the Rha, an ancient name for the Volga.

Vervain (or verbena) was thought to cure headaches, and liquorice was used for throat and chest complaints. However, Grainger probably refers to Caribbean substitutes for the Old World plants commonly so called: see notes on I, 538, and IV, 123.

155 Grainger now moves on to a discussion of various insect-pests of the sugar-cane. Kevan notes that 'It is somewhat surprising that there is no mention of one of the worst pests of cane at the present time, the Sugarcane moth-borer, *Diatraea saccharalis* (Fabricius)', although this appears to have been mentioned by Sloane. However, Kevan argues that none of Grainger's descriptions fit the moth-borer, and he suggests identifications for the pests Grainger has described; these have been drawn on heavily by the present writer.

166 See note on I, 4.

168 Kevan suggests that the 'yellow fly' is most probably the large Neotropical grasshopper, *Schistocerca pallens*, which is resident in St. Kitts and has been known to be a serious pest of sugar-cane at different periods, though he discusses other possibilities. The African locusts mentioned as a comparison are most likely either the African Migratory locust (*Locusta migratoria migratorioides*) or the Desert locust (*Schistocerca gregaria gregaria*).

171, n. 'Cochinille,' or cochineal, is a scarlet dye obtained from an insect (*Dactylopius coccus*) which lives on the nopal plant (*Nopalia coccinellifera*), a type of cactus (Grainger's 'Indian fig') native to Mexico, where the dye had been used since Aztec times. As Grainger noted in *TCD* (f. 36$^v$) it was a different species of plant from the various kinds of prickly pear (*Opuntia*) found in the Caribbean islands. The belief that cochineal was a kind of seed continued to be widespread until about 1725, although the insect had been identified as such by Anthony van Leeuwenhoek in 1703. It has been generally superseded by artificial dyes, but cochineal was a significant export from Mexico in Spanish colonial times, and it was used to provide the 'bright scarlet' of British military uniforms; see ll.

*Additional Notes to* The Sugar-Cane. *Book II* 253

174–5. Some of Grainger's information could have come from Sloane, *A Voyage to the Islands*, II, 152–4, or from Ulloa, *A Voyage to South America [...]*, I, 341–7.

Cochineal is mentioned by Dyer, *The Fleece*, Book III (*Poems*, 1761, p. 131).

Note the use of 'reptile' in a manner typical of the period to refer to almost any sort of 'creeping thing', including insects; see also II, 213, and IV, 311 (where it refers to intestinal worms).

175 The 'British Wolf' is James Wolfe (1727–59) who commanded the British expedition against Quebec in 1759, which arrived at Halifax, 20 April 1759. Wolfe's death in the moment of victory after the capture of Quebec, 13 September 1759, made him a national hero. Other editions, such as Chalmers (1810) and Anderson (1836) correctly give 'Wolfe.'

Grainger had left England for St Kitts in April 1759 (Grainger to Thomas Percy, 9 April 1759, Bod. MS Percy c.10, ff. 25–6) and this passage suggests that he must have begun the poem soon after his arrival in St Kitts, before news of Wolfe's victory and death; if so, it is strange it was not revised later before publication. Grainger may have known Wolfe personally, or at least met him; Wolfe was at both Falkirk and Culloden, and later periods of service in Scotland (1749–52, 1753) overlapped with Grainger's regiment, the 13th Foot, being stationed there (1751–3).

181–93 Although the transition is unclear in the poem, Kevan suggests that this passage refers to 'the greasy fly' which is mentioned after 'the yellow fly' in the Argument to Book II. The 'greasy fly' is perhaps either the Yellow sugar-cane aphid (*Sipha flava*) or the Corn-leaf aphid (*Rhopalosiphum maidis*); Kevan notes that 'greasy' may refer to the sticky 'honeydew' produced by aphids.

182–3 Note the military metaphor.

186 That is, wash the leaves of the canes with sea-water. The 'Augæan toil' refers to the classical legend of the labours of Heracles (Hercules) in which the hero cleaned the stables of King Augeas by diverting the river Alpheus through them.

194–269 A long account of 'the blast' and of not very effective remedies for it. Kevan notes:

A reference to the Kentish 'hop-grounds' is in respect of the winds bringing the 'Hop fly', or Hop-damson aphid, *Phorodon pruni* (Scopuli) [= *Ph. humuli* (Schrank)], which, in the 18th and 19th Centuries, frequently brought ruin to the hop gardens of Kent, but which no longer presents so serious a threat. Smudge fires (particularly incorporating sulphur) were used in an attempt to drive it away. The analogy is obvious here. 'The blast' is clearly the same affliction as has been called 'black blight' in the West Indies. This is a result of a combined infestation by the 'Cane fly', *Saccharosydne saccharivora* (Westwood), a delphacid plant-hopper, and sooty moulds that grow on their excretions. The 'Black blight' seems to have been a much more serious pest than it now is [...] – another analogy to the 'Hop fly'! It seems also to have had its most serious effects after hurricanes (as here implied in verses 233–4), for Schomburgk (1848) notes that, in Grenada, after the hurricane of 1831, it destroyed half of the sugar crop in some areas [...]

Martin (*Essay upon Plantership*, pp. 40–1 and footnote) says of the blast, 'All the schemes hitherto proposed for curing that evil, that fore-runner of the planter's ruin, are vain, impracticable speculations, or a waste of time and labor, to little purpose [...] the best and only effectual cure is wiping the blades by wet cloths, until wet weather completes the cure.'

The mention in connection with the blast of 'ants' (l. 229) and of attacks on the roots of the canes (ll. 254–5; possibly also implied by the 'Pernicious pioneers!' of l. 235) perhaps indicates termites rather than ants; Kevan suggests *Heterotermes tenuis*, which has been known to attack canes, as the most likely species. Compare Caribbean English use of 'wood-ants' for termites, which dates back to the eighteenth century (e.g., Hughes, *Natural History*, p. 93).

On the other hand, Schomburgk (*History of Barbados*, pp. 640–3) gives a lengthy description of the great damage to agriculture caused in several different Caribbean islands in the mid-eighteenth century by the Sugar Ant (*Formica omnivera*, Linn.).

198–9   Eurus (also at II, 231, 303, 501; IV, 359) is the East Wind; compare Smart, *Hop-Garden*, I, 72 (Williamson, ed., p. 44): 'when whistling Eurus comes'. Boreas is the North Wind.

205, n.   The quotation from Pliny (*Natural History*, XIII, vii, 28, 'It likes running water, and to drink all the year round') refers to the palm-tree; see Rackham et al., IV, 114–15.

# Additional Notes to The Sugar-Cane. Book II

213   See note on II, 171.

214   The 'filmy jail' is perhaps suggested by the lines in Philips which describe the use of treacle to catch wasps

> that with fruitless Toil
> Flap filmy Pennons oft, to extricate
> Their Feet, in liquid Shackles bound [...]
> (*Cyder*, I, 432–4; Lloyd Thomas,
> *Poems of John Philips*, p. 57)

218, n.   The 'Jamaica plumb tree' is *Spondias purpurea*. The panspan is *Spondias mombin*, also known as the hog plum. The golden apple or pomme cythère (*Spondias cytherea*) is a related species.

231–2   A rather obscure mythological allusion: 'the bright God of day' is presumably Apollo (compare III, 256), but Rhea is usually the wife of Chronos (and, as such, Apollo's grandmother), and neither Apollo nor Rhea are normally thought of as parents of winds. Some of the winds, e.g. Boreas, were conventionally said to be children of Eos (Dawn). Since Rhea is an earth-goddess, it is possible these lines are a convoluted way of suggesting that the sun's heat brings the east wind off the African continent and across the Atlantic.

233   Auster is the South Wind.

270–361   Grainger's description of the hurricane includes a number of verbal and structural echoes of the storm in *G*, I, 311–34. There may also be echoes of Virgil's own models in Homer (*Iliad*, XVI, 384–92), Hesiod (*Works and Days*, 507–16), and Lucretius (*De Rerum Natura*, I, 271–6 and VI, 253–61). Grainger also seems to have been influenced by Virgil's description of the portents which greeted the death of Julius Caesar (*Georgics*, I, 466–88).

One important difference is that while Virgil explicitly claims that his description of stormy weather is based on personal experience (*saepe ego ... vidi* ... , 'I have often seen ... ,' *G*, I, 316–18), Grainger's invocation of his muse is much more ambiguous. There had been two major hurricanes in the Leeward Islands in 1747, and Martinique was devastated by a hurricane in 1756, but the Eastern Caribbean does not seem to have been affected again until 1766; it seems likely that Grainger's description of the hurricane is based on what he had heard from others, and on literary models (see list of Caribbean hurricanes in Schomburgk, *History of Barbados*, pp. 689–95).

There may also be echoes of Philips' description (itself partly based on Virgilian models) of the destruction of the Romano-British town of Ariconium by an earthquake (*Cyder*, I, 173–247; Lloyd Thomas, *Poems of John Philips*, pp. 49–51).

There is a hurricane passage in Chapman, *Barbadoes, and other poems*, pp. 69–70.

275–84   Ætna (in Latin; Etna in Italian) is a volcano on the east coast of Sicily. Many legends were associated with it in classical times, including that it was the workshop of Hephæstus and the Cyclops (see note on I, 407); e.g., the Cyclops are referred to in connection with Ætna in *G* I, 471–3; IV, 170–5, in Book III of the *Aeneid*, and also in *Ætna*, a Latin poem of the first century AD, once commonly attributed to Virgil (ll. 37–40, though this dismisses the legend as baseless). For text and translation of *Ætna*, see Duff, *Minor Latin Poets*.

Grainger may have seen volcanic activity at Etna in the course of a visit to Italy in 1750 (see Introduction), but there were no major eruptions between 1669 and 1830, and his description closely resembles that in *Aeneid* III, 571–7.

285   Virgil similarly ascribes the storm to the direct intervention of Jupiter, *ipse pater* (*G*, I, 328).

286   Grainger's 'all the battles of thy winds' echoes Virgil's *omnia ventorum ... proelia* (*G*, I, 318).

287–9   That is, during August to September, the height of the hurricane season. See also notes on I, 417, 483–4, and 489, above.

293, n.   The 'stocks' are the arms of the windmill used for grinding the sugarcane. 'Points, are those parts of a wind mill, to which the sails are fastned' – note by Grainger in *TCD*, f. 55$^v$ (with reference to III, 202, below).

294   The Royal Palm is *Roystonea regia*, but Grainger may refer to the Cabbage Palm (*Roystonea oleracea*).

306–9  Possibly an echo of Hesiod: see Wender's translation, p. 75. Virgil mentions only the fleeing of wild beasts (*fugere ferae* – *G*, I, 330).

310–12  An echo of Milton, *Samson Agonistes*, ll. 86–9:

> The sun to me is dark
> And silent as the moon,
> When she deserts the night
> Hid in her vacant interlunar cave.

Like Milton, Grainger uses 'interlunar' in the sense of 'Belonging to the time when the moon, about to change, is invisible' (Johnson), but note Grainger's search for more elevated diction in the substitution of 'palace' for 'cave.'

317–18  Virgil has *nunc nemora ingenti vento, nunc litora plangunt* ('now the woods, and now the coasts wail with a mighty wind,' *G*, I, 334).

322  The 'brazen engineries' are cannon. Philips, *Cyder*, I, 195, has 'brazen Enginry' in the same sense (Lloyd Thomas, *Poems of John Philips*, p. 50.) Milton uses 'engines' of cannon several times in the description of the war in heaven in *Paradise Lost*, VI.

326  'whirl'd aloft in air' is very close to Virgil's *sublimem expulsam eruerent* (*G*, I, 320), which refers to the winds tearing up the crop and hurling it into the air; the phrase 'whirled aloft' also occurs in Dryden's translation of this passage.

327–8  The words in inverted commas are not an exact quotation, but an echo of Shakespeare, *Hamlet*, II, ii (ll. 485–6 in the Riverside Edition): 'and the orb below/As hush as death'. They come from a simile of a storm in a speech by one of the Players, describing the destruction of Troy, and the allusion may perhaps be intended by Grainger to lend additional dignity to his description of the hurricane.

332–3  Possible echo here of *G*, I, 468, 'impiaque aeternam timuerunt saecula noctem', which Dryden translates as 'And impious mortals feared eternal night' (Walker, ed., p. 478), a line copied by Trapp (*Works of Virgil*, I, 125), or perhaps of *G*, I, 330–1, 'mortalia corda/per gentis humilis stravit pavor' which Dryden gives as 'Deep horror seizes every human breast' (Walker, ed., p. 474).

The effect of the terrors of the hurricane on a bad conscience is echoed by Chapman ('All, all are self-convicted') in a long passage (*Barbadoes, and other poems*, pp. 13–15) describing the effects of a fall of volcanic dust in Barbados which was so heavy it obscured the sun, following the eruption of the Souffrière in St Vincent (1 May 1812):

> Terrors, unmasked, upon the impious seize —
> Who never prayed before, are on their knees;
> [...]
> There in the dust low grovelling is laid
> The base betrayer of an artless maid:
> Terror and madness cloud his aching brain;
> That trembling wretch will never smile again.

Chapman's description has a number of points in common with Grainger's and may have been directly influenced by it, as well as by the Virgilian and other classical models they have in common and by the Biblical description of the destruction of Sodom and Gomorrah (Genesis, xix). For a discussion of this passage in Chapman and its place in the Caribbean literary tradition, see Kamau Brathwaite, *Barabajan Poems*, pp. 86–9, notes 26–9 on p. 305, and Appendix II, pp. 335–7.

336–42 Virgil's description of the storm includes several uses of military language to depict the struggle between the farmer and nature (see Richard F. Thomas' notes on *G*, I, 311–50), though this is not apparent in Dryden's translation, where the only example in this passage is his 'warring winds' for Virgil's *omnia ventorum ... proelia*. Grainger picks this up, but gives it a New World reference: the nearby description of the palm as 'pride of Indian groves' (l. 346) suggests that the 'Indian forests' where the 'Barbaric armies suddenly retire' are located, not in India, but in 'the Indies' in the broadest sense. Compare note on II, 55 above, and see also notes on I, 586 and II, 294.

345 Virgil describes the destruction of crops in detail, and refers to Jupiter casting down mountain-tops with his thunderbolts, but apart from the wailing of the woods (see note on 317–18 above) he makes no specific mention of damage to trees. Topless palm-trees are a common enough sight after high winds in the Caribbean, but Grainger may also have been influenced here by Lucretius, I, 273–5:

# Additional Notes to The Sugar-Cane. Book II

> [...] rapido percurrens turbine campos
> arboribus magnis sternit montisque supremos
> silvifragis vexat flabris [...]

Hastening with a swift whirlwind across the plains it [the force of the wind] covers them with mighty trees and troubles the lofty mountains with its forest-breaking blasts ...

346   Compare IV, 522.

347–50   The name Theodorus (implying 'divine gift' or 'offering to God') has been chosen to complement the reference to 'devotion'. He may well be a symbolic figure rather than a real individual; note how he echoes the character of the good planter in the Montano episode (I, 579–646), the implication being that natural disasters are not necessarily indications of divine wrath. Contrast the English poet William Cowper's 'The Negro's Complaint' (1788) where hurricanes are invoked as showing God's disapprobation of the slave trade, or the Antiguan poet William Gilbert's *The Hurricane* (1796), which makes the same suggestion.

350–3   Virgil has *sata laeta boumque labores*, 'abundant crops and the labours of cattle,' being swept away by heavy rain, and describes swollen rivers; Grainger's 'billowy main' echoes Virgil's *fretis spirantibus aequor*, 'sea with roaring waters' (*G*, I, 325–7). There is also an echo of G, I, 481–3:

> proluit insano contorquens vertice silvas
> fluviorum rex Eridanus camposque per omnis
> cum stabulis armenta tulit.

> Then, rising in his might, the king of floods
> Rushed through the forests, tore the lofty woods,
> And rolling onward with a sweepy sway,
> Bore houses, herds and labouring hinds away.
> 
>                         (Dryden's translation, in Walker,
>                                 ed., *John Dryden*, p. 479)

> [...] Eridanus, Supreme of Rivers,
> With roaring Inundation, o'er the Plains,
> Swept Woods away, and Cattle, with their Stalls.
> 
>                         (Trapp, *Works of Virgil*, I, 126)

Dryden's 'labouring hinds' are not in the Latin, but may have influenced Grainger's inclusion of 'Men'. On the other hand, Grainger's 'A river foams, which sweeps, with untam'd might' is perhaps closer to *insano contorquens vertice* than Dryden's 'sweepy sway' or Trapp's 'roaring Inundation'.

Dyer has a similar passage (*The Fleece*, Book I; *Poems*, 1761, p. 79).

356 Compare Virgil's *corusca fulmina*, 'flashing thunderbolts' (*G*, I, 328–9), and see also II, 421 below.

358 'Earth trembles' translates Virgil's *terra tremit* (*G*, I, 330). Trapp (*Works of Virgil*, I, 116) uses the same phrase, but it is so obvious a translation that this does not necessarily demonstrate influence.

398 The first appearance of the coconut tree (*Cocos nucifera*); see Grainger's note on II, 438, and note below. Also mentioned at III, 205; IV, 558.

428–553 The whole of the Junio and Theana episode was reprinted in the *Gentleman's Magazine* (XXXIV, 342; July 1764). As was usual with the 'Poetical Essays' published or reprinted in the *GM*, there was no editorial comment, but this represented generous coverage and suggests that the story was well calculated to appeal to a contemporary readership. The whole episode was also quoted by John Langhorne in his review, describing it as 'a very tender story of two Lovers, which, we suppose, may be more generally acceptable to our Readers than any precepts of cultivation contained in this poem' – *Monthly Review*, XXXI, 105–18 (August 1764), at pp. 112–15.

In response to a query from Grainger's editor Robert Anderson, Percy claimed 'The tale is probably founded on fact but I know not the particular personages' (W. E. K. Anderson, *Percy Letters*, IX, 67). Perhaps, but it would have reminded many eighteenth-century readers of the Celadon and Amelia episode in Thomson's *Seasons* (Summer, ll. 1169–1222), which in turn may have been inspired by Pope's well-known epitaph on John Hewet and Sarah Drew, two real-life lovers who had been struck dead by lightning at Stanton Harcourt in Oxfordshire in 1718. With the lightning replaced by a man-eating shark, Grainger returns to the theme of love and sudden death in his 'Bryan and Pereene' (see Appendix).

There may also be an echo of the Hero and Leander story, which appears in Virgil (*G*, III, 258–63), and another version of which (from

Ovid's Heroides) was translated by Grainger (*Poetical Works*, ed. Anderson, 1836, II, 91–115). While there is a sort of Romeo and Juliet feel to the hostility between the lovers' families, it is not implausible in the context of planter families in Caribbean: in 1765 Governor George Thomas (see note on I, 19–20 above) suspended a member of the Council of Antigua for having 'basely and treacherously seduced his Daughter' and married her without her father's consent (Oliver, *History of Antigua*, I, 266).

429–34   It was common for the children (especially the sons) of planter families to be sent to England for their education. Eton is the famous public school; the Isis is the local name given to the River Thames where it flows through the university city of Oxford; 'the Nine' are the Muses.

438, n.   In an undated letter to Thomas Percy (Bod. MS Percy. c.10, ff. 34–5), Grainger mentions 'I have sent you two carved Coco-Nuts, we drink water out of them in this Country.'

Grainger is here careful to distinguish between the coconut palm (modern scientific name *Cocos nucifera*), the coca bush (*Erythroxylum coca*, now all too well known as the source not only of coca leaves, but also of cocaine), and the cocoa tree (*Theobroma cacao*) whose beans produce the main ingredient of chocolate.

441, n.   The sapodilla is *Manilkara zapota*.

445–6   Sheen was an old name for Richmond in Surrey (nine miles from central London), for centuries the location of a royal palace. This had fallen into decay by the early eighteenth-century, but Grainger's 'royal walks' probably refer to Richmond Park, then (and now) a royal park and a popular outing for Londoners.

452   First appearance in the poem itself of Grainger's friend Thomas Percy (also mentioned at III, 509), for whom see Introduction.

456   Hymen is the classical god of marriage.

469   The allusion is perhaps to the fertility of the Low Countries; 'Saturn's reign' translates the Latin *Saturnia regna* (*E*, IV, 6) referring to the mythical Golden Age when the earth provided freely for its inhabitants without their having to labour.

471  Ausonia is a synonym (taken from classical Latin poetry) for Italy.

476  The Venus de Medici, a Roman copy of a Greek marble statue of the second or third century BC (now in the Uffizi Gallery in Florence) was highly regarded in eighteenth century Europe as a representation of female beauty. In his 'Three Elegies written from Italy', Grainger claimed 'The Medicean Venus I have seen,/Ausonia's noblest boast, the pride of art' (Anderson, ed., *Poetical Works of James Grainger*, 1836; II, 55).

477  When Grainger refers to Theana as Junio's 'Indian fair' or as 'His Indian bride' (II, 512), the word is used in a purely geographical sense as a synonym for 'West Indian' (see note on I, 586). We should not assume that Grainger intends Theana for an Amerindian, a mistake Fairchild (*Noble Savage*, p. 69) makes about Pereene, 'the pride of Indian dames' (see Grainger's 'Bryan and Pereene' in Appendix II).

485  The *Po* was the name of the ship on which Grainger travelled from England to St Kitts in 1759 (Grainger to Percy, 1 June 1760; NLS Adv. MS. 22.3.11, ff. 1–2). The River Po is mentioned by Virgil, under its Latin names of Eridanus and Padus (*G*, I, 482; II, 452; IV, 372), but this is, at most, a secondary consideration.

487–8  The Charente is a river in western France, which flows into the Bay of Biscay.

496  'The Thunderer' (Latin *tonans*) was a conventional epithet for the god Jupiter in classical poetry, and has a certain appropriateness as a name for a warship; Grainger may have known of a real French ship called *Le Tonitruant*, or it may simply be his invention.

499, n.  Porto Santo, capital of the island of the same name in the Madeiras, is 33° 4' N, 16° 20' W.

500  *1764* has 'Like clouds dim rising in the distant sky' but the *Errata* say 'for *sky*, read *air*.' The change avoids the rhyme with the previous line.

504, n.  Grainger's 'boneta' is most likely the bonito (*Sarda sarda*), though the skipjack tuna (*Katsuwonus*, or *Euthynnus*, *pelamis*) is another possibility. Several families of sharks are found in the Caribbean; that still known as a guinea-shark is *Rhincodon typus*.

Additional Notes to The Sugar-Cane. Book II

505–6, n. 1764: The *Errata* supply these lines in place of the following in 1764:

> The little nautilus with purple pride
> Expands his sails, and dances o'er the waves:

Similarly, *1764* has 'nautilus' instead of 'urtica' as the introductory word to the note. These changes, and that at l. 500, are followed by both Chalmers (1810) and Anderson (1836). Both the original version and the alteration have some resemblance to Pope (*Essay on Man*, III, 177–8):

> Learn of the little Nautilus to sail,
> Spread the thin oar, and catch the driving gale.

Grainger was originally thinking of members of the pearly nautilus (Nautilus) or paper nautilus (Argonauta) genera, but his reference to its purple colour better fits the Portuguese man of war, i.e. one of the many species of Physalia, perhaps the common *Physalia physalis*. The Latin name *urtica* (meaning a stinging nettle) was applied to this or some other stinging marine creature in classical times.

507, n. A number of different species of flying-fish (Exocoetidae) are found in the Caribbean; the reference may be to the Atlantic flying-fish (*Cypselurus heterurus*), though the species 'commonly sold at Barbadoes' (where it is regarded as a national emblem) is *Hirundichthys affinis*. The albacore is *Thunnus alalunga*, or perhaps a related species. 'Garayio' looks like a word imported from the Hispanic Caribbean; Emilio Rodríguez Demorizi, *Del Vocabulario Dominicano* (p. 125) defines 'guaraguao' as 'ave de rapiña' ('bird of prey') but gives no scientific name. 'Garra' is Spanish for 'claw' or 'talon'.

508, n. In the Caribbean, a dolphin is not any of the species of seamammal which share the same name in English (Delphinidae), but a fish (*Coryphaena hippurus*) which makes excellent eating.

509, n. At least in modern usage, the Tropic-bird and the Frigate-bird are different species; the former is *Phaeton aethereus*, the latter *Fregata magnificens*.

514 The 'purple main' is 'the dark sea'; πορφυρεος (literally 'purple') is a

conventional epithet for the sea in Homer: e.g. *Iliad*, I, 481–2, κυμα ...πορφυρεον ('dark wave'); *Iliad*, XVI, 391, 'αλα πορφυρεην ('dark sea').

## Book III

6    *1764*: 'At last, from some long eminence, descries'; *TCD* (f. 50ʳ): 'At last from some lone Eminence descries'. 'Long' for 'lone' here is mentioned by Grainger in a letter to Percy (undated, but c. February 1765, NLS Adv. MS. 22.4.10, ff. 3–4) among 'some very unpoetical Blunders of yᵉ press' he had discovered in *1764*. See also note on IV, 253. Chalmers (1810) and Anderson (1836) print 'long'.

21   The phrase 'Cane-land isles' appears again at IV, 243. This adjectival use is perhaps influenced by Smart's references to 'hopland shades', 'yonder hop-land close', 'hop-land groves' (twice) and 'the hopland state' (twice) (*Hop-Garden*, I, 33, 127; II, 2, 28, 92, 242; Williamson, ed., pp. 43, 45, 55, 57, 63). Grainger also uses 'Cane-lands' as a substantive at I, 612, 645; II, 353, 383.

25, n.   There are several species of Smilacaceae found in the Caribbean, and more than one of them seems to have been known as sarsaparilla. Plants of this genus were regarded in the eighteenth century as useful for 'purifying the blood' and as offering cures for a wide range of ailments, including venereal disease. On lignum vitae, see note on I, 34–7 above.

27   Kevan suggests that this refers to what 'are presumably native bees (? *Trigona* or *Melipona* species)'. Grainger noted (*TCD*, f. 50ᵛ) 'There are Bees in yᵉ Mountains of this Island, & their honey is very delicious.'

31   Percy (in W. E. K. Anderson, *Percy Letters*, IX, 183) thought this 'certainly applied to' Daniel Mathew (1718–77), who is referred to by name in Grainger's note to IV, 523. He was a cousin of Grainger's wife, and owned plantations in St Kitts, Antigua and Tobago; see pedigrees of Burt and Mathew families in Oliver, *Antigua*, I, 88–91 and II, 251–58, and *Caribbeana*, I, 369. Grainger dedicated his *Essay on the more common West-India Diseases* to Daniel Mathew, 'as it affords me a pleasing opportunity of recommending to others, that distinguished humanity, wherewith your Negroes have ever been treated' and as an expression of his 'high regard' for him.

However, the passage appears in substantially the same form in *TCD* (f. 51ʳ), where the name is given as 'Martyn' (i.e., Colonel Samuel Martin, for whom see note on Grainger's Preface). It is possible that Grainger replaced this with 'M * * *' so that both Mathew and Martin might feel it applied to them.

46–7 The repetition emphasises not only the cyclical nature of agriculture but also, more specifically, the fact, already mentioned in ll. 12–30, that the beginning of crop (the sugar-cane harvest) coincides with the beginning of the calendar year, unlike the autumn harvest of temperate countries. This adds some variation to the fact that Grainger is here echoing *G*, II, 401–2 (*redit agricolis labor actus in orbem/ atque in se sua vestigia volvitur annus*, 'the completed task comes back again in a circle to the farmers, and the year rolls round in its own tracks'), and may have been influenced by Trapp (*Works of Virgil*, I, 158):

> The Farmer's Labour, with the circling Year,
> Turns on it's self, and in a Round revolves.

Dryden here (Walker, ed., p. 494) has the rather different

> Thus in a circle runs the peasant's pain,
> And the year rolls within itself again.

The same lines of Virgil were imitated by others, e.g., Thomson, *Autumn*, 1233–4. Philips (*Cyder*, I, 65; Lloyd Thomas, *Poems of John Philips*, p. 46) refers to 'revolving Years'.

52–90 This passage in some ways echoes the destructive fire in a grove of olive-trees in *G*, II, 303–14.

Virgil's fire occurs *incautis pastoribus*, 'because of the carelessness of shepherds,' and the destructiveness of the cane-fire is similarly ascribed to the carelessness of watchmen, though Grainger also mentions (ll. 53–4) how it could have been started by lightning, accident, or arson (there are other hints of arson at I, 494 and IV, 574; see also note on IV, 605). Since burning canes reduced the amount of sugar which could be obtained from them, this form of arson was a common form of revenge against plantation owners or managers during slavery and has survived into modern times; Grainger's reference to it also echoes the fire in Virgil which takes hold *furtim*, 'stealthily, in a thief-like manner.' Note also 'The spreading vengeance'; if this is also intended to suggest arson, it would seem that Grainger does not approve and nor is divine vengeance appropriate here, in view of the fact that the plantation owner is called 'the virtuous, and the wise.' Both Virgil and Grainger refer to the power of the wind to increase the blaze. However, Virgil's fire rages without any human attempt to check it, while Grainger, by contrast, once more shows man engaged in a struggle – this time unsuccessful – with nature. This time the slaves are given pride of place; the description of them as 'dæmon-like' (l. 69) as they attempt to control the blaze by creating a fire-break suggests more than human effort and is not necessarily negative in connotation – compare Bailey's definition of 'dæmon' as 'a Spirit either Good or Bad.' It also hints that while the 'hand of malice' is a threat to be reckoned with, while some slaves will commit arson, most of them will side with their masters in an emergency.

Grainger's 'the flame burst forth' echoes Virgil's description of the fire as *elapsus*, 'escaped,' while his 'clouds of white smoke load the sky' is (except for the – realistic – change of colour) close to Virgil's fire which *ruit atram/ ad caelum picea crassus caligine nubem*, 'thick with pitch-black gloom hurls a black cloud into the sky.' Grainger emphasises the noisiness of the cane-fire (the 'deafning bells' which sound the alarm, 'the cries of horror,' the 'tumultuous bands,' the 'crackling flames,' the reference to 'loud it roars'), which is perfectly in keeping with the reality of such a scene, but compare Virgil's saying his fire *ingentem caelo sonitum dedit*, 'gave a mighty roar to the heavens.' Similarly, in l. 72, 'branches' is a strange word to use with reference to canes (unless we assume that 'these' in the same line refers to some otherwise unspecified trees, in contrast to 'those Canes' in l. 70), but 'topmost branches' echoes Virgil's *alta cacumina*.

In turn, Grainger appears to have influenced Chapman. The description of a cane-fire in *Barbadoes, and other poems*, p. 57, seems to be more closely related to Grainger than the resemblance one might expect from the coincidence of subject. Chapman asks

>What gleaming lights bring back the parted day?
>What lurid brightness scares the night away?

He has 'horrid cries' and 'deafening bells'; his 'zealous negroes' are an 'eager throng' of 'swart forms that dash the flames among'. 'These canes they cut, and those they tear away [...] but all is vain [...]' Where Grainger calls the slaves 'dæmon-like', Chapman compares them to 'the

# Additional Notes to The Sugar-Cane. Book III

demons sung/By poets, whom the incensed father bound/In Etna's entrails' in a manner reminiscent of Grainger's reference to Etna at the beginning of his hurricane passage (II, 275–84) and to the Cyclopes (I, 407–8).

59   If Palæmon was intended to be any particular individual, identification is now impossible. The name appears as that of the shepherd who judges the singing contest in *E*, III, and in several other places in classical literature as that of a sea-god. Palamon is also a character in Chaucer's Knight's Tale, paraphrased by Dryden under the title 'Palamon and Arcite.'

61   The fire is hard to suppress, like the hydra in classical mythology, a many-headed monster which grew two new heads whenever Hercules cut one off. This is echoed by the 'serpent-error' in l. 71 (following the double sense of 'to err' as 'to go out of the Way, or mistake' – Bailey).

73   This suggests the use on the plantation of some sort of hand-pumped fire-engine; these had existed since ancient times but were given a number of major improvements in the later seventeenth century. The first fire-engine which successfully used steam-power for pumping was not made until 1829. Note the contrast between the 'watery engines' and the 'burning deluge' and 'blazing torrent' in the next two lines.

80   The 'cypress-roofs' may refer to the *Cordia alliodora*, sometimes referred to as 'cypre' (pronounced 'sip') in the Caribbean, which provides 'a good furniture wood' (Gooding et al., *Flora of Barbados*, p. 347).

81, n.   Grainger's supposition is correct. 'Magasse' and 'megasse' are still used in St. Kitts and some other parts of the Caribbean as alternatives to 'bagasse.' The 'large stacks' of bagasse were used as fuel in the plantation's boiling house and were normally piled up near to it; if they caught fire, the plantation's working buildings would be endangered, and perhaps also the owner's 'mansion,' which was often nearby.

Philips list various uses of 'the dry Refuse' of apples which have been crushed for cider: *Cyder*, II, 100–14; Lloyd Thomas, *Poems of John Philips*, p. 71.

92   See note on II, 293 n., above.

94   The 'coppers' are the vessels in which the cane-juice was boiled. They are 'late-hung' because they have recently been put into place for the beginning of Crop.

98–101   It was often suggested that the slaves were happier in crop-time as, although they had more work to do, they were allowed to eat as much of the ripe cane as they wanted and were thus better fed – e.g., Edwards, *West Indies*, II, 259–60. Compare also ll. 407–12 below. On the bill, see note on I, 175.

103   'Wanes' are wains (i.e., wagons); compare III, 128 below. *TCD* has the same spelling (f. 53$^r$, 54$^r$), and also has 'wane' (f. 13$^r$) at what is I, 182 in *1764*, where 'wain' is printed.

106–7   Perhaps inspired by Shakespeare, *Romeo and Juliet* (I, v, 45–6): 'It seems she hangs upon the cheek of night/As a rich jewel in an Ethiop's ear'. In his minor poems, Grainger twice uses 'negro-darkness' with reference to night (Anderson, ed., *Poetical Works of James Grainger*, 1836; II, 18, 37).

108   Phosphor is the Morning-Star.

111–12   The 'sapless burden' is the dried leaves or 'trash' surrounding the cane (which is now 'yellow' because it is ripe), which is removed before the canes are taken to the mill for grinding. The trash is either left in the field to cover the soil and prevent its being dried out by the sun, or used as fuel in the boiling house. See also I, 230, and note on the Argument to Book I.

127   As the context indicates, junks are short pieces; see note on I, 260 n.

130–40   Dyer was a Lincolnshire rector, and there is a clear reference here to the description of sheep-shearing at the end of Book I of *The Fleece* (*Poems*, 1761, pp. 77–85). Tar was applied to cuts and nicks caused by shearing in order to prevent infection and, particularly, to stop insects laying their eggs in the wounds.
   On the other hand, some of this passage may be based on Grainger's personal observation. His patron John Bourryau owned an estate at Blyborough (or Blighborough) in Lincolnshire, and Grainger dated a letter from there in 1758 (Oliver, *Caribbeana*, III, 251–4; Grainger to Percy, 18

## Additional Notes to The Sugar-Cane. Book III

October 1758, Bod. MS Percy c.10, ff. 16–17). The detail about the 'infant throng' and the 'struggling ram' is not in Dyer, nor is that about 'Their master's cypher.' As Tobias Döring has pointed out, this last suggests the branding of slaves as a mark of ownership – something which Grainger does not mention.

153 Annan is a town in Dumfries and Galloway (formerly Dumfrieshire), not far from the border between Scotland and England – l. 154 refers to border raids in the days when the two were separate countries, as well as to feuds between local lords. The passage suggests that Grainger knew the area at first hand; it is just north of Cumberland, from where his father is said to have come, and Percy thought that Grainger's father might have settled in Annandale after the Jacobite rebellion of 1715 (W. E. K. Anderson, *Percy Letters*, IX, 75). However, this is no more than speculation (see Introduction).

160–4 Grainger here gives a picture of grain being harvested to the sound of a bagpipe. On Ceres, see note on I, 64–72; on the dog-star, note on I, 55.

168, n. To 'put the mill out of the wind' was to use the tail-tree to turn the round-house so that the sails were no longer catching the wind; when the sails ceased to turn, the grinding rollers would also stop, of course. However, 'instantly' is here a relative term, as this process would have required a number of men to move the tail-tree and several minutes to accomplish.

In his *Essay on the more common West-India Diseases* (1764; p. 66), Grainger suggested that the owner could 'prevent this horrid accident' by not having the mill work at night, 'or if that cannot be done, at least change those who supply the mill every two hours; by this means their growing sleepy may be prevented.'

Labat's comment occurs in his account of his visit to Barbados (*Nouveau Voyage aux Isles de l'Amerique*, 1724, II, 134–5) where he says of rebellious slaves that 'Those who are captured and sent to prison are condemned to be passed through the mill, burnt alive or exposed in iron cages [...]' (trs. Connell, p. 169). The burnings alive and the iron cages can be documented from other sources (e.g., Edwards, *History ... of the British West Indies*, II, 78–9), but Grainger's scepticism about grinding slaves to death is probably justified. It is questionable whether it would be possible to pass a complete human body through the rollers of a cane-mill, and

Labat's entire account of his voyage to Barbados may be fictitious – see Chatillon.

The last paragraph of Grainger's note ('Daily observation [...]') is the only place in the book he comes close to admitting the essential nature of slavery; when one human being is the 'absolute property' of another, the relationship between them can only be one of arbitrary power, and not one of justice, morality or humanity. The ideal of the virtuous slave-owner, which Grainger describes so skilfully in the Montano episode in Book I, is a chimaera.

184–5  Perhaps a reference to Virgil's insistence (*G*, III, 468–9) that a diseased sheep should be killed before it can infect others.

188  See note on I, 260 n.

191–8  Vulcan is the classical god of fire (compare II, 9); Amphitryte was the wife of Neptune and goddess of the sea, whose name was thus used in classical poetry as a synonym for the sea, or sea-water. Nepenthe (originally an adjective) referred to a drug which took away grief, described by Homer in the *Odyssey* (IV, 220–32) as given to Helen in Egypt by Polydamna. 'Thone's imperial queen' is influenced by Pope's *Odyssey* (where this passage, like the rest of Book IV, was translated by Elijah Fenton), which has 'Thone's imperial wife', where Homer calls her simply Θωνος παρακοιτις 'Αιγυπτιη, 'the wife of Thone, an Egyptian woman.' However, Grainger clearly had the original in mind as well: nepenthe (νηπενθες) is not mentioned as such by Fenton, who refers simply to 'drugs' (Chapman calls it 'a medcine' and 'this Juyce'), nor does Fenton give Polydamna's name (which means 'taming much'), though it does appear in Chapman's translation; in their versions of this passage neither Chapman nor Fenton call Helen 'Jove-born,' but this translates Homer's Διος 'εκγεγαυια and Διος θυγατερ.

The 'evasive spirit' whose superiority to nepenthe is praised by Grainger, is, of course, rum. Chapman, *Barbadoes, and other poems*, picks up the idea of rum as 'a new nepenthe' (p. 11) and refers again to 'cane-distilled nepenthe' (p. 72).

See also note on III, 489–506.

199–203  The image of the mariner furling his sails during a storm appears in Virgil (*G*, I, 370–3), but is here aptly applied to the sails of a windmill for grinding canes, which was often described in nautical terms, and the man who fed the canes into the mill and was in charge of the grinding operations was called the bo'sun: see Anon., 'Old plantation customs'; Carstensen, *Betty's Hope*, Cassidy and Le Page (under 'boatswain'), and Dash, 'Windmills and copper walls.' On the 'points' (l. 202), see note on II, 293 n., above.

205   A reference to the branches of the coconut palm (*Cocos nucifera*).

209   The 'Informer of the planetary train' is the sun; the phrase is taken from Thomson, *The Seasons* (Summer, l. 104). A little further (ll. 113–14), Thomson has 'Parent of Seasons! who the pomp precede/That waits thy throne [...]'

222, n.   By 'a seasonable year', Grainger means one with good rainfall (compare his note on I, 482). Antigua is 17° 6' N, 61° 45' W. Grainger's estimate of Antiguan sugar production seems somewhat exaggerated; according to the figures in Deerr, *History of Sugar* (I, 195), the highest level in years immediately preceding publication of *The Sugar-Cane* was 12,459 tons for 1753 (one of the most productive years of the century). If we allow a fairly normal 15 or 16 hundredweight to the hogshead, this makes no more than about 16,000 hogsheads.

225–51   Grainger's detailed description here of an animal-powered mill for crushing the canes is ultimately based on Virgil's description (*G*, I, 160–75) of the *duris agrestibus arma* ('implements of hardy farmers'), the plough and other tools of cultivation. However, Grainger is much more detailed, perhaps to the point of sacrificing poetry for exactness; by contrast, a modern commentator on Virgil (H. H. Huxley, quoted by R. D. Williams, p. 142) says of the Roman poet's plough that 'we have here an impressionist painting, not a blueprint for an agricultural engineer.'

There are parallels in other writers of English georgic poetry. Philips has a rather shorter account of how to make a cider-press:

> [...] now exhort
> Thy Hinds to exercise the pointed Steel
> On the hard Rock, and give a wheely Form
> To the expected Grinder: Now prepare
> Materials for thy Mill, a sturdy Post
> *Cylindric*, to support the Grinder's Weight
> Excessive, and a flexile Sallow' entrench'd,
> Rounding, capacious of the juicy Hord.

(*Cyder*, II, 78–85; Lloyd Thomas, *Poems of John Philips*, p. 70)

Dyer gives descriptions of the construction and use of a loom, and of the operation of a fulling mill (*The Fleece*, Book III; *Poems*, 1761, pp. 128–31). In his review of *The Fleece*, in *Monthly Review*, XVI, 328–40 (April 1757) at pp. 338–40, Grainger quotes much of this and says of it and another passage, 'What [...] can be more poetically expressed [...]?'

227, n. For the Tobago 'hiccory', which Wright identified as *Juglans baccata*, Kevan suggests 'possibly *Sterculia apetala*, the Coolie Pistache which is native – and which produces nuts of about the same size'. Another possibility is the bully-tree (a name applied to both *Dipholis salicifolia* and *Manilkara bidentata*): a late seventeenth-century account of Tobago's timber-trees (quoted at length in Archibald, *Tobago: 'Melancholy Isle'*, pp. 65–8) does not mention 'hiccory' but says 'Bully-tree is a ponderous, durable and compact Wood; that sinks if put in Water: they use it in Barbados for Rolers, but principally Coggs, to Spindles, and shafts in their Windmills: besides several other uses.'

Grainger's mastic or calaba is probably not the Barbados mastic (*Mastichodendron sloaneanum*) but *Calophyllum calaba*, commonly known as galaba or galba.

St Croix was then a Danish colony; it became part of the United States Virgin Islands in 1917.

Crab Island is what is now known as Vieques, just east of Puerto Rico; its possession was disputed between the Spanish and the British from the late seventeenth century until the mid-nineteenth, with Britain not finally abandoning its claims until 1863, and in the eighteenth century visits by ships from the British Caribbean colonies to obtain hardwood posts were one of the causes of conflicts with Spanish officials based in Puerto Rico. See Dookhan, 'Vieques or Crab Island', who notes that in 1833 'Daniel Bryan Mathew, a proprietor of St Christopher,' petitioned the British government, claiming that Vieques was 'his property in virtue of a grant made to his ancestor in 1748.' This may be Daniel Byam Mathew, son of Grainger's wife's cousin Daniel Mathew (for whom see note on III, 31 above).

Tobago, previously a sparsely inhabited 'neutral island' (not formally owned by any European power) was officially recognised as a British possession by the Treaty of Paris in 1763.

233–4 The 'worm, that pest/Of mariners' is the *Teredo*.

241 Cassidy and Le Page, *Dictionary of Jamaican English*, define 'capoose' as 'Each of the pivots on which the rollers in sugar-mills formerly turned;

# Additional Notes to The Sugar-Cane. Book III

they were shaped like cones rounded at the top and flanged below' though their earliest citation is 1790. The word is not in OED. Cassidy and Le Page suggest derivation from Spanish or Portuguese *capuz*, a cowl, or Venezuelan Spanish *capúza*, arrowhead. Compare Bailey: 'CAPUCHE [...] a Monks Cowl or Hood' (similar definition in Johnson, under 'Capouch').

247   Note that while Grainger has previously (III, 92) spoken of windmills, the present description refers to an animal-powered mill.

252   *1764* has 'thro'' rather than 'through'; the change is called for by the *Errata*. See note on III, 285 below.

253   Strained through a sieve-like mesh. Philips mentions the cidermaker's use of strainers made from goat's hair: *Cyder*, II, 86–90; Lloyd Thomas, *Poems of John Philips*, pp. 70–1.)

255–7   Muscovado is moist unrefined sugar; the normal Caribbean product of this period, exported to Europe for refining. The casks would be supported above ground – the 'staunchions' or stanchions are 'supporters in buildings' (Bailey), though the word is often used of vertical pillars (but see III, 428 n.) – so that as much molasses as possible would drip from the sugar over a period of several weeks before it was shipped. The molasses could later be distilled into rum (III, 439–43). 'Day's bright god' is Apollo; the reference is to the myth of him driving the chariot of the Sun across the sky each day before taking it into the sea at dusk. The suggestion is that the mill will produce ten casks of sugar in a working week; if the casks are taken as equivalent to the usual hogshead of 15 or 16 hundredweight, this works out at about eight tons of sugar a week. This is probably a reasonable average for a small estate depending on an animal-mill; a more powerful windmill could produce perhaps two tons of sugar a day in the eighteenth century (see Carstensen, *Betty's Hope*, pp. 7–9). The change from vertical to horizontal rollers begun at the end of the eighteenth century improved efficiency, and in the last phase of windmill use in the early twentieth century a good mill might produce as much as four tons of sugar a day (Dash, 'Windmills ... of Barbados', p. 58).

259, n.   Raleigh mentioned above, I, 598. Egg Harbor is in what is now New Jersey.

261   The belief that the night air is injurious is still common in the Caribbean.

274                  *The Poetics of Empire*

272    Machaon (also at IV, 121) is a physician mentioned several times in Homer. Hence, 'Machaon's art' is simply an elegant reference to medical skill in general. However, the allusion suggests a specific — and boastful — reference to Grainger himself, for Homer describes Machaon as a warrior as well as a physician: he is not only 'Ασκλεπιου υ‘ιον, 'αμυμονος 'ιητηρος ('son of Asclepios the excellent physician'; in post-Homeric times Asclepios came to be recognised as a son of Apollo and a god of medicine) but also 'ηρωα Μαχαονα ('the hero Machaon') and ποιμενα λαων ('shepherd of the people', i.e., a prince; compare the way Dyer refers to George II as the 'people's shepherd' at the beginning of *The Fleece*); see, e.g., *Iliad*, IV, 194, 200; XI, 506.

273    'Cattle' perhaps refers to draught-animals in general; Bailey defines 'farcy' as 'a Disease in Horses' and 'tabid' as 'dry, lean, wasting away' (Latin *tabes*, dwindling, consumption, plague).

278    'Indesinent': unceasing.

282–3, n.    After a campaign of several months, the French island of Guadeloupe capitulated to the British, 1 May 1759. Fort Royal (Fort-de-France), capital of Martinique, was captured by the British, 3 February 1762, and the rest of the island reduced by 12 February. Havana surrendered to the British on 10 August 1762, after a two months' siege. These conquests were restored to France and Spain by the Treaty of Paris, 10 February 1763. See Fortescue, *History of the British Army*, II, 362, 547–53.

The passage suggests that this part of the poem was composed about the second quarter of 1762. Grainger anticipated the capture of Havana in a letter to Percy, 25 July 1762 (Bod. MS Percy c.10, f. 28–9), though he feared that Britain might not do so well out of the peace: 'we never yet could cope w$^t$ the French at negociation'.

284–8    A reference to water-mills for grinding canes.

285    *1764* has 'thro'' rather than 'through'; the change (like that at III, 252 above) is called for by the *Errata* but the reason is obscure. In the first case it affects a stressed syllable, in the second an unstressed one. In both cases *TCD* (ff. 59$^r$, 61$^r$) has 'thro''. Both 'thro'' (I, 80; II, 300, 351, 395; III, 106, 148, 157; IV, 341, 551) and 'through' (II, 15; III, 193, 235, 340, 564, 575, 625; IV, 21, 22, 45) are found elsewhere in *1764*, and both forms also appear in different places in *TCD*. Here and at III, 252, Chalmers (1810) and Anderson (1836) follow the *Errata*.

Additional Notes to The Sugar-Cane. Book III    275

289–307    Robert Marsham (1712–93), 2nd Baron Romney (succeeded to title, 1724) had in 1742 married Priscilla, daughter and heiress of Charles Pym of Old Road, St Kitts. There is still a place in St Kitts called Romney Manor. The Pyms were related to Grainger's wife's family, the Burts.
    The reference to 'civil armies' alludes to the campaign for the establishment of a revived militia in Britain following the outbreak of hostilities with France in 1755; an invasion scare in 1759 led to the creation of an effective militia in that year. Lord Romney was described by the *Gentleman's Magazine* at the time of his death as 'Indefatigable in his endeavours to promote the establishment of a national militia' and from 1759 he was Colonel of the West Kent Militia. See C[ockayne], *Complete Peerage*, XI, 85, and Western, *English Militia*, pp. 127–61.

308    Having finished his descriptions of mills and the grinding of the canes to extract their juice, Grainger now proceeds to discuss the boiling of the cane-juice to produce sugar.

312–13, n.    Iron vessels are those 'from the martial mine' while 'thine ore, bright Venus' is copper (one source of which in ancient times was Cyprus, traditional home of the goddess).

318    The zodiacal sign Cancer is used to refer to June, the height of the crop-season. See also note on I, 417, above.

334–41    Sugar-boilers were considered to be particularly prone to dropsy. Writing of the St Kitts slaves in 1775, Janet Schaw says 'They are also very subject to dropsies, by which they [the planters] lose many of their boilers, who are always the best slaves on the plantation' – (Andrews, *Journal of a Lady of Quality*, p. 128). The boilers were skilled workers who were among the most valuable slaves on a plantation: compare III, 427–8.

350, n.    The Latin phrase *pocula morte carent* means 'the cups lack death,' i.e., the poison is harmless if drunk.
    The arrow-poison is described by Ulloa, *A Voyage to South America* [...], I, 414–15, and by La Condamine, *Journal du Voyage*, pp. 189–90. Both mention the use of sugar as an antidote; however Ulloa notes 'this specific, though often salutary, is not infallible', and La Condamine says it 'ne produit souvent aucun effet' ('often has no effect at all').

352    The chemical complexity of cane-juice: acor refers to acidity, mucilage to viscous properties.

357, n.   Dumb cane is *Dieffenbachia seguine*; it is described by Hughes, *Natural History of Barbados*, p. *252, which could have given Grainger his reference to using it for dropsy (though Hughes mentions only external use and places the physician concerned in the time of the Duke of Albemarle's governorship, i.e., in the reign of James II, not Charles II). Sloane, *A Voyage to the Islands*, I, 168, says of the dumb cane that 'Pieces of this Stalk are cut, and put into Baths and Fomentations for Hydropick Legs, and are thought very effectual.' There may be a connection here (Sloane went to Jamaica as the Duke of Albemarle's physician) but the details given by Hughes (who mentions mixing the juice with fat and using it as an ointment) do not match exactly.

Xantippe was the wife of the Greek philosopher Socrates (5th century BC) and from classical times her name was proverbial as that of a nagging, quarrelsome woman.

361   Bailey defines 'cade' as 'a Barrel, a Cag [i.e., keg], or Cask.' Although a Latinate word (from *cadus*, a vessel of any kind, especially a wine-flask), it was not a particularly poetic term in the eighteenth century. Grainger uses it again (III, 467) and it appears in Philips (*Cyder*, II, 311, 363; Lloyd Thomas, *Poems of John Philips*, pp. 77, 79).

An earlier version of this line had 'Mark' instead of 'cades', with the note 'Planters put the initial Letters of their Name upon their sugar H[ogs]h[ea]ds – & y$^e$ Sugar Brokers will give more Money for certain Marks than for others' (*TCD*, ff. 65$^v$, 66$^r$).

363, 381–400   A small quantity of '*temper*, which is commonly Bristol white-lime in powder' was routinely added to the boiling cane-juice: 'One great intention of this is to neutralize the superabundant acid, and which to get properly rid of, is the great difficulty in sugar-making' (Edwards, *History ... of the British West Indies*, II, 267).

366–80   These lines refer to 'An Hymn to the Nymph of Bristol Spring' (1751) by William Whitehead (1715–85, poet laureate from 1757 until his death); see Chalmers, *Works of the English Poets*, XVII, 210–14.

At the beginning of the passage, 'to thy waters only trust for fame' is an echo of Whitehead's line 'Nor yet for waters only art thou fam'd,' rather than an exact quotation; Grainger may have paraphrased intentionally or made a mistake in quoting from memory. The 'waters' were those of the Bristol hot wells, which had become fashionable in the reign of Queen Anne; they were believed to be medicinal and were even bottled for export. Grainger refers to this in his note on the bath at Nevis (I, 134) and Whitehead suggests that the waters of the Bristol spring were used not only by the English merchant who fell victim to tropical disease, but even by colonial slaves:

> Thee the glad merchant hails, whom choice or fate
> Leads to some distant home, where Sirius reigns,
> And the blood boils with many a fell disease
> Which Albion knows not. Thee the sable wretch,
> To ease whose burning entrails swells in vain
> The citron's dewy moisture, thee he hails [...]

Grainger's interest in Whitehead's poem may also have been aroused by its claim for the value of the Bristol waters as a cure for venereal disease:

> Thence the boy,
> Who mourns in secret the polluted charms
> Of Lais or Corinna, grateful feels
> Health's warm return, and pants for purer joys.

The 'beamy diamonds' were semi-precious stones found in the vicinity of Bristol and mentioned in Whitehead's poem. The reference to Shakespeare depends on the fact that the Bristol Avon is a different river from the Warwickshire Avon, on which stands Shakespeare's birthplace, Stratford-on-Avon (though *TCD*, f. 65ᵛ-66ʳ, shows Grainger was originally unaware of the distinction). Compare also Milton, *L'Allegro*:

> Then to the well-trod stage anon,
> If *Jonsons* learned Sock be on,
> Or sweetest *Shakespear* fancies childe
> Warble his native Wood-notes wilde [...]

Grainger earlier had 'the wild Drama's Child'. The 'ideal' (or imaginary) 'sword' is the dagger in *Macbeth*, II, i, perhaps referred to by Grainger because of its Scottish subject. 'Sabrina' is the Latin name for the river Severn, into which the Bristol Avon flows.

The passage is described in the index to *1764* as 'Whitehead, praise of.' In response to a query from Anderson, Percy said he did not know if Grainger had been a friend of Whitehead, and there appears to be no other evidence on this, but Percy said 'An Hymn to the Nymph of Bristol

Spring' was 'a popular poem at that time' (W. E. K. Anderson, *Percy Letters*, IX, 67). Even when *The Sugar-Cane* appeared, Whitehead was seldom regarded as a poet of the first rank, and his tenure of the laureateship brought him some ridicule.

395   On Danae, see note on I, 542–50 above.

401–6   Bermuda was famous in the eighteenth century for ships built from its native cedar. Edmund Waller (1606–87) was the author of 'The Battel of the Summer-Islands' (1645), a mock-heroic poem set in Bermuda (often called the Summer or Somers Islands in the seventeenth century after Sir George Somers or Summers, who claimed them for Britain in 1609). Waller's poem gives an idealised picture of Bermuda and describes the combat between 'Two mighty whales' which had been trapped close inshore by rough seas and their human would-be captors. Waller still enjoyed some popularity in the eighteenth century: the prominent London publisher Jacob Tonson (d. 1767) brought out an edition in 1758, and he is mentioned by Akenside, *The Pleasures of Imagination*, III, 558 and note (ed. Dix, pp. 151, 173).

414   See note on I, 399 above.

425   *1764* has 'weighed'; change as called for in *Errata*, which is followed by Chalmers (1810) and Anderson (1836). TCD (f. 68ᵛ) has 'weighd'.

451–4   The simile is taken from Virgil's combat between two swarms of bees (*G*, IV, 67–87), especially the end of the passage, where he says how it can be quelled by throwing a little dust on them:

> hi motus animorum atque haec certamina tanta
> pulveris exigui iactu compressa quiescunt.
>
> Yet all these dreadful deeds, this deadly fray,
> A cast of scattered dust will soon allay [...]
> (Dryden's translation, in Walker, ed., *John Dryden*, p. 524)

455–76   Both Philips (*Cyder*, II, 136–145; Lloyd Thomas, *Poems of John Philips*, p. 72) and Dyer (*The Fleece*, Book II; *Poems*, 1761, pp. 90–91) warned against adulteration.

### Additional Notes to The Sugar-Cane. Book III

Note the use of 'hoe' (rather than 'plough') which is more in accord with Caribbean reality than English poetic convention – though of course it was not 'Gallia's sons' but rather their slaves who actually wielded the hoe. Grainger earlier had 'cultivate these Isles' (*TCD*, f. 69ʳ).

463 After the attack on the French, the details of the example Grainger gives indicate a planter in a British colony. The use of 'Avaro' as the name of a real or imaginary character obviously suggests avarice; earlier (*TCD*, f. 70ʳ) he was called 'Guloso' ('Greedy').

466 The 'Sugar-bakers' are the refiners in Britain, who processed muscovado imported from the Caribbean into white sugar.

476 The rivers are used for the cities which stand on their banks: Bristol (the Avon) and London (the Thames). 'Thame' for 'Thames' was acceptable poetic diction; compare, e.g., Milton, 'At a Vacation Exercise in the College,' l. 100, or Pope, *Pastorals: Summer*, l. 2.

482 Baynard, or Bayard, was a conventional name for a horse or mule; Bailey defines 'bayard' as 'a bay horse', but its popularity seems ultimately to derive from the name given to the horse of Rinaldo, a hero of mediaeval and later romance. Philips has 'Blind *Bayard* ... worn with Work, and Years' providing the power for a cider-press: *Cyder*, II, 95; Lloyd Thomas, *Poems of John Philips*, p. 71.

'Old' seems to have been an afterthought, and makes the line a syllable too long. *TCD* (f. 71r) has 'Give Dobbin these' with 'Dobbin' altered to 'Baynard.'

489–506 Grainger clearly did not share the views of Akenside, who appears to have thought that poets should be water-drinkers: *Hymn to the Naiads*, 314–7 (ed. Dix, p. 368).

Dyer mentions 'heart-chearing wine' from Spain (*The Fleece*, Book IV; *Poems*, 1761, p. 157).

Philips has an extended passage praising the merits of Herefordshire cider as superior to those of imported wines (*Cyder*, I, 521–41; Lloyd Thomas, *Poems of John Philips*, pp. 59–60). Grainger goes a step further by claiming that rum-punch is superior to Burgundy, Champagne, beer ('Ceres' – see note on I, 64–72 above) and cider. To any reader who recalled the end of Philips' or Smart's poems, Grainger might well have seemed to be making a political statement about the importance of the

Caribbean, rather than simply expressing a preference in drinks; compare the following:

> [...] where-e'er the *British* spread
> Triumphant Banners, or their Fame has reach'd
> Diffusive, to the utmost Bounds of this
> Wide Universe, *Silurian* Cyder borne
> Shall please all Tasts, and triumph o'er the Vine.

(*Cyder*, II, 665–9; Lloyd Thomas, *ed. cit.*, p. 87; *Silurian* refers to the Silures, an ancient British tribe who inhabited south-eastern Wales, and Siluria is defined by Dyer in a footnote to *The Fleece*, Book I (*Poems*, 1761, p. 54) as 'the part of England which lies west of the Severn, viz. Herefordshire, Monmouthshire, &c.' Herefordshire was and is famous for its cider.)

> [...] France
> Shall bow the neck to Cantium's peerless offspring,
> And as the oak reigns lordly o'er the shrub,
> So shall the hop have homage from the vine.

(*Hop-Garden*, II, 301–4; Williamson, ed., p. 65; these words are spoken by Neptune; Cantium is the Latin name for the English county of Kent, famous for its hops).

Grainger's 'golden fruit' (l. 496) are probably ripe limes (or perhaps lemons). 'Vigornian hills,/Pomona's lov'd abode' refers to Worcestershire (from Vigornia, Latin name for the city of Worcester), which was, like Herefordshire, famous for its cider.

Philips also mentions (along with coconut-water) what appears to be some sort of brandy-punch in connection with the Caribbean (*Cyder*, II, 265–81; Lloyd Thomas, *ed. cit.*, p. 76).

507   Bailey bluntly defines 'ebriety' as 'Drunkenness.'

509   The first two are Grainger's friends Samuel Johnson (1709–84) and Thomas Percy (1729–1811), for whom see Introduction. According to Percy, White 'was Mr. James White a native of Edinburgh, who resided in London and taught the learned Languages viz. Latin and Greek to Grown Gentlemen whose Education had been neglected.' He published a translation of *The Clouds* of Aristophanes (1759) and a work on *The English Verb* (1761), and

# Additional Notes to The Sugar-Cane. Book III 281

died c. 1811 (W. E. K. Anderson, *Percy Letters*, IX, 59, 67–8, 269). He is mentioned in several of Grainger's surviving letters to Percy. *TCD* (f. 72ʳ) shows White's name was substituted for two others which Grainger tried first and then deleted to the point of illegibility, though this may have had more to do with metrical considerations than the degree of affection involved.

510, n. Mrs Charlotte Lennox (1720–1804), best known for *The Female Quixote* (1752), had edited a translation of *The Greek Theatre of Father Brumoy* (3 vols., London, 1759), to which Grainger had contributed. Percy later recalled that Grainger had been a 'great admirer' of her (W. E. K. Anderson, *Percy Letters*, IX, 68).

Mrs Lennox was probably, as Grainger suggests, born in Gibraltar (referred to here by its Latin name Calpe), though she is sometimes claimed as a native of the colony of New York (where she did spend part of her early life); see introduction by Margaret Anne Doody in Margaret Dalziel's edition of *The Female Quixote*. In *TCD* (f. 72ʳ), Grainger first wrote 'Skullkills Banks' (presumably meaning the Schuylkill River in Pennsylvania) before changing 'Skullkills' to 'Hudsons'; the correction to 'Calpe's rocks' is later than *TCD*.

514 'my Pæon's son' *TCD* (f. 71ᵛ) reads 'my Pæan's Son'. Pæan or Pæon (Gr. Παιαν, epic Παιηων) is mentioned in Homer (*Iliad*, V, 401, 899) as the physician of the gods. Some classical writers treat Pæan as an epithet of Apollo, while others make him a separate deity. Who Grainger intends by this reference is unclear, but it may be Oliver Goldsmith, a friend who was (like Apollo) both physician and poet. Percy later suggested (W. E. K. Anderson, *Percy Letters*, IX, 183) that it might have been John Armstrong, but admitted he had never heard Grainger speak of Armstrong as someone he knew personally.

Armstrong begins his *Art of Preserving Health* with an invocation to 'Daughter of Pæon, queen of every joy,/Hygeia [...]' (1744 ed., p. 1).

522, n. The sand-box tree is *Hura crepitans*; the reference to its shade needs some qualification, as the tree is partly deciduous and will have few leaves left after a period of severe drought.

531 The dwellings of the slaves.

532 Adapted from Milton, *Comus*, l. 30: 'And all this tract that fronts the falling Sun'.

533   Closely related to each other, bananas and plantains are both complex hybrids of two ancestral *Musa* species; Grainger associates them with each other again, IV, 569–73. See also note on I, 430.

546   *TCD* (f. 72ᵛ) shows that 'airies' was Grainger's spelling for 'eyries.'

549, n.   For panspans, see Grainger's note on II, 218, and note above. The papaw is *Carica papaya*.

550   See note on I, 397.

555   The Latin *Hesperia* can refer to either Italy or Spain, but the allusion here is almost certainly to Italian opera, which aroused strong partisanship, both for and against, in eighteenth-century Britain; compare II, 479. The 'unnatural quavers' may, specifically, be those of castrato singers; compare Johnson's 'warbling eunuchs' (*London*, l. 59).

556–60   The references are clearly to European song-birds; the 'chaste poet of the vernal woods' is perhaps the nightingale (*Erithacus megarhyncus*), while the 'herald-lark' is the skylark (*Alauda arvensis*).

562   See note on I, 386.

564   A reference to the broad leaves of the plantain; compare IV, 573.

568–72   Kevan suggests that 'If one had to hazard a guess at the identity of these iridescent little insects "that hover round us" and hum, and whose wings have a purplish sheen, one might reasonably suggest metallic sweat-bees (Halictidae), such as tiny *Augochlora* or only slightly larger *Agapostemon* species.'

573   See note on II, 116.

577 ff.   Compare Virgil's famous passage (*G*, II, 458–74) beginning *O fortunatos nimium, sua si bona norint,/agricolas!* ('How very happy farmers would be, if only they knew their own happiness!') This was imitated by many eighteenth-century writers (e.g., Thomson, *Autumn*, 1235–1351), but Grainger gives it a twist of his own. While Virgil praises a simple rural life in contrast to the luxury and corruption of the city, Grainger encourages West Indian Creoles to stay at home rather than 'spend their opulence

# Additional Notes to The Sugar-Cane. Book III

in other climes' by suggesting that the Caribbean can rival or surpass whatever Europe has to offer. Contrast Smart's more austere advocacy of rural simplicity:

> Hail heroes, hail invaluable gems,
> Splendidly rough within your native mines,
> To luxury unrefined, better far
> To shake with unbought agues in your weald,
> Than dwell a slave to passion and to wealth,
> Politely paralytic in the town!
> (*Hop-Garden*, I, 164–9; Williamson, ed., p. 46)

587 Bellona was the Roman goddess of war. These lines are given point by the military and naval campaigns fought in the Caribbean during the Seven Years War (1756–63). These were not purely a matter of conflict between troops sent out from Europe and creole colonists were sometimes actively involved: ten companies of Barbadian volunteers took part in the British capture of Martinique in 1762. The converse of this display of patriotic 'martial ardour' was the employment as pioneers of slaves who had rather less choice in the matter; slaves from both Antigua and Barbados were used in the Martinique campaign (Fortescue, *History of the British Army*, II, 547, 550).

592 The 'heaven-favoured bard' is the Tyrtæus named in l. 600, a Greek elegiac poet of the seventh century BC, whose songs were supposed to have inspired the Spartans with martial ardour. Grainger's wish echoes that of Dryden in the epilogue to his play *Amboyna* (1673):

> A Poet once the *Spartans* led to fight,
> And made 'em Conquer in the Muses right:
> So wou'd our Poet lead you on this day [...]
> (Gardner, *Prologues and Epilogues
> of John Dryden*, p. 55)

595–8, n. The 'Man of Norfolk' is George Townshend (1724–1807), later fourth Viscount (1764) and first Marquis (1787) Townshend, one of the leading promoters of the revived militia (see notes on ll. 289–307 above). He served as brigadier-general under Wolfe in the Quebec expedition of 1759 and took over command after Wolfe's death (see note on II, 175).

Grainger may have known or met Townshend, who had served in the Duke of Cumberland's army and fought at the battles of Culloden and Laufeld.

TCD (f. 74ʳ) has 'British Ardour', and (instead of 'England's swains' and 'swains of England'), 'Britains Sons' and 'Sons of Britain', while 'their native shore' was previously 'the Mother Isle' (f. 75ʳ).

601 The luxurious life-style – and especially the luxurious tables – of many West Indian planters in the period before the American War of Independence was proverbial. Janet Schaw mentions a 'family dinner' at an Antiguan planter's house in 1774, 'which in England might figure away in a newspaper, had it been given by a Lord Mayor, or the first Duke in the Kingdom.' She asked 'Why should we blame these people for their luxury? since nature holds out her lap, filled with every thing that is in her power to bestow, it were sinful in them not to be luxurious.' She went on to give a long description of this particular dinner and of the food she encountered in general (Andrews, *Journal of a Lady of Quality*, pp. 95–100) which indicates that a large part of what visitors to the Caribbean regarded as luxury was the ready availability of turtle-meat (see note on III, 606) and other tropical foodstuffs (especially the wide variety of fruits) which in a northern climate were either high-priced rarities or, as she put it elsewhere (p. 92), 'delicacies, which the utmost extent of expence is unable to procure in Britain.' Turtle-meat is now forbidden to the ecologically conscious, but in recent years the widespread use of airfreight has stocked the shelves of British supermarkets with a range of 'exotic' produce which the eighteenth century would have regarded as 'luxurious' in the extreme.

604 The name of Marcus Gavius Apicius, a Roman epicure of the first century AD, became proverbial for luxurious eating. The *De re coquinaria*, a Latin recipe book of the third century AD, was ascribed to another Apicius.

606 Both the Hawksbill turtle (*Eretmochelys imbricata*) and the Green turtle (*Chelonia mydas*) were eaten in the Caribbean, but it was the Green turtle which was especially prized as a delicacy, both in the Caribbean and in Europe. Grainger mentions turtle again, but as invalid food (IV, 146, 267).

608, n. The Jewfish (*Epinephelus itajara*) is a member of the Serranidae family, which includes Groupers and Sea Basses.

Additional Notes to The Sugar-Cane. Book III                285

610   On crabs, see note on I, 342.

611–12   Cambria and Scotia are Latinate names for Wales and Scotland; Scotia, or the adjective Scotian, is used again (IV, 178, 437, 618).

613, n.   Barbuda (now part of the country of Antigua and Barbuda) was held by the Codrington family on a lease from the British Crown from 1685 to 1870. Christopher Codrington (1668–1710) left his estates in Barbados to the Society for the Propagation of the Gospel for the establishment of what became Codrington College, though for many years this did little for the conversion of slaves.

614, n.   Grainger considerably overestimates the size of Anguilla, which is about 35 square miles. The 'war preceding the last' was that of 1739–48 (see Introduction).

616   Lusitanian means Portuguese; Hesperian could mean either Spanish or Italian (see note on III, 555).

618   A reference to the repeated warfare of the period. *TCD* (f. 75$^r$) has 'dyed'.

627–32   This passage is reminiscent of Edgar's description of the view from the cliff-top in Shakespeare, *King Lear*, IV, vi, 10–24, and also of Philips, *Cyder*, I, 105–14 (Lloyd Thomas, *Poems of John Philips*, p. 47), but there are no exact verbal resemblances. Grainger's quotation at l. 631 is unidentified; it may derive from Thomson, *The Seasons* (Summer, ll. 649–50):

> Majestic woods of every vigorous green,
> Stage above stage high waving o'er the hills [...]

The phrase 'Stage above stage' also appears in Pope's *Odyssey* (XVII, 316; this Book translated by Elijah Fenton) and Christopher Pitt's translation (1740) of Virgil's *Aeneid* (IX, 718), but in both of these refers to buildings rather than natural scenery.

637   The quotation is from Philips, *Cyder*, I, 98: 'Thus naught is useless made;' (Lloyd Thomas, *Poems of John Philips*, p. 47). The next line and a half in particular, and the passage as a whole, echoes Philips' description of the 'Honest Man' (*Cyder*, I, 730):

> [...] he to his Labours hies
> Gladsome, intent on somewhat that may ease
> Unhealthy Mortals, and with curious Search
> Examines all the Properties of Herbs,
> Fossils, and Minerals, that th'embowell'd Earth
> Displays, if by his Industry he can
> Benefit Human Race [...]
>
> (*Cyder*, I, 754–60; Lloyd Thomas,
> *Poems of John Philips*, p. 66)

In a slightly later letter to Percy (25 March 1765; Bod. MS Percy c.10, ff. 31–33) Grainger expressed his hopes of 'becoming a planter in S$^t$ Vincent' and having time to devote to his botanical 'Enthusiasm' there, and suggested that Percy might be able to use his contacts to get him a government job as 'a Botanist & Inspector of his Majesties reserved Woodlands in y$^e$ new Isl$^{ds}$' (i.e. those in the Windward Islands which Britain had acquired by the Treaty of Paris).

A number of other physicians in the eighteenth-century Caribbean were actively involved in botanical research: see Howard, 'Eighteenth Century West Indian Pharmaceuticals.'

*Book IV*

1  See note on I, 4.

4  The third largest river in Africa (2,600 miles), the Niger reaches the sea through an extensive delta in what is now Nigeria. In Grainger's day, its source and course were unknown to Europeans (although European geographers had speculated about a large African river of this or similar name since classical times): the first edition (1771) of the *Encyclopædia Britannica* incorrectly described it as 'a great river of Africa, which runs from east to west through the middle of Negroland, and discharges itself into the Atlantic ocean by three channels, called Rio Grande, Gambia, and the river Senega.' The Rio Grande (referred to by Grainger in l. 9) is the Koliba River in what is now Guinea-Bissau, while Grainger's 'black Sanaga' is the Senegal River; both of these (like the Gambia) are not in fact connected with the Niger.

Additional Notes to The Sugar-Cane. Book IV

6   See III, 549 and Grainger's note.

9   See note on IV, 4.

11   Under 'brede' Johnson simply has 'See BRAID' and quotes 'a curious brede of needlework' from Addison's 'Essay on Virgil's Georgics' (cf. Guthkelch, ed., II, 5).

22   'Libya' (here and at IV, 290) is 'that Part of the World commonly called *Africa*' (Bailey) and not the modern country of that name; 'Libyan' (IV, 42) and 'Lybians' (IV, 144) have a similar extended reference.

25   'my Melvil' is Robert Melville (1723–1809), a Scottish military officer who became lieutenant-governor of Guadeloupe in 1759 (governor from 1760) and was governor of the ceded islands, 1763–70. He later recalled that he had not actually met Grainger, but that they had corresponded while they were both living in the Caribbean (General Robert Melville to Robert Anderson, 24 April 1801, NLS Adv. MS 22-3-11, ff. 15–16)

Melville was a classical scholar, and was also responsible for the establishment (1763) of the Botanical Garden in St. Vincent – see John Ellis, *Some additional observations [...]*, pp. 10–11, where the garden is described as 'for the culture of the most useful plants, intended for the general benefit of the American Islands, many of which may, in time, become profitable articles of commerce.' This is also described at length in Melville's letter to Anderson, and may have been the origin of Grainger's interest in him.

An almost completely different version of this passage in *TCD* (ff. 81ʳ, 82ʳ) invokes the patronage, not of Melville, but of Pitt the Elder, whose name is written over another which has been deleted, apparently that of Bute (see Introduction).

28   See note on I, 586.

36–7   Compare the end of the preface to his *Essay on the more common West-India Diseases* (1764; p. vi), where Grainger wrote: 'if this performance shall produce the salutary effects for which only it was written, I shall think my leisure well employed; for though the diseases of Blacks are its primary object, *Homo sum & humani nihil a me alienum puto.*' The quotation is a famous line from the Roman playwright Terence (*Heautontimorumenos*, I, i, 25: 'I am a man: I think nothing that is human foreign to me'). Note the stress placed on the humanity of the slaves.

38–9   See note on II, 75 n., above. Grainger has a similar description in his *Essay on the more common West-India Diseases* (1764, pp. 7–8). The belief in differing national characteristics among the slaves was widespread among the planters and is echoed by Janet Schaw (Andrews, *Journal of a Lady of Quality*, p. 128):

> [...] it behoves the planter to consider the country from whence he purchases his slaves; as those from one coast are mere brutes and fit only for the labour of the field, while those from another are bad field Negroes, but faithful handy house-servants. There are others who seem entirely formed for the mechanick arts, and these of all others are the most valuable; but want of attention to this has been the ruin of many plantations.

It is also mentioned in a footnote to his 'Jamaica, A descriptive and didactic poem', *Poems, written chiefly in the West-Indies*, p. 7, by Bryan Edwards.

55   Bryan Edwards also refers to 'ambrosial cane' in his 'Jamaica, A descriptive and didactic poem', and again in his 'Elegy, Written in Jamaica, 1773', in *Poems, written chiefly in the West-Indies*, pp. 13, 44.

58   *1764* has 'art' instead of 'want'; change as called for in *Errata*. *TCD* (f. 83$^r$) has 'Art', but while 'art' (in the sense of technical skill) might well be the 'Offspring of rude necessity' (*TCD* originally had 'harsh' before changing it to 'rude'), 'want' makes better sense as the agent of compulsion. Chalmers (1810) has 'Want'; Anderson (1836) 'want'.

62   The 'Golden Coast' was an area along the Gulf of Guinea, more or less coterminous with the later British colony of the Gold Coast (modern Ghana).

63   'Papaws' was the name given to slaves shipped from the port of Whydah in Dahomey (the modern Ouidah in the Republic of Benin).

65   The River Volta is formed by the confluence of the Black Volta and White Volta, both of which rise in Burkina Faso, and flows through Ghana to the Gulf of Guinea. The 'Rey' is the Rio-del-Rey in Cameroon.

## Additional Notes to The Sugar-Cane. Book IV

72   See note on I, 4.

82   'Cormantee' (also Coromantee, Coromantine and other spellings) was a name given to a slave shipped from what is now Kromanti in Ghana, or a descendant of these slaves. Grainger's description of the Cormantee character was a traditional one; such slaves were prominent in rebellions during the eighteenth century.

94   Although it is the same plant (*Oryza sativa*) as that cultivated in wet paddies in many parts of Asia, Grainger refers to the dry cultivation of rice in West Africa, in a manner still to be seen among the Maroons (descendants of escaped slaves) in Suriname. On yams, see note on I, 237. 'Lofty maize' may refer either to guinea corn (*Sorghum vulgare*), or to Indian corn (*Zea mais*), which although a New World plant was being grown in West Africa by the mid-sixteenth century; see note on IV, 567 n.

99   'Minnah' is probably Elmina (in modern Ghana), which was the earliest European settlement on the Gold Coast and an important slaving port. It was a Dutch possession from 1637 to 1872, when it was transferred to the British.

102   'Moco' is defined by Cassidy and Le Page, *Dictionary of Jamaican English*, as 'An African tribal name of doubtful identity'; Edwards (*History ... of the British West Indies*, II, 90) included them among the 'Eboes', suggesting an origin in what is now south-eastern Nigeria.

103 ff.   Armstrong, *Art of Preserving Health* (III, 533–618; 1744 ed., pp. 93–8) has a long description of the sweating sickness (or some similar human epidemic) in England, and Dyer has a long passage on various diseases of sheep (*The Fleece*, Book I; *Poems*, 1761, pp. 63–5). However, Grainger's ultimate model for his account of the diseases of slaves is Virgil's description of the plague at Noricum (*G*, III, 478–566), which destroyed both livestock and humans. In Virgil's plague, human intervention is unavailing, and his vivid and horrific details are difficult to reconcile with the symptoms of any actual disease. Grainger is (unsurprisingly) both more naturalistic in his descriptions, and much more positive about the potential of medicine to prevent, cure or at least alleviate disease. In the same way that Virgil's plague parallels his account of the storm, and of the portents which foreshadowed the Civil War (*G*, I, 311–34, 463–97), so Grainger's diseases of slaves parallel his account of the pests of the sugar-cane in Book II.

103–7 Kevan suggests that tapeworms are referred to, especially the Beef tapeworm (*Taenia saginata*). He argues that this would explain the reference to 'Mundingo,' presumably the Mandinga (including the Malinke) people, who lived in the region in and around what is now Mali and who were probably brought to the Caribbean via Senegambia: 'That they are singled out as being particularly liable to have "worms" on arrival in the West Indies would, if the Beef tapeworm were involved, be explicable on the basis of the "Mundingo" being mainly stock-raisers and naturally more frequent beef-eaters than most of the tribes which provided the bulk of the slaves. To this day, the people of the lands adjacent to the southern Sahara are widely and commonly infected with this tapeworm.'

108–11 This passage has its origin in what *TCD* (f. 87ᵛ) originally offered as an alternative to IV, 166:

> Tho doomd from Rise to Set, in Phœbus' Eye
> Indesinent to labour —
> How far more pleasant &c

As Grainger noted in *TCD*, this echoes Shakespeare, *Henry V*, IV, i, where the King – restless the night before battle – claims that

> No, not all these, laid in bed majestical,
> Can sleep so soundly as the wretched slave;
> Who, with a body fill'd and vacant mind,
> Gets him to rest, cramm'd with distressful bread,
> Never sees horrid night, the child of hell;
> But like a lackey, from the rise to set,
> Sweats in the eye of Phoebus, and all night
> Sleeps in Elysium [...]

The Shakespearian allusion is used to imply that the slave was better off in some ways than his social superiors as well as than other kinds of labourers around the world (IV, 165 ff.).

113 The 'Quanza's lucid stream' is the River Kwanza in Angola.

121 For Machaon, see note on III, 272.

123 The statement in ll. 124–5 that 'These, in every hedge,/ Spontaneous grow' suggests that Grainger refers not to the European ver-

Additional Notes to The Sugar-Cane. Book IV    291

vain (*Verbena officinalis*) and sempre-vive (*Sempervivium tectorum*) but to Caribbean equivalents. The vervain is probably the West Indian vervain (*Stachytarpheta jamaicensis*) widely regarded as a panacea. In his *Essay on the more common West-India Diseases* (1764; p. 19), Grainger specifically identifies semprevive as aloes, i.e., what is now well-known as *Aloe vera*, still widely popular in the Caribbean as a purgative. It would seem that this is also what is meant here, though Kevan suggested the leaf-of-life or wonder-of-the-world (*Bryophyllum pinnatum*), originally a native of Madagascar, but now widespread in the Caribbean, where a number of medicinal properties are claimed for it (though acting as a vermifuge does not seem to be one of them).

Ligon (pp. 98–9) refers to aloes, 'which we call *semper vivens* in *England*'.

127   A note in *TCD* (f. 85ᵛ) explains 'the white eagle' as 'Aquila Alba the Alchymical Term for that preparation of Mercury commonly called Calomel', i.e., mercurous chloride, long popular as a purgative.

136–7, n.   *1764* has 'rhinds' instead of 'rinds'; change as called for in *Errata*; followed by Chalmers (1810) and Anderson (1836).

The tree referred to is *Anacardium occidentale*, whose seed, when roasted, is the well-known cashew nut. The fruit has an astringent flavour and is said to be good for upset stomachs (compare l. 138). As Grainger describes in his note, the oil depends for its somewhat drastic cosmetic effects on the fact that it blisters and removes the skin. The 'American fortune-tellers' are almost certainly Amerindians.

142   'Hydrops' is 'a Disease, otherwise called *Diabetes*' (Bailey).

144   See note on IV, 22.

146   The mention of turtle as invalid food for slaves perhaps raised a few eyebrows among Grainger's British readers, who would have been more accustomed to thinking of it as a luxury item (notes on III, 601, 606). See also IV, 267.

150   One possible cause of dirt-eating (or 'pica') is hookworm infestation; see note on IV, 290–305. 'Chlorotic' is the adjective from chlorosis, 'the Green-sickness, a Disease in young Virgins, which makes them look of a wan sallow Complexion' (Bailey) – a popular diagnosis in the eigh-

teenth and nineteenth centuries for a variety of symptoms which would now be attributed to anaemia.

156   Pæan is Apollo, as god of healing (see note on III, 514).

163, n.   The conch is a large marine gastropod (*Strombus gigas*) whose shell can be blown as a sort of trumpet – this, or a bell, was used to summon plantation workers to their early morning tasks until well into the twentieth century in parts of the Caribbean. As Grainger mentions (IV, 267) the flesh of the conch is also used as food; it is considered a great delicacy in parts of the region.

Chapman, *Barbadoes, and other poems*, p. 10, similarly has 'The conch or shrill-toned bell' summoning the slaves at sunrise.

165–82   If Grainger compares the position of Caribbean slaves with that of European miners, the comparison could also be reversed. The Rev. John Dalton described 'Two Ladies' visiting the mines near Whitehaven:

> AGAPE the sooty collier stands,
> His axe suspended in his hands,
> His Æthiopian teeth the while
> 'Grin horrible a ghastly smile,'
> To see two goddesses so fair
> Descend to him from fields of air.
> Not greater wonder seiz'd th'abode
> Of gloomy Dis, infernal god,
> With pity when th'Orphean lyre
> Did ev'ry iron heart inspire,
> Sooth'd tortur'd ghosts with heavenly strains,
> And respited eternal pains.
> (*A Descriptive Poem [...]* (London, 1755), lines 65–76, p. 6)

Dalton makes much of the subterranean scenery, and there are passing references to fire-damp (pp. 1, 5) and in a prose note (p. 2) to 'dreadful explosions, very destructive to the miners', but there is not much on the nature of the miners' work (unless it is implied in the allusion to Orpheus' descent into the underworld and the reference to 'tortur'd ghosts'. A little later, describing miners cutting through rock to reach coal-seams, he says (lines 107–8, p. 9):

*Additional Notes to* The Sugar-Cane. *Book IV*    293

Thus, urg'd by Hunger's clamorous call,
Incessant Labour conquers all.

(This echoes *G*, I, 145–6, one of the most famous passages in Virgil.) The 'sooty collier' and his 'Æthiopian teeth' seem to imply a comparison with Caribbean slaves – Whitehaven (in Cumberland, a northern English county bordering on Scotland, which was also the county where Grainger's father seems to have had his original home) was a minor but still significant slave-trading port.

Grainger's comparison is given added point by the fact that for most of the seventeenth and eighteenth centuries a large proportion of the coal-miners in Scotland (though not in England) were legally serfs, bound for life to the mines in which they worked, and 'In practice serfdom almost invariably was hereditary, in the sense that sons followed fathers whatever the niceties of the law.' The parallel was sufficiently close that when in 1770 a Caribbean slave who had been brought to Scotland sought to obtain his freedom from the Court of Sessions in Fife, his case was supported by funds raised by the local colliers, salters and farm-workers. Serfdom among the coal-miners (who were the third largest group in Scotland's working class) was not finally abolished until 1799, a generation after Grainger's death. See T. C. Smout, *A History of the Scottish People, 1560–1830*, pp. 167–70, 403–12.

More generally, compare Goldsmith, *The Deserted Village* (1776), ll. 103–4, where miners (like sailors) are 'wretches, born to work and weep' (ed. Mack, p. 53).

In his 'Jamaica, A descriptive and didactic poem', Bryan Edwards describes 'Th'unhealthful mine' with reference to Mexico and Potosi (Bolivia) and 'Darien's marshy shores, and the rank plains/Of hot Guiana' before claiming the Caribbean islands are more fortunate: 'ye beauteous isles! whose happier shores/Nor foul contagion blots, nor births obscene/Dare enter', *Poems, written chiefly in the West-Indies*, pp. 4–5.

Chapman, *Barbadoes, and other poems*, pp. 27–8, also draws a parallel between Caribbean slaves and European miners (in this case, the mercury miners of Idria, the modern Idrija in Slovenia) and goes on to suggest that both the miners and 'those wretches of the lead-like hue', the 'nerveless children, wo-begone, and pale' of England's industrial towns were much worse off than 'The happier negro.' Similarly, one of the characters in a play performed in Barbados in 1832 says of an Englishman who has just been given a tour of a sugar plantation, 'let him, now that he has an opportunity of forming a fair opinion and an honest judgment, determine whether West India slaves do not possess more actual comfort and personal liberty than the unhappy, gagged, maimed and deformed white children of the factory mills of Leeds and Manchester; or the inhumed miners of Cumberland and Cornwall!' (Orderson, *The Fair Barbadian and Faithful Black*, p. 17).

Grainger begins by discussing mining in general terms (though he is probably thinking of coal-mining) and then specifically mentions mining for lead and mercury ('silver's fluent ore,' a variation on the traditional name of quicksilver for mercury), both of which were likely to poison those who worked with them. The Drave (l. 181 and note), or Drava, runs through several modern European countries before becoming a tributary of the Danube.

166   *TCD* (f. 88$^r$) originally had 'Tho doomd to labour in the Mid-day Sun:' before changing it to the version used in 1764. See also note on IV, 108–111.

183–198   The comparison now moves on to Amerindians forced to work in the mines of South America. The 'proud insulting tyrants' are the Spanish; once again, the superiority of British rule is implied.

Grainger may have taken a hint here from a passage in *The Fleece*, Book III (*Poems*, 1761, p. 140), where Dyer compares the lot of English weavers with that of South American miners:

> But chearful are the labors of the loom,
> By health and ease accompany'd: they bring
> Superior treasures speedier to the state,
> Than those of deep Peruvian mines, where slaves
> (Wretched requital) drink, with trembling hand,
> Pale palsy's baneful cup.

He might also have got some ideas from the descriptions of mines in Ulloa, *Voyage to South America* (esp. I, 466–79; II, 145–56), though these play down the hazards. Compare also Thomson's reference to 'sad Potosi's mines/Where dwelt the gentlest children of the Sun' (*Summer*, ll. 871–2).

193–4   Probably a reference to mercury poisoning; as mercury will dissolve most other metals, it was widely used in the extraction of precious metals from their ores. Mercury poisoning is still a widespread hazard in small-scale gold-mining in South America.

### Additional Notes to The Sugar-Cane. Book IV

196   *TCD* (f. 89ʳ) has 'Their glorious God, the Sun' ; compare II, 232; III, 256, and note how Grainger conflates what he has read about sun-worship in pre-Columbian America with European classical mythology.

199   See note on I, 4.

211–31   For Dyer, the slave trade was 'the valued trade', 'this advent'rous traffic' and 'The gainful commerce' which provided those who 'till our fertile colonies', but he also said that it

> [...] in telling, wounds
> The gen'rous heart, the sale of wretched slaves;
> Slaves, by their tribes condemn'd, exchanging death
> For life-long servitude; severe exchange!

He advised those involved in the trade to pursue it 'With just humanity of heart' and warned that

> [...] wickedness is blind:
> Their sable chieftains may in future times
> Burst their frail bonds, and vengeance execute
> On cruel unrelenting pride of heart
> And av'rice. There are ills to come for crimes.
> (*The Fleece*, Book IV; *Poems*, 1761, p. 164.)

Compare also Chapman's discussion of the slave-trade (*Barbadoes, and other poems*, pp. 26–30). While Chapman refers to the

> [...] dire thirst of gold,
> [...]
> At whose fierce bidding comes the armed band,
> And tears the peasant from his native land [...]

he also says of the trade's victims that

> They changed their country, but their life the same —
> In wide-spread Libya freedom is a name.

Chapman admits that they might have felt homesick, but by the time he is writing (1833), the slave trade has been abolished and, in Barbados at least, '[…] the race has vanished from the land,/Whose hopes lie buried in far Guinea's sand', conditions have improved, and the slaves (who are now being christianised) are perfectly happy:

> Now that a brighter faith their children warms,
> And hope delights them in a thousand forms;
> Now that brute force and cruelty are gone,
> Their hearths are sacred and their store their own;
> Now that the brand, the torture, and the chain,
> The sharp wild shriek of agonizing pain,
> The sobbing accents that in vain implore,
> And slavery's blotch, are seen and heard no more –
> Change but the name – hunt freedom o'er the waves,
> Search through the earth for happier than the slaves; —
> Vain is the search! and when their minds shall be
> Free as their persons, will the slaves be free.

By contrast, Grainger's recognition of the 'tyrannic sway' of 'heart-debasing slavery' (235–6) is far more honest. In *TCD* (f. 89$^v$) there is a note opposite this passage: 'The great, because pious Boerhaave used to say, that he never saw a prisoner carried to Execution, without asking his own soul, who knows whether this man is not less guilty than I?' (Hermann Boerhaave [1668–1738] was a celebrated Dutch physician and scientist.)

A much longer note on the same passage (*TCD*, f. 89$^v$, 90$^v$, 91$^v$, not used in the published version) attempts to justify slavery as an economic necessity, claims 'it is a Masters Interest to treat his Bondslave w[i]t[h] humanity' and insists that 'an African who has a tollerable Master, not only does less Lab[ou]r y$^n$ [than] a Common Man in great Britain, but that Apprentices in general are not better treated y$^n$ our Negroes in y$^e$ West Indies.' A great deal is made to depend on that 'tollerable'.

243   See note on III, 21 above.

244–5   Much of the material in this and the following sections can be paralleled in Grainger's *Essay on the more common West-India Diseases* (1764).

245–55   This describes the Guinea-worm or 'dragon worm' (l. 256) which grows up to three feet (approximately one metre) in length and whose thickness has been compared to a horse-hair or the wire of a paper-clip; the scientific name is *Dracunculus medinensis*. Humans can become infected by drinking water in which a kind of minute water-flea (*Cyclops* spp.) is present; the water-flea acts as a host to immature worms, but while the flea is destroyed by human digestive juices, the worms are not, and they continue to develop within the human body, where they settle in connective tissue. They eventually find their way to the skin, where they create an ulcer through which they emerge. The infection is often extremely painful and can cripple. It is not clear why Grainger refers specifically to 'A leaden cylinder', but the method of extraction he describes, removing the worm by winding a very little of it at a time around a thin stick or similar object, remains the only treatment; complete removal of the worm can take weeks or months. Kevan mentions another method of extraction, sucking the worm into a conical metal tube, and suggests that Grainger is confusing the two; this seems unlikely, his *Essay on the more common West-India Diseases* (1764; p. 63) simply refers to winding the worm round 'a small cylinder'. Lead piping would have been easy to come by on an eighteenth-century plantation, as it was used in the equipment for distilling rum.

The exact process of infection was not understood until the twentieth century; Grainger correctly associates it with contaminated water (l. 247), though he was 'not convinced it ever gets into the human body by drinking water' (*West-India Diseases*, 1764, p. 63). The reference to 'native streams' is given point by his observation that 'I fancy it is not a Disease of the West-Indies; for all those I ever saw afflicted therewith, had brought it with them to the new world from Guinea' (ibid., p. 62); as Kevan notes, 'The Guinea worm never became widely established in tropical America [...] perhaps because of a relative lack of suitable species of *Cyclops*.' His 'annual lameness' (l. 255) may refer to the fact that it takes about a year after infection for the worms to reach maturity and emerge through the skin (at which point they are at their most painful and can render the sufferer incapable of work for up to three months). If a victim with an open Guinea-worm ulcer enters water, the worm will emerge and release thousands of immature worms, creating the possibility of re-infection.

As the name suggests, Guinea-worm disease (dracunculiasis) was brought from Africa to the Caribbean, where it is no longer found. Since 1986, when there were an estimated 3.5 million victims, an international campaign has greatly reduced the incidence of the disease, which is now found only in parts of Africa between the Sahara and the Equator (mostly in southern Sudan), in the Yemen, and in isolated parts of Rajastan in India. (See dracunculiasis web-page hosted by the National Center for Infectious Diseases, Atlanta).

A rather similar description is given by Hughes, *History of Barbados*, p. 41.

253    *1764* has 'surely' for 'surly', but Grainger noted this as an error of the press, along with that at III, 6 (see note above on that passage). In *TCD* (f. 91ʳ) the passage reads:

>    [...] but O beware
> No Roughness practise: else 'twill surly snap,
> And suddenly retreating, dire produce
> An annual Lameness to the tortur'd Limb.

The 'surly' (and perhaps also the absence of a comma after 'suddenly') add to the personification of the Guinea-worm which is begun by the 'subtly' (l. 246) and 'It may be won' (l. 251). Chalmers (1810) and Anderson (1836) follow *1764*.

255    Only here in the poem is 'Moor' used as a synonym for 'African' or 'Black.'

257, n.    For various names current in Caribbean English, see Allsopp, under 'chigo(e).' Grainger refers to a kind of flea (*Tunga penetrans*), his description is generally accurate, though Kevan points out that he is in error in calling them 'winged' and that the Spanish name 'Miguas' should be 'niguas' – this, like 'chigo(e)' and its variants, is a word of Amerindian origin; see Luis Hernández Aquino, *Diccionario de voces indígenas de Puerto Rico*, under 'nigua.' From personal experience, Kevan questioned Grainger's reference to the itching as 'not unpleasing'; Ligon (1673, p. 65) said they caused 'much smarting pain', while Hughes, *History of Barbados* (p. 42) refers to 'a throbbing itching pain', but as Virgil puts it, *trahit sua quemque voluptas* (*E*, II, 65; 'his own desire draws each one on').

265–89    Yaws (framboesia) is a contagious disease caused by a spirochæte, *Treponema pertenue*, which is very similar to that which causes syphilis (*T. pallidum*). The causes of the two diseases were only fully identified in the early twentieth century, but their resemblance was long recognised; for example, Hooper, *Quincy's Lexicon-Medicum* (under 'Framboesia') remarks that yaws 'is somewhat similar in its nature to the lues venerea, and is endemic to the Antillia islands.' However, yaws is not normally contracted through sexual activity, and while later and potentially fatal complications of the sort associated with tertiary syphilis are possible, they are much rarer. The disease manifests itself in raspberry-like eruptions (hence the name framboesia, first used in 1759) which are usually painless and normally will eventually drop off of their own accord. As Grainger notes (l. 273), material from the sores is extremely contagious. His description of the disease is evidently based on close observation, and his suggested remedies are about as much as medical science could offer before the advent of penicillin (which was found to provide a cure): isolation of the infected to prevent wider contagion, a good diet, and various topical applications to the eruptions. The use of sulphur (l. 268) taken internally was still common in the early twentieth century, and the use of mercury ('live-silver', l. 276) was similar to treatments for syphilis. Infection often (though not invariably, as Grainger suggests, ll. 286–7) confers a high degree of immunity in later life.

Yaws is now believed to have been eliminated from the Caribbean, as a result of mass campaigns by the World Health Organisation some forty years ago.

265  As printed, this line is too long (eleven syllables instead of ten). *TCD* (f. 91ʳ) has 'The Yaws infectious bane? – such far remove'. Grainger then crossed out the last three words, substituting 'the infected far' and inadvertently adding an extra syllable, as well as making other alterations in the preceding and following lines. The problem is easily solved by elision ('th'infected') which many of Grainger's readers would probably have done unconsciously, but the fact that the line was not printed like this suggests hasty revision and/or proof-reading. Chalmers (1810) prints 'th'infected'; Anderson (1836) keeps 'the infected' but changes the apostrophe in 'yaw's' to follow the s, which makes better grammar but does nothing for the scansion.

Compare IV, 534, where 'the anata' has to be elided to make the line scan; Anderson (1836) – but not Chalmers – prints 'th'anata'.

267  On turtle, see note on III, 606, and on conch, see note on IV, 163.

268, n.  The 'niccars' are the seeds of the shrub *Caesalpinia bonduc*, whose Caribbean English names still include nickers or horse-nickers. Grainger is wise to prescribe them 'burnt' as they are poisonous if not roasted.

283  The 'turpentine' is identified by Wright in the index to Anderson

(1836) as the 'Turpentine tree, (West-India) [...] *Bursera gummifera* (modern scientific name *Bursera simaruba*); this is probably suggested as a substitute for other trees from different parts of the world which were all referred to as turpentine and employed in medicine primarily for their laxative properties, though such products were also popular in the treatment of 'gleets' (discharges caused by gonorrhœa); see Hooper, Robert, *Quincy's Lexicon-Medicum*, under 'Turpentine'. The guaiac is *Guaiacum officinale*, introduced here through the association of yaws with syphilis (see note on I, 34–7).

290–305    Grainger's reference to worms is rather general; Kevan points out that some of the symptoms described in this passage could have had other causes, but that where helminth parasites were involved, these would have been nematodes, and the tropical hookworm (*Necator americanus*) would have been the most prevalent. Introduced to the Caribbean from West Africa, this 'can cause many of the kinds of symptoms mentioned by Grainger'.

291    In classical mythology, Proteus was a sea-god who could change his shape at will (described in *G*, IV, 405–14, 440–44).

300    With the possible exception of 'the sweltering fever' (IV, 510) this is the only reference to malaria in the poem; Kevan comments: 'This may not, however, be surprising when one considers that this mosquito-borne disease was quite commonplace in Europe, including England, at the time. There is, alas, no revolutionary suggestion that this, or any other disease, might be carried by insects!'

305    Adapted from Armstrong, *Art of Preserving Health*, III, 196–202, from a passage on the perils of sudden exertion:

> Besides, collected in the passive veins,
> The purple mass a sudden torrent rolls,
> O'erpowers the heart and deluges the lungs
> With dangerous inundation: Oft the source
> Of fatal woes; a cough that foams with blood,
> Asthma, and feller Peripneumonie,
> Or the slow minings of the hectic fire.

In a footnote, Armstrong defines 'Peripneumonie' as 'The inflammation of the lungs' (1744 ed., p. 73). Grainger's meaning appears to be that

# Additional Notes to The Sugar-Cane. Book IV

worm infestation can produce symptoms similar to those of consumption (tuberculosis); compare Bailey's definitions of 'hectica' as 'an hectic Fever; a slow habitual Fever, gradually preying on and consuming the Moisture of the Body, often accompanied with an Ulcer in the Lungs and a Cough' and of 'hectick' as 'subject to such a Fever, Consumptive.'

In his *Essay on the more common West-India Diseases* (1764, p. 21), Grainger claimed that 'The truth is, there is scarce one symptom with which the animal œconomy may be affected, which Worms are not capable of exciting.'

309, n.   See note on II, 123, n.

311   See note on II, 171.

313   See note on II, 119.

317, n.   'The mineral product of the Cornish mine' is tin. In the note, *1764* gives the Greek word for tin (in the accusative), Κασσιτερον (which Grainger glosses with its Latin equivalent, *stannum*) as two words, Κασσι τερον. The correct form is noted in the *Errata*; in some eighteenth-century (though not in modern) typography, this involved a change in the form of the letter τ. Chalmers (1810) and Anderson (1836) correctly give it as one word.

Akenside refers to British tin as 'mineral treasure' and associates it with the Phœnicians (*Hymn to the Naiads*, 119–25; ed. Dix, p. 363). It is also mentioned by Dyer (*The Fleece*, Book II; *Poems*, 1761, p. 104).

The 'polished Tyrians' of l. 319 are the 'Phænicians' mentioned in Grainger's note, i.e., the Phoenicians, renowned for their commerce throughout the ancient Mediteranean. Their territory was roughly equivalent to modern Lebanon, and its chief city was Tyre. Strabo was a Greek geographer of the late first century BC; the story to which Grainger refers is in his *Geography*, 3, 5, 11 (see Loeb trs. by H. L. Jones, II, 157–9).

325   A reference to either the unsuccessful invasion of Greece (480 BC) by the Persian king Xerxes, or to the defeat of Darius III by Alexander the Great (333 BC).

330   'Enna' is used for Sicily as a whole; see note on I, 64–72. 'Belgian' was used for the Low Countries in general, and not just for modern Belgium (in Grainger's time, the Austrian Netherlands); compare

Akenside's 'On leaving Holland' where he refers to the Dutch university town of Leiden as 'The Belgian Muse's sober seat' (Dix, ed., *Poetical Works*, p. 262). Lines 332–6 suggest Grainger is in fact referring to the Dutch Republic, which was no longer as prominent in European affairs and international commerce as it had been in the seventeenth century.

336   After the digression, we return to 'Mighty commerce' (l. 322) which is to be identified with the 'Parent of wealth'.

345–6   Sylvanus was the Roman god of woods and fields. On Ceres, see note on I, 64–72 above.

360   Compare I, 97–126. 'That world' is of course the Americas, while 'those realms' are the coasts of Africa explored by command of the kings of Portugal ('Lusitania's chiefs'). Grainger neatly ends his digression on the blessings of commerce, and returns to 'the subject of my song', by alluding to the slave trade – without being unduly specific once more on such an awkward subject.

381–405   Compare the description of European magic in classical antiquity at II, 131 ff.
  Commenting on the St Kitts slaves in 1775, Janet Schaw wrote (Andrews, *Journal of a Lady of Quality*, p. 128) that 'Strange as it may seem, they are very nervous and subject to fits of madness. This is looked on as witchcraft by themselves, and there is a seer on every plantation to whom they have recourse when taken ill.'
  Other eighteenth-century accounts of obeah (or at least of the slave-owners' views of it) such as those in Hughes, *Natural History of Barbados*, pp. 15–16, or Edwards, *History ... of the British West Indies*, II, 106–19, offer details similar to those given by Grainger.

382   See note on I, 4.

406   'Lucifer' used in the literal sense of 'bringer of light,' referring to 'the Morning or Day-Star, the Planet *Venus*, when it rises before the Sun' (Bailey).

410, n.   A number of different species are called broom in the Eastern Caribbean. Grainger's description suggests he is referring to *Sida acuta*;

## Additional Notes to The Sugar-Cane. Book IV 303

another possibility is *Malvastrum americanum* but *Sida* opens in the morning, *Malvastrum* in the afternoon.

The marvel of Peru is *Mirabilis jalap* (former scientific name *Mirabilis Peruviana*), perhaps best remembered in literature for its appearance in 'The Mower against Gardens' (first published 1681), by Andrew Marvel (1621–78):

> Another world was searched, through oceans new,
> To find the *Marvel of Peru*.

Compare Chapman's 'The four-o'clocks their shrinking petals close' and his note: 'This is the American clock; which is also known as the "marvel of Peru." ' (*Barbadoes, and other poems*, pp. 40, 99). Chapman mentions it again, p. 65.

415 n.   The solanum or fire-weed is *Datura stramonium* L., which has been used for a number of medicinal purposes, although it is in fact poisonous. 'Dr. Stork' is Anton, Freiherr von Störck, (1731–1803), who recommended an extract prepared from the seeds of this plant 'in maniacal, epileptic and convulsive affections', though other physicians of the period expressed scepticism – see Hooper, *Quincy's Lexicon-Medicum*, under 'Stramonium.' A member of the same family, *Solanum americanum*, shows some similarities; see II, 95, and note above.

416   Kevan indicates that 'crickets' could refer to both true crickets (Grylloidea) and bush-crickets or katydids (Tettigonioidea).

435   'Ïerne' is poetic diction for Ireland (from Greek Ἰερνη, found in Aristotle and other classical authors). Compare, e. g., Philips, *Cyder*, II, 223 (Lloyd Thomas, *Poems of John Philips*, p. 75).

449, n.   Grainger's note is paraphrased from John Ogilby (not 'Ogilvy'), *America: Being the latest, and most accurate description of the New World [...]* (London, 1671), p. 357.

454, n.   The modern scientific name of the pigeon-pea is *Cajanus cajan*.

456, n.   The bonavist is *Lablab niger*.

457, n.   'Ochra' (now usually spelt okra) is *Hibiscus esculentus*. It is still widely used in Caribbean cooking, and is used in the gumbos of the southern United States. In Britain, it is perhaps best known as an ingredient of some dishes served in Indian restaurants, where it is known as bhindi. Also known as 'lady's finger.' It is a member of the mallow family (Malvaceae).

459, n. As Grainger's note makes plain, he refers to sweet potatos (*Ipomoea batatas*) and not what is commonly called in the Caribbean the 'English potato' or 'Irish potato' (*Solanum tuberosum*). Grainger appears to believe that the latter is an Old World plant, but both originate in the Americas, and the sweet potato is 'of Indian original' in the sense that it was grown in the Caribbean in the pre-Columbian period.

461, n. See note on I, 596, n.

462, n. 'Indian cale' (or Kale) is defined by Cassidy and Le Page, *Dictionary of Jamaican English*, as 'Plants of the closely related genera *Xanthosoma* and *Colocasia*, the leaves of which are cultivated and eaten as greens and in soups'; eddoes and tannias come from the same genera (see note on I, 596, n.). Calaloo (also calalu and other spellings) is *Amaranthus spinosus* or related *Amaranthus* spp.; Grainger is probably right in thinking the common name is Amerindian, though African origins have also been suggested. 'Mezembay' is probably *Cleome gynandra*, still known as masambay in St. Kitts; a native of Africa, widely naturalised in the Caribbean, it is used as a spinach in Ghana. The 'Jamaica prickle-weed' is perhaps *Amaranthus spinosus*, sometimes called 'prickly calalu' in Jamaica.

463 The European herbs referred to are probably spearmint (*Mentha spicata*), common thyme (*Thymus vulgaris*) and lemon balm (*Melissa officinalis*). *Thymus vulgaris* and a number of mint species are cultivated in the Caribbean.

466 The 'bushy citrons' may possibly be, not the citron (*Citrus medica*), but the sweet lime (*Triphasia trifolia*), which is widely cultivated as a hedge in the Caribbean – when mature, it is virtually impenetrable. It bears a small red berry vaguely resembling a miniature lime.

474–81 The cocoa tree (*Theobroma cacao*) and the Madre de Cacao (*Gliricidia sepium*); see I, 604, n. and note on that passage. The 'food of health' is chocolate.

488–95 This passage is perhaps an inversion of Philips' description of how Mediterranean fruits were acclimatised in Britain:

Additional Notes to The Sugar-Cane. Book IV          305

> Now turn thine Eye to view *Alcinous'* Groves,
> The Pride of the *Phæacian* Isle, from whence,
> Sailing the Spaces of the boundless Deep,
> To *Ariconium* pretious Fruits arriv'd [...]
> (*Cyder*, I, 457–60; Lloyd Thomas,
> *Poems of John Philips*, pp. 57–8)

Phæacia was another name for Corcyra (Corfu), whose king, Alcinous, entertains Odysseus in Homer's *Odyssey*, where the king's luxurious palace and supernaturally abundant gardens are described at length (VII, 82–132) There is also an echo of *G*, IV, 116–24, where Virgil says that he would sing of *pinguis hortos* ('fertile gardens') if only he were not anxious to finish his task (compare note on IV, 552–3), but nevertheless goes on to sketch an idealised garden and introduce the old man of Tarentum (see note on I, 579). Although there is an element of fancifulness in Grainger's description (see note on IV, 518) this entire passage (down to IV, 553) makes the claim that Caribbean reality exceeds the fantasies of Europe. Again, however, some of Grainger's inspiration is literary; in a note on this passage in *TCD* (f. 96v) he says 'That the following is not meerly a poetical Garden, those who will take y*e* trouble to consult Ulloa's Description of the province of Quito may be convinced.' Ulloa, *A Voyage to South America [...]*, I, 310–498, is a long 'Description of the Province of Quito' emphasising its varied and equable climate and its fertility.

498   See note on I, 418, n.

500   Adapted from Milton, *Paradise Lost*, IV, 138: 'Insuperable highth of loftiest shade'. Grainger previously (*TCD*, f. 75*v*) had 'Insuperable Heigth of loftiest shade' following what is now III, 630.

502, n.   The mammey's modern scientific name is *Mammea americana*. In Europe, noyau was a liqueur made of brandy flavoured with fruit-kernels; Grainger is describing a Caribbean adaptation of it. In a codicil (1801) to his will, the Barbadian planter Sir John Gay Alleyne left 'two cases of extraordinary fine Noyau [...] of different sorts' but it is not clear whether these were imported or locally made; see Louise R. Allen, 'Alleyne of Barbados,' in Brandow, *Genealogies of Barbados Families*, at p. 45.

504   There may be an echo of Shakespeare, *Othello*, I, iii, 144, but anthropophagi was a standard term for 'Men-eaters; Savages, that eat

Man's Flesh' (Bailey), and the allegation that this was true of the original Amerindian inhabitants of the Caribbean was a common one.

509, n.   See note on I, 624, n.

513, n.   The cassia is *Cassia fistula* (also mentioned at I, 36). Hooper, *Quincy's Lexicon-Medicum* (under 'Cassia fistularis'), says of the pulp of its seed-pods that 'It has been long used as a laxative medicine, and being gentle in its operation, and seldom disturbing the bowels, is well adapted to children, and to delicate or pregnant women.'

518   Grainger specifically notes that the chirimoia is not found in 'these torrid isles' (see also his note on I, 418); there is a cherimoya which is a subtropical species of *Annona*, i.e., a soursop relative. On the other hand, chirimoya is one of the Spanish names for *Annona squamosa* (Caribbean English: sweetsop or sugar apple) which is in fact quite widespread in the Caribbean, and which is mentioned by Grainger in his note to I, 597; it may be that Grainger simply means he had not seen it in St Kitts or Nevis. Chirimoya can also refer to the custard apple (*Annona reticulata*). Yet another possibility is suggested by Wright's identification of Grainger's chirimoia as *Averrhoe acida*; this perhaps suggests the carambola, also known as five-fingers or star-fruit (modern scientific name *Averrhoa carambola*) – while this is (at least at the present day) fairly common in some Caribbean islands, it is also associated with Central and South America.

519   See note on I, 418, n.

522–5, n.   Compare II, 346, and see note on II, 294. Grainger refers to the English architects Inigo Jones (1573–1652) and Sir Christopher Wren (1632–1723), and to the Italian architect Andrea Palladio (1518–80), who developed a style based on ancient Roman models which influenced many later architects in Europe (including Jones and Wren) and in the Americas. A number of impressive eighteenth- and nineteenth-century buildings in a Palladian style survive in the Caribbean; outstanding examples are those in the square in Spanish Town, Jamaica, with its colonnaded monument (about 1819) to Admiral Lord Rodney.

Daniel Mathew was Grainger's wife's cousin (see note on III, 31). Grainger had travelled extensively in Europe, but I have come across no indication that he had got as far as the Levant. His reference to Palmyra

## Additional Notes to The Sugar-Cane. Book IV

(in what is now Syria) is almost certainly based on *The Ruins of Palmyra* (1753), an influential work by Robert Wood (?1717–71) with numerous engraved plates after drawings by the Italian architect G. P. Borra. Plate XXXV, a large part of which is taken up by 'one side of the long portico' of the Temple of the Sun, might have been what Grainger was remembering when he saw the avenue of palms, though columns and colonnades are much in evidence in several of the other plates. Under its alternative name of Tadmor, Grainger had mentioned Palmyra in his 'Solitude' (1755), and Percy, *Reliques*, I, 314, noted that this was an allusion 'to the account of Palmyra published by some late ingenious travellers,' i.e. Wood and his companion James Dawkins (1722–57, a Jamaican by birth).

527    See note on I, 132, n.

534–40, n.    'Anata' (now usually anatta or anatto) is *Bixa orellana*. It is a tropical plant, which makes Grainger's reference to 'the tribes/Of Northern-Ind' somewhat implausible (though this may have been influenced by recent events in the Seven Years' War (see II, 55–61 and note on that passage). However, it was used as a body-paint by the Amerindian inhabitants of the Caribbean (a detail Grainger could have found in Ogilby, *America*, p. 359, which he cites at IV, 449, n.). It is still used as a food-colouring, particularly in the French Caribbean, where the name roucou is used. It was also supposed to have medicinal properties.
See also note on IV, 265, above.

543, n.    The granadilla is *Passiflora quadrangularis*, the water-lemon is *Passiflora laurifolia*. On Linnæus, see note on I, 503, n. Grainger's reference to Charles Plumier (author of a number of botanical works, such as *Description des Plantes de l'Amérique*, Paris, 1693, and *Nova Plantarum Americanarum genera*, Paris, 1703) is possibly lifted from Hughes, *Natural History of Barbados*, p. 187.

552–3    Virtually a literal translation of *G*, IV, 116–17: [...] *extremo ni iam sub fine laborum/vela traham et terris festinem advertere proram* ('if I were not now furling my sails at the very end of my labours, and hastening to turn my prow towards land').

558    The coconut-palm (*Cocos nucifera*); see note on II, 398.

563, n. The scientific name of the bay-grape (now more commonly referred to as the sea-side grape, or simply sea-grape, in many parts of the Caribbean) is *Coccoloba uvifera*; *acini* is the plural of the Latin word *acinus*, meaning a berry, or the stone contained within it.

567, n. The name 'Indian millet' is obsolete in Caribbean English, and the plant is commonly referred to as guinea corn; there are a number of varieties (*Sorghum vulgare* or *S. durra*). In modern English, maize generally refers to Indian corn (scientific name, *Zea mays*), commonly called simply 'corn' in Caribbean English.

569–73 Both bananas and plantains have broad leaves, suggesting winnowing-fans ('vans'). See also note on III, 533.

582–605 The description of the slaves' dance is based in part on the festivities in Philips' *Cyder*, II, 411–23:

> Perpetual Showers, and stormy Gusts confine
> The willing Ploughman, and *December* warns
> To Annual Jollities; now sportive Youth
> Carol incondite Rhythms, with suiting Notes,
> And quaver unharmonious; sturdy Swains
> In clean Array, for rustic Dance prepare,
> Mixt with the Buxom Damsels; hand in hand
> They frisk, and bound, and various Mazes weave,
> Shaking their brawny Limbs, with uncouth Mein,
> Transported, and sometimes, an oblique Leer
> Dart on their Loves, sometimes, an hasty Kiss
> Steal from unwary Lasses; they with Scorn,
> And Neck reclin'd, resent the ravish'd Bliss.
>             (Lloyd Thomas, ed., *The Poems of John Philips*, p. 80)

While Grainger has made a number of explicit references to Philips in *The Sugar-Cane*, it is worth pointing out that this particular borrowing is unacknowledged.

Smart's scene of boisterous horse-play among hop-pickers (*Hop-Garden*, II, 181–9; Williamson, ed., p. 60), does not seem to have influenced Grainger here. Nor does the shearing festival in Dyer (*The Fleece*, Book I; *Poems*, 1761, pp. 79–85) where the 'swains' address each other at

# Additional Notes to The Sugar-Cane. Book IV

length in blank verse, unless it be in the references to dancing in circles (ibid., p. 79: 'on the grass/The mingled youth in gaudy circles sport'; p. 84: 'and now the mossy bank/Is gayley circled'), but this is hardly conclusive. Thomson (*Winter*, ll. 617–29) has a passage on 'Rustic mirth'.

There is a 'negro-festival' in Chapman, *Barbadoes, and other poems*, pp. 72–3, but this is a sentimentalised picture of 'Saturn's reign of revelry' which does not seem to owe anything directly to Grainger.

605 One of the few references to slave rebellion or resistance in the poem; compare the allusions to arson at I, 494, III, 54, and IV, 574, and the description of the 'Cormantee', IV, 81–8.

611 The 'prickly vine' is probably *Hylocereus trigonus*.

613 The candle-weed is probably *Tecoma stans*, known as Christmas hope or golden seal in some parts of the Caribbean.

615 See notes on I, 417, and I, 433, above.

620–9 The reference is to Louis XIV, king of France from 1643 to 1715, who suppressed duelling, encouraged the arts, and improved the administration of justice (Themis is the classical goddess of justice, also mentioned at I, 330), and particularly to the *Code Noir*, the regulations on the treatment of slaves which had their basis in a royal edict of 1685 and later laws. They were perhaps 'mild' in comparison with those which obtained in the British colonies, but as they were not always enforced, and as changes were introduced in the eighteenth century, it is difficult to demonstrate any real difference in the treatment of slaves in the French and British Caribbean. See Goveia, 'West Indian slave laws.'

Compare Grainger's comment, *Essay on the more common West-India Diseases* (1764, p. 70), that 'Where neither humanity nor self-interest, are able to make masters treat their slaves as men, the Legislature should oblige them. This the French have done much to their honour.'

630–4 Compare Philips, *Cyder*, I, 368–9: 'oft at Midnight Lamp/Ply my brain-racking Studies' (Lloyd Thomas, *Poems of John Philips*, p. 55).

635 Pope refers to the river as 'Old Father *Thames*' in *Windsor-Forest* (1713), 330. For the invocation of the Thames as the home and symbol of British commerce, compare Sir John Denham, *Cooper's Hill* (1642–55), 179–188:

> Nor are his Blessings to his banks confin'd,
> But free, and common, as the Sea or Wind;
> When he to boast, or to disperse his stores
> Full of the tributes of his grateful shores,
> Visits the world, and in his flying towers
> Brings home to us, and makes both *Indies* ours;
> Finds wealth where 'tis, bestows it where it wants
> Cities in deserts, woods in Cities plants.
> So that to us no thing, no place is strange,
> While his fair bosom is the world's exchange.
> (Banks, ed., *Poetical Works of Sir John Denham*, pp. 75–7)

In *Windsor-Forest*, 355–422, Pope has the Thames hail the blessings of peace and commerce in a prophetic strain of which Grainger's conclusion is in some ways reminiscent: compare especially ll. 377–84, 397–402. Compare also Thomson, *The Seasons*, Autumn, 118–33, and Dyer's conclusion to Book III of *The Fleece* (*Poems*, 1761, pp. 151–2), where the 'stately Thamis' flows

> To great Augusta's mart, where lofty trade,
> Amid a thousand golden spires enthron'd,
> Gives audience to the world [...]

('Augusta' was a conventional poetic name for London; see also note on I, 19–20 above.)

A number of other passages in Dyer emphasise the importance of trade, e.g., *The Fleece*, Book II: 'Ingenious trade, to clothe the naked world,/Her soft materials [...] collects sagacious' (*Poems*, 1761, pp. 107 ff.); 'For it suffices not [...] /Only to tend the flock, and shear soft wool:/Gums must be stor'd of Guinea's arid coast [...]' (ibid., pp. 115 ff.). Particularly important is the ending of Book IV and the whole poem, where Dyer uses a passage describing the circumnavigation of the globe (1740–4) by George Anson (1697–1762; later Admiral Lord Anson) to suggest that the use of naval force to open up the world to British commerce is entirely justified and ultimately to everybody's benefit:

> Rejoice, ye nations, vindicate the sway
> Ordain'd for common happiness. Wide, o'er
> The globe terraqueous, let Britannia pour
> The fruits of plenty from her copious horn.
> (*Poems*, 1761, pp. 183–8; this quotation at p. 186)

638   Thomson, *Summer*, 843 ff. refers to the vast size of 'The sea-like Plata' compared to European rivers.

645   Compare Pope, *Essay on Criticism*, 231-2:

> Th'*increasing* Prospect *tires* our wandring Eyes,
> Hills peep o'er Hills, and *Alps* on *Alps* arise!

Grainger discussed the whole of this passage (ll. 225-32), referring to it as 'the celebrated simile of the Alps' in his review of [Joseph Warton], *An Essay on the Writings and Genius of Pope* in *Monthly Review*, XIV, 528-54, XV, 52-78 (June, July 1756), at XV, 54-5, where Grainger suggests that Pope might here have been indebted to the Scottish writer William Drummond of Hawthornden (1585-1649).

657   This is misnumbered 655 in *1764*, and the rest of the numbering is out accordingly (corrected in this edition).

667   The version of this passage in *TCD* (f. 99ᵛ) invokes not Wisdom, but 'Great Pitt' (i.e., Pitt the Elder).

683-4   There is perhaps a faint echo of Pope's reference to Queen Anne as 'Empress of the Main', *Windsor-Forest*, 164.

# Bibliography

## a) Works by James Grainger

This listing is confined to works used or referred to in the present study, and is not intended as a complete bibliography of Grainger's works.

### I. Manuscripts

A: *Literary works*
1. Bodleian Library MS Percy e. 8, ff. 11$^v$–29$^v$, 'Leander to Hero,' translation by Grainger of Ovid, Epistles xviii, copy in Thomas Percy's hand.
2. Bodleian Library MS Percy e. 8, ff. 1–4, 'Hero to Leander,' translation by Grainger of Ovid, Epistles xix, in Grainger's hand.
3. Bodleian Library MS Percy e. 8, f. 31, Opening (first eight lines only) of a revised version of Grainger's 'Hero to Leander' (translation by Grainger of Ovid, Epistles xix), in Thomas Percy's hand.
4. Trinity College, Dublin, MS. 880. This is, as described in T. K. Abbott's *Catalogue*, a 'foul copy, much corrected, about 1762', of *The Sugar-Cane*. See Introduction.

B: *Letters*
Most of Grainger's surviving letters are printed in Nichols, *Illustrations*, VII, 240–95. I have used the originals in Bodleian Library, MS Percy c.10, and in National Library of Scotland, Advocates' MSS 22-3-11 and 22-4-10. For the remaining letters I have used Nichols and transcripts of the originals generously supplied by Peter Jackson, who is, together with the present editor, preparing an edition of the correspondence of Thomas Percy with Thomas Apperley and James Grainger.

C: *Miscellaneous items*
1. Medical notebook, c.1745–c.1751, Edinburgh University Library, MS. La. III. 186. 96 numbered pages, plus other unnumbered pages. A few brief entries in English, but most of the content is in Latin, a

large part of it apparently notes for, or a draft of, Grainger's *Historia febris anomalae.*)
2. St Christopher Deed Book G No. 2., National Archives of St Christopher and Nevis, Basseterre. Includes will of James Grainger, 17 July 1763, proved 9 June 1767.

## II. printed works

A: *Collections (two or more works)*
1. 'The Poetical Works of James Grainger, M.D. [...]', in Robert Anderson (ed.), *A Complete Edition of the Poets of Great Britain* (14 vols, London and Edinburgh, 1792–1795), X, 889–935. Separate title-page for Grainger dated 1794. Includes 'The Life of Grainger' (pp. 891–5), 'The Sugar Cane' (pp. 896–932), 'Solitude' (pp. 932–4) and 'Bryan and Pereene' (pp. 934–5).
2. [Alexander Aikman, ed.], *Three Tracts on West-Indian Agriculture, and subjects connected therewith; viz. An Essay upon Plantership; By Samuel Martin, Senior, Esq. of Antigua: The Sugar-Cane, A didactic poem, in four books: And, An essay on The Management and Diseases of Negroes, with the easiest means of cure: The two latter, by James Grainger, M.D. of St. Christopher's* (Kingston, Jamaica, 1802). There is a copy of this item in the Goldsmiths'-Kress Library of Economic Literature (no. 18485) in the library of the University of London. There is a general title-page, and a dedication leaf: 'To the Honourable *House of Assembly of Jamaica*, This republication of these scarce and valuable tracts, is very respectfully inscribed, By their most faithful and devoted servant, the Printer', i.e., Alexander Aikman, senior (died 1838). The three items have separate title-pages and separate pagination; the pagination suggests that each item had a half-title (not present in the Goldsmiths' copy) and they appear to have been issued individually as well as in this collection (see D4 and G6 below).
3. 'Select Poems', in Thomas Park (ed.), *Supplement to the British Poets*, Vol. IV, (London, 1809). This volume has two separate paginations; Grainger is represented only by 'Solitude' and 'Bryan and Pereene' (pp. 165–73 and 173–5 of the second pagination). Facing p. 174 is an illustration to 'Bryan and Pereene' which is 'Drawn by Rich$^d$ Cook', 'Engrav'd by A. Cardon' and 'Publish'd April 19. 1809 by John Sharpe, Piccadilly'; this is the same illustration as used in the 1822 *British Poets* edition of Grainger.

4. 'The Poems of James Grainger, M.D.', in Alexander Chalmers (ed.), *The Works of the English Poets* ... (21 vols, London, 1810), XIV, 467–511. Includes 'The Life of Grainger, by Mr. Chalmers' (pp. 469–74), 'Solitude' (pp. 475–7) 'Bryan and Pereene' (pp. 477–8) and 'The Sugar-Cane' (pp. 478–511).
5. 'The Poems of James Grainger, M.D.', in *The British Poets* (100 vols, Chiswick, 1822), LIX, 7-146. Includes 'The Life of Grainger' (pp. 7–16; this is 'By R. A. Davenport, Esq.'), 'Solitude' (pp. 17–25), 'Bryan and Pereene' (pp. 25–7) and 'The Sugarcane [sic]' (pp. 28–146). The rest of the volume (pp. 147–260) is an edition of the poems of Samuel Boyse (1708–49).
6. 'Select Poems', in Ezekiel Sanford and Robert Walsh, Jr. (eds), *The Works of the British Poets, with lives of the authors* (50 vols, Philadelphia, 1819–23), XXVII, 271–373. This volume was published in 1822, and includes works by Charles Churchill (1731–64) and William Falconer (1732–69) as well as those by Grainger. Includes 'The Life of James Grainger' (pp. 271–4; a précis of that by Chalmers), 'Solitude' (pp. 275–83) and 'The Sugar-Cane' (pp. 285–373; apparently complete, but without Grainger's notes).
7. Robert Anderson (ed.), *The Poetical Works of James Grainger, M.D., with Memoirs of his Life and Writings, by Robert Anderson, M.D., and an Index of the Linnean names of plants, &c., by William Wright, M.D., F. R.S., Physician to his Majesty's Forces* (2 vols, Edinburgh, London and Dublin, 1836).

## B: 'Solitude: An Ode'

'Solitude: An Ode' was first published in Vol. IV (1755), pp. 233–43, of *A Collection of Poems [...] By Several Hands*, edited and published by Robert Dodsley (6 vols, London, 1748–58 and later editions).

## C: Grainger's translations of Tibullus and Sulpicia

*A poetical translation of the Elegies of Tibullus; and of the poems of Sulpicia. With the original text, and notes critical and explanatory* (2 vols, London, 1759 [in fact published November 1758]).

The first edition is the only one to include Grainger's version of the Latin text, but his translations were reprinted in Anderson's *Poets of Great Britain*, in Chalmers' *English Poets* and in a number of other collections. The latest I have seen is a 1910 reprint of the Bohn's Classical Library edition of *The poems of Catullus and Tibullus [...]*, edited by Walter K. Kelly, which was first published 1854 and includes Grainger's translations along with those of other writers.

*D: The Sugar-Cane*
1. *The Sugar-Cane: A Poem. In Four Books. With Notes.* (London, 1764). 'Printed for R. and J. DODSLEY, in Pall-mall' pp. vii, 167; frontispiece.
2. *The Sugar-Cane: A Poem. In Four Books. With Notes* (London, 1766). 'LONDON: Printed and sold by the Booksellers' pp. ix, 180, advertisement leaf; frontispiece.
3. *The Sugar-Cane: A Poem. In Four Books. With Notes* (Dublin, 1766). 'Printed by WILLIAM SLEATER, on Cork-Hill' pp. ix, 180, advertisement leaf; frontispiece.

D2 and D3 appear to be identical except for the title-page and the London imprint is possibly spurious. The advertisement leaf in both is for 'BOOKS, &c. printed and sold by W. *Sleater*, at Pope's-Head on Corkhill.' They also include 'Beauty: A Poem', said to be 'By the same Author' but is in fact not by Grainger, but by Robert Shiels (d. 1753); see W. E. K. Anderson, *Percy Letters*, IX, 33.

*4. *The Sugar-Cane: A Poem. In Four Books. With Notes* (Kingston, Jamaica, 1802). 'London: Printed. Jamaica: Re-printed by Alexander Aikman […]' pp. ix, 170
I have not seen this item, but it appears to be identical with the edition in *Three Tracts on West-Indian Agriculture* (see A2 above). There is a copy in the Beinecke Library at Yale; another copy, in the West India Reference Library of the Institute of Jamaica, is bound with Aikman's 1802 edition of the *Essay on the more common West-India Diseases*.

*E: 'Bryan and Pereene'*
'Bryan and Pereene' was first published in Thomas Percy, *Reliques of Ancient English Poetry* (3 vols, London, 1765), I, 313–16.

*F: Other poetry*
A number of miscellaneous poems and an unfinished verse drama ('The Fate of Capua') were published in the second volume of Robert Anderson's 1836 edition of Grainger's works, from material supplied by Thomas Percy, or previously published in the *Grand Magazine* and the *European Magazine*. A few additional items were published in Nichols, *Illustrations*, VII, 234–40.

## G: Medical works

1. *Dissertatio Medica Inauguralis, de Modo excitandi Ptyalismum; et Morbis inde pendentibus* (Edinburgh: Hamilton, Balfour and Neill, 1753) pp. iv, 34.
2. *Historia febris anomalae Batavae, annorum 1746, 47, 48, &c. Accedunt Monita Siphylica* (Edinburgh: Hamilton, Balfour and Neill, 1753) pp. xii, 196, iv, 34.
    The last section, pp. iv, 34, is a reprint of the MD dissertation.
3. 'An obstinate Dysentery cured by Lime-Water' in *Essays and Observations, Physical and Literary. Read before a Society in Edinburgh and published by them*, Vol. II (Edinburgh, 1756) pp. 257–63.
    Appears in the 1770 edition of the same volume at pp. 282–9.
4. *An Essay on the more common West-India Diseases; and the Remedies which that Country itself produces. To which are added, some hints on the Management, &c. of Negroes. By a Physician in the West-Indies.* (London, 1764) pp. (viii), vi, [7]–75.
    Grainger's authorship is not given in the work, but see the next item..
5. *An Essay on the more common West-India Diseases; and the Remedies which that Country itself produces: to which are added, some hints on the Management, &c. of Negroes* (Edinburgh, 1802) pp. xii, vi, [7]–98.
    'Second Edition' of the previous item, identifying Grainger as the author and 'With practical notes and a Linnaean index, by William Wright, M.D., F.R.S. [,] Physician to His Majesty's Forces.'
*6. *An Essay on the more common West-India Diseases; and the Remedies which that Country itself produces: to which are added, some hints on the Management, &c. of Negroes* (Kingston, Jamaica, 1802) pp. xii, vi, [7]–98. 'Edinburgh: Printed. Jamaica: Re-printed by Alexander Aikman [...]'
    Not seen, but a reprint of G8 above and apparently identical with the edition in *Three Tracts on West-Indian Agriculture* (see A2 above). There are two copies in the West India Reference Library of the Institute of Jamaica, one of which is bound with Aikman's 1802 edition of *The Sugar-Cane.*

## H: Contributions to the Monthly Review

These (and those of other contributors) were identified by Nangle, *Monthly Review ... Indexes*, from information in a marked file of the magazine (now in the Bodleian) kept by Ralph Griffiths, its proprietor and editor. I have given full references to individual items as used.

*I: Miscellaneous items*
1. Contributions to William Maitland, *The History and Antiquities of Scotland from the earliest account to the death of James I., ... 1437; and from that period to the accession of James VI. to the Crown of England, 1603, by another hand* (London: A. Millar, 1757) 2 vols, folio.
2. Translation (from French) of Pierre Brumoy's version of the *Cyclops* of Euripides, in Charlotte Lennox, ed. and trs., *The Greek Theatre of Father Brumoy* (3 vols, London: Millar, 1759), III, 452–78.
3. *A Letter to Tobias Smollet, M.D. occasioned by his Criticism upon a late Translation of Tibullus* (London: Sold by T. Kinnersley, in St. Paul's Church-yard, 1759) p. 25.

*b) Other works consulted in the preparation of this edition*

*I. Manuscripts*

*British Library, London*
Journal of Thomas Percy, Add. MS 32,336.
William Strahan's account book for printing work, 1739–68, Add. MS 48800, in Reel 1 of *Printing and Publishing History Series One: The Strahan Archive from the British Library*, published on microfilm by Research Publications (Woodbridge, Connecticut and Reading, England, 1990).

*Public Record Office, London*
War Office papers:
Commission Book, WO 25/22
Notification Book, WO 25/136
'Regimental List of Successions in the Army, from 1st January 1754, to 1st January 1764,' WO 25/209
MS Army List for 1752 (with additions to 1757), WO 64/11
Colonial Office papers
CO 152/28
CO 153/18
CO 241/8

*General Register Office for Scotland, Edinburgh*
Testament Dative of Dr. James Granger [sic], registered in Commissariat Record of Edinburgh, 8 April 1790; CC8/8/128/1.

*National Library of Scotland, Edinburgh*
Advocates' Manuscripts 22-3-11 and 22-4-10: letters from William Wright, Robert Melville and others about Grainger and his family, as well as letters from James Grainger and his wife Daniel Mathew Grainger.

*National Archives of St Christopher and Nevis, Basseterre*
St Christopher Assembly Minutes 1761–69
St Christopher Marriage Bond Book, 1771–1780

## II. Published works

Abbott, T. K., *Catalogue of the Manuscripts in the Library of Trinity College, Dublin*, (Dublin, 1900).
*Academiæ Oxoniensis Comitia Philologica In Theatro Sheldoniano Decimo Die Julii A.D. 1713. Celebrata: In Honorem Serenissimæ Reginæ Annæ Pacificæ* (Oxford, 1713).
Addison, Joseph, 'An Essay on Virgil's Georgics,' in A. C. Guthkelch, (ed.), *The Miscellaneous Works of Joseph Addison* (2 vols, London, 1914), II, pp. 2–11.
Alleman, G. S., letters to editor, *Times Literary Supplement*, 13 August 1938 and 30 May 1951.
Allen, Robert Porter, *Birds of the Caribbean* (New York, 1961).
Allsopp, Richard, *Dictionary of Caribbean English Usage* (Oxford, 1996).
Anderson, Phillip B., 'Mr. Young, Meet Mr. Pope: James Grainger's 'Solitude: An Ode", *Publications of the Arkansas Philological Association*, XI, (Spring 1985) pp. 1–11.
Anderson, W. E. K., *The Percy Letters* [Vol. IX]: *The Correspondence of Thomas Percy and Robert Anderson* (New Haven and London, 1988).
Andrews, Evangeline Walker and Charles McLean Andrews (ed.), *Journal of a Lady of Quality; Being the Narrative of a Journey from Scotland to the West Indies, North Carolina, and Portugal, in the years 1774 to 1776* (New Haven and London, 1921).
Anon., 'The Pleasures of Jamaica: In an Epistle from a Gentleman to his Friend in London', *Gentleman's Magazine*, VIII, 158, 213–14 (March, April 1738).
Anon., review of *The Sugar-Cane*, in *Gazette Littéraire de l'Europe*, Vol. IV, No. 49 (5 December 1764), pp. 14–16.
Anon., *Jamaica, A Poem, in three parts. Written in that Island, in the Year MDCCLXXVI. To which is annexed, A Poetical Epistle From the author in that Island to a Friend in England* (London, 1777).

Anon., 'Old plantation customs,' *Journal of the Barbados Museum and Historical Society*, VII, No. 3 (May 1940), pp. 109–15.

Anon., 'Dr. Grainger's "Sugar Cane",' *Times Literary Supplement*, 16 February 1951.

Archibald, Douglas, *Tobago: 'Melancholy Isle': Volume I, 1498–1771* (Port of Spain, Trinidad, 1987).

[Armstrong, John, M.D.], *The Art of Preserving Health: A Poem* (London, 1744).

Aubin, Robert Arnold, *Topographical Poetry in XVIII-Century England* (New York, 1936; reprinted Millwood, New York, 1980).

Bailey, N[athan], *An Universal Etymological English Dictionary* ... (6th edn, London, 1733).

Banks, T. H. (ed.), *The Poetical Works of Sir John Denham* (2nd edn., New York, 1969).

Barclay, Alexander, *A Practical View of the Present State of Slavery in the West Indies* (3rd edn, London, 1828; facsimile reprint Miami, 1969).

Barlow, Virginia, *The Nature of the Islands: Plants and Animals of the Eastern Caribbean* (Dunedin, Florida, 1993).

Beckles, Hilary and Verene Shepherd (eds), *Caribbean Slave Society and Economy: A Student Reader* (Kingston, Jamaica, 1991).

Benson, Larry D. (ed.), *The Riverside Chaucer* (Oxford, 1988).

Black, Jeremy, *Culloden and the '45* (corrected paperback edn, Stroud, Gloucestershire, 1993).

Brandow, James C., compiler, *Genealogies of Barbados Families: From Caribbeana and The Journal of the Barbados Museum and Historical Society* (Baltimore, 1983).

Brathwaite, Edward Kamau, *X/Self* (Oxford and New York, 1987)

Brathwaite, Kamau, 'Creative Literature of the British West Indies during the period of slavery' (first published 1970) in Brathwaite, *Roots* (Ann Arbor, 1993), pp. 127–70.

—— *Roots* (Ann Arbor, 1993).

—— *Barabajan Poems* (Kingston, Jamaica and New York, 1994).

Brissenden, R. F. (ed.), *Studies in the Eighteenth Century: Papers presented at the David Nichol Smith Memorial Seminar, Canberra 1966* (Canberra 1968).

Brown, Lloyd W., *West Indian Poetry* (second edn, London, 1984).

Brumoy, Pierre, S. J., *Le Théâtre des Grecs* (3 vols, Paris, 1730).

Buisseret, David, *Historic Architecture of the Caribbean* (London, 1980).

Butt, John (ed.), *The Poems of Alexander Pope: A one-volume edition of the*

Twickenham text with selected annotations (London, 1965; University Paperbacks).

Campbell, P. F., 'Barbados: The Early Years,' *Journal of the Barbados Museum and Historical Society*, XXXV, No. 3 (1977), pp. 157–77.

Carey, John and Alastair Fowler (eds), *The Poems of John Milton* (London, 1968).

Carrington, Sean, *Wild Plants of the Eastern Caribbean* (London and Basingstoke, 1998).

[Carstensen, Birgit], *Betty's Hope: An Antiguan Sugar Plantation* (St John's, Antigua, [1993])

Cassidy, Frederic G., *Jamaica Talk: Three Hundred Years of the English Language in Jamaica* (2nd edn, Kingston, Jamaica and Basingstoke, 1971)

Cassidy, F. G. and R. B. Le Page, *Dictionary of Jamaican English* (2nd edn, Cambridge, 1980).

Cave, Roderick, *Printing and the Book Trade in the West Indies* (London, 1987)

Chalker, John, *The English Georgic: A study in the development of a form* (London, 1969).

Chalmers, Alexander, (ed.), 'The Poems of William Somervile,' *Works of the English Poets* (21 vols, London, 1810) XI, pp. 147–240.

—— *Works of the English Poets, from Chaucer to Cowper; including the series edited, with Prefaces, biographical and critical, by Dr. Samuel Johnson: and the most approved translations* (21 vols, London, 1810).

[Chambers, Robert], *Chambers' Eminent Scotsmen* (rev. edn, 3 vols, London, 1875).

Chapman, M[atthew] J[ames], *Barbadoes, and other poems* (London, 1833).

Chapman, R. W., 'Dodsley's *Collection of Poems*, (collations, lists and indexes),' *Oxford Bibliographical Society Proceedings & Papers*, Vol. III, Pt. III (Oxford, 1933; repr. Nendeln, Liechtenstein, 1969), pp. 269–316.

—— (ed.), *James Boswell: Life of Johnson* (Oxford, 1980: World's Classics ed., intro. by Pat Rogers, repr. 1989)

Chatillon, Marcel, *Le Père Labat à travers ses manuscrits* (n.p., n.d.; reprint from *Bulletin de la Société d'Histoire de la Guadeloupe*, Nos. 40-2, 1979).

Clifford, James L. (ed.), *Eighteenth-Century English Literature: Modern Essays in Criticism* (New York, 1959, 1971).

C[ockayne], G. E., *The Complete Peerage or a History of the House of Lords and all its Members from the Earliest Times*, revised edn, Vol. XI, Geoffrey H. White (ed.) (London, 1949).

Colley, Linda, *Britons: Forging the Nation 1707–1837* (New Haven and London, 1992).

Collymore, Frank A., *Notes for a Glossary of Words and Phrases of Barbadian Dialect* (5th edn, Barbados, n.d.).

Connell, Neville, trs., 'Father Labat's Visit to Barbados in 1700', *Journal of the Barbados Museum and Historical Society*, XXIV, No. 4 (August 1957), pp. 160–74.

Courtney, William Prideaux and David Nichol Smith, *A Bibliography of Samuel Johnson* (Oxford, 1925: 'A Reissue of the Edition of 1915 Illustrated with Facsimiles').

Craton, Michael, *Testing the Chains: Resistance to Slavery in the British West Indies* (Ithaca and London, 1982).

Crawford, Robert, *Devolving English Literature* (Oxford, 1992).

Dabydeen, David, 'Eighteenth-century English literature on commerce and slavery,' in David Dabydeen (ed.), *The Black Presence in English Literature* (Manchester, 1985), pp. 26–50.

—— (ed.), *The Black Presence in English Literature* (Manchester, 1985).

Dallett, Francis James, Jr., 'Griffith Hughes dissected', *Journal of the Barbados Museum and Historical Society*, XXIII, No. 1 (November 1955), pp. 3–29.

Dalton, John, *A Descriptive Poem, addressed to Two Ladies, At their Return from Viewing The Mines near Whitehaven. To which are added, Some Thoughts on Building and Planting, To Sir James Lowther, of Lowther-Hall, Bart.* (London, 1755).

Dash, J. Sydney, 'The windmills and copper walls of Barbados,' *Journal of the Barbados Museum and Historical Society*, XXXI, No. 2 (May 1965), pp. 43–60.

Davis, Bertram H., *Thomas Percy: A Scholar-Cleric in the Age of Johnson* (Philadelphia, 1989).

Davison, Dennis (ed.), *Eighteenth-Century English Verse* (London, 1988: Penguin Classics; first published 1973 as *The Penguin Book of Eighteenth-Century English Verse*).

Deane, C. V., *Aspects of Eighteenth Century Nature Poetry* (Oxford, 1935).

Deerr, Noel, *The History of Sugar* (2 vols, London, 1949–50).

Denham, Woodrow W., *West Indian Green Monkeys: Problems in Historical Biogeography* (Basel, 1987).

Dix, Robin (ed.), *The Poetical Works of Mark Akenside* (Madison, Teaneck and London, 1996).
Dobrée, Bonamy, 'The Theme of Patriotism in the Poetry of the Early Eighteenth Century,' *Proceedings of the British Academy*, XXXV (1949), pp. 49–65.
[Dodsley, Robert, ed.], *A Collection of Poems in Six Volumes[:] By Several Hands* (London, 1775; originally published 1748–58).
Dookhan, Isaac, 'Vieques or Crab Island: Source of Anglo-Spanish Colonial Conflict', *Journal of Caribbean History*, VII (November 1973), pp. 1–22.
Drayton, Arthur D., 'West Indian Consciousness in West Indian Verse: A Historical Perspective,' *Journal of Commonwealth Literature*, No. 9 (July 1970), pp. 66–88.
Duff, J. D., trs., *Lucan: The Civil War (Pharsalia)* (Cambridge, Mass. and London, 1928, repr. 1969: Loeb Classical Library).
Duff, J. Wight and Arnold M. Duff, *Minor Latin Poets* (London and Cambridge, Mass., rev. edn, 1935; repr., 1961: Loeb Classical Library).
Dyer, John, *Poems* (London, 1761; facsimile reprint, Farnborough, 1969)

Eatough, Geoffrey, *Fracastoro's Syphilis: Introduction, Text, Translation and Notes, with a computer generated word index* (Liverpool, 1984).
[Edwards, Bryan, et al.] *Poems, written chiefly in the West-Indies*, (Kingston, Jamaica, 1792).
Edwards, Bryan, *The History, Civil and Commercial, of the British West Indies* (5th edn, 5 vols, London, 1819).
Edwards, George, *A Natural History of Birds* (London, 1743).
Ellis, John, *Some additional observations on the Method of Preserving Seeds from Foreign Parts, For the Benefit of our American Colonies. With an Account of The Garden at St. Vincent, under the care of Dr. George Young* (London, 1773).
Ellis, Keith, 'Images of Sugar in English and Spanish Caribbean Poetry,' *Ariel: A Review of International English Literature*, Vol. 24, No. 1 (January 1993), pp. 149–59.
*Encyclopædia Britannica*, (3 vols, Edinburgh, 1771)
*Encyclopædia Britannica*, 11th edition (29 vols, Cambridge, 1910–11).
Everett, Sir Henry, *The History of the Somerset Light Infantry (Prince Albert's) 1685–1914* (London, 1934).
Fairchild, Hoxie Neale, *The Noble Savage: A Study in Romantic Naturalism* (New York, 1928).

Fausset, Hugh l'Anson (ed.), *Minor Poets of the Eighteenth Century* (London, 1930).
Ferguson, Moira (ed.), *The History of Mary Prince, a West Indian slave, related by herself* (London, 1987).
[Foote, Samuel], *The Dramatic Works of Samuel Foote, Esq; to which is prefixed A Life of the Author* (2 vols, London, 1809; facsimile reprint, New York and London, n.d.).
Fortescue, J. W., *A History of the British Army*, Vol. II (2nd edn, London, 1910, repr. 1935).
Fraser, Henry and Sean Carrington, Addinton Forde, John Gilmore, *A-Z of Barbadian Heritage* (Kingston, Jamaica, 1990).

'G.', 'The Poet Grainger,' *Notes and Queries*, 3rd Series, Vol. VI, 19 November 1864.
Gardner, William Bradford, *The Prologues and Epilogues of John Dryden: A Critical Edition* (New York, 1951).
Gaspar, David Barry, *Bondmen & Rebels: A Study of Master-Slave Relations in Antigua, With Implications for Colonial British America* (Baltimore and London, 1985).
Gilbert, William, *The Hurricane: A Theosophical and Western Eclogue. To which is subjoined, A Solitary Effusion in a Summer's Evening* (Bristol, 1796).
Gilfillan, George, *Specimens with Memoirs of the Less-Known British Poets* (3 vols, Edinburgh, 1860).
Gilmore, John (ed.), *Chester's Barbados: The Barbados chapters from* Transatlantic Sketches *(1869) by the Rev. Greville John Chester* (Barbados, 1990).
—— 'Tibullus and the British Empire: Grainger, Smollett and the Politics of Translation in the Mid-18th Century,' *The Translator*, Vol. 5, No. 1 (April 1999), pp. 1–26.
Goldsmith, Oliver, *An History of the Earth and Animated Nature* (8 vols, London, 1774).
[Goldsmith, Oliver], *The Complete Works of Oliver Goldsmith* ('new edition', London, 1867).
Gooding, E. G. B. and A. R. Loveless, G. R. Proctor, *Flora of Barbados* (London, 1965).
Goold, G. P. (ed. and trs.), *Manilius: Astronomica* (Cambridge, Mass. and London, 1977: Loeb Classical Library).
Gosse, Edmund, *A History of Eighteenth Century Literature (1660–1780)* (London, 1889).

Goveia, E. V., 'The West Indian slave laws of the 18th century', in *Chapters in Caribbean History*, No. 2 (Barbados, 1970), pp. 7–53.

Hargreaves, Dorothy and Bob Hargreaves, *Tropical Trees found in the Caribbean, South America, Central America, Mexico* (Portland, Oregon, 1965).

Henige, David P., *Colonial Governors from the Fifteenth Century to the Present* (Madison, Wisconsin, 1970).

Hernández Aquino, Luis, *Diccionario de voces indígenas de Puerto Rico* (3rd ed., 1993; no place of publication; printed Hato Rey, Puerto Rico).

Hill, G. B. and L. F. Powell (ed.), *Boswell's Life of Johnson* (6 vols, Oxford, 1934).

Hogg, Peter Carlquist, *Slavery: The Afro-American Experience* (London, 1979).

Honychurch, Penelope N., *Caribbean Wild Plants and their Uses: An illustrated guide to some medicinal and wild ornamental plants of the West Indies* (London and Basingstoke, 1986 [first pub. 1980]).

Hook, Andrew (ed.), *The History of Scottish Literature: Volume 2, 1660–1800* (Aberdeen, 1987).

Hooper, Robert, *Quincy's Lexicon-Medicum: A New Medical Dictionary* (London, 1811).

Howard, Richard A., 'Eighteenth Century West Indian Pharmaceuticals,' *Harvard Papers in Botany*, V, (1994) 69–91.

Hughes, Griffith, *The Natural History of Barbados* (London, 1750; facsimile reprint, New York, 1972).

Huntingford, G. W. B. (trs. and ed.), *The Periplus of the Erythraean Sea* (London, 1980).

IJsewijn, Jozef, *Companion to Neo-Latin Studies, Part I: History and Diffusion of Neo-Latin Literature* (2nd edn, Leuven, 1990).

Inniss, Sir Probyn, *Historic Basseterre: The Story of its growth* (Basseterre, St Kitts, 1979).

—— *Historic Basseterre: The Story of a West Indian Town* (Basseterre, St Kitts, 1985) [printed St John's, Antigua; revised edition of preceding item].

Ireland, Stanley (ed.), *Apollodorus: The Argonauts & Herakles* (London, 1992).

[Johnson, Samuel and Thomas Percy], review of *The Sugar-Cane*, in *London Chronicle*, XVI, 12, 20, 28 (3–5 July, 5–7 July, 7–10 July 1764).

[Johnson, Samuel], review of *The Sugar-Cane*, in *Critical Review*, XVIII, 270–7 (October 1764).

—— *A Dictionary of the English Language [...]*, (4th edn, 2 vols, London, 1773; facsimile, Beirut, 1978).

—— *Lives of the English Poets*, Everyman edition, introduced by L. Archer-Hind (2 vols, London, 1925, reprinted 1964).

Johnston, Col. William, (ed. by Lt. Col. Harry A. L. Howell, RAMC) *Roll of Commissioned Officers in the Medical Service of the British Army who served on full pay within the period between the Accession of George II and the formation of the Royal Army Medical Corps, 20 June 1727 to 23 June 1898, with an Introduction showing the Historical Evolution of the Corps* (Aberdeen, 1917).

Jones, Horace Leonard, trs., *The Geography of Strabo* (8 vols, London and New York, 1917–32; Loeb Classical Library).

Keener, Frederick M. (ed.), *Virgil's Aeneid translated by John Dryden* (Harmondsworth, 1997).

Kevan, D. Keith McE., 'Mid-eighteenth-century entomology and helminthology in The West Indies: Dr. James Grainger,' *Journal of the Society for the Bibliography of Natural History* (1977) 8 (3): 193–222.

Kinsley, James (ed.), *Scottish Poetry: A Critical Survey* (London, 1955).

Kirkpatrick, J[ames], *The Sea-Piece: A narrative, philosophical and descriptive Poem. In Five Cantos.* (London, 1750).

Knox, Ronald, 'A Neglected Poet (James Grainger)' in Knox, *Literary Distractions*, (London and New York, 1958) pp. 98–108.

—— *Literary Distractions* (London and New York, 1958).

La Condamine, Charles Marie de, *Journal du Voyage fait par ordre du Roi, à l'Equateur, servant d'introduction historique à la Mésure des Trois Premiers Degrés du Méridien* (Paris, 1751).

[Labat, Jean-Baptiste], *Nouveau Voyage aux Isles de l'Amerique* (2 vols, The Hague, 1724).

[Lanaghan, Mrs], *Antigua and the Antiguans: A Full Account of the Colony and its Inhabitants from the time of the Caribs to the present day, Interspersed with Anecdotes and Legends* (2 vols, London, 1844; facsimile reprint, London and Basingstoke, 1991).

[Langhorne, John], review of *The Sugar-Cane*, in *Monthly Review*, XXXI, 105–18 (August 1764).

Lennox, Charlotte, *The Female Quixote* (Oxford, 1989; World's Classics edn, ed. by Margaret Dalziel, intro. by Margaret Anne Doody).

—— *The Greek Theatre of Father Brumoy* (3 vols, London, 1759).

Lewis, Charlton T. and Charles Short, *A Latin Dictionary* (Oxford, 1879).

Lewis, D. B. Wyndham and Charles Lee (ed.), *The Stuffed Owl: An Anthology of Bad Verse* (London and Toronto, 1930).

Liddell, Henry George and Robert Scott, *A Greek-English Lexicon* (9th edn, revised by H. S. Jones et al., 2 vols, Oxford, 1940; repr. 1951).

Ligon, Richard, *A True & Exact History of the Island of Barbadoes* (London, 1657; 2nd edn, 1673; facsimile reprint of 2nd edn, London 1970 and 1976).

Lindsay, David W., intro., *The Beggar's Opera and other Eighteenth Century plays* (London and New York, 1975; Everyman's Library, reprint with new introduction of selection [by John Hampden] first published 1928).

Lloyd Thomas, M. G. (ed.), *The Poems of John Philips* (Oxford, 1927).

Lonsdale, Roger (ed.), *Thomas Gray and William Collins: Poetical Works* (Oxford, 1977; repr. 1985; Oxford Standard Authors series.)

—— (ed.), *The New Oxford Book of Eighteenth Century Verse* (corrected paperback edn, Oxford, 1987).

Mack, Robert L. (ed.), *Oliver Goldsmith* (London, 1997: Everyman's Poetry series).

[Mackay, Charles], *The Poetical Works of Charles Mackay* (London, n.d., c. 1876: Chandos Classic edition).

MacQueen, John and Tom Scott (eds), *The Oxford Book of Scottish Verse* (Oxford, 1966).

Marshall, Nelson, *Understanding the Eastern Caribbean and the Antilles* (St. Michaels, Maryland, 1992).

Martin, Samuel, *An Essay upon Plantership [...]* (4th edn, Antigua printed, London reprinted, 1765).

Martinius, Matthias, *Lexicon Philologicum, præcipuè etymologicum, in quo Latinæ et a Latinis auctoribus usurpatæ tum puræ tum barbaræ voces ex originibus declarantur ...* (Bremen, 1623; later editions: Frankfurt am Main, 1655, Amsterdam, 1701; Amsterdam, 1703).

Merrill, Gordon C., *The Historical Geography of St. Kitts and Nevis, The West Indies* (Mexico City, 1958).

Millar, J. H., *A Literary History of Scotland* (London, 1903).

Munk, William, *The Roll of the Royal College of Physicians of London* (2nd edn, 3 vols, London, 1878).

Murray, A. T. (ed.), *Homer: The Iliad, with an English translation* (2 vols; Cambridge, Mass. and London, 1924–5, 1978, 1976: Loeb Classical Library).

Murray, A. T. (ed.), *Homer: The Odyssey ... with an English translation* (2nd ed., revised by George E. Dimock, 2 vols; Cambridge, Mass. and London, 1995: Loeb Classical Library).

Murray, Dea, *Birds of the Virgin Islands* (St Thomas, USVI, 1969).

Mynors, R. A. B. (ed.), *P. Vergili Maronis Opera* (Oxford, 1969).

Nangle, B. C., *The Monthly Review, First Series 1749–1789: Indexes of Contributors and Articles* (Oxford, 1934).

National Center for Infectious Diseases, Atlanta, Georgia: dracunculiasis web-page, (http://www.cdc.gov/ncidod/dpd/dracunc.htm (consulted 12 April 1999).

Nichols, John and John Bowyer Nichols, *Illustrations of the Literary History of the Eighteenth Century* (8 vols, London, 1817–58).

Nicholson, Desmond V., *Antigua, Barbuda and Redonda: A Historical Sketch* (St John's, Antigua, 1991).

Nicoll, Allardyce (ed.), *Chapman's Homer* (2 vols, London, 1957).

Ogilby, John, *America: Being the latest and most accurate description of the New World; Containing The Original of the Inhabitants and the Remarkable Voyages thither* (London, 1671).

Oliver, A. M., 'The Scottish Augustans,' in James Kinsley (ed.), *Scottish Poetry: A Critical Survey* (London, 1955), pp. 119–49.

Oliver, Vere Langford, *History of the Island of Antigua, One of the Leeward Caribbees in the West Indies, from the first Settlement in 1635 to the Present Time* (3 vols, London 1894–99).

—— *Caribbeana: Being Miscellaneous Papers relating to the History, Genealogy, Topography and Antiquities of the British West Indies* (6 vols, London, 1910–19).

—— *Registers of St. Thomas, Middle Island, St. Kitts* (London, 1915; published as supplement to *Caribbeana*, Vol. IV).

Orderson, J. W. [i.e., Isaac Williamson Orderson], *The Fair Barbadian and Faithful Black; or, A Cure for the Gout. A Comedy in Three Acts* (Liverpool, 1835).

Partington, Angela, ed., *Oxford Dictionary of Quotations* (revised 4th ed., Oxford, 1996).

Percy, Thomas, *Reliques of Ancient English Poetry: Consisting of Old Heroic Ballads, Songs and other Pieces of our earlier Poets, (Chiefly of the Lyric kind.) Together with some few of later Date* (3 vols, London, 1765).

Pineda, Peter, *A New Dictionary, Spanish and English and English and Spanish [...]* (London, 1740).
Popham, Hugh, *The Somerset Light Infantry (Prince Albert's) (The 13th Regiment of Foot)* (London, 1968).
Porter, Roy, *The Greatest Benefit to Mankind: A Medical History of Humanity from Antiquity to the Present* (London, 1997).
Pottle, Frederick A., *James Boswell: The Earlier Years 1740–1769* (London, 1966).
Prebble, John, *Culloden* (Penguin edn, Harmondsworth, 1967).

Rackham, H., W. H. S. Jones and D. E. Eichholz (ed. and trs.), *Pliny: Natural History* (10 vols, London and Cambridge, Mass., 1938–63: Loeb Classical Library).
Ramsay, James, *An Essay on the Treatment and Conversion of African Slaves in the British Sugar Colonies* (London, 1784).
Reese, M. M. (ed.), *Gibbon's Autobiography* (London, 1970).
Reid, Hugh, 'A Note on James Grainger's "Ode to Solitude",' *Notes and Queries*, CCXXXI (December 1986), p. 518.
Rodríguez Demorizi, Emilio, *Del Vocabulario Dominicano* (Santo Domingo, Dominican Republic, 1983).
Rolfe, John C. (trs.), *Quintus Curtius* (2 vols, London and Cambridge, Mass., 1946: Loeb Classical Library).
Rouse, W. H. D. (ed. and trs.), *Lucretius: De Rerum Natura, with an English translation* (3rd edn, London and Cambridge, Mass., 1937, 1947: Loeb Classical Library).
Royle, Trevor, *The Macmillan Companion to Scottish Literature* (London and Basingstoke, 1983; repr. 1985).
Rudd, Niall (ed.), *Johnson's Juvenal: London and The Vanity of Human Wishes* (Bristol, 1981, 1988).

Sambrook, James (ed.), *James Thomson: The Seasons and The Castle of Indolence* (Oxford, 1972, 1991; Oxford Paperback English Texts).
—— (ed.), *James Thomson: Liberty, The Castle of Indolence and other poems* (Oxford, 1986).
—— (ed.), *William Cowper: The Task and Selected Other Poems* (London and New York, 1994; Longman Annotated Texts).
Sandiford, Keith A., 'The Sugared Muse: or the case of James Grainger, MD (1721–66)', *Nieuwe West-Indische Gids/New West Indian Guide*, LXI (1987), pp. 39–53.
Schomburgk, Sir Robert H., *The History of Barbados; comprising a*

*geographical and statistical description of the island; a sketch of the historical events since the settlement; and an account of its geology and natural productions* (London, 1848; facsimile reprint, London, 1971).

Scott, Mary Jane, 'James Thomson and the Anglo-Scots,' in Andrew Hook (ed.), *The History of Scottish Literature: Volume 2, 1660–1800* (Aberdeen, 1987), pp. 81–99.

Senior, Olive, *A–Z of Jamaican Heritage* (Kingston, Jamaica, 1983).

[Shakespeare, William], *The Riverside Shakespeare* (Boston, 1974).

Shankman, Steven (ed.), *The Iliad of Homer translated by Alexander Pope* (Harmondsworth, 1996).

Sheridan, Richard B., *Doctors and Slaves: A medical and demographic history of slavery in the British West Indies, 1680–1834* (Cambridge, 1985).

Shields, David S., *Oracles of Empire: Poetry, Politics and Commerce in British America 1690–1750* (Chicago and London, 1990).

Shyllon, Fọlarin, *James Ramsay: The Unknown Abolitionist* (Edinburgh, 1977).

Singleton, John, *A General Description of the West-Indian Islands, As far as relates to the British, Dutch and Danish Governments, from Barbados to Saint Croix. Attempted in Blank Verse* (Barbados, 1767).

Sloane, Hans, 'An Account of a prodigiously large feather of the Bird *Cuntur*, brought from *Chili* and supposed to be a kind of Vultur; and of the *Coffee-Shrub*,' *Philosophical Transactions: Giving some Accompt of the present Undertakings, Studies and Labours of the Ingenious in many considerable parts of the World*, XVII (No. 208, February 169$\frac{3}{4}$), pp. 61–4.

Sloane, Hans, *Catalogus Plantarum quæ in Insula Jamaica sponte proveniunt, vel vulgò coluntur, cum earundem Synonymis & locis natalibus; adjectis aliis quibusdam quæ in Insulis Maderæ, Barbados, Nieves, & Sancti Christophori nascuntur[,] Seu Prodromi Historiæ Naturalis Jamaicæ Pars Prima* (London, 1696).

—— *A Voyage to the Islands Madera, Barbados, Nieves, S. Christophers and Jamaica, with the Natural History of the Herbs and Trees, Four-footed Beasts, Fishes, Birds, Insects, Reptiles, &c. of the last of those Islands* [...] (2 vols, London, 1707–25).

Smith, G. Gregory, *Scottish Literature: Character and Influence* (London, 1919).

Smout, T. C., *A History of the Scottish People, 1560–1830* (London, 1969; repr., 1985).

Spate, O. H. K., 'The Muse of Mercantilism: Jago, Grainger and Dyer,' in

R. F. Brissenden (ed.), *Studies in the Eighteenth Century: Papers presented at the David Nichol Smith Memorial Seminar, Canberra 1966* (Canberra, 1968), pp. 119–31.

Spevack, Marvin, *The Harvard Concordance to Shakespeare* (Cambridge, Mass., 1973).

Story Donno, Elizabeth (ed.), *Andrew Marvell: The Complete Poems* (Harmondsworth, 1972).

Swan, Bradford F., *The Caribbean Area* (Amsterdam, 1970; part of series *The Spread of Printing*, ed. Colin Clair).

Sypher, Wylie, *Guinea's Captive Kings: British Anti-Slavery Literature of the XVIII$^{th}$ Century* (Chapel Hill, 1942).

Tatlock, John S. P. and Arthur G. Kennedy (eds), *A Concordance to the complete works of Geoffrey Chaucer and to the Romaunt of the Rose* (Washington, DC, 1923; repr. Gloucester, Mass., 1963).

Templeman, Thomas, *A New Survey of the Globe: Or an Accurate Mensuration of all the Empires, Kingdoms, Countries, States, principal Provinces, Counties, & Islands in the World* (London, n.d., c. 1729).

Thomas, Richard F. (ed.), *Virgil: Georgics* (2 vols, Cambridge, 1988).

Tierney, James E. (ed.), *The Correspondence of Robert Dodsley 1733–1764* (Cambridge, 1988).

Tillotson, Geoffrey, 'Eighteenth-Century Poetic Diction,' in James L. Clifford (ed.), *Eighteenth-Century English Literature*, (New York, 1959, 1971) pp. 212–32.

Trapp, Joseph, *The Æneis of Virgil, translated into blank verse* (2 vols, London, 1718, 1720).

—— *The Works of Virgil: translated into English Blank Verse. With large Explanatory Notes and critical observations* (3 vols, London, 1731).

Ulloa, Jorge Juan de and Antonio de Ulloa, *Relación historica del viage a la America Meridional [...]* (3 vols. in 2, Madrid, 1748)

Ulloa, George Juan [Jorge Juan de] and Antonio de Ulloa, *A Voyage to South America [...] Translated from the Original Spanish* (2nd. edn, 2 vols, London, 1760).

Vaughan, H. A., *Sandy Lane and other poems* (n.p., n.d. [Barbados, 1945]).

Venuti, Lawrence, *The Translator's Invisibility: A history of translation* (London and New York, 1995).

Veyne, Paul (trs. David Pellauer), *Roman Erotic Elegy: Love, Poetry and the West* (Chicago and London, 1988).

Viola, Herman J. and Carolyn Margolis (ed.), *Seeds of Change: A Quincentennial Commemoration* (Washington, DC, 1991).

Walcott, Derek, *Omeros* (London, 1990).

Walker, Keith (ed.), *John Dryden* (Oxford, 1987; Oxford Authors series).

Waller, Edmund, *The Works of Edmund Waller, Esq; in Verse and Prose* (London, 1758).

Warrack, Alexander, compiler, *Chambers Scots Dictionary* (Edinburgh, 1911, repr. 1977).

Watson, J. S. (ed.), *The Odyssey of Homer: Translated by Alexander Pope* (London, 1862).

Watson, Roderick, *The Literature of Scotland* (Basingstoke and London, 1984).

Weekes, Nathaniel, *Barbados: A Poem* (London, 1754).

Wender, Dorothea, trs., *Hesiod: Theogony, Works and Days; Theognis: Elegies* (Harmondsworth, 1973).

Western, J. R., *The English Militia in the Eighteenth Century: The Story of a Political Issue, 1660–1802* (London and Toronto, 1965).

White, William C. (intro. and ed.), *Flowering Trees of the Caribbean* (New York and Toronto, 1951; reprinted 1959).

Wilkinson, L. P., *The Georgics of Virgil: A Critical Survey* (Cambridge, 1969).

Williams, Eric, *Capitalism and Slavery* (Chapel Hill, 1944).

Williams, R. Deryck (ed.), *Virgil: The Eclogues & Georgics* (London, 1979, 1996).

Williamson, Karina (ed.), 'The Hop-Garden: A Georgic,' in *The Poetical Works of Christopher Smart*, Vol. IV, Miscellaneous Poems, English and Latin (Oxford, 1987), pp. 41–65 (and notes, pp. 416–19).

Wood, Robert, *The Ruins of Palmyra, otherwise Tedmor, in the Desart* (London, 1753).

Wright, Richardson, *Revels in Jamaica 1682–1838* (New York, 1937; facsimile reprint, Kingston, Jamaica, 1986).

Young, Edward, *The Universal Passion. Satire III. To the Right Honourable Mr. Dodington* (London, 1725).

Young, Edward, *Love of Fame, The Universal Passion* (2nd edn, London, 1728).

Young, Edward, *The Poetical Works of the Reverend Edward Young, LL.D. Rector of Wellwyn in Hartfordshire and Chaplain in Ordinary to His Majesty* (2 vols, London, 1741).

# *Index*

This index includes: (a) persons and topics mentioned or discussed in the Introduction; (b) names of persons and places mentioned by Grainger in the text of *The Sugar-Cane* or in Grainger's notes to the poem (except mythological personages, large geographical areas such as Africa or the West Indies, and adjectival forms; places referred to by Grainger under poetical or obsolete names have been cross-referenced to their usual modern names); (c) plant and animal species mentioned by Grainger (and indexed under the names he uses, though modern scientific names are supplied where possible). References to the text of *The Sugar-Cane* are given by book and line numbers as well as by the page numbers of the present work. Grainger's notes are indexed only in so far as they refer to items not actually mentioned in the poem itself; the reader is referred to these, and to the Additional Notes, for further details on many of the subjects indexed here. For the sugar-cane itself, and the order in which Grainger discusses the various stages involved in its cultivation and manufacture into sugar, see the Arguments prefixed to each book of the poem.

13th Foot: *see* Pulteney's Regiment

acajou (*Anacardium occidentale*), 149 (IV, 136–8)
acassee (*Acacia tortuosa*), 104 (I, 510)
Acosta, José de, 168
Addison, Joseph, 26, 27, 32, 62–3
Ætna: *see* Etna
Akenside, Mark, 11, 25–6
albacore (*Thunnus alalunga*), 187
Albion, 113 (II, 59), 124 (II, 483), 135 (III, 283), 140 (III, 508), 155 (IV, 353), 158 (IV, 472), 161 (IV, 630); *see also* Britain
Alleman, G. S., 199
alligators, 114 (II, 74)
aloes: *see* sempre-vive
Amazon (river), 191
Amerindians, Grainger and, 36, 61
Amyntor (character in *The Sugar-Cane*): *see* Payne, Ralph
anana (pineapple, *Anana comosus*), 102 (I, 418), 158 (IV, 498), 159 (IV, 519)
anata (anatto, *Bixa orellana*), 159 (IV, 534–40)
Anderson, Phillip B., 10, 53
Anderson, Robert, 2–6, 11, 20, 38, 48
Andes mountains, 182, 186
Anguilla, 143 (III, 614)
Annandale, 4, 132 (III, 153)
Anne, Queen of Great Britain and Ireland, 173
*Annual Register*, 20
Antigua, 2, 3, 15, 46, 59, 88, 133 (III, 222), 173, 187, 192
ants, 117–8 (II, 229–37)
Apicius (Roman epicure), 143 (III, 604)
Arabia Felix, 181
Armstrong, John, 11; quoted by Grainger: 153 (IV, 305)
Arrian (Greek historian), 165
arrow-poison, 190–1
arsenic, 114 (II, 83)

Atenca, Pedro de, 166
Augustus (Roman emperor), 33
Aurelius (character in *The Sugar-Cane*): see Thomas, George
Ausonia: *see* Italy
Avaro (character in *The Sugar-Cane*), 139–40 (III, 463–76)
avocado pear: *see* sabbaca
Avon (river), 137 (III, 371), 140 (III, 476)
Azores, 165

Bahamas, 22
balm (? lemon-balm, *Melissa officinalis*), 157 (IV, 463)
bananas (*Musa*), 52–3, 141 (III, 533), 160 (IV, 569–71), 181
Barbadoes: *see* Barbados
Barbados, 31, 46, 65, 91, 95 (I, 132–3), 172, 187, 192
Barbary Coast, 165
Barbuda, 143 (III, 613)
Basseterre (St Kitts), 2, 3, 20, 46, 89
*Battle of the Frogs and the Mice*, 200–1
bay-grape (*Coccoloba uvifera*), 160 (IV, 563–5)
bearded fig-tree (*Ficus citrifolia*), 95 (I, 132–3), 159 (IV, 526–33)
bees, 128 (III, 27), 139 (III, 451–4)
Belgium (used by Grainger to refer to the Low Countries in general), 123 (II, 469), 154 (IV, 330)
bellyache bush: *see* physic-nut
Bentley, Richard, 24
Bermuda, 127, 138 (III, 401), 167
Biscay, Bay of, 124 (II, 487)
Blackmore, Sir Richard, 11
Black Sea, 165
blast (pest of sugar-cane, *Saccharosydne saccharivora*), 106 (I, 558), 111, 117–8 (II, 194–269)
bonavist (*Lablab niger*), 157 (IV, 456)
boneta (bonito, *Sarda sarda*), 124 (II, 504)
Boswell, James, 5, 10, 19, 31, 38, 64, 200–1
Bourryau, John, 9, 12–3, 14, 17
Bourryau, Zachariah, 9
Brathwaite, Kamau, 54–5, 59, 65

Brazil, 166
Breda, Treaty of (1667), 166, 173
Bristol, 127, 137 (III, 364–5, 367, 381), 173, 189
Britain (and Britannia), 97 (I, 211), 103 (I, 464), 104 (I, 489), 112 (II, 24), 123 (II, 444), 135 (III, 291), 137 (III, 365, 368), 139 (III, 458), 143 (III, 615), 154 (IV, 318), 162 (IV, 660), 163 (IV, 676, 683); *see also* Albion
broom-bush (? *Sida acuta*), 156 (IV, 410)
Brown, Lloyd W., 201
Brumoy, Pierre, 12
Burt, Daniel Mathew: *see* Grainger, Daniel Mathew
Burt, Mary: *see* Spooner, Mary
Burt, Penelope: *see* Verchild, Penelope
Burt, William, 13
Burt, William Mathew, 13
Burt, William Pym, 13
Bute, John Stuart, 3rd Earl of, 16

Cabot, Sebastian, 189
cacao (cocoa, *Theobroma cacao*), 107 (I, 604), 158 (IV, 474–6), 187
calaba (*Calophyllum calaba*), 133–4 (III, 227–36)
calaloo (*Amaranthus* spp.), 157 (IV, 462)
Calpe: *see* Gibraltar
Cambria: *see* Wales
Camões, Luis Vaz de, 41
Canary Islands, 165
candle-weed (? *Tecoma stans*), 161 (IV, 613)
cane-piece rat: *see* rats
cane-fire (passage in *The Sugar-Cane*), 29, 37, 55, 127, 129–30 (III, 55–90)
Cape Verde Islands, 165
'Caraccas,' the, 181
Carlisle, James Hay, 1st Earl of, 172
carnation (*Caesalpinia pulcherrima*), 105 (I, 520–31)
cashew: *see* acajou
Caspian Sea, 165
cassada (cassava, *Manihot esculenta*), 107 (I, 595), 114 (II, 84), 157 (IV, 449–53), 181
cassia (*Cassia fistula*), 93 (I, 36), 159 (IV, 513–7)

# Index

castor-oil plant (*Ricinus communis*), 177
Catháy: *see* China
Cayenne, 180
ceiba (*Ceiba pentandra*), 93 (I, 36)
Celsus (Aurelius Cornelius Celsus, Roman medical writer), 107 (I, 617)
Chalker, John, 53, 200
Chalmers, Alexander, 49, 53, 56
Chapman, Mathew James, 47
Chapman, Robert William, 200
Charente (river), 124 (II, 488)
Charles I, King of Great Britain and Ireland, 172
Charles II, King of Great Britain and Ireland, 171, 172, 191
Chaucer, Geoffrey, 167
cherimoya (or chirimoia), 159 (IV, 518), 176
chickweed (*Drymaria cordata*), 115 (II, 128)
chiggers (*Tunga penetrans*), 31, 145, 152 (IV, 257–62)
Chile, 186
Chili: *see* Chile
China, 118 (II, 265), 188
china (plant): *see* smilax
Christobelle (character in *The Sugar-Cane*), 105 (I, 544)
ciguaterra: *see* fish-poison
citron (*Citrus medica*), 106 (I, 555), 157 (IV, 466)
coca bush (*Erythroxylum coca*), 186–7
cochinille (cochineal, *Dactylopius coccus*), 116 (II, 171–3)
cockroaches, 100 (I, 337–9)
cocoa: *see* cacao
coconut tree (*Cocos nucifera*), 122 (II, 398), 123 (II, 438), 133 (III, 205), 160 (IV, 558)
Codrington, Christopher, 192
coffee (*Coffea arabica*), 107 (I, 605), 158 (IV, 471–3)
Coleridge, Samuel Taylor, 49
*Collection of Poems ... By several hands* (ed. Robert Dodsley), 9–10
College of Physicians of London (now Royal College), 8–9
Colley, Linda, 29, 33

Collins, William, 10, 38
Columbus, Christopher, 21, 39, 91, 94–5 (I, 93–126), 155 (IV, 360), 162 (IV, 643), 169, 173, 186
conch (*Strombus gigas*), 150 (IV, 163), 152 (IV, 267)
condor: *see* zumbadore
Congo, 147 (IV, 44)
Constantinople, 181
Corcyra, 158 (IV, 489)
Cornwall, 154 (IV, 317)
cotton (*Gossypium barbadense*), 107 (I, 600–602), 157 (IV, 468–9)
cow-itch (*Mucuna pruriens*), 115 (II, 123–7), 153–4 (IV, 308–11)
Cowper, William, 201
Crab Island: *see* Vieques
crabs, 100 (I, 342), 114 (II, 78), 143 (III, 610)
Craufurd, John, 8
crickets, 156 (IV, 416)
*Critical Review*, 9, 11, 19, 41–3
Cromwell, Oliver, 171
Crump, George, 15
Culloden, Battle of (1746), 6–7
Cumberland (former English county), 3
Cumberland, Richard, 35
Cumberland, William Augustus, Duke of, (son of George II), 6
Cuming, William, 4, 21
Curtius (Quintus Curtius Rufus, Roman writer), 171
custard-apple (*Annona reticulata*), 180
cypress (? *Cordia alliodura*), 130 (III, 80)

Dabydeen, David, 29
Danae (character in *The Sugar-Cane*), 107 (I, 606)
Darwin, Erasmus, 28
Davenport, Richard Alfred, 49–50, 56, 58
Davis, Bertram H., 38
Davison, Dennis, 53
Depoinci: *see* Poincy
Diseases of slaves, 37–8, 58, 145, 148–50 (IV, 103–57), 152–4 (IV, 244–317); *see also* Grainger, James, Works of, under *Essay on the more common West-India Diseases*

Dobrée, Bonamy, 29
Dodsley, James, 18–9
Dodsley, Robert, 9, 18–9
dolphin (*Coryphaena hippurus*), 124 (II, 508)
Dominica, 19
Donne, John, 51
Dorchester, 98 (I, 233)
Douglas, Gavin, 51
dragon-worm (or guinea-worm, *Dracunculus medinensis*), 31, 145, 152 (IV, 245–255)
Drave (river), 150 (IV, 181)
Drayton, Arthur D., 54
Dryden, John, 26, 29
dumb cane (*Dieffenbachia seguine*), 127, 137 (III, 357–9)
Dunse (Berwickshire; now Duns, Scottish Borders), 3–4
Durante (Castor Durante da Gualdo, Italian writer), 182
Dyer, John, 22, 25, 26, 28, 33, 38, 42, 62, 89, 92 (I, 12), 131 (III, 131)

Easton Mauduit (Northamptonshire), 17–8, 38
'edda': *see* 'tanies'
Edwards, Bryan, 14, 46–7
Edwards, George, 178
Egg Harbour (New Jersey), 190
Egypt, 165, 181
Elizabeth I, Queen of England, 189–90
Elmina, 148 (IV, 99)
England, 143 (III, 595–6)
Enna (Sicily), 93 (I, 64), 154 (IV, 330)
Etna, 119 (II, 278, 280)
Eton, 63, 123 (II, 431)

Falkirk Muir, Battle of (1746), 6–7
Ferdinand, the Catholic, King of Castile and Aragon, 95 (I, 113, 119–20), 166
ferns, 155 (IV, 387), 159 (IV, 548)
fern-tree (*Cyathea arborea*), 102 (I, 393)
fireflies, 108 (I, 643)
fish-poison, 115 (II, 139–46)
Florida, 166
fly, greasy (? *Sipha flava* or *Rhopalosiphum maidis*), 111, 116–7 (II, 181–93)

fly, large (pest of coffee: ? *Xyleutes lillianae*), 181
fly, yellow (? the Neotropical grasshopper, *Schistocerca pallens*), 111, 116 (II, 168)
flying fish (? *Cypselurus heterurus*), 124 (II, 507)
Foote, Samuel, 35
forbidden fruit (*Citrus paradisii*), 93 (I, 44)
Fracastoro, Girolamo, 21
France (Gallia, Gaul), 97 (I, 216), 114 (II, 81), 116 (II, 177), 123 (II, 469), 139 (III, 442, 455), 165, 181
Fraser, Thomas, 15
French and Indian War: *see* Seven Years' War
frigate-bird (*Fregata magnificens*), 188

Gallia: *see* France
gallinazo (? *Cathartes aura*), 114 (II, 72)
Ganges (river), 139 (III, 443)
garayio ('a sea fowl'), 187
Garth, Sir Samuel, 11
Gaul: *see* France
*Gazette Littéraire de l'Europe*, 20, 43–5
*Gentleman's Magazine*, 2, 19, 36
George II, King of Great Britain and Ireland, 5–6, 33
George III, King of Great Britain and Ireland, 33, 92 (I, 20), 116 (II, 176), 163 (IV, 682)
Gibraltar, 140 (III, 510)
Gilfillan, George, 51
ginger (*Zingiber officinale*), 107 (I, 598)
Gold Coast, 147 (IV, 62)
Goldsmith, Oliver, 11, 29, 65
Goodwin, Gordon, 7
Gosse, Edmund, 51, 57
Grainger, Daniel Mathew (née Burt; wife of James Grainger), 2, 13–4, 19, 20
Grainger, Eleanora (daughter of James Grainger), 2, 14
Grainger, James, birth (date of), 2, 3, 5; parentage, 3, 4; Scottishness of, 4, 35, 46; at University of Edinburgh, 5; military service, 6–8; MD degree, 8; admitted Licentiate of the College of Physicians, 8–9; as writer in London,

# Index

9–12; goes to St. Kitts, 12–3; marriage, 13–4; visit to British Isles (1763–4), 17–9; death, 2; burial, 3; will, 3; Hanoverianism, 6–7, 33; and slavery, 13, 17, 20, 34–5, 40, 43, 49–50, 52–3, 54–65; and British Empire, 33–4; view of Irish, 33; hostility to French, 33; anti-Catholicism, 33; coat of arms, 7; library, 19, 20; portrait, 20.

Grainger, James, works of: book reviews, 7–8, 9, 32, 33; 'Bryan and Pereene', 18, 48, 51–2, 53, 202–4; *Dissertatio Medica Inauguralis*, 4, 8; *Essay on the more common West-India Diseases*, 10, 15, 61–2; *History and Antiquities of Scotland*, 9; *Historia febris anomalae*, 8; *Poetical Translation ... of Tibullus*, 11, 54, 63; *Solitude*, 2, 9–10, 48, 51, 53; 'Three Elegies written from Italy', 7; translation from *The Greek Theatre of Father Brumoy*, 12; translations from Ovid, 11; *see also: Sugar-Cane, The*

Grainger, John (probable father of John Grainger), 3

Grainger, Louisa (daughter of James Grainger), 14

Grainger, William (half-brother of James Grainger), 3, 5, 6, 19–20

Grainger, Mrs. William, 3

Grampian Mountains, 105 (I, 517–8)

granadilla (*Passiflora quadrangularis*), 159 (IV, 543)

Gray, Thomas, quoted by Grainger, 108 (I, 634)

Greece, 94 (I, 78), 123 (II, 470), 154 (IV, 324–5)

Grenada, 17

Guadaloupe: *see* Guadeloupe

Guadeloupe, 127, 135 (III, 282), 182

guaiac (or lignum-vitae, *Guaiacum officinale*), 93 (I, 37–42), 95 (I, 126), 153 (IV, 283), 188

guava (*Psidium guajava*), 93 (I, 37–9)

Guayaquil, 113–4 (II, 69–74)

Guiana, 166

Guinea, 153 (IV, 287), 174, 177, 187

guinea-corn: *see* 'maize'

guinea-worm: *see* dragon-worm

Hadzor (or Hadzer), John, 7

Havana, 190

Havannah, The: *see* Havana

Henry VII, King of England, 189

Hesiod (Greek poet), 25, 39, 44, 89, 92 (I, 8)

hiccory (? *Sterculia apetala*), 133–4 (III, 227, 239)

Hispaniola (St.-Domingue, Santo Domingo), 166, 170, 196

Homer (Greek poet), 185, 199–201

Horace (Quintus Horatius Flaccus, Roman poet), 24

Hughes, Griffith, 22, 32

hummingbird (passage in *The Sugar-Cane*), 30, 32, 37, 105 (I, 520–31)

Hungary, 193

hurricane (passage in *The Sugar-Cane*), 29, 37, 40, 42, 45, 55, 60, 118–121 (II, 270–361)

Hutchinson, Benjamin William (nephew [-in-law] of James Grainger), 16

Iërne: *see* Ireland

iguana, 175

'Indian cale', 157 (IV, 462)

Indian fig (*Nopalia coccinellifera*), 116 (II, 172)

'Indian millet': *see* 'maize'

insects (as pests of sugar-cane), 55, 60, 116–8 (II, 174–269)

Ireland, 33, 157 (IV, 435)

Isis (river), 123 (II, 433)

Italy (also Ausonia), 100 (I, 315), 106 (I, 551), 124 (II, 471), 171

Jacobite Rebellion, (1715), 3–4; (1745), 6–7, 33

Jamaica, 39, 46, 59, 91, 94 (I, 88–93), 167, 171, 187, 191

*Jamaica, A Poem* (anon.), 47–8, 55

'Jamaica plumb tree' (*Spondias purpurea*), 117 (II, 218–20)

Jamaica prickle-weed (? *Amaranthus spinosus*), 196

James II, King of Great Britain and Ireland, 4, 170

'James III': *see* Stuart, Prince James Francis Edward

Jewfish (*Epinephelus itajara*), 143 (III, 608)
Johnson, Samuel, 10, 11, 14, 18, 19, 21, 29, 32, 34, 38, 41, 43, 45, 58, 60, 61, 140 (III, 509), 200–1; reviews of *The Sugar-Cane*, 36–8, 41–3, 58, 60
Jones, Inigo, 159 (IV, 524)
Junio and Theana (episode in *The Sugar-Cane*), 16, 19, 34, 36, 40, 58, 63, 122–6 (II, 425–553)
Juvenal (Decimus Junius Juvenalis, Roman poet), 29

Kames, Henry Hume, Lord, 17
Karukera: *see* Guadeloupe
Keats, John, 55
Kent, 117 (II, 197), 135 (III, 306)
Kerr, John, 5
knotted grass (or worm-grass, *Spigelia anthelmia*), 115 (II, 119), 154 (IV, 313)
Knox, Ronald, 52–3, 63
Koliba (river), 146 (IV, 9)
Kwanza (river), 149 (IV, 113)

Labat, Jean-Baptiste, 58, 88, 182, 183, 188–9
La Condamine, Charles Marie de, 43, 190–1
Langhorne, John, 38–41, 42
Langhorne, William, 38
lark (skylark, *Alauda arvensis*), 142 (III, 558–60)
Lauder, George, 5
Lauffeld, Battle of: *see* Val, Battle of
Lee, Charles, 51–2
Leeward Islands, 13, 33, 46, 59, 167, 171, 173, 192
lemon (*Citrus limon*), 102 (I, 427), 104 (I, 499), 175
Lennox, Charlotte, 12, 140 (III, 510)
Lewis, Dominic Bevan Wyndham, 51–2
Lewis, Dr (? William Lewis, English chemist), 183
Liamuiga: *see* St Kitts
lignum-vitae: *see* guaiac
lime (*Citrus aurantifolia*), 102 (I, 427), 104 (I, 499), 140 (III, 496)

lime, sweet (*Triphasia trifolia*), 157 (IV, 465–6)
Lincolnshire, 9, 131 (III, 130–1)
Linnæus (Carl von Linné), 176, 194, 197
lizards, 100 (I, 341 n.), 155 (IV, 389), 156 (IV, 416); *see also* speckled lizard
locusts, African, 116 (II, 163–6)
locust tree (*Hymenæa courbaril*), 93 (I, 34)
logwood (*Hæmotoxylum campechianum*), 104 (I, 503)
London, 181
*London Chronicle*, 36–8
Lonsdale, Roger, 53
Louis XIV, King of France, 145, 161 (IV, 622–9)
Luard, Peter Robert (brother-in-law of John Bourryau), 14
Lucan (Marcus Annaeus Lucanus, Roman poet), 165
Lucretius (Titus Lucretius Carus, Roman poet), quoted by Grainger, 89
Lusitania: *see* Portugal

Mackay, Charles, 50
Madeira Islands, 165–6; *see also* Porto Santo
madre de cacao (*Gliricidia sepium*), 158 (IV, 478–9), 180–1
mahoe-berry (? *Thespesia populnea*), 176
Maitland, William, 9
'maize' (either *Sorghum vulgare* or *Zea mais*), 148 (IV, 94), 160 (IV, 567)
Maldives, 186
Maldivy Islands: *see* Maldives
mammey (*Mammea americana*), 158 (IV, 502–8)
mangrove (*Rhizophora mangle*), 113 (II, 69)
Manilius, Marcus (Roman poet), 23–5, 87
Marcley Hill (Herefordshire), 96–7 (I, 190–3)
Markham, Benjamin Pym (nephew [-in-law] of James Grainger), 16
Marlborough, James Ley, 1st Earl of, 172
Marne (river), 140 (III, 501)
Martin, Samuel, 34, 88, 129 (III, 31); *Essay upon Plantership*, 205–7
Martinico: *see* Martinique

# Index

Martinique, 127, 135 (III, 283), 170
Martinius, Matthias, 180
Martinus: *see* Martinius, Matthias
marvel of Peru (*Mirabilis jalap*), 156 (IV, 414)
Matanina: *see* Martinique
Mathew, Daniel, 15, 34, 129 (III, 31), 196
Mathew, Sir William († 1704), 13
Mathew, William († 1752), 13
Maupertuis, Pierre Louis Moreau de, 174
melon (*Cucumis melo*), 158 (IV, 497)
Melville, Robert, 4, 34, 146 (IV, 25)
mezambay (? *Cleome gynandra*), 196
mice, 199–201
Millar, Andrew, 9
Milton, John, 10, 29, 32, 52; quoted by Grainger, 94 (I, 90–2), 112 (II, 29), 158 (IV, 500), 171–2
*Mimosa pudica*, 115 (II, 129)
miners, sufferings of (compared to those of Caribbean slaves), 43, 60, 150–1 (IV, 165–205)
Minnah: *see* Elmina
mint (? *Mentha spicata*), 157 (IV, 463)
Mithridates, King of Pontus, 115 (II, 130)
Mocha, 181
Modyford, Sir Thomas, 171
mongoose (*Herpestes auropunctatus auropunctatus*), 183–4
monkeys (*Cercopithecus aethiops*), 42, 96 (I, 173), 111, 113 (II, 34–54), 201
Monro, Alexander, 5
Montano (character in *The Sugar-Cane*), 16, 34, 42, 57, 63, 106–8 (I, 579–646)
*Monthly Review*, 9, 33, 38
Montserrat, 91, 95 (I, 135–7), 186
mosquitos, 100 (I, 334)
mountain dove (*Zenaida aurita*), 115 (II, 116), 142 (III, 573)
Mountserrat: *see* Montserrat
'Mundingo', 148 (IV, 104)
myrtle (*Myrtus communis*), 91, 92 (I, 6), 106 (I, 551–6)

Nevis, 91, 95 (I, 134), 170, 173
Newfoundland, 157 (IV, 436)

niccars (*Caesalpinia bonduc*), 152 (IV, 268)
Nichols, John Bowyer, 2
Niger (river), 146 (IV, 4)
nightingale (*Erithacus megarhyncus*), 142 (III, 556)
nightshade (? *Solanum americanum*), 114 (II, 95)
nopal plant: *see* Indian fig
Norfolk, 143 (III, 596)

obeah, 62, 145, 155–6 (IV, 365–405)
ochra (okra, *Hibiscus esculentus*), 157 (IV, 457–8)
Ogilby, John, 195
Ogilvy: *see* Ogilby
orange, sweet (*Citrus sinensis*), 102 (I, 427), 104 (I, 501), 157 (IV, 466–8)
Orinoco (river), 186
Oronoko: *see* Orinoco
Ovid (Publius Ovidius Naso, Roman poet), 11, 24

Palæmon (character in *The Sugar-Cane*), 130 (III, 84–90)
Palladio, Andrea, 159 (IV, 525)
Palmyra, 196
panspan (*Spondias mombin*), 141 (III, 549), 185
papaw (*Carica papaya*), 141 (III, 549), 146 (IV, 6–7)
Pasqua (coffee-house proprietor), 181
Payne, Ralph, 34, 100 (I, 329–32)
Percy, Thomas, 2, 3, 4, 10–11, 13–22 *passim*, 36, 38, 45, 48, 61, 65, 123 (II, 452), 140 (III, 509), 200, 202
*Periplus of the Erythraean Sea*, 165
Persia, 165
Peru, 181
Phæacia: *see* Corcyra
Philips, John, 25, 27, 28, 30, 42, 59, 89, 92 (I, 12), 97 (I, 191); quoted by Grainger, 144 (III, 637)
*Philosophical Transactions*, 182
physic-nut, 176–7
pigeon-pea (*Cajanus cajan*), 157 (IV, 454)
pineapple: *see* anana
Pineda, Peter, 167, 179

plantain (*Musa*), 102 (I, 430), 141 (III, 533), 142 (III, 564), 160 (IV, 572)
Plata (the River Plate), 162 (IV, 638)
'Pleasures of Jamaica' (1738), 30
Pliny (the Elder: Gaius Plinius Secundus, Roman writer), 165, 180, 184, 185
Plumier, Charles, 197
Plymouth (Montserrat), 173
*Po* (ship), 124 (II, 485–6, 497)
Poincy, Phillippe de Longvilliers de, 177
Pompey (Gnaeus Pompeius Magnus, Roman general), 165
Pontus, 115 (II, 130)
Pope, Alexander, 21, 36, 54, 56, 64
Porto Santo (Madeira), 124 (II, 499)
Portugal, 155 (IV, 363), 187
potatos, 'English' or 'Irish' (*Solanum tuberosum*), 195; sweet (*Ipomoea batatas*), 157 (IV, 459)
prickly pear (*Opuntia dillenii*), 105 (I, 536)
prickly vine (? *Hylocereus trigonus*), 161 (IV, 611)
Pride of Barbados: *see* carnation
Prince, Mary, 59
Pringle, John, 8
Prior, Matthew, 54
privet (*Clerodendrum aculeatum*) 105 (I, 515–9)
privet, European (*Ligustrum vulgare*), 105 (I, 515–9)
Pulteney's Regiment (the 13th Foot), 6–8
pummelo: *see* shaddoc

Quanza: *see* Kwanza

Rae, James, 5
Raleigh, Sir Walter, 107 (I, 598), 134 (III, 259)
Ramsay, James, 15, 49, 59; *Essay on the Treatment and Conversion of African Slaves*, 208–211
rats (cane-piece rat, *Oryzomys antillarum*), 31, 96 (I, 172), 111, 113–4 (II, 62–98), 199–201
rats, domestic (*Rattus rattus*), 182
Ray, John, 177
Red Sea, 165

*Reliques of Ancient English Poetry* (Thomas Percy), 18, 61, 202
Rey: *see* Rio-del-Rey
Reynolds, Sir Joshua, 19, 200
Rhine (river), 143 (III, 617)
rhubarb, 115–6 (II, 149–52)
rice (*Oryza sativa*), 148 (IV, 94)
Richmond, 123 (II, 445–6)
ricinus, 104 (I, 508); *see also* physic-nut
Rio-del-Rey, 147 (IV, 65)
Rio Grande: *see* Koliba
Romney, Robert Marsham, 2nd Baron, 34, 60, 127, 135 (III, 289)
royal palm (*Roystonea regia*), 119 (II, 294), 120 (II, 345), 159 (IV, 522–5)
Royle, Trevor, 201
rum, 35, 40, 42–3, 127, 140 (III, 489–506)
Ryswick, Treaty of (1697), 170

sabbaca (also avocato, the avocado pear, *Persea americana*), 93 (I, 45), 102 (I, 420)
Sabrina: *see* Severn
St Christopher: *see* St Kitts
St Clair, George, 8
St Croix, 189
St Jago de la Vega: *see* Spanish Town
St John's (Antigua), 3, 46
St Kitts, 2, 3, 9, 12, 13, 14–5, 17, 18, 19, 24, 37, 39, 45, 46, 49, 56, 57, 59, 60, 88, 91, 93–4 (I, 60–83), 97 (I, 206), 113 (II, 47), 118 (II, 265), 173, 182, 188, 202, 208
St Lucia, 19
St Vincent, 17, 19
Sambrook, James, 201
Sanaga: *see* Senegal
sand-box tree (*Hura crepitans*), 141 (III, 522)
sand-flies, 100 (I, 334)
Sandiford, Keith A., 55–6
Santo Domingo: *see* Hispaniola
sappadilla (sapodilla, *Manilkara zapota*), 123 (II, 441–2)
Scotia: *see* Scotland
Scotland, 143 (III, 612), 150 (IV, 178)
sea-grape: *see* bay-grape
sempre-vive (*Aloe vera*), 149 (IV, 123)

# Index

Senegal (river), 146 (IV, 9)
Seven Years' War, 16, 17
Severn (river), 137 (III, 380), 138 (III, 406)
shaddoc (or shaddock, *Citrus grandis*), 93 (I, 44)
Shakespeare, William, 29, 137 (III, 372–6); quoted by Grainger, 120 (II, 327–8), 169
sharks, 124 (II, 504), 203
Sheen: *see* Richmond
Shenstone, William, 17, 111, 112 (II, 23), 113 (II, 31)
Shields, David S., 56–7
Shirley, Sir Anthony, 171
Shyllon, Folarin, 208
Sicily, 93 (I, 64–6), 119 (II, 275–280), 165; *see also* Enna, Etna
Sidney, Sir Philip, 51
silk-cotton tree: *see* ceiba
Singleton, John, 46
Sixtus V, Pope, 182
slave-dance (passage in *The Sugar-Cane*), 30, 38, 40, 42, 45, 55, 59–60, 145, 160–1 (IV, 582–605)
Sloane, Sir Hans, 22, 169, 171, 185, 187
Smart, Christopher, 25, 31, 51, 62, 92 (I, 13)
smilax ('broad-leafed china'), 128 (III, 25)
Smollett, Tobias, 11, 32
snakes, 113 (II, 68), 155 (IV, 389), 156 (IV, 416)
solanum (*Datura stramonium*), 156 (IV, 415)
Somervile, William, 18, 25, 32, 92 (I, 13)
soursop (*Annona muricata*), 107 (I, 597)
Spain, 154 (IV, 335), 165, 178
Spanish Town (Jamaica), 171
speckled lizard (? *Ameiva* sp.), 100 (I, 341)
Spooner, Charles, 14, 18
Spooner, Mary (née Burt), 14
star-apple (*Chrysophyllum cainito*), 180
Störck, Anton, Freiherr von, 194
Strabo (Greek geographer), 194
Strahan, William, 19
Stuart, Prince Charles Edward, 5, 6
Stuart, Prince James Francis Edward, 4, 5

sugar-apple (*Annona squamosa*), 180
*Sugar-Cane, The* (James Grainger), 3, 4, 7, 11–2, 16, 19; composition of, 16–8, 22; printing, 18–9; as georgic, 16, 21–35, 38–9, 44–5, 52–3, 56–7, 63–4; contemporary reception, 36–45; reception and influence in the Caribbean, 45–8; later editions, 48; later criticism, 49–53; in relation to modern Caribbean, 54–65; and Caribbean English, 32, 39, 64–5
Surinam (river), 166
Swift, Jonathan, 51, 64
Syria, 181

tamarind (*Tamarindus indica*), 107 (I, 624), 141 (III, 549), 158–9 (IV, 509–12)
'tanies' (? tannia, *Xanthosoma sagittifolium*), 107 (I, 596)
Tempé, 93 (I, 61)
Templeman, Thomas, 169
Tennyson, Alfred, Lord, 49
Thame: *see* Thames
Thames (river), 122 (II, 430), 140 (III, 476), 141 (III, 521), 162 (IV, 634–5, 663)
Theodorus (character in *The Sugar-Cane*), 120 (II, 347–350)
Theodosia (character in *The Sugar-Cane*), 107 (I, 606)
Thévenot, Jean de, 181
thistle, yellow (*Argemone mexicana*), 115 (II, 114)
Thomas, George, 33, 92 (I, 19)
Thomson, James, 21–2, 25, 32, 49, 54; quoted by Grainger, 133 (III, 209)
thyme (*Thymus vulgaris*), 157 (IV, 463)
Tibullus (Roman poet), 11–2, 28, 32, 63
Tille (river), 140 (III, 501)
tin, 154 (IV, 317)
tobacco (*Nicotiana tabaccum*), 107 (I, 598), 148 (IV, 90)
Tobago, 19, 133 (III, 226)
Tonson, Jacob, 18
Tournefort, Joseph Pitton de, 177
Townshend, George (4th Viscount and 1st Marquis Townshend), 34, 143 (III, 595–8)

Trapp, Joseph, 26, 29
tree-fern: *see* fern-tree
tropic-bird (*Phaeton aethereus*), 124 (II, 509)
Tull, Jethro, 34, 99 (I, 290)
turpentine-tree (*Bursera simaruba*), 153 (IV, 283)
turtle, 35, 143 (III, 606), 149 (IV, 146), 152 (IV, 267)
Tyrtæus (Greek poet), 143 (III, 600)

Ulloa, Jorge Juan and Antonio de, 168, 178, 182, 183, 190
urtica (? Portuguese man-o'-war, *Physalia physalis*), 124 (II, 505)
Utrecht, Peace of (1713), 64, 170

Val, Battle of (1747), 7
Vaughan, Hilton, 65
Vega, Garcilaso de la (c. 1501–36), 41
Vega, Garcilaso de la (the Inca, c. 1535–1616), 41
Venus de Medici, 34, 124 (II, 476)
Venuti, Lawrence, 63
Verchild, James, 13
Verchild, Penelope (née Burt), 13
vervain (*Stachytarpheta jamaicensis*), 115 (II, 148), 149 (IV, 123)
Vieques (Crab Island), 189
Virgil (Publius Virgilius Maro, Roman poet), 23–31, 33–4, 39, 42, 44, 45, 52, 63, 89, 92 (I, 11), 100 (I, 313), 115 (II, 132), 185, 201
Virginia, 189–90
Virgin Islands, 117 (II, 217), 182
Vitruvius (Marcus Vitruvius Pollio, Roman architect), 105 (I, 534)
Volga (river), 115–6 (II, 150–1)
Volta (river), 147 (IV, 65)

Walcott, Derek Alton, 65
Wales, 143 (III, 611)
Waller, Edmund, 138 (III, 402)
War of Jenkins' Ear, 5
War of the Austrian Succession, 5, 7, 192
Warton, Joseph, 10, 27, 30

Warton, Thomas (the younger), 10
water-lemon (*Passiflora laurifolia*), 159 (IV, 544)
Weekes, Nathaniel, 22, 31
White, James, 140 (III, 509)
white acajou (? *Anacardium occidentale*), 93 (I, 45)
white eagle (calomel, mercurous chloride), 149 (IV, 127)
'white grub' (pest of coffee: ? *Planococcus citri*), 181
Whitehead, William (quoted and referred to by Grainger), 137 (III, 366–80)
wild liquorice (*Abrus precatorius*), 105 (I, 538), 115 (II, 148)
wild pineapple (? *Bromelia plumieri*), 176
wild red cedar (? *Tabebuia heterophylla*), 93 (I, 34)
William III, King of Great Britain and Ireland, 173
Wiltshire, 161 (IV, 616)
Wolfe, James, 16, 34, 116 (II, 175)
Worcestershire, 140 (III, 503)
Wordsworth, William, 49
worm-grass: *see* knotted grass
worms (infesting humans), 115 (II, 120–2), 145, 148 (IV, 103–7), 149 (IV, 127, 150), 153–4 (IV, 290–317); (pest of cotton, *Alabama agrillacea*), 107 (I, 601); (*Teredo*), 134 (III, 233–5); *see also* dragon-worm
Wren, Sir Christopher, 159 (IV, 524)
Wright, William, 3, 4, 15, 51

Xantippe, 137 (III, 359)

yams (*Dioscorea var species*), 52–3, 98 (I, 236–43), 107 (I, 595), 148 (IV, 94), 157 (IV, 449)
yaws, 145, 152–3 (IV, 263–289)
Young, Edward, 10; quoted by Grainger, 100 (I, 332)

Zaire (river), 147 (IV, 45)
zumbadore (condor), 108 (I, 641–2)

CPSIA information can be obtained at www.ICGtesting.com
Printed in the USA
LVOW010730221212